Andy Warhol's
Blow Job

Roy Grundmann

Temple University Press

PHILADELPHIA

Temple University Press, Philadelphia 19122

Copyright © 2003 by Temple University Press

All rights reserved

Published 2003

Printed in the United States of America

Library of Congress Cataloging-in-Publication Data

Grundmann, Roy, 1963–

Andy Warhol's "Blow job" / Roy Grundmann.

p.   cm. — (Culture and the moving image)

Includes bibliographical references and index.

ISBN 1-56639-971-8 (cloth : alk. paper) — ISBN 1-56639-972-6 (pbk. : alk. paper)

1. Blow job (Motion picture : 1963).   2. Gays—Identity.   3. Gays in popular culture—United States.

I. Title.   II. Series.

PN1997.B6735 G78 2003

791.43'72—dc21   2002020422

Images on pages 23, 32, 33, 34, 35, 50, 51, 52, 53, 104,

105, and 106 © 2002 The Andy Warhol Museum, Pittsburgh, PA,

a museum of Carnegie Institute.

2 4 6 8 9 7 5 3 1

Für meine Eltern und meinen Bruder

CONTENTS

ACKNOWLEDGMENTS

This book had its origins in my doctoral dissertation, "The Politics of Performance and Andy Warhol's Films," which I wrote at the Department of Cinema Studies at New York University. Reasonably enough, I was then confining myself to treating Andy Warhol's film *Blow Job* in but one chapter, but during the writing I was beginning to realize—with a mixture of great excitement and some anxiety—that *Blow Job* may well merit a book-length study. The present book is the result of this realization, of overcoming the anxiety, of throwing caution to the wind, and of my decision to embark on the project and indulge in it. Since then, much of the original treatment has been changed, some of the material has been deleted, the scope expanded, and so on. Yet, crucial sections have, in one way or another, found their way into this final product. I thus feel the need to express my thanks, first, to those who supervised my thinking and writing about this film, Warhol's cinema, and Warhol himself as I prepared my dissertation.

My deepest gratitude goes to Robert Sklar, Chris Straayer, and Art Simon, who have all been connected with my work on Warhol in an intrinsic manner. Robert Sklar taught me to think like a historian, and his approach to analyzing and understanding film has had a strong impact on the way I now look at cinema and culture in general. It was during one of his lecture classes that I first encountered an Andy Warhol film, and it was he who encouraged me to write about Warhol's cinema. Chris Straayer's fierce, unrelenting support during the writing stages significantly contributed to my being able to complete the first stage of this project. In addition, her critical thinking and expertise—especially with regard to issues of gender, sexuality, and sexual representation—have inspired me to the present day. I am also indebted to Art Simon, whose work on Warhol and American popular and underground culture influenced crucial aspects of my discourse. A fourth person whose influence became widely visible in my work on Warhol's films in general is Callie Angell. As the curator for the Andy Warhol Film Project at the Whitney Museum of American Art, Callie supervised my internship there and significantly influenced my thinking about Warhol the filmmaker. Over several years, I benefited not only from her professional expertise and great knowledge but also from her personal friendship and generosity. Once her catalogue raisonné on Warhol's films is completed, it will profoundly change the way we think about Warhol's cinema.

My warmest thanks go also to my New York University dissertation writing group, whose members, Antje Ascheid, Melinda Barlow, Marcos Becquer, Bruce Brasell, Alex Keller, Cindy Lucia, David Lugowski, Valerie Manenti, Paula Massood, Jill O'Brian, and Kirsten Thompson, gave me so much valuable feedback and support as they tirelessly read and reread drafts of my chapters. While this group as a whole set new standards for me in terms of support and loyalty, I need to specifically single out four persons. My professional dialogue and personal friendship with Marcos Becquer significantly helped shape what became the second and fourth chapters of this book. Whenever I thought I had covered the territory, Marcos's comments helped me to push myself even further. Paula Massood and Kirsten Thompson witnessed my work on this project from the very first page, and their countless good suggestions, references, and comparisons were incredibly stimulating and helpful. The same is true of my good friend and *Cineaste* editor Cindy Lucia, who also took on the martyr-like task of proofreading and copyediting many early drafts. Further thanks go to José Esteban Muñoz, Tobi Miller, and David James, whose general concern for my work and assistance with this project made a significant difference. They provided me with valuable perspectives as to how I could broaden my investigation toward the spectrum of concerns now present in this book In this vein, I would also like to thank Noll Brinckmann, Professor of Film Studies at the University of Zürich, and Stanislaus von Moos, Professor of Art History at the University of Zürich, for inviting me to present a section of this book to their students. Noll also has my warmest love for her long-time friendship, unflagging support, and spiritual guidance.

In addition, several friends were helpful and supportive during the dissertation phase of my work on *Blow Job*. I would like to thank Richard Porton for reading parts of my work, Arjun Bhasin for his love, support, and for helping me compile visual materials during the early writing process, and Jörg Bettendorf for his patience and his quick, effective intervention whenever I had problems convincing my computer of my intentions. Winfried Hohmann and Georgetta Stonefish are simply great friends. They taught me to love New York and how to survive in it.

During my years as a graduate student, the Department of Cinema Studies at New York University provided a nurturing research environment , trained me as a teacher, and came to groom and respect me as an intellectual. My special thanks go to the department as well as to Ken Sweeney for his help with tricky matters of school bureaucracy and for his decade-long support and patience. Deutsches Haus at New York University gave me loyal support and steady employment, without which my life and studies in New York would have been impossible. Gary Crowdus, editor-in-chief of *Cineaste* magazine, and my fellow editors at *Cineaste* helped me become a writer and editor and, during the crucial first phase of my project, generously exempted me from many of the commitments and responsibilities.

The transformation of *Andy Warhol's Blow Job* from dissertation chapter to book took place in Boston. I would like to thank the Department of Film and Television at Boston University, where I have been teaching film studies for the past four years. My special thanks go to Dean Brent Baker and his faculty and staff, especially to Marilyn Root, Debbie Northall, Amy Buswell, Ray Carney, Bill Lawson, Nancy Maguire, Jennifer Morcone, and Ken Holmes, who have all made me feel at home and have helped create a supportive environment for my teaching, research, and writing. By assisting me with teaching and research, Fonda Chin, Derek Frank, Kate Guiney, Zachary Lee, Alex Lykidis, Mel Osborne, Luigi Scarcelli, and Lisa Terry made it much easier for me to juggle my many responsibilities and, thus, to fulfill my book contract. Additional thanks go to Kate Guiney and Cynthia Rockwell for indexing this book.

I would also like to thank several institutions and individuals for providing me with materials and information about Warhol's life and work and for helping make this book a reality. Tom Sokolowski and his staff at the Andy Warhol Museum in Pittsburgh were extremely cooperative and made my research in Pittsburgh fruitful and thrilling. My special thanks go to Geralyn Huxley, Greg Pierce, and Lisa Miriello, who gave me access to *Blow Job* and other Warhol images and provided stills from the film. My research is also greatly indebted to Matt Wrbican, head archivist at the museum, who provided me with a flood of archival materials, images, and a never ceasing stream of valuable background information on Warhol. I greatly benefited from Matt's incredible knowledge about Warhol the artist and the person. In addition, Eileen Doyle at Art Resources and Michael Herrmann at the Andy Warhol Foundation for the Visual Arts were very helpful in making additional images available to me. Further thanks go to Bill Hunt, executor of the Wallowitch estate, and to John Wallowitch, brother of the late Ed Wallowitch, for his patient and helpful correspondence about Warhol's relationship with Ed and their collaborations during the 1950s and early 1960s. I would also like to thank Janet Francendese at Temple University Press for her editorial comments and for overseeing this project.

Finally, my biggest thanks and all my love go to Mark Hennessey, who has been sustaining me with his love and without whose patience, advice, and support I would not be where I am today.

Andy Warhol's Blow Job

INTRODUCTION

hen Andy Warhol began making films in 1963, blow jobs, although widely given and received, to be sure, were still a taboo subject. Any claim that, today, this taboo has been lifted, is a misjudgment, despite the sexual liberation of the 1970s, the public sphere's acknowledgment of "alternative lifestyles," the media industry's ever more aggressive exploitation of racy sex, the proliferation of Internet chat rooms, and a recent presidential sex scandal. Especially the last example makes clear just how deeply American culture continues to be pervaded by the private/public split. Apart from the fact that genital sex in general is still a queasy subject (its representations relegated to the realm of the pornographic), sex of the nonmarital, nonreproductive kind is entertained with even greater anxiety.

As far as blow jobs are concerned, sex censorship is firmly ritualized and yet (or therefore?) highly ironic. Representations of blow jobs are precise indices of how a modern, basically liberal, secular society determined by the private/public split visually serves up sex to its media consumers. On one level, the physical particularities of blow jobs are a godsend for Hollywood and cable television: The partner who moves down the anatomy invariably exits the frame—the realm of what is deemed representable—without disturbing the viewer's connectedness to the overall act. Even so, these physical specifics, in themselves, still pose a particularly slippery area. They foreground in charged manner that sex is about power, and power is what determines the status of gender and gender relations under patriarchy. Lacking naturalizing paradigms (the teleology of reproduction; the missionary position as centerpiece of Western sexual tradition), representations of such devious variants as fellatio and, of course, anal intercourse immediately beg the question—even more so than naturalized and accepted forms of sex do—of who may do what to whom and in which constellation. Answering this question is risky because it is potentially compromising.

One thing that makes it hard to talk about sex is that any such talk always reveals something about the talker. To simply observe and describe sex without revealing some form of personal affect is the clinician's domain, and while most of us may have little desire to excel in this speech genre, even the banal act of substituting such terms as fellatio and oral sex with "blowing" or "getting sucked off" means going out on a limb. It may reveal that, for better or worse, one knows what one is talking about. This is only compounded by the allusive—read, connotative—aspects that inhere the (self-)censoring nature of much sexual representation. Granted, Warhol's 1964 film *Blow Job* presents these issues with highly unusual charge, provocation, and irony. But *Blow Job*'s exceptional status lies less in the way the film exploits sex than in the degree to which it exploits the trappings of sex talk and foregrounds the basic operative principle guiding such talk. *Blow Job*, which shows the face of a young man having his cock sucked (or so its title alleges), but which depicts neither sucking nor sucker, potentially makes a sucker out of anyone who attempts to summarize the film's "content" (the use of quotation marks is no saving grace). If I do just this in this book, it is because the chance of earning the just-mentioned attribute puts me in good company. The perusal of much of what has been written about *Blow Job* has shown me that it is very difficult to talk about *Blow Job* without being partial to the film. To write a whole book about it in the absence of partiality is outright impossible.

The silent *Blow Job*, thirty-six minutes long,[1] consists of a black-and-white close-up of the handsome face of an unidentified young man leaning against a brick wall. The film begins by showing the man looking half down. His face is cast in shadow, as his head blocks the film's light source, located off-screen at the upper left corner above his head. Nonetheless, one can see that his head indicates body movements that possibly result from the unzipping of his fly. He may be getting ready for the blow job. Then his head tilts up, whereby more light is thrown on his face, which soon registers signs of what could be sexual pleasure. From then on, this male beauty periodically looks up or down, to the right or the left, his movements and sensations possibly caused by the off-screen blow job. Once or twice one can see the upper part of his shoulder, the collar of his black leather jacket, and his right or left hand moving through his wavy hair, indicating that he is more and more turned on. Toward the end of the film, his body movements seem more pronounced and rhythmic; they might be caused by the motions of whoever may be sucking the man off below frame. At this point, the man's facial expressions are consistently dramatic; his eyes seem to glaze over and he begins to stare; his head trembles slightly; and he bites his lip as he seems, one might assume, to be coming close to orgasm. Near the film's end, he lights a cigarette which, considering his now more relaxed facial expressions, appears to be that famous "cigarette after."

In the course of the many times I have shown this film to friends, acquaintances, and students, many have expressed views that support the description just given as being plausible if somewhat suggestive. Talking about *Blow Job* brings viewers out of the woodwork, especially when assumptions about the blow job are fed by—and, in turn, feed into—projections of gender pairings. But there have also been a smaller, consistent number of perspectives that stubbornly ward off any assumption of sex as a presumptuous encroachment on the invisible. It would be easy to dismiss these arguments for what might be their lack of imagination. But the imagination has room for more than the sexual, just as a viewer's conclusion that *Blow Job* is not about sex offers no conclusive proof that the viewer has not entertained sex as at least one possibility before (consciously or subconsciously) dismissing it. Finally, there are those who consider *Blow Job*—sex or no sex—simply boring and tedious. These views are the most alien to me. I can rehearse them rationally, but my prolonged involvement with *Blow Job*, informed by my own position (constituted, like anyone's, by multiple qualities—in my case being a white gay man, a historian, and someone who is personally and professionally fascinated with Warhol's cinema) have minimized the sense of being bored by the film. The experience of boredom would surely have taken this book in a different direction.[2]

Diverse as these views are, one aspect unites them. In their respective ways, they all respond to the discrepancy between the two levels on which *Blow Job* produces meaning: the denotative level, minimalist as it is in the film, and the rich connotative range opened up by the film's suggestive title, its framing, the chiaroscuro lighting, the background, the solitary male figure, the lack of what one would ordinarily call "plot" or even mundane actions, and even the slowed-down projection speed. These qualities make the film at once full and empty, lending the image a certain aesthetic intensity that, however, the film leaves "unsupported" or "unredeemed," stopping short, as it does, of anchoring its strongly saturated signifiers through designated signifieds.[3] This tension between the film's concrete surface display and its highly unconcrete meaning confronts those scanning the image with the fact that their own (and possibly any) reading process entails transference, reconfiguration, and abstraction. Indeed, the fact that the film's highly concrete image tilts over at times into semi-abstract segments, showing the young man's head shrouded in darkness or bathed in light, further compounds the reading process. Viewers thus have to negotiate the image's own abstracting qualities in addition to experiencing somewhat self-consciously the necessarily abstracting nature inherent in any reading process. In this way, *Blow Job* not only leads to interpretations that diverge particularly widely, but it also triggers similarly diverse emotive responses, depending on such vectors as spectatorial excitement, an appreciation for the image's oneiric qualities, thwarted expectations, and the experience of tedium.

It is perhaps no coincidence that Warhol often chose the topic of sex (whether explicitly articulated or merely alluded to in some form) as a privileged site for this complex tension between concreteness and abstraction. Because sex and sexual arousal produce direct bodily reactions, we always think of sex as something concrete—an immediate experience. But for Warhol, sex had a distinctly abstract quality. This notion may easily mislead us into accepting the cliché that Warhol was sexless and afraid to have relationships (neither of which is true). Rather, Warhol saw the world through the eyes of an artist, and a gay one at that. While gay men have been known for their proclivity to detach sex from the contexts that surround it (enjoying sex in *any* context and for sex's own sake), they have also shown a particular talent for putting sex into multiple contexts—that is, for seeing sex connected to myriad mundane, seemingly nonsexual aspects of life. This is what Warhol did. He consistently saw and depicted sex as an aesthetic experience mediated by the many contexts in which it occurred, none of which, as the heterogeneity of his work attests, was privileged. Given this particular approach, Warhol's oeuvre has provided rich fodder especially for theorists who have stressed and argued the discursive nature of sex. One scholar who has broached this topic particularly with regard to Warhol is Linda Nochlin, who in her essay, "'Sex Is So Abstract': The Nudes of Andy Warhol," discusses Warhol's sexual imagery in several contexts—the artist's own attempts to seek arousal, his first career as a commercial artist versed in the techniques of advertising, his second nature as a compulsive collector of high and low art, of porn, painting, and photography, and his tremendous knowledge of art history and the history of visual representation in general.[4] When Nochlin asserts that Warhol's nudes are art, she does not deny their prurience. Warhol's sexual images are, in fact, about sex; they are sexy and sometimes "dirty." And they always put sex in a certain context, citing it along with the artwork's object and theme: sex-in-advertising, sex-in-high-art, sex-in-portrait photography, and so on.

Blow Job may be less raunchy than Warhol's nudes. What it shares with them, as part of the Warhol canon, is the artist's pronounced aesthetic sensibility, his impulse for placing sex in multiple contexts, and the tension between the abstract and the concrete. These qualities profoundly contribute to the pleasure of looking at Warhol's images and films. They have also paved the way for a flood of research and scholarship on Warhol's artistic output from such diverse areas and disciplines as cultural studies, psychoanalysis, narratology, semiotics, and queer studies, all of which may, at times, take cues from one another or intersect in some way and all of which have come to supplement art history as the discipline traditionally concerned with artists such as Warhol.

Warhol's multifaceted artistic sensibility compelled me to draw on several of these approaches and disciplines for the present study. My analysis of *Blow Job*, then, treats the film as being about gay sex and gay identity without dismissing other contexts through which a reading of the film may proceed. Indeed, because of homosexuality's complex position—it is Other, yet it has evolved neither in complete secrecy nor in a cultural vacuum—I will argue that to read the film in terms of homosexuality necessarily means considering multiple contexts apparently not related (or only superficially related) to it. In some cases, this has required me to launch into fairly elaborate excursions when discussing the cultural, historical, and theoretical discourses I bring to the topic. In this sense, this book is at once about much more and much less than this one film. It is about high art, popular culture, and representation in general, but it is also about a specific medium, film, and subcategory of this medium. It is about Warhol's art in general, but it is also about the gay aspects of it in particular. And it is about sex and sex talk in general (including rumors, assumptions, rhetoric, and polemics), but it is also about the history and culture of one particular form of sex and desire and about the oppression it has suffered, the survival strategies it has taken, and the problems and dysfunctions it may have.

This generously staked out field provides multiple entry points for a systematic introduction of my agenda. My decision to begin discussion of this film by placing it in the context of Warhol's overall cinematic output is simply a pragmatic choice. It is one of several possible ways of placing *Blow Job* in one of several possible contexts. It establishes a particular time, place, and mode of production to which subsequent discussions can be related.

Warhol made over 650 films, about 500 of which are three-minute portrait films, so-called screen tests, that feature Warhol's friends, acquaintances, and members of the New York art world. The other 150 or so titles are experimental shorts and features ranging in length from twenty minutes to twenty-five hours.[5] While this level of creativity is staggering, even more surprising is that all of these films were made in a period of only five years, 1963 to 1968. Of course, these five years were not just any five years—they are, in and of themselves, worth discussing to a degree that would inexorably explode the framework of this book. Thus, historiographic shorthand will have to do. Even though the following account is a standard one, proffered before by multiple sources, it is worth recalling for its suggestive heft: When Warhol began making films, President John F. Kennedy was alive, the cold war climate had begun thawing, the United States was harboring (perhaps unfounded) hopes of reaching widespread prosperity and domestic peace, the civil rights movement was harboring (perhaps legitimate) hopes of effectively combating and decreasing racism, the American art scene was more lively, diverse, and provocative than ever, and, despite the fact that Doris Day ruled at the box office, sex was becoming more accessible for many, especially women. By the end of the year in which Warhol handed film production over to Paul Morrissey, this same country was steeped in the multiple morasses known as Vietnam; a series of American leaders, political and civic, had been assassinated; American cities were plagued by inner-city poverty, decay, and racial uprisings; the divorce rate was up; the counterculture was blooming openly; the artistic underground was already dead; Hollywood as producer of dominant entertainment was in deep crisis; film censorship had been radically modified;

and sexual and pornographic representations had found legal protection and were poised to expand into broader markets.

Suggestive as this account may be, one would be mistaken to consider the events that transpired during the 1960s simply as *causes* for the profound changes that occurred in American culture and society. One must also look at these events as *symptoms* of developments that began before this time. The seeds for America's various domestic crises were not sown with the assassination of John F. Kennedy but long before Kennedy assumed office. The same can be said about the conflict in Indochina. The fragmentation of American culture began after World War II, although it was largely ignored by consensus culture and simultaneously fueled and patched over by suburbia. Hollywood's demise (and with it that of the Production Code) can be dated back to the late 1940s. And if sex and sex talk became more explicit during the 1960s, it was not until the 1970s, and only among two groups—the gay male population and a small, white, upper middle class segment of straight society—that some of the promises the previous decade held out were finally being met in the flesh, the former group strutting its stuff in the public sphere, the latter predictably remaining behind closed doors.

Warhol's cinema, too, can be discussed in terms of both its originary influence and its transformative impact on a cultural-aesthetic vocabulary that was already in place before Warhol emerged as an artist. If Warhol is considered one of the fathers of the kinds of aesthetics now found in commercial advertising, music video, and movies, his oeuvre is also marked by a distinct impulse to seize on and transform preexisting images. His film work, in particular, evidences both change and unifying constants. Warhol began making films in 1963 with a sixteen-millimeter silent Bolex camera. His earliest films, produced in that year—*Tarzan and Jane Regained . . . Sort of*, *Haircut* (No. 1), and *Sleep*—show the first steps Warhol took in experimenting with the medium. *Tarzan and Jane* is much closer to such slightly earlier Beat films as Ron Rice's 1959 *The Flower Thief* and Vernon Zimmerman's 1960 *Lemon Hearts* than to Warhol's later cinematic output. A feature-length, densely edited travelogue of sorts with retroactively added sound, *Tarzan and Jane* was made during Warhol's road trip to California that year and features underground performer Taylor Mead, the "star" of Zimmerman's and Rice's films and of many Beat and underground films of the late 1950s and 1960s. *Haircut* (No.1) also shows a strong Beat sensibility: A twenty-seven-minute film comprising, exclusively, a series of static shots, each taken from a different perspective, of a playfully homoerotic all-male haircutting party in a Lower East Side apartment, *Haircut* (No. 1) is remarkable for its high-contrast expressionist lighting and aesthetic exploration of depth of field, which later Warhol films would partially or completely abolish. *Sleep* is a nearly five-and-a-half-hour minimalist film of poet John Giorno sleeping. The film's structure, consisting of multiple spliced-together camera rolls of silent, black-and-white film, provides an early indication of Warhol's desire to transcend the limitations of the equipment, which allowed for only four minutes of uninterrupted filming before the camera had to be reloaded. Even though *Sleep* is carefully edited and has multiple camera perspectives within each roll of film, the film's length, its slowed-down projection speed to sixteen (later eighteen) frames per second, and its repeated use of the same footage may paradoxically produce the false impression that the film is simply one static shot of Giorno's breathing torso.[6]

This effect is exactly what Warhol sought to produce more systematically in his most famous minimalist films of the following year: *Eat, Blow Job, Henry Geldzahler,* and

Empire. The first two were still shot with the Bolex, which Warhol mounted on a tripod to keep it static. He refrained from editing these films, letting the splices between the rolls, which register as white flashes, determine their structure.[7] As in *Sleep* and *Haircut* (No. 1), Warhol slowed down the projection speed of these films, which enhanced their length and the trance-like effect of the minimalist actions they feature. *Henry Geldzahler* and *Empire* were shot with an Auricon sound camera that could hold fifty-minute cartridges of film,[8] but Warhol was not yet utilizing sound. Both films are similarly slowed-down and silent explorations of their respective objects. The former film is a feature-length static shot of Warhol's friend Henry Geldzahler sitting on the famous Factory couch and struggling with the persistent gaze of Warhol's camera. The latter is an eight-hour, five-minute static shot of the Empire State Building, during which the viewer's observation of the pro-filmic object is gradually supplemented, perhaps even largely replaced, by an exploration of the material property of the filmstrip itself with its chemical irregularities, blemishes, and varying degrees of graininess. The crude means of Warhol's filmmaking belie these films' formal sophistication. As Callie Angell has pointed out, the films constitute an early achievement in purist style: "a single shot on an entirely stationary camera continued over multiple assembled rolls to record a single preconceived action. By reducing his film production to these basic elements of the medium, Warhol was able to transcend the limitations of his equipment and accomplish the paradoxical effect of stillness and monumental duration in his moving images."[9]

But Warhol did not refrain for long from using the Auricon's capacity to record sound. The year 1965 saw a prolific output of Warhol films based on the basic unit of a static, thirty-three-minute-long shot (often accumulated into two- or three-reel films) featuring many of the Factory's guests and hangers-on in sometimes comical, sometimes cruel verbal and erotic interactions. For many of these films, Warhol asked scriptwriter Ronald Tavel to write scenarios and dialogue, but he often manipulated the performers to disregard any preexisting script or treatment, trusting that the often charged relations between cast members would spark conflicts and repartees more original, witty, and spontaneous than those conceived by Tavel.[10] Warhol's production of alternately (or simultaneously) funny and scandalizing sound films based on the thirty-three-minute unit culminated in the 1966 three-and-a-half-hour film *The Chelsea Girls*, which is an assemblage of twelve such reels (black-and-white as well as color) projected in double screen and featuring many of Warhol's friends and acquaintances. *The Chelsea Girls* not only became a cause célèbre of underground cinema, but by the following year it had accomplished what no underground film had before: It moved into commercial theaters, was exhibited across the United States, and became a genuine commercial success.[11]

With *The Chelsea Girls* being reviewed in mainstream publications, the underground had gone above ground—and relinquished itself in the process. But Warhol was able to add to his growing fame as a pop artist a reputation for infamous (and, as some perceived it, simply "bad") filmmaking. The success of *The Chelsea Girls* led to the re-circulation of some of Warhol's earlier films. In addition, the growing crisis in the dominant entertainment industry, the influx of European art and soft-core porn films into the U.S. market, and the burgeoning sexploitation exhibition circuit led exhibitors to encourage Warhol in 1967 to make a string of feature-length sexploitation films with such titles as *The Nude Restaurant; Bike Boy; I, a Man;* and *Lonesome Cowboys*.[12] These films retained some of the minimalism of Warhol's earlier films, but all of them had sound and color. In addition, their static camera position was interrupted by a cluster of techniques, including pans, zooms, strobe cutting, and postproduction editing, some of which Warhol first explored in the 1965 gay sex farce *My Hustler*.[13] The 1967 cycle of sexploitation films showed little sex, and from today's perspective, much of the nudity featured in these films is actually rather coy. Warhol would push the envelope one more time with the 1968 hard-core fuck-and-talk tryst *Blue Movie*, but after he was shot by Valerie Solanas and nearly died, he handed over the creative rudder to Paul Morrissey, whose films of the late 1960s and 1970s he merely signed as producer.

Blow Job is thus part of merely one phase of Warhol's massive and heterogeneous cinematic output; however, conceptually it is a highly typical, perhaps even the quintessential, Warhol film. Its minimalism enables and encourages a prolonged scrutiny of the image, which has certain effects on the viewer. Some spectators may become bored very quickly. Others may be taken in by the camera's gaze onto its object, the young man in front of the camera who may be receiving a blow job. Yet others may temporarily shift their attention away from the young man and focus on the film's chiaroscuro play of light and dark or on its background, the brick wall. And some spectators may engage all of these impressions and activities during one and the same viewing. What *Blow Job* has most notably in common with many Warhol films is the concept of the tease—the promise, rarely kept yet integral to much of Warhol's filmic oeuvre, of revealing information about their pro-filmic objects, of revealing their desires, jealousies, rages, and, last but not least, sexual activities and sexual identities. When *Blow Job* premiered on July 16, 1964, at the Washington Square Gallery in New York, its title was not announced to the audience attending that evening's set of screenings,[14] but the film was subsequently exhibited under this title, which is bound up with the film's concept as a tease. In *Blow Job*, the tease is pared down to a minimalist extreme, triggering a host of questions: How much will the film show of the sex act? Can this act be verified through the young man's facial expressions? Does this act actually take place? If the film is really about a blow job, who is or are the fellators? Is this a gay sex act, a straight one, or a bisexual one, which would suggest the kind of polymorphous sexuality often associated with Greenwich Village bohemia during the 1960s?

These questions point to certain qualities and raise issues that make *Blow Job* an integral part not only of Warhol's cinematic canon but also of the 1960s' underground cinema in general. Parker Tyler, who wrote an important early history of underground film, noted as early as 1969 that this cinema was marked by the scandalizing visualization of what was taboo to the mainstream proffered, among other things, by the queer sexual and gender exhibitionism of the denizens of the underground.[15] It seems that, in the United States, there has traditionally been a close link between homosexuality and avant-garde film production. Even before World War II, when there was no avant-garde film *scene* in this country to speak of, the avant-garde films that were produced often featured homosexuality or at least a certain queerness.[16] In the postwar 1940s and early 1950s, such important filmmakers as Kenneth Anger (*Fireworks*, 1947), Curtis Harrington (*Fragments of Seeking*, 1946), and James Broughton (*The Adventures of Jimmy*, 1950) brought discourses of homosexuality under their own authorial control. These films were not free of homophobia, but unlike prewar efforts, they explored the traumas and pleasures of gay awakening from a gay point of view. At least Anger's and Harrington's films engaged and furthered a particular avant-garde subgenre, the trance film or psychodrama.[17] As the avant-garde in the United States slowly gathered steam during the 1950s through the immeasurable influences of such key figures as Maya Deren and, slightly later, Jonas Mekas, avant-garde filmmaking increasingly comprised a myriad of approaches and styles. These ranged from Deren's own carefully choreographed and highly stylized explorations of female subjectivity, power, and movement to the aesthetic-discursive maturation of Stan Brakhage's mythopoeia and to the epic mythologies of Harry Smith's experiments with animation and graphic cinema. These artists were not concerned with homosexuality. If they treated sexuality at all, they did so as a universal force into which one had to tap to assert one's place in the world.

The continuing activities of some of these artists into the 1960s, their legacies found in the work of others, and newly emerging and reemerging avant-garde approaches, such as the compilation film and structural film, made the 1960s' American avant-garde the most richly diverse in the world. Treatments of homosexuality and gay sensibility made up merely a portion of this spectrum. However, from the late 1950s on, with the emergence of Beat cinema, gay and queer discourses began to proliferate and shed the seriousness of the psychodrama in favor of adopting a spirit of subversive, indeed, polymorphously perverse, playfulness. By 1963, a vibrant avant-garde and underground film scene was burgeoning especially in New York City's Greenwich Village with its multiple intersecting networks of artists, filmmakers, and their friends, most of whom knew one another and many of whom were involved in one another's projects in multiple functions.[18] The year 1963 alone saw the production of three of the most notorious queer-themed underground films of the period: Kenneth Anger's *Scorpio Rising*, Jack Smith's *Flaming Creatures*, and Barbara Rubin's *Christmas on Earth*. But the list of films featuring queer performers and/or themes could easily be expanded to include, among others, such films as *The Flower Thief, Lemon Hearts,* and a group of films ranging from Jack Smith's 1963 *Normal Love* and Ron Rice's *The Queen of Sheba Meets the Atom Man* (1962–1967) to the Kuchar brothers' playfully queer pop fantasy, *Sins of the Fleshapoids* (1965). The diverse cultural and demographic makeup of this scene attests to the great heterogeneity of avant-garde films, only some of which were underground films, some of which (as evinced in Warhol's early films) mixed elements of Beat sensibility with other concerns, and some of which also received other labels and classifications, such as Baudelairean cinema.[19] In addition to being an underground film, *Blow Job* also fits into the third category, with its impulse toward negating time in the decadent space of the Baudelairean elsewhere, its articulation of mnemonic impulses, its would-be defiance of social codes and contemporaneous mores, and its ironic-demonic inversion and overlap of opposite signifiers and values, such as Christian versus satanic iconography and innocuous posing versus stimulation through sex and/or drugs and pain.

Whatever subversive and transgressive qualities underground cinema possessed that made it a school for scandal, this cinema also tended to be carefully self-censoring—and there is no better example for this than *Blow Job*. On the one hand, the film's self-imposed censorship is symptomatic of the repressive context of the period. In the early 1960s, underground films became the target of police raids in New York and elsewhere. Some films, such as *Flaming Creatures*, were temporarily seized by the police; others, such as Warhol's *Andy Warhol Films Jack Smith Filming "Normal Love,"* were confiscated and lost forever.[20] Warhol, who was then moving within the underground film scene in Greenwich Village, quickly learned to negotiate, in films such as *Blow Job*, the oppressive conditions brought about by the repressive state apparatus's "interest" in this form of art. Like most of Warhol's cinematic ventures prior to *The Chelsea Girls, Blow Job* would have been exhibited on a relatively modest scale—in small, ever shifting hush-

hush-and-rush basement screenings—as part of the underground cinema it now emblematizes. But it was, of course, precisely the concept of the tease that made Warhol's films palatable to a gradually increasing audience. Even when the film was exhibited on the growing college campus screening circuit, into which Warhol gradually tapped, audience exposure west of the Hudson River was able to increase precisely because of the stable duality between the film's provocative title and its self-censorship: It could—and always can—be appropriated by straight college students and young "hip" heterosexuals in general, as it affords a certain degree of aesthetic transgression that makes these viewers feel special about their role as avant-garde consumers while shielding them from the more explicit, dramatic, and confrontational aspects of transgressiveness and taboo.

I believe it is of extraordinary importance for us to pay close and consistent attention to the film's cautious negotiation of transgression, its shielding of taboo, and, indeed, its aesthetic-discursive makeup *as* a shield. While 1960s underground film may generally be said to explore the boundaries between the permissible and the forbidden (hence, its label), homosexuality constituted a particularly charged area. A review of underground cinema's negotiation of this area may yield insight into a specific historical moment that saw alternative cultural production collide with external efforts of repression. But, in addition, the self-censorship of many of these films, and of *Blow Job* in particular, may proffer insights into the epistemology of the *discursive production* of gender and sexuality, which is inherently linked to an *epistemology of interdiction* that goes far beyond the random casting about of the NYPD. In other words, if it is true, as Richard Dyer writes with specific reference to Warhol's cinema, that "*Couch, Blow Job* and the other early films are thus not just about breaking the taboo on seeing gayness, but exposing some of the aesthetic mechanisms of the proscription and the lifting of it,"[21] *Blow Job*'s self-censorship may not simply be the result of a repression imposed from above. Rather, it must be understood as the discursive production of what it purports to suppress—and, in turn, as the very suppression of what it purports to produce. *Blow Job*'s minimalist aesthetics and provocative framing impose a set of conditions and demands on the viewer. Reading and interpreting the film require reading into it, and these modes of reading and hypothesizing say more about the reader's psychosexual and cultural mind-set than about the film itself. What gets exposed in these readings are assumptions about gender, sexuality, morals, and truth that are deeply ingrained in Western culture and have evolved over a long period of sociopolitical and cultural engagement with gender and sexuality. I submit that *Blow Job* must be understood as a meta-commentary on a number of regimes—political and cultural, scientific and artistic—that have utilized regulatory discourses of gender and sexuality to construct identities.

At the heart of the history of sexuality itself is a whole cluster of discursive regimes that have produced a myriad of intersecting discourses and polemics. Michel Foucault has characterized this cluster as *scientia sexualis*.[22] He has argued that for two centuries, enlightenment society and culture have produced a proliferating welter of discourses on sex, seizing on sexuality's polymorphous shape to establish categories and subcategories of perversions, pathologies, and sexual identities in the name of and as products of "scientific truth." *Scientia sexualis* has intersected with social discourses, pronouncing itself the authority on hygiene and regulating behavior with regard to all areas of the body. It has intersected with and produced legal discourses, setting up punishments and punitive categories with regard to sex both as practice and as the sole foundation of identity. And it has intersected with evolutionist myths, seeking to classify and "eliminate defective individuals, degenerate and bastardized populations"[23] for the safeguarding, indeed, for the production, of the narrowly sanctioned category of orderly and acceptable biological reproduction for family, society, and nation.

But Foucault emphasizes that particularly this last aspect indicates that what *scientia sexualis* constructed was actually the opposite of knowledge. *Scientia sexualis* became a "blanket guarantee under cover of which moral obstacles, economic or political options, and traditional fears could be recast in a scientific-sounding vocabulary":[24]

> It is as if a fundamental resistance blocked the development of a rationally formed discourse concerning human sex, its correlations, and its effects. A disparity of this sort would indicate that the aim of such a discourse was not to state the truth but to prevent its very emergence. . . . The learned discourse on sex that was pronounced in the nineteenth century was imbued with age-old delusions, but also with systematic blindnesses: a refusal to see and to understand; but further—and this is the crucial point—a refusal concerning the very thing that was brought to light and whose formulation was urgently solicited. For there can be no misunderstanding that is not based on a fundamental relation to truth. Evading this truth, barring access to it, masking it: these were so many local tactics which, as if by superimposition and through a last-minute detour, gave a paradoxical form to a fundamental petition to know. Choosing not to recognize was yet another vagary of the will to truth.[25]

Describing Jean-Martin Charcot's Salpêtrière, an early scientific-clinical hospital and laboratory, as an exemplification for *scientia sexualis*'s dubious double take on knowledge, Foucault makes clear that the extraction of knowledge had another far-reaching consequence—it profoundly changed the role of the observer from someone who would, as it were, stumble upon a preexisting knowledge or scientific detail in unassuming fashion and would then proceed to contemplate it to someone who became much more actively involved in the discursive production of knowledge. The sex researcher and regulator became a participant, performing experiments, examining, interrogating, displaying intricacies of sex and gender, producing confessions from scientific "objects," inducing ritual crises, inciting psychosexual reactions.[26] In other words, interrogators of sex became *participants* and *performers* in their own theater.

This theater of science-as-performance relied heavily on the visual: Being able to see meant being able to determine the truth. The mastery of the object became synonymous with ocularcentric mastery. But this form of mastery replicated for the self-positioning of the observer the same duality Foucault identifies at the heart of *scientia sexualis:* The will to know and the stubborn refusal to know resurface in the observer's self-understanding as the duality between the frantic activity of producing specific acts of observing and the compulsion to disavow one's partiality to these acts in favor of the conceit of having stumbled upon a preexisting reality and truth. Decades before a specifically Foucauldian concept of the disciplined subject was extended to the concept of the disciplined viewer, Walter Benjamin theorized this viewer as both producer and observer, subject and object, of modern visual culture, which had become the culture of the mechanical reproduction of images.[27] For Benjamin, the medium of film, in particular, epitomized this new visual culture. The photographic and, later, the film camera were capable of seeing details foreclosed to the human eye.[28] Film itself thus became a scientific tool. But film also subjected its viewers to a frenzy of rapidly changing images, shifting the viewers' activity to one of reaction rather than action and forcing viewers to abjure the traditional mode of contemplation in favor of a new mode of distracted observation.[29] In this new mode, the viewers' responses to the image were preordained and fairly accurately overlapped with—and thus became symptoms of—the discursive regimes that underscored the production of images and that largely determined the context, if not the complete outcome, of their reception.

But for Benjamin the disciplinization of the viewer of mechanically reproduced art is founded on more than the technological specificity of visual stimuli. It is also founded on the shift in content that came with mechanical reproduction. Art itself profoundly changed: The boundaries between high art and mass culture became more blurred than ever, and mechanically reproduced mass culture images themselves produced a proliferation of iconographies and iconologies that would have a lasting effect on the cultural vocabulary of twentieth century Western society.[30] This society became a society of reified types and stereotypes, and its culture became a culture of citationality. The tremendous impact of this mode of expression can be seen in the fact that some areas of high art that sought to reinsert themselves into the social and reinstall a link between art and everyday life did so by "stooping" to low art and using the latter as raw material for discursive rearticulations. While this was occurring long before the 1960s, the 1960s was a decade that celebrated the blurring of high and low art and of discourses of humanism and science with renewed force. The 1960s witnessed a vigorous leap into a certain postmodern sensibility that oscillated between self-consciousness and disaffection. This sensibility, emblematized by the "new sensibility" of Susan Sontag, Norman Mailer, and others, optimistically championed the playful leveling of art and mass culture, of art and science, and of documentation and fictionalization, whereby all cultural artifacts would now have equal "validity."[31] Consumption became an integral part, indeed, the driving force, of this approach to culture, and citation became its modus operandi. Citation enabled the promiscuous seeking out of, celebration of, and pleasurable consumption of aesthetic-discursive idioms formerly deemed discrete, incompatible, or even inimical to one another. In addition, the move to the surface, emblematic of 1960s art and culture, facilitated the spatialization of philosophical and cultural binaries in close cohabitation and proclaimed that this could be done with self-confidence and seeming impunity.

Scientia sexualis, the disciplined viewer, and the citation of such binary opposites as high and low art and fact and fiction are the concepts that define the first part of my discussion of Andy Warhol's *Blow Job* in this book. Spectatorial assumptions about *Blow Job* are worth considering with regard to how they reflect Western paradigms of producing knowledge about sexuality, sex acts, and the kinds of individuals who engage in them. And because spectatorial assumptions about *Blow Job* are just that—speculations—they also place viewers in a position that marks their responses to the film firmly with regard to discursive manipulation. These rhetorics may be triggered by the film itself, but they are part of a much larger historical and cultural environment. *Blow Job* mobilizes them not only via its self-conscious framing, its lack of sound, its tightly constructed, minimalist mise-en-scène, and its lighting but also through the kinds of visual associations and memories *Blow Job* can arguably be said to trigger—and these associations have to do as much with the individual viewer's history of personal experiences and encounters as with his or her status as a socialized individual and consumer of mass culture.

One further area that is important to the first two chapters of this book—and weaves through most of the discussion in those chapters—is myth. To even so much as narrow down myth from an "area" to a concept is problematic, for there are many notions and concepts of myth, some of which will be explained later. Suffice it to say at this point that myth pertains to a discussion of *Blow Job* on multiple levels. First, *Blow Job* has garnered a mythological currency of its own. The title's denotative aspect aside, the internal censorship of *Blow Job*'s image, self-imposed and flaunted, provides the link between *Blow Job*'s content and its now mythical underground status. *Blow Job* became one of the most notorious films of 1960s underground cinema, and the fact that it was much more talked about than seen only increased this currency.

Second, *Blow Job*'s carefully crafted mise-en-scène makes it an emblematic example of the citational frenzy of the culture of the 1960s, spatializing a number of binary opposites without resolving them. On this level, *Blow Job* can be most clearly linked to myth, for, like myth, it functions as a vehicle that structures and negotiates binaries. For example, the film negotiates the relation between nature and culture, one of myth's traditional operational premises, by mobilizing several discursive regimes that articulate this great divide, including the tension between the "objective" recording and the fictionalization of an event, the tension between a "raw," purely physical and "prediscursive" sexuality and a discursive production of the latter, and the tension, on a somewhat broader, if clichéd, level, between life and art. Moreover, *Blow Job*'s intensely citational surface display alludes to a number of visual traditions and movements from the history of modern art and film, such as dadaism and surrealism, documentary and ethnographic film, Hollywood aesthetics, and pornography. What results from the act of enfolding these diverse discourses onto one picture plane is the image's high degree of reflexivity. I will argue that the film's self-reflexive properties question conventional ways of looking at gender and sexuality, but I will also ask to what extent *Blow Job*'s reflexivity really constitutes an epistemological advance over the paradigms it appropriates. By spatializing and foregrounding certain myths and conditions that pertain to myth's structuring impact, *Blow Job* performs a dual operation that, in turn, is closely related to *scientia sexualis* and the disciplined observer. On the one hand, the film's reflexivity tends to foreground the rhetorical nature of discourses of sex, gender, and sexuality and, as such, enables us to link these discourses to the discursive operations of myth itself. On the other hand, *Blow Job* also teases spectators into investing into these same discourses, and investing into them in a way that points to spectatorial desires to have knowledge produced as a coherent knowledge, to have truth extracted as a preexisting truth, and to have contradictions and aporias seemingly resolved in the teleology of achieving epistemological mastery.

Blow Job's mobilization of truth discourses and their questioning is actually much more complex than this description would suggest. The tension in *Blow Job* between an impression of aestheticization, fabrication, and artifice, on the one hand, and the pervasive if residual generic presence of documentary and its ethos and aspiration to simply (however "inadequately") record a preexisting event, on the other hand, also influences our dual impression of the young man's relation to the camera in the film. As Douglas Crimp observes, since the young man's eyes and gaze are for the most part obscured by shadows, it is very hard to state with any certainty that the young man acknowledges this camera. This leads Crimp to assert that *Blow Job*'s sitter does not perform but is performed upon.[32] This is an important perspective to bring to the film, because, as Crimp rightly claims, it offers viewers the freedom to revise conventional notions and expectations of textual/filmic content.[33] Crimp's reading is useful in that it suggests a general spectatorial potential to appropriate the image in the imaginary for specific purposes. But while *Blow Job* enables this spectatorial freedom, the aesthetic qualities that make the film a teaser also provoke very much the opposite: They tease viewers into scanning the image, into attempting to possess it by studying it for a truth value it never delivers. The freedom Crimp attributes to spectatorship in *Blow Job* is thus, indeed, only a *potential* one—on this level, it is an unlimited freedom in that it also enables, precisely with the same means, a range of readings that go in very diverse directions. And these depend more on the viewer than on the film, on what kind of viewer we are talking about, on the historical moment this viewer is confronted with *Blow Job*, and on how much knowledge the viewer brings to the film about its context. (Does the viewer know the title? Has the viewer heard about the film before, and if so, in what context and with what information? Does the viewer know the film's production context and its participants? To which of the multiple visual genres alluded to by *Blow Job* is the viewer sensitized and likely to respond?) Crimp, for his part, is implementing a highly specific spectatorial position and vantage point here—that of the gay historian whose hindsight vantage point of the film's "content" and insider knowledge determine his reading.

In this sense, Crimp's reading must be placed in a spectrum of possible readings and, as such, is no less partial than any other. Coming from a position similar to Crimp's, I identify with his mode of appropriating the film. Yet, having observed time and again how *Blow Job* generally tends to turn its viewers into readers very partial to their own respective and diverse interpretations, my own set of readings of the film investigates the dynamics of partiality that *Blow Job* mobilizes. The kinds of responses triggered by *Blow Job*'s charged allusions to sexuality can be witnessed on a broader level with regard to the generally polysemic quality of Warhol's larger image canon—cinematic or otherwise —which has recently prompted Hal Foster to conclude in a related context that certain "camps make the Warhol they need, or get the Warhol they deserve; no doubt we all do."[34]

The point for me, then, is not to cite visual proof to contradict Crimp. Indeed, those moments when one of the eyes of *Blow Job*'s young man is visible and is pointing roughly in the direction of the camera are easily outnumbered by moments when his eyes are obscured and cannot be unproblematically isolated from the larger sequence of his movements. However, while the young man's movements seem unrehearsed and spontaneous and while his facial expressions can be read as registering self-absorbed sexual pleasure, the film's overall setup makes it difficult to fully relinquish the impression that the young man in *Blow Job* at no point acknowledges the presence of the camera. (Given this setup, to what extent does my impulse to entertain the idea that the young man is aware of the camera, which is more or less directly placed in front of him, even depend on his eye contact for additional visual "proof"? To exhibit oneself to the camera does not always entail making eye contact with it, and spectatorial doubt or uncertainty as to the object's awareness of being filmed does not *necessarily, consistently* mitigate against the spectator's visual/sexual pleasure.) For me, it is primarily the context that counts here, and this context cannot be dissociated from any assumption, made in the absence of empirical proof, of what *Blow Job*'s young man may look at—and be aware of—at any given moment.

I will also argue in this book that *Blow Job*'s incitement of the desire to scan and "master" the image is itself foregrounded in and undermined by citation, whereby the impression of a seemingly "objective" filmic record of a preexisting event is produced, paradoxically, because of the film's very inadequacy as a reliable document. It is nothing less than the film's insinuating force that encourages us to read the young man's gestures and motions as undisturbed and self-absorbed, potentially freeing some of us from the doubt of fakery, authenticating the visual and sexual pleasure some of us have as particular kinds of viewers. Crimp rightfully points out that *Blow Job*'s setup and lighting disallow ocularcentric mastery, that they refuse to yield knowledge, and that they thwart voyeurism. To add to this, one might, in fact, entertain the claim that voyeurism is predominantly a heterosexual phenomenon—it is one of the staples of heterosexual (and heterosexist) exploitation of sexual representation, and it has been theorized by psychoanalytic discourses as a straight male domain. But if *Blow Job* thwarts voyeurism, it nonetheless makes us partial to our own readings of its image; it encourages some of us (as well as discourages others) to grant authenticity to the blow job itself, to invest in it, and even to claim, as Crimp does, that it is possible to pinpoint exactly when *Blow Job*'s young man reaches orgasm.[35] If this claim does not quite demonstrate ocularcentric mastery of the image, it does demonstrate a will to knowledge through scrutiny of the image and, most important, a will to take possession of the image, albeit in a very particular context and in a highly specific way. So even though *Blow Job* may ultimately disallow voyeurism, as Crimp asserts, Crimp's own reading tells me that *Blow Job* also constantly mobilizes the possessive aspects, implications, and consequences that underscore the basic act of using visual (and other) texts as evidence on which to "build a case," as it were.

In this sense, the claim that *Blow Job* unambiguously enables viewers to glean the young man's orgasm reminds me of Jonathan Flatley's useful analogy between *Blow Job* and the Kuleshov effect: "Precisely in the way that we are led to imagine that each tilt of the head and squinting of the eyes means something more than itself, *Blow Job* foregrounds how all face-reading is a matter of 'feeding the imagination.'"[36] Having enjoyed the kind of reading Crimp proffers, I support it for reasons of pleasure; however, I also agree with Flatley, who claims that "it is impossible to tell if the person is 'actually' being fellated"[37] and rightfully invokes David James's evaluation that performance in Warhol films is inevitable, as Warhol's cinema "constitutes being as performance."[38] It is for this reason, and not because I do not believe that a blow job is given in the film, that I will henceforth call *Blow Job*'s young man a "poser." In addition, my analyses throughout this book are meant to focus on the pose as a central element in epistemologies of gender and sexuality, in identity construction, in political activism, and in historical appropriations of heroes, role models, and mythologized icons.

This, then, brings me back to my discussion of myth. As an example of Warhol's particular brand of pop art, *Blow Job* engages a number of particular mid-twentieth century pop culture myths, mythical stereotypes (such as the teenage rebel), and mythologized stars (such as James Dean). I will place these myths into the context of Warhol's larger canon of images and will discuss the particularly pronounced iconic qualities of the Warholian image, which make Warhol's canon itself citational and highly intertextual. In fact, these qualities render Warhol's canon into a veritable boutique of mythical types, stereotypes, and pop culture icons, which can be drawn into different social, cultural, and political arenas, providing a further basis for locating and debating specific spectatorial positions, readings, and appropriations. While Chapter 1 and most of Chapter 2 of this book discuss *Blow Job*'s most important aesthetic properties and how they bear on the discursive production of gender and sexuality, toward the end of Chapter 2,

I begin to narrow the focus to the main group of interest for me—white gay men. Because the film may be regarded, as I argue in Chapter 2, as a historical reservoir or "archaeological site" of mythological types and popular stereotypes, it may allow us access also to white gay male appropriations of these types via the structure of memory and the operation of intertextuality. (In this sense, my analysis of *Blow Job* is based on the premise that the film is at least as much about the decade that preceded it as it is about the decade during which it was made.) I thus move into a discussion of how, in *Blow Job* and Warhol's larger canon of images, some of these mythological types, such as Christ and "the sad young man," gained currency particularly for white gay male self-stylizations.

By discussing *Blow Job* as the product of gay sensibility and an expression of white gay male identity, I attempt to wrest the film away from heteronormative ways of thinking that deny the visibility of homosexuality. But in doing so, I also seek to problematize the very mode of this kind of appropriation—not for the purpose of striking some kind of "humanist balance" or "objectivity" but, indeed, to infuse politically partisan appropriations of images with new methodological subtlety and strength. I believe that for these appropriations to survive in the current era of potentially homophobic "post-identity discourses," their limitations must be attended to with critical acumen and their virtues must be explored and pushed into new directions. But a discussion of gay appropriations of popular culture and mythology, while integral to this book, is only one of its aspects. Indeed, the trajectory I chart rests on a paradox: On the one hand, because homosexuality is a modern invention, a product of *scientia sexualis*, and because white gay male identity in particular is largely contingent on and contiguous to larger historical designs of masculinity and white male power and privilege—in the sense that it emerged from the latter and is constantly threatened to be subsumed by it—it is important for us to acknowledge that *Blow Job*, emphatically, is *not* a gay film at all. Further, *Blow Job*'s refusal to unambiguously visualize homosexuality is not an exact correlative to its refusal to unambiguously visualize heterosexuality. To the extent that the discourses that constructed homosexuality during the past 100 years are heterosexual(izing) and heteronormative discourses, *Blow Job*, if seen as a template of these discourses, is *profoundly* heteronormative (one might even go so far as to say profoundly heterosexual). On the other hand, precisely because *scientia sexualis* has systematically othered same-sex desire into homosexuality, making it one of the Others on which it has erected heterosexuality, homosexuality has come to be the Other that simultaneously supports and disturbs modernist systems of thought. Its existence is virtually guaranteed by the very regime that oppresses and disavows it. Therefore, if *Blow Job* rehearses some of these heteronormative discourses, homosexuality must then also be an important part of the film. Homosexuality's existence in the film, however disavowed and suppressed, must be integral to *Blow Job*—and may possibly be so in ways much more basic than the host of gay stereotypes that can be gleaned from the film. These stereotypes may themselves be only the tip of the iceberg, second- or third-order indications of larger, deeper dynamics at the heart of homosexual signification.

The middle section of this book explores these issues through historiographic and theoretical ways of thinking about homosexuality and Otherness. As a first step, it is justified to ask the question of what role, if any, *Blow Job* has played for homosexuals and, particularly, for white gay men. It becomes clear very quickly that the answer to this question has much to do with the paradox mentioned earlier and with underground cinema's own paradoxical way of visualizing scandal. While *Blow Job* is now considered one of the most prominent and enduring examples of the canon of gay cinema, during the first decade of its circulation it likely had very little direct impact on homosexuals. Its relatively confined, if gradually expanding, circulation foreclosed its mass exposure to homosexuals in that decade. Nonetheless, while many gay men might never have set eyes on a Warhol film for much of the 1960s, by the end of the decade, Warhol's cinema, as it existed and expanded in popular discourses, served as important evidence of the existence of homosexuality in America. The mere fact that somewhere in the homophobic American public sphere there existed a film titled *Blow Job* was sufficient evidence of homosexuality—even though those gay men who actually did get to see *Blow Job* were, of course, under similar strains as their heterosexual co-spectators to read the film as "proof" of their own conjectures.[39]

The main thrust of *Blow Job*'s currency for white gay men in the 1960s and into the 1970s may best be understood and measured by invoking myth. The fact that the screening of a Warhol film and the reaction of its audience would become inscribed into popular memory and circulated through gossip and anecdotes is symptomatic of the status of Warhol's films since the 1960s—they were much more talked about than seen and gained near-mythic status possibly even before Warhol withdrew his films from circulation in 1972. These films' and particularly *Blow Job*'s complex position within the public sphere—the tension between their elusive, almost hypothetical existence and their growing currency in prurient anecdotes and gay gossip—to some extent mirrors the situation of postwar, pre-Stonewall homosexuals in America. It would not be wrong to draw an explicit parallel between both as spectacles that are much more talked about than actually encountered by the mundane person. In this sense, while the mythical status of *Blow Job* may have been produced and amplified through gay gossip (thus serving as a catalyst for the proliferation of discourses of homosexuality in a public sphere that, on one level, homophobically ignored gayness), *Blow Job* also always serves as an allegory for the limitations and interdictions homosexuality has encountered on public *as well* as private levels of acknowledgment.

Because the position of homosexuality and particularly white gay male identity in the postwar American public sphere is very complex, it needs to be explored more systematically. In Chapter 3, I theorize and historicize the reemergence particularly of white gay male identity during the postwar 1940s and the 1950s with regard to the tension between invisibility and visibility, latency and manifestation. There are several conditions that produced this tension: First, the historically unprecedented privileging of large-scale homosocial spaces during World War II played an important role in allowing gays and lesbians to encounter and act upon same-sex desires even in the face of massive interdiction and punishment. Second, while many lesbians and homosexuals of color went back into their old civilian habitats after the war, white gay men used their relative freedom and mobility to move away from their prewar communities and began creating a fledgling network of urban subcultural scenes. The cultural productions of gayness that thrived in these scenes bore the stamp of the war years such that masculine identification became a pivotal idiom of white gay male sensibility. Third, the findings of the 1948 Kinsey Report on sexual behavior in the human male depathologized homosexuality and put it on a sliding scale with heterosexuality. As Kinsey's findings trickled down into the mainstream, they caused rampant homophobia, which, partly because of the inability to identify homosexuality on a mundane level, came to be displaced onto discourses of gender. But mainstream anxiety over effeminacy in men occurred concurrently with a proliferation of "alternative" masculinities, registering, among other things, in the emergence of new types of masculine idols, such as James Dean and Montgomery Clift. In turn, while gay life was beginning to flourish in subcultures in the United States, homosexuals remained largely closeted and developed sophisticated ways of communicating with one another in the hostile public sphere—ways that increasingly exploited the newly emerging "acceptable" if alternative masculinities. In Chapter 3, I analyze these historical factors in greater depth. I discuss the self-stylizations of white gay men with regard to their responses and counterstrategies against the homophobic yet highly unstable cluster of discursive productions of masculinity.

If the reemergence of white gay male identity during the 1950s evinced a strong tendency to insert homosexuality in subtle ways into the public sphere, this very subtlety also testifies to the complex relationship of masculine-identified white gay men to public America. By appropriating and manipulating discourses of masculinity, white gay men have demonstrated that they can pass successfully for straight, protecting themselves in some instances from homophobic persecution. In this way, white gay men have also capitalized on the fact that they can always be subsumed under the category of white men, which has enabled many of them to reap most of the privileges afforded to white men in our society. Chapter 4 proceeds from these insights with a discussion theorizing the relation between gender and sexual orientation through current paradigms of identity theory. By claiming that sexual and gender identities are firmly constructed in and by the social, queer theory and historiography (following in the footsteps of feminist theory's deconstruction of the concept of "woman") have systematically analyzed historical forms of anti-gay oppression and have persuasively conceptualized counterstrategies and reverse discourses. I look at some of these theories in Chapter 4, but I also ask whether they can be brought to bear on white gay male identity to the same extent and with similar benefits as they have on the theorization of, say, lesbian subject positions and the signification of drag. Analyzing white gay men's complex position as socialized males, I rehearse the deconstruction of white gay male identity specifically with regard to the relationship between the penis and the phallus, and I debate the virtues, limitations, and discursive limits of this theoretical approach for historical and political discourses of identity politics. I then juxtapose this approach to recent models that have sought to depart from theorizing identity in this way, as they have argued that the deconstruction of gender and sexual identity and some effects of gay rights activism have largely taken the specificity out of such terms as "gay" and "lesbian," threatening to make gays and lesbians once more invisible by prepping them for assimilation into the mainstream.

While *Blow Job* hovers in the background of much of my discussion in Chapter 3, serving as an exemplary reenactment of some of the problematics of the tension between invisibility and visibility particularly with regard to the immediate postwar years, Chapter 4 draws on the film as an example for discussing the theoretical implications of the virtues and limitations of deconstructing white gay male identity. I use the film to demonstrate the central paradox involving white gay men: On the one hand, they have been apprehended and socialized simply as white men; on the other hand, the set of qualities that make male homosexuality inimical to heterosexual masculinity have constituted a persistent, perhaps even essential, gap that sets gay men apart from heterosexual men. The discussion in Chapter 4 explores the question of whether this gap registers in *Blow Job*'s aestheticization of masculinity and, thus, whether this gap can be visually apprehended.

Rather than producing a definitive answer to these complex questions, my discussion of white gay male identity provides a set of arguments that can be inserted into current debates around theorizing identity. In the last two chapters of this book, I draw on these arguments to resume a historically focused analysis of the evolution of white gay male identity into the 1960s. In Chapter 5, I expand my discussion of *Blow Job* to a group of images Andy Warhol produced from the mid-1950s into the 1960s—images that I view as not only expressing white gay sensibility but also arguably rehearsing the evolution of white gay male identity in a shifting historical context. The early 1960s saw a proliferation of mainstream discourses of homosexuality. No longer an unspoken or unambiguously demonized taboo, homosexuality became the target of liberal mainstream efforts to ethnicize and incorporate sexual Otherness in new ways. Thus, in Chapter 5, I read several of Warhol's images that depict gay icon James Dean or Dean look-alikes against this new context, and I trace two antithetical processes in these images: First, they can be read in a trajectory that exemplifies the evolution of white gay male identity via appropriations of and identifications with public figures, evincing strong parallels to major psychoanalytically defined processes of identity formation. Second, they persistently index the traumatic repressions at the heart of identity formation, and, further, they point to a certain dysfunction in the relationship of white gay male identity to masculinity.

For much of this book I focus on white gay male identity with regard to sexual orientation and masculinity. Some of these discussions are punctured by a discussion of race, pinpointing the whiteness of white gay men. Chapter 6 focuses on race more systematically, drawing on my arguments and insights from previous chapters. If white gay men's relation to masculinity has placed these men in a hegemonic position with regard to the stratum of social and sexual groups (oppressed yet privileged, persecuted yet also celebrated and integrated), how does the whiteness of white gay men intersect with their masculinity and their social positioning? In Chapter 6, I compare white gay male self-stylizations to a figure that became notorious in the early 1960s and to which white gay men have a historically close and theoretically complex relation—the white heterosexual hipster. In addition to discussing *Blow Job* as a template of whiteness as a hegemonic construct, I also consider other images from the Warhol canon with regard to questions of race and late 1950s and early 1960s hipsterism.

1

MYTHS FROM THE UNDERGROUND

The range of *Blow Job*'s self-reflexive devices—along with all that they enable—must be understood to derive from the interplay of several "classically Warholian" features. One of these features is the mobilization of diverging generic markers, rhetorics, and spectatorial assumptions without apparent conflict, such that cinema's dual abilities to document and fictionalize are exploited simultaneously. A second feature is a minimalist style that enables a dissection of the image into its basic formal properties of time and space and that further decomposes these properties into mutually foregrounding tendencies toward motion and stasis, depth and flatness, and realism and fragmentation. Considering each of these aspects in turn and discussing, when apposite, how they are influenced by a third feature—the incorporation without "value judgment" of elements from high and low art—I shall argue that *Blow Job*'s self-reflexive devices constitute a unique kind of spectatorial address that dislodges audiences from their contemplative positions and makes them react and respond to the film in a number of ways. *Blow Job*'s reflexivity makes spectators intensely aware that seeing a film means projecting onto and investing into the image a part of one's own self, which is always a socialized, acculturated self. Yet, even though *Blow Job* troubles the assumption that spectator and artwork exist in autonomous, ontologically separate worlds and that the viewing process proceeds in an analytically neutral and objective vacuum, this troubling realization does not completely foreclose some of the implications of the practice of contemplation. Indeed, it may be taken as a confirmation of the viewer's supreme cognitive and analytical capacities. More particularly, the awareness self-consciously experienced by many viewers that they are being addressed and provoked by the film implies the promise that vision is a tool central to their epistemological advancement. It seems, then, that precisely because *Blow Job* also invites spectators to invest back into the image *epistemologically as well as libidinally*, it coerces a form of spectatorship that runs counter to—yet seems to coexist with—aspirations of obtaining any kind of "higher" analytical knowledge. Viewers thus oscillate between an awareness of their contingency on larger schemes and the promise of ocularcentric mastery of the image. It is not that *Blow Job* thereby completely voids or neutralizes its self-reflexive aspects. Rather, *Blow Job*'s spectators may become aware that their deductive, analytical activities become integral to the film's conceptual success as a tease. Textual reflexivity and spectatorial contemplation are themselves part of a broader ocularcentric discourse that presumes—but also consistently seems to have to reconfirm—the viewer's perceptual and epistemological autonomy. *Blow Job* consistently feeds into aspirations to such autonomy even as it undermines them.

This dual spectatorial address never confines itself to the strictly cerebral play of formal properties and details. However, there are two particular areas—to be discussed later in this chapter—where the film subverts and mocks the form/content split very concretely with regard to the representation of sex. The first area seizes on the way we interpret facial expressions as indices of particular sensations. Does the face of the poser in *Blow Job* betray lust, pain, intoxication, or the desire to pull the wool over our eyes by "faking" any or all of the above? And what do our approaches to the image, methodological or seemingly "instinctual," say about our much-famed perceptual and epistemological autonomy? The second area, the symbolically charged division between on- and off-screen space, even more blatantly foregrounds the precariousness of spectatorial autonomy. The image demonstrates that its viewer is an acculturated viewer whose interpretations of on- and off-screen space reveal his or her own contiguity to socio-cultural and historical contexts.

THE MYTH OF REFLEXIVITY

One of the most striking features of *Blow Job*'s reflexivity is the tension in the image between documentation and denaturalization/fictionalization—a tension, that is, between the illusion of unmediated visual presence and an acknowledgment of the mediating presence of illusion. On one level, *Blow Job* can be said to simply display the face of a man who is positioned in front of a camera and who goes through certain motions with his head and body. The static camera and the absence of editing help the film capture "objectively" the spontaneous details of the poser's movements and facial expressions as they unfold. The minuteness of the unfolding act produces an impression of authenticity and immediacy not unlike that which earlier film theorists such as Siegfried Kracauer attributed to the close-up's capacity to reveal small material phenomena and thus to disclose new aspects of physical reality.[1] Of course, the opposite is also true; as Kracauer points out, these acts of disclosure almost immediately assume a defamiliarizing effect. The details of the poser's face with regard to these antithetical aspects are thus of considerable interest.

However, the poser's face is not the only object *Blow Job* offers for scrutiny. Another very prominent aspect of the image is its background, the brick wall, which also, on one level, contributes to the impression of documentary authenticity. The film's static camera, absence of editing, and overall minimalism enable an unusually extensive, undisturbed perusal of the brick wall, much like with a photograph. Viewers have enough time to behold this backdrop, and the brick wall's dense surface texture itself produces an impression of unforced documentary immediacy. Yet, it is also true that the brick wall's visual qualities are aestheticized simply by the fact that they are an important part of the *fabricated* mise-en-scène. The black-and-white image artistically enhances the surface qualities of diverse materials that make up the wall (the irregularities in the lines of brick, the uneven application of mortar) and amplifies the bricks' chipped and coarse condition. In this regard, an analysis of *Blow Job*'s mise-en-scène can be compared to analytical approaches to certain generic qualities in black-and-white social realist photography (such as Walker Evans's *Kitchen Wall, Hale County, Alabama/1936*) via Gestalt theory, where the discovery of surface contrasts and structural irregularities and, paradoxically, their promotion to an overall structuring principle aestheticizes in the very act of documenting.[2]

Hence, what is important for us to note at this point is that the dual qualities of documentation and aestheticization far from neutralize any documentary aspects. Creating the *illusion of a referent*, they are an inherent part of the documentary tradition itself—even though this tradition has been re-theorized, along with Western visual culture's mode of mechanical reproduction, as being completely determined by the simulacrum. *Blow Job* is not a documentary, but whatever else it does with this duality, however else it tips the scale away from documentation, the film also always invokes documentary at least as a genre.

The formal and generic conventions of the documentary tradition also consistently if latently inform our complex readings of other aspects of the film, such as whether the poser acknowledges the camera. We need to note, too, that the documentary element is not necessarily abolished for those viewers who allow the film's title to inform their reading of the image. If a reading of *Blow Job* allows the off-screen act to become part of the on-screen content, the concept of transgressiveness enters the picture and arguably heightens the impression that what we see is part of a sex act that actually took place, possibly in public. In the manner of a particular nonfiction film genre— ethnographic cinema—*Blow Job* may then be regarded as a sort of undercover exposé of illicit sex practices, a film seeking to document the existence of blow jobs and to capture the specific "types" who might be presumed to be practicing fellatio. (What better ethnological territory for this kind of study than Warhol's famed Factory?) From this perspective, precisely because the scene *Blow Job* depicts comes across as transgressive and "exotic," it implicitly authenticates the existence of a subcultural world with which certain sex acts are associated. In this sense, *Blow Job* at least holds out the promise for viewers to read its documentary/ethnographic lens, in David James's words, as a "means to the unhindered passage of content, and so to construct a documentarist Warhol, valuable precisely for his depiction of an otherwise unrepresented social milieu."[3]

All this said, we must not ignore the other set of qualities of *Blow Job*'s mise-en-scène—manipulation and aestheticization, which are manifold and complex and which are indissociable from the film's documentary impulse. Any spectatorial ambivalence as to whether the poser acknowledges or denies the existence of the camera (or oscillates between the two) prompts at least two readings. One such reading is that the poser may be faking the blow job, which leads to questioning the whole scenario and which contributes to the film's dual status as real event and put-on. Another reading is that the poser's movements represent the kind of self-conscious behavior of someone who, while actually having sex, is being filmed. Either reading places the poser squarely within the performance parameters so characteristic of many Warhol films, indicating the pressure that comes to rest on the subject simply by virtue of being placed in front of Warhol's camera. Read this way, the poser's *complicity* in being filmed makes the whole scenario into what David James has termed "a theatre of self-presentation,"[4] to which the presence of the camera is integral.

Any attempt to clarify the relation between poser and camera and to put a definitive label on the film is further foiled by the strong aestheticization of *Blow Job*'s mise-en-scène. For example, the film temporalizes its image by producing a tension between stasis and motion. It makes temporality palpable as it gestures toward stillness. The slowed-down projection speed of the image to sixteen (or eighteen) frames per second dramatizes the poser's convulsions and thereby renders the act somewhat inauthentic and trancc-like. One gets the impression that the film seems to aspire almost to a negation of time and a transcendence of material reality when it celebrates sexual pleasure in a hidden and protected underground space. This self-conscious temporalization helps to define *Blow Job*'s space as an "other" space, or an elsewhere. Its effect is even compounded by the unstable relationship between the poser and the visual environment in which he is placed. Not only do the poser's erratic movements carry him, at times, half out of the frame, but the minimalist lighting in which they appear (and that they themselves help produce) destabilizes the ontological separation between figure and ground. At certain times, the poser's head moves forward and appears clearly set off from the background; at other times, especially when he throws his head back, his head seems to blend in with the brick wall. The image's overall impression is therefore neither one of depth nor one of complete flatness. Film theorists as early as Rudolf Arnheim have noted that if this effect is carried too far, it not only strongly aestheticizes an image but threatens to undermine any documentary function that is supposed to inhere in its pictorial carriers.[5]

Finally, *Blow Job*'s image produces strong chiaroscuro patterns. More accurately, we witness the fragmentation of the picture plane into smaller, semiabstract parts. This effect is produced by the movements of the poser's head, which all but completely determine the distribution of light across the frame. Depending on the degree to which the poser's head is tilted away from the light source, located just beyond the upper left frame, the lighting of his face appears in various patterns of chiaroscuro and ranges from evenly lit to completely obscured. For example, at certain times, the poser's face is completely shrouded in darkness because his head is tilted down. At other times, when his face is directed toward the camera, the subtle motions of his head generate undulating patterns of light and shadow across his face. At yet other times, when he throws his head back and deep into his neck, his face is bathed in light. Sometimes, the poser turns his face sharply to the left, a position that would display his head in profile were it not for the fact that his face is actually off frame, so that all we see is one of his ears and the back of his head. At other times he makes a similar movement to the right, so that his other ear becomes fully visible. As the film progresses, the dramatic patterns of light and shadow are further complicated by the poser using his hands to touch his nose, forehead, and hair. Sometimes, he seems to rotate through his motions in a regular, almost rhythmic order. At other times, the film shows him moving his head directly and rapidly from a low angle to a high angle.

Blow Job's mise-en-scène thus dissects its object by sequencing the same array of corporeal gestures over time, a process that causes the poser's seemingly unified image to become segmented into recurrent, semiabstract visual constellations of light and shadow. Intermittently, viewers begin to focus on particular parts of the image. They may become intrigued by, say, the shadow under the poser's nose and chin; they may begin to pay attention to his right ear or the conspicuous spot of light on the tip of his nose; they may start noticing the light reflected in his hair (Figure 1.1). This kind of segmentation of *Blow Job*'s image somewhat qualifies the commonly held assumption that Warhol's early films, because of their static camera and lack of editing, exclusively and by definition constitute a unified image. While *Blow Job*, on one level, never quite ceases to produce the impression of a unified image, on another level, its play of light and shadow also generates varying and broadly recurring *fragments* of the poser's face. One might argue that the poser's head rotates through its various positions—shifting up, down, and sideways, sometimes thrusting forward, at other times moving backwards—so that audiences, rather than seeing only this one face, actually see different versions of the face dissolve and reconstitute themselves. In addition, even as viewers may apprehend the same face in ever new versions and visual constellations, the image's fleeting visual quality may trigger spectatorial anxiety, as details within the image constantly change even though the overall image seems to stay the same. The effect is a vague sense of distraction—a distraction not from the image, but by and within the image. In sum, *Blow Job*'s space appears simultaneously more real (because it is captured momentously with very basic, even crude, means) and more artificial (because of its semiotic instability). As the tension between authenticity and fabrication then becomes one of the basic effects of *Blow Job*'s self-reflexive aesthetics, the film's visually unstable mise-en-scène

Figure 1.1
Blow Job. Film still courtesy of the Andy Warhol Museum.

invites comparison with many of Warhol's silk screens in that it obtains a double status as both referent and simulacrum. As a visual document of a young man, the film appears to have a clear referent. But this status is constantly undermined by the image's fabricated quality. The simulacrum both constitutes and simulates its own content. It looks like "the real thing," yet it also looks like a "bad," low-quality copy.

Blow Job's unstable visuals arguably trigger a shift in perception. Rather than making the viewer search for a hidden, preformulated "message," the film produces a series of cognitive frissons through its self-reflexive devices. These devices are self-reflexive in part because they draw attention to the film's means of production but mostly because they draw attention to the act of viewing and questioning the image. Critics have argued that the reflexivity of Warhol's early minimalist films makes the viewer not only the subject who analyzes the film but also the object of this analysis. Stephen Koch, for example, claims that Warhol's early films make one "peculiarly aware of the process of looking, itself, conscious not merely of the object, but also the feel, the nature, the very matrix and interplay of your perceptions. The object will thus refer you again to yourself and your own personal capacity to transform objects and their environments."[6] Koch traces this quality to dadaism and, more particularly, to the conceptual legacy of Marcel Duchamp. Part of this legacy is that the image is only secondarily concerned with displaying an object; its raison d'être is the act of showcasing as such—an act it declares as worthy of attention and celebration. Thomas Elsaesser has traced this polemic further in dadaist cinema, characterizing it as the Duchampian shift from ends to means, which "is always doubled by what might be called a process of semiotization, where an object of little or no value is transformed not into a value but into an (ironic) signifier of value."[7] *Blow Job* can be said to emblematize this shift in more than one way: For example, the tension between documentation and fictionalization may be regarded as a self-conscious act of simultaneously mobilizing and frustrating the two basic conditions of spectatorship that attend cinema's double function as scientific device and aesthetic medium—scopophilia and epistemophilia[8]—aspects that will be reencountered frequently in this book especially with regard to the film's discourses on sexuality. This simultaneous celebration and mitigation of the desire for accessing and mastering the visual field finds an analogy in the film's ironic comment on the status of the image as a commodity. *Blow Job* simultaneously defamiliarizes and endorses its own mercantile function. It lures the viewer with its aesthetically and sexually intriguing spectacle, and it flaunts its own strategies of pandering without delivering.

One of the values *Blow Job* can thus be said to resignify via its ironic shift from ends to means is that of commercial exchange. In this respect, a comparison seems apposite between *Blow Job* and pornography, one of the most blatantly mercantile genres of visual culture. *Blow Job*'s relation to pornography is examined in more detail in the next section of this chapter. The focus here is on *Blow Job*'s seeming deviation from one of hard-core pornography's staples, the cum shot or money shot—that is, the ejaculation outside the sex partner's body as visual proof for the camera that male satisfaction has been obtained. In the commercial regime of porn, the money shot operates like a fetish in that it masks commercial porn's main raison d'être, which is not to arouse but to turn a profit.[9] Linda Williams argues that "perhaps in the money shot's repeatedly inflated, 'spending' penis we can see condensed all the principles of late capitalism's pleasure-oriented consumer society: pleasure figured as an orgasm of spending; the fetish not simply as commodity but as the surplus value of orgasm."[10] The money shot thereby becomes an illusion whose seeming visual truth eclipses the oppressive power hierarchies and the human exploitation that go into producing it as a commodity. By contrast, *Blow Job* withholds this money shot from viewers and teases them by making them read the poser's face for signs of orgasm, not the least because they *want* to believe in the blow job. The absence in *Blow Job* of a cum shot—of barely so much as an unequivocal facial twitch—would then separate exchange value and surplus value and seemingly denaturalize—the commodity aspect of visual imagery. The image's defalcation and the spectatorial frustrations that result help transform value into its own signifier and thereby foreground that in our culture images are always subject to commercial valuation. If they are not always issued as merchandise, they still end up mercenaries.

However, this observation must be qualified by another aspect that signals that *Blow Job* also significantly departs from most original Dada discourses (if not from the appropriation of Dada by the museum as a bourgeois institution): Even though *Blow Job* ironically foregrounds that viewers of any kind of image are also always consumers, the film nonetheless makes us invest in—and thus pay for—the image with ever greater frenzy. In other words, while the film self-reflexively transforms value into its own signifier, it does not abjure value altogether. In fact, by denying the cum shot, *Blow Job* places viewers merely on the other side of the "frenzy of the visible," to borrow Williams's term, as it makes them scrutinize the poser's face for signs of orgasm. (In this sense, *Blow Job* is in close conceptual proximity to pornography's display of female orgasm, which is marked by apocryphal surface qualities.)[11] The depth with which even 1960s audiences, who viewed *Blow Job* at a moment right before the money shot would come into its own as an integral part of the soon-to-emerge genre of hard-core pornography, were invested in such frenzied valuation of the visual can be gleaned by the frustrated reaction of an audience of *Blow Job* consisting of students from Columbia University, who impatiently cheered, "We shall never come!"[12] *Blow Job*'s early audiences may not have expected an actual cum shot, but the Columbia University audience's reaction to *Blow Job* suggests that the viewer's need for visual proof was already conditioned to such an extent that the development of a logical outcome for this need, only a few years later, in the unabashedly capitalist nature of hard-core porn comes as no surprise. Of course, one could easily object to this reading of *Blow Job*'s refusal to feature the cum shot by claiming that the reading derives from a discussion of heterosexual porn. But if the cum shot in gay male porn were to function differently for gay male spectators (in the sense, as Richard Dyer has pointed out, that its stress on visibility and plenitude, while inherent to male sexuality in general, potentially harbors certain "politically progressive" aspects with regard to gay men[13]), *Blow Job*'s refusal to provide such visual/sexual pleasure is even more obnoxious. Refusing to desublimate its otherwise tactile beauty to this end, *Blow Job* chooses to remain tactful—a fact to be kept in mind by those who insist on extolling the purported defiance of 1960s underground cinema.

The Duchampian shift from ends to means thus effects a transformation of *Blow Job*'s image, so that the functions one might assume to inhere in the image are actually cited by it as reified qualities. This transformation then also reflects the status of the film's self-reflexive devices and their alignment with discourses of realism and modernism. One might initially—but, as we shall see, falsely—assume that *Blow Job* represents a basically realist image that operates within the aesthetic/discursive parameters in which low art and mass culture produced and exploited realist imaging and that this realist image is distorted "from above," as it were, by the "intervention" of the high art influence of, say, dadaism. Yet, our discussion of *Blow Job*'s self-reflexive devices makes clear that the film's reflexivity operates on several levels. Thus, *Blow Job*'s undermining of its own purported documentary realism, the slowed-down projection speed, and the destabilization of the figure/ground relation are not simply aberrations from the conventions of realism but can, in fact, also be found, in one way or another, in much of realist-based mass culture to this day. Recent historicizations on the evolution of visual representation from nineteenth to twentieth century Western visual culture have stressed that the conceptual implications and effects linked to an *anti*-ocularcentric image did not come about with a certain modernist "distortion" of the realist image (of which the semiotic fragmentation of *Blow Job*'s image into chiaroscuro patterns may be taken as one instance) but that they must be regarded as being part and parcel of the overall conditions of the production and reception of mass-marketed realist imagery itself. So the relationships within *Blow Job* between realism and its distortion, and between low art and high art, are quite complex. Not only do these terms have a complicated genealogy, but they also complicate any discussion of the film's reflexivity.

Reflexivity in visual representation has more often than not existed in dialectical relation to the contemplative viewer. It functions as a kind of culturally sanctioned advancement of the viewer's analytical capabilities. Robert Stam and Jonathan Crary have, from different perspectives, critiqued the myth that reflexivity per se comes to be the guarantor for the subject's autonomy in that it is considered to disturb the discursive regime that naturalizes the subject in the process of constructing it. Stam reminds us that the realism of mimetic representation and its distortion through reflexivity are not necessarily conceptual antitheses. As he notes,

> They illuminate the everyday realities of the social conjunctures from which they emerge, while also reminding their readers or spectators of the artificiality of their mimesis. . . . Realism and reflexivity are not strictly opposed polarities but rather interpenetrating tendencies quite capable of coexistence within the same text. It would be more accurate to speak of a 'coefficient' of reflexivity or mimesis, while recognizing that it is not a question of a fixed proportion.[14]

The critical focus, Stam goes on to say, therefore shifts away from investigating the formal properties of realism and mimesis toward spectatorial investment and complicity in it.[15] With *Blow Job*'s sex act suspended between reality and illusion, we turn from asking whether its representation is "true" to investigating what we want from the film and how we project our own investments onto its image. From this perspective, *Blow Job* may well denaturalize the sitter's status as referent by subverting its own documentary realism, but in the process of doing so, the film also foregrounds our desire for that referent as a knowable, coherent entity and, by implication, our desire, relayed through our investment in realism, for reality. The capacity of the image to transform human perception becomes enfolded with its antithetical function of affirming conventional spectatorial notions of mimesis and, linked to these notions, the desire to see particular social contexts represented with which viewers identify. This process is significant, as it indicates the dual status of *Blow Job*'s viewer as both subject and object: The viewer is the film's viewing subject in that it is he or she who is addressed by the film as viewer. Yet, to the extent that the viewer's epistemological mastery of the image is foiled, he or she ends up viewing the film subjectively. The viewer is turned into an object because his or her subjective reading of the film becomes an index of his or her existence as a socialized individual and, even further, as an object of certain historically accrued physical technologies and rhetorical techniques of representation—a disciplined subject, a docile viewer, to borrow from Foucault.

Jonathan Crary has described this dual status of the viewer as subject/object as emblematic of a shift in the conceptualization of perception that took place in the early nineteenth century. Thus, as Crary points out, this shift occurred somewhat before the emergence of, in this case, modernist reflexivity and its respective incarnations in abstract painting and avant-garde film. According to Crary, it was not the advent of photography but the earlier emergence of what he calls "new technologies of the observer" that replaced the notion of vision as an objective tool of knowledge by relocating it inside the viewing subject, who, along with his or her now subjectivized vision, became the object of study and technological experimentation. Crary adds that this subjectivization of vision was already accompanied by a general fragmentation of space, by the exchangeability of images, and by the severing of the referent. The refraction of the classical perspectival space of the camera obscura was then not instigated by late nineteenth century high modernist visuals but, rather, had been informing both modernist abstraction and mass culture realism even before that time.[16]

This insight pertains to our analysis of *Blow Job*. Reading *Blow Job* in a way that aligns reflexivity entirely with the influence of high art and realism entirely with low art would be too simplistic. Even though high appears to defamiliarize low, the fragmentation of *Blow Job*'s image also references specifically the fragmentation of the overall body of images produced by mass culture. *Blow Job* here suggests that low art and realist visual documentation themselves consist of nothing but fabricated fragments and that each mass-produced image is itself a fragment in the frantic exchange of mass cultural imagery. The conditions for this fragmentation, which Crary traces in nineteenth century culture but which, of course, continue to exist to the present, also underscore some of the ways in which *Blow Job* places viewers in relation to their own fragmented realities by confronting them with a series of images they feel they have encountered before. For example, even though *Blow Job* does not avail itself of found images (in the manner of dadaism and especially surrealism), the film nonetheless alludes to them. *Blow Job*'s image simulates the iconographic and fetishistic features of Hollywood publicity stills and film posters and temporalizes their generic identity as still images. But while the film's slowed-down projection speed, on one level, gestures toward this stillness, on another level, it also works against this effect. The film comes to be a reverse correlative of surrealism's stilling of objects associated with motion:[17] It animates a formerly still representation of well-known status, such as the publicity poster from *Rebel Without a Cause* that shows James Dean leaning against a brick wall, and thereby defamiliarizes it and brings it back to life.

What is usurped, then, by *Blow Job*'s simulacrum is not the referent but other simulacra. To the extent that the chiaroscuro patterns fragment *Blow Job*'s image into blotches of light and dark, they can be regarded as giving the image a semiabstract quality; to the extent, however, that these blotches reconfigure the poser's face into diverse face fragments, they are far from anti-mimetic. On this level, they can be regarded as producing a series of fragmented allusions to such pop icons as James Dean and to broadly mythological figures such as the juvenile delinquent and the suffering martyr.[18] In this sense, *Blow Job*, once again, "disciplines" viewers by making them "respond" to their own history of encountering popular culture even as they take this response for an original, personal, intimate eureka effect. The way in which *Blow Job*'s simulacrum addresses viewers is, thus, yet another instance of what Crary describes as the production of a new kind of observer who was calculable and regularizable and whose vision could be measured and exchanged.

As noted earlier, *Blow Job* constructs the viewer as both subject and object. While the film flaunts its illusionistic qualities and tempts viewers to lose themselves in the ethereal aesthetics of the image, to dream, to speculate, and to ruminate about it, it also acknowledges and mobilizes the spectatorial desire for access—access to the epistemological and ethnographic truth of the image; access to unmediated sexual pleasure; and access to experience per se, experience that is unmediated by time and space. In other words, the desire that *Blow Job* both mobilizes and frustrates is the aspiration for a time and space prior to reading, interpretation, and the pitfalls attached to them. In fact, by articulating the reality of desire, the film promotes a desire for a reality that could be called "truth." Even if (or precisely because) *Blow Job*'s viewers may recognize themselves in the dual role of subjects being subjected to the tease, they go right on to place their historically accrued investments into the image. The film makes them realize—but may also make them experience with pleasure—just how deeply they are implicated in the rhetorics of representation.

The disciplinary aspects of what one may call a relation of contiguity of viewer and image are themselves highly suggestive of the shift in consciousness brought about by nineteenth-century visual cultures' stress on automation and mechanization. In this regard, one may recall Warhol's own notorious remark, "I want to be a machine." If the ironic paradox between the remark's declared desire for deindividuation and its deadpan, one-of-a-kind notoriety mythologizes the artist once again as a highly individual, unique personality, it also points to precisely the kind of shift in relation to images that Crary discusses. Crary compares the nineteenth-century observer's metonymic relation to techniques of visualization to the ways in which industrialization inverted the relationship between man and tool, whereby man became the tool of his own man-made machines—strictly functional and, as such, irreplaceable only as a general category.[19] While the automatism aspect of the machine metaphor rings somewhat totalizing and defeatist in its extremely disciplinary nature, the actual "machine" part harbors an element of productivity, which potentially leads to ever new ways in which humans remake themselves within and through the disciplinary operations that produce them. A Foucauldian discourse would thus argue that while we never free ourselves of discipline, our engagement with it over a period of time nonetheless leads to myriad redefinitions and evolutions of the very categories of disciplinary production. Therefore, particularly the production aspect of this machine metaphor may be linked to several areas of Foucauldian discourse, such as the heterogeneity of forms of power, the productive and strategic character of cultural and subcultural practices, and, closely related, the productive and strategic nature of reverse discourses and countermemories. They are worth mentioning here because they figure directly or indirectly in *Blow Job*'s mobilization of popular myths and in the film's construction of gender and sexuality.

To the extent that the disciplined viewer is contingent with—indeed, the product of—larger technologies of cultural production, the viewer is no less imbricated with the social than is the "classical" contemplative viewer. But while the latter is called upon to seek out the image as a means of resisting the ideologically inflected space of the social, the former—as a subject/object, machine/tool—consumes and converts images (converts them partly by consuming them) into cultural and subcultural practices that always take place within the social. These practices may then also include imaging and *reimaging*, but image production is now just one single aspect of a much larger cultural production of discourses and practices. And these practices take place as much outside any *particular* image as they take place within it. *Blow Job*'s self-reflexive features do not exempt the film from this dynamic. On the contrary, this is their focus, as they paradoxically and hyperbolically identify the image's minimalist content and its spatial isolation with their respective opposites—the dense charge of activity and the intricate involvement with the world outside. As an ironic interface between subject and object, *Blow Job* shows that the act of viewing is a process that links the individual to the outer world and links the inside of an image to its outside—a process that involves viewers' libidos as much as their intellects. It is this contiguity of viewer/image that helps the film both demythologize and remythologize such cherished notions as spectatorial self-awareness and textual reflexivity. *Blow Job* demythologizes the importance conventionally ascribed to spectatorial autonomy by demystifying its impact—by helping viewers, at best, to become aware of their own historically and socioculturally conditioned perception of images. In other words, the film demythologizes the viewer as subject by showing the viewer his or her status as an object. But *Blow Job* also remythologizes the viewer's aspiration to master its object, even as the film foregrounds the myths that plague the seemingly autonomous viewer. The film lures viewers to enter the exchange the film initiates. We view an enigmatic and alluring image, and, in turn, we attempt to possess it and then pander this possession to the rest of the world, whereby we help mythologize the film as well as ourselves as viewers, commentators, truth-seekers, advisers, and so on. Thus, *Blow Job* does not destroy myth but perpetuates myth as a category. Not the least effect of this operation is the film's own mythical status: *Blow Job* is remembered as an explicit document of forbidden sex, which it is not; as an underground film widely seen in its own day, which it was not (neither by gay nor straight viewers); and as Warhol's paean to the gay male subculture, which it became only slowly, over an extended period that involved a number of events that took place without the image much more so than within it, including the Stonewall "revolution," gay gossip, and a little false detail Stephen Koch added to his description of *Blow Job*.[20]

The visual incompleteness of *Blow Job*'s image causes viewers to speculate not only on whether a sex act is actually taking place and who the young man's putative partner may be but also on the type of persons who would engage in public fellatio. Among the factors that would have influenced such speculations, both Kinsey reports (the 1948 study of sexual behavior in the human male and the complementary study, published in 1953, focusing on sexual behavior of females) are arguably central here. These reports not only depathologized homosexuality (see Chapter 3) but also revealed a host of statistical data about sex practices of American men and women of all sexual persuasions.[21] As the publication of Kinsey's research forced public discourses to acknowledge that Americans were having sex for more reasons than to make babies, it also prompted postwar American culture to mobilize with renewed fervor certain clichés and stereotypes, which helped to newly stigmatize nonreproductive sex because its existence could no longer be denied and which also negotiated notions of gender linked to nonreproductive sex. In this light, at least certain portions of *Blow Job*'s initial audiences were likely to imagine either a gay man, a prostitute, or a "bad" girl at the poser's cock. But the film refuses to bear out any such assumptions. Neither does it give unequivocal proof that the poser actually reaches orgasm. The notion that orgasm is proof of the existence of a sexual act can also be attributed to Kinsey's work,[22] for Kinsey claims that orgasm is a prerequisite for the proper scientific verification of both homosexual and heterosexual sex acts, which he has termed "outlets." It is, of course, exactly the determination of this "outlet" that *Blow Job* frustrates and, in fact, displaces onto a perusal of the poser's face.

Our search for particular sexual clues in the poser's face derives from a subliminal dynamic that informs a much broader range of human encounters, some of which might be categorized as overtly sexual and some as mundane. And yet, even on a mundane level, the study of the face may be characterized as pornographic, for it contains a certain feature Stephen Koch has singled out as being central to pornography: that is, because of the central role of fantasy, "the other" becomes a mere extension of one's own desires and fantasies.[23] *Blow Job* aptly exemplifies this dynamic. That the film is capable of triggering sexual fantasies without showing sex indicates that our erotic imagination can be sparked easily without the help of naked bodies, genitals, or intercourse. *Blow Job*, then, arguably combines the mundane, seemingly nonsexual with the pornographic. Or, more accurately, it hints at the latent existence of the sexual in all human encounters; it locates the nonsexual and the sexual on a sliding scale, and it designates the human face as a privileged site of these readings. But if *Blow Job* reveals that the nonsexual and the sexual are never too far apart, what exactly happens to the pornographic impulse? While I believe that *Blow Job* significantly differs from pornography, to usefully isolate the pornographic impulse in *Blow Job*, we need to compare the film to pornography itself. More particularly, while the semiotic implications of the facial expressions of hard-core porn performers are quite different from those of *Blow Job*'s poser, from an anthropological perspective they share the same territory: the realm of myth. By juxtaposing *Blow Job* to pornography, I will argue herein that *Blow Job* constitutes a complex response to two particular myths—first, the myth that nonreproductive sex is degenerate and, second, the myth that gender is natural. I will also discuss how these myths arose in connection with the emergence of a set of social laws whose superimposition has been registered as nothing less than traumatic.

While hard-core pornography did not become commercialized on a large scale until the late 1960s, its existence is virtually contemporaneous with the invention of the moving image.[24] Its transgressive and forbidden status in Western culture has been marked not simply by its graphic depiction of genital sex but also by the facial expressions of its protagonists. Facial expressions in pornography are often perceived as obscene not merely because of their varying degrees of exaggeration but also because of a much more basic impulse inherent in them. The fact that even subtle and almost casually performed changes in the human face may be registered as obscene points to the existence of a powerful and long-standing semiotic code that relates the range of facial expressions to what a given civilization may consider acceptable or taboo. Anthropologists and semioticians know that this code relates the sexual aspects of the face to its seemingly nonsexual functions, such as the utterance of speech. Speech itself is intrinsically bound up with the evolution of civilizations and thus with what Dean MacCannell calls "the regime of grammar"[25]—a set of dos and don'ts that lays down the rules of what is deemed civilized and uncivilized. The linguistic codes of this social grammar have discursively regulated human sexuality. The incest taboo, meant to sponsor and protect exogamy, has divided sex into lawful and unlawful sex. MacCannell, on whose influential work much of the discussion in this section draws, points out that in the evolution of humankind, sex must obviously have existed *before* speech, but the specific facial expressions during intercourse nevertheless evolved *with reference to the possibility of speech.*[26] In other words, before the firm linguistic establishment of civilizational rules, procreation and sexual intercourse would have had a purely incidental relation. But the political interests and power relations of exogamy led to the stigmatization of nonreproductive sex. More specifically, to demarcate procreative sex from sex that exists solely for the sake of "getting off," these operations merely reinscribed the latter into the preverbal and posited it as ontologically prior and, therefore, as "primitive," animalistic, and hedonistic. The divide between acceptable and taboo sex is thus fully a product of those postlinguistic regimes that seek to maintain exogamy and procreation through a division between both kinds of sex. MacCannell suggests that since facial expressions during sex are *alternately readable as prelinguistic and postlinguistic,* their existence must be seen in relation to the erection of this mythological divide. These facial expressions, then, indicate something about the initial reception of and response to the deeply disruptive, regulatory, and ultimately violent imposition of language, of such social institutions as kinship, and of morals. As MacCannell argues, they indicate a reaction to the establishment of exogamy as a requirement.

We may add that since facial expressions of sexual pleasure obviously persist, they constantly threaten to debunk this divide as what it is—a myth. For anthropologists, the facial expressions in hard-core porn are among the few easy-to-come-by examples that may help us understand how dividing sex into "acceptable" sex and "unacceptable," "taboo" sex rests on an oftentimes political and ideological motivation of drawing artificial boundaries. Hard-core porn's face work highlights the fact that sex spans the divide between preverbal and fully verbalized speech; porn's regressive verbalizations reference speech as a possibility, but they also reference humans' capacity and intent to resist speech.[27] For their study of facial expressions in hard-core porn, anthropologists have developed their own, very scientific, method of describing and categorizing sexual and nonsexual elements in the porn performer's face work. Such jargonistic terms as "upper and lower face agreement" (for nonsexual facial expressions) and "upper and lower face muscular antagonisms" (for sexual expressions) may appear too technical and over-wrought to us, but this impression, justified as it may be, also indicates how deeply in-grained, intuitive, and unreflected our own perceptions of these facial expressions are.[28]

But there is more than one reason why anthropologists have seized on hard-core pornography to trace the linguistic regulation of sex: For them, facial expressions in hard-core porn are also semiotic proof that the prohibitions and taboos produced by the linguistic regulation of sex took the form of a *trauma*. Facial expressions in hard-core porn can be said to reenact this trauma by expressing the agony of whether to speak or not speak during sex. In other words, for anthropologists it is less crucial that porn per-formers use their faces to express *moral* obscenity than it is that the compulsive reenact-ment of the simultaneous defiance and articulation of linguistic and social codes in these facial expressions identify hard-core porn as a *privileged performative response* to the trau-matic imposition of culture onto nature.

It is important to note that this is not an argument about a simple binary of re-pression and release. We all know that pornography does not simply show "real" sex—the sex, as it were, that we have always practiced but that our culture does not want us to see. Instead, pornography is, of course, a highly strategic and highly artificial pro-duction. But it is also important to note that as a genre that traffics in obscenity, porn is not to be regarded simply as a more or less precise index of a postlinguistic culture's commercial exploitation of what it projects as transgressive. Facial expressions in pornography are to be understood as more than the commodification of the punitive implications of the set of prohibitions that spark and accompany the production of porn in the first place. They must be regarded, paradoxically, as *the site where the original, trau-matic encounter with prohibition remains screened and unavailable.* Thus, in the facial ex-pressions it features, porn's amplification of sexual transgressiveness corresponds to the traumatized subject's inability to fully grasp and successfully integrate the traumatic event into the symbolic. Porn performers' failed efforts to integrate the traumatic en-counter with prohibition differ from any such efforts located outside of the porno-graphic only in so far as the particular symbolic arena that is the home of porn is already that of obscenity. However, this obscenity is not to be understood as unsignifiable in the psychoanalytic/linguistic sense (as abject and literally obscene—that is, as not part of the scene of the enunciable). Rather, porn's obscenity merely operates in the realm of what postlinguistic regimes have constructed as the immoral. In other words: because porn is a strategic, thoroughly linguistic production, we must not confuse the impossibility of visualizing abjectness with porn's strategic signification of immorality. But again, porn's display of immoral sex does not constitute an act of "working through" the original trauma; instead, it is primarily a failure with regard to the latter—a failure that implies a screening of the traumatic redefinition of sex by language, a failure that indicates that the original trauma eludes porn's grasp.[29]

In sum, face work in hard-core porn becomes, first, an archeological trace of the moment when sex became colonized by culture—a trace that enables us to see that the divide between acceptable and taboo sex is first and foremost a mythical divide, a gigan-tic attempt to regulate sex for purposes that have nothing to do with sex at all and that must be seen as a violent imposition with punitive consequences and traumatic implica-tions. Second, porn's compulsive, repetitive, and automatic enactment of moral obscen-ity indicates the failure to "normalize" and integrate the original event into the sym-bolic. While porn's heightened obscenity would seem to give the impression that porn "knows too much" about sex, the facial expressions of porn performers actually indicate the opposite—that the original trauma is hidden from the knowledge of these performers. However, to this we must add that the original trauma may well become insignificant because the continuous, subtly diversified, and insidiously amplified regulation of sex (the division into acceptable and taboo sex) functions over time to produce the unlawful *as* the traumatic.

How does *Blow Job* relate to this mythical divide, and how does the film's display of face work compare to porn's face work in its function as a response to trauma? *Blow Job*'s provocative title, its capacity for prompting sexual fantasies, and its mythical status as an underground film would seem to suggest that the film is somewhat cognate to hard-core pornography. But does *Blow Job* offer itself as a deconstructive tool for the particular anthropological discourse outlined herein? Anyone obsessed enough to subject *Blow Job* to this particular kind of perusal may use those times when he or she is not "otherwise busied" by the film to search for certain anthropological indications in the poser's face of sexual activity. And, lo and behold, certain moments in *Blow Job* make the porn anthropologist's heart beat faster. For example, if we follow MacCannell's characterization of face work in pornography, we can read as more or less unambiguously *sexual* certain moments in which the poser presses his lips together in a particular way, such as when he pulls his lips fairly tightly around his teeth (Figure 1.2). His mouth here is also slightly distorted—the chin muscle is pulled up and slightly creased, which indi-

Figure 1.2
Blow Job. Film still courtesy of the Andy Warhol Museum.

Chapter 1

Blow Job. Film still courtesy of the Andy Warhol Museum.

cates the kind of facial asymmetry MacCannell attributes to sexual expressions. Sometimes, the poser also opens his mouth "asymmetrically," pulling his upper lip around his teeth (Figure 1.3). However, these expressions hint at sexual activity in a much more subtle way than those commonly seen in hard-core porn. For example, the area of the poser's eyes in these moments appears fairly relaxed and cannot be likened to the semiotic contrast found in porn performers' faces. Alas, scientific methodology can go only so far in manifesting sexual activity in *Blow Job*.

The face work of the poser in *Blow Job* frustrates the porn anthropologist for several reasons. There is, of course, that obnoxious detail in *Blow Job* that MacCannell's study of hard-core porn did not have to negotiate—that is, the fact that *Blow Job* makes the sex act itself unverifiable. While the film's framing is partly responsible for this modesty, an equally or even more important determining factor is the overall subtlety of the poser's facial expressions. These expressions constantly blur the sexual with the nonsexual. For example, the use of the tongue—a hard-core porn staple for expressing obscenity[30]—is very inconspicuous in the case of *Blow Job*'s poser. In the absence of an explicit and verifiable sexual context, *Blow Job*'s poser's face work garners a semiotic valence that somewhat differs from that of hard-core porn. The signification of sex itself is constantly threatened to be subsumed under the possibility of heightened nonsexual extremes, such as pain and psychological anguish (Figure 1.4). Oftentimes, the poser's face simply signifies a vague sort of trance, which could be drug-induced (Figures 1.5 and 1.6). These

Myths from the Underground

Figure 1.4
Blow Job. Film still courtesy of the Andy Warhol Museum.

expressions have the potential to transport the whole scenario completely outside the realm of the sexual.

One could then argue that *Blow Job* is not an example of pornography, that *Blow Job*'s poser, even if he were attuned to the demands of pornographic performance, is simply not "the type" for spectacular face work, or that there are several kinds of pornography (gay versus straight) as well as several periods, genres, and modes of porn production, not all of which require the production of conspicuously obscene facial expressions. All of these arguments would certainly influence any further analysis of the poser's face work. Without denying the validity of any of these qualifications and modes of inquiry, let us focus on one particular aspect that places *Blow Job* in juxtaposition to the semiotic conditions underlying porn, but let us note that this juxtaposition is superficial precisely to the extent that *Blow Job*'s poser's face work constitutes merely an alternate surface response to the broader determinants that affect both the poser and the performers in hard-core porn. The aspect on which we will focus is this: While the heightened facial expressions of hard-core porn performers screen the traumatic imposition of culture in one way (they repeatedly reenact the "clash" between sex and speech in a heavily histrionic and, thus, less threatening form), *Blow Job*'s "muted" face work screens this trauma in another way—by literally trying to cover it up.

The poser's repetitive movements and his often trance-like facial expressions, which some viewers experience as a boring monotony and which, it might be argued,

Figure 1.5
Blow Job. Film still courtesy of the Andy Warhol Museum.

Figure 1.6
Blow Job. Film still courtesy of the Andy Warhol Museum.

empty the image of any meaning, could be read as a defense against affect and thus as analogous to the traumatized subject's efforts to "master" the traumatic event. The repetitive signification of affectlessness appears as though its function is to pretend that normalization has already taken place. But it is only in this superficial sense that the face work of *Blow Job*'s poser and the face work of porn performers are diametrically opposed, constituting opposite surface reactions to the same phenomenon—the fact that the trauma itself remains not fully available to the subject. Whatever respective strategies these performances take to negotiate the relation sex/law, both *produce* their own respective trauma, constituted by the moments when this relation can be inferred as being unbearable. In this sense, then, the moments in each respective performance paradigm when this screening process fails must also be regarded as related. The brief, fleeting, and erratic moments of this failure in the face work of *Blow Job*'s poser are located at the points where his face does, in fact, appear to index unambiguous sexual pleasure via certain "genuine," that is, nonstrategic facial contortions. Correlatively, in the face work of porn performers, the failure to screen the trauma can be located in those moments that indicate the subject's momentary loss of control over his or her own strategic signification—a process one may describe for porn as "professional failure." This failure can take two forms: First, it may be registered as an expression that becomes briefly yet unambiguously identified as "phoniness," and, second, taking the same effect as with *Blow Job*'s poser's failure, it may be registered in an expression of genuine (nonprofessional) sexual pleasure. (However, as I will argue shortly with regard to spectatorship, the distinction between these two effects is ultimately unimportant.)

The poser's repetitive, trance-like expressions and gestures are of further interest if we regard them as not only a response to the broader trauma of the imposition of culture (which, if one follows MacCannell's argument, pornography's face work responds to) but also as a response to a particular if fundamental aspect of this imposition: To the extent that culture and the codes of civilization became imposed in the name of exogamy, they constitute the imposition of discursive heterosexuality, which is, of course, the imposition of fixed gender positions. In this sense, the poser's face work may be argued to screen the violent moment that linguistic-psychoanalytic accounts of our psychosexual development have characterized as the traumatic assignment of gender—norms of femininity and masculinity—effected by the subject's plunge into language and the symbolic. The poser's compulsive repetitions may thus be read as indicators of the subject seeking to "fulfill" his gender assignment. Correlatively, his "lapses" into uncontrolled sensation, to the extent that they register as sudden, reactive, and non-strategic moments that occur literally in the blink of an eye, is what we perceive as the puncturing of the screen of performance; the failure to assume the assigned position.[31] This observation potentially complicates any characterization of *Blow Job*'s portrayal of masculinity: Even if *Blow Job* impels us to read masculinity as the gender the poser is assigned to, the film far from supports the idea that masculinity is a natural, essential quality. Indeed, the poser's repetitive motions and irregular twitches suggest the incredibly laborious—if compulsory—character of the assignment called gender. *Blow* Job thus questions the notion that gender is natural; the film presents gender as yet another myth it engages with. Gender as an assigned quality is discussed in much greater detail in Chapter 4 with regard to gay men's relationship to masculinity. At this point, let us return to our discussion of the traumatic implications of the imposition of culture as a broader set of laws and relate this discussion to considerations of how the screened trauma (in *Blow Job* as well as in pornography) registers with the spectator.

According to recent art historical discourses, the signification of trauma in Warhol's art can take complex and multiple forms. For example, Hal Foster argues that, at least with regard to spectatorship, Warhol's reenactment of trauma is not restorative. Foster has discussed this phenomenon with regard to a series of Warhol's silk screens, the "Death in America" series.[32] In this series, the repetition and aestheticization of the image not only responds to an original trauma (in this case located in the images' brutal, shocking content), but also produces a second shock effect for the spectator through aesthetic and technical irregularities and "impurities" (such as a torn or faded image or some other jarring detail).[33] Foster compares these visual blemishes to Roland Barthes's definition of the punctum, a visual detail that goes against the grain of the overall image and holds the viewer's attention.[34] Within the aesthetic parameters of Warhol's art, marked as it is by the reified context of repetition and similarity, the punctum becomes an accident, or even, if you wish, a minor incident or an event. For the viewer of Warhol's death and disaster silk screens who is shocked by their content, the punctum breaks through the screening of the trauma in a way that the viewer experiences as "the return of the real," to cite the title of Foster's study, even though the punctum is, in fact, no more real than its visual environment.[35] For Foster it is thus the interplay of repetition and punctum in Warhol's images that makes them complex responses to trauma. He notes that, "For one thing the Warhol repetitions not only *re*produce traumatic effects; they also produce them. Somehow in these repetitions, then, several contradictory things occur at the same time: a warding away of traumatic significance *and* an opening out to it, a defending against traumatic affect and a producing of it."[36]

Although *Blow Job*'s viewers are not technically traumatized by the content of the film in the way that may be attributed to viewers of Warhol's death and disaster silk screens, the film confronts them with the poser's repetitive movements and facial expressions in a way that is comparable to the repetitive structure of Warhol's silk screens. Whether viewers are lulled by the film or view it with anxiety (many may oscillate between these two responses), certain twitches or sudden intensifications in the poser's face may be perceived as disruptions and irregularities that may well have an effect on viewers that is *analogous* to the one Foster attributes to the silk screens. In fact, viewing these twitches and irregularities may even, at certain moments, convey the impression that the poser has reached orgasm. In other words, the accidental, nonstrategic effect of these irregularities may be experienced by viewers as a quasi-documentary effect that is comparable to the way Foster characterizes the puncturing of the silk screens—that is, as moments when the real briefly erupts on the screen and "catches up" with the viewer.[37]

My reading of *Blow Job* converges with Foster's argument about the silk screens' multiple responses to trauma with regard to yet another aspect: the construction of *Blow Job*'s viewer as a disciplined viewer. As Foster points out, repetitions in Warhol's images fix on the traumatic real *as well as* screen it *as well as* produce it. Thus, they go a long way toward accounting for how Warhol's aesthetics elicit diverse readings and spectatorial reactions. These repetitions, but also the regular and irregular variations against which they emerge, make Warhol's works some of the more apposite examples for demonstrating that the concept of disciplining the viewer is much more heterogeneous than that of interpellating the viewer (in the traditional Althusserian sense). Discussing the multiple effects of Warhol's aesthetics, Foster writes: "And this multiplicity makes for the paradox not only of images that are both affective and affectless, but also of viewers that are neither integrated (which is the ideal of most modern aesthetics: the subject composed in contemplation) nor dissolved (which is the effect of much popular culture: the subject given over to the schizo intensities of the commodity-sign)."[38]

Warhol's art and films hold viewers in a particular kind of spell that pulls them in and yet gives them the feeling that they are left out, a spell that suspends them between anxiety and frustration, between being teased and being bored. It seems that the punctum has no small role in this construction of the disciplined viewer. Particularly, *Blow Job*'s punctum, constituted by the poser's brief, irregular, and inadvertent facial twitches, becomes the marker of two impressions that, though fleeting and barely noticeable, come to haunt the poser's performance and its effect on viewers. The first is the impression that there may be "something wrong" with this man, something strange that may pertain to the very qualities that cause us to identify him as a man—in the natural, essential sense of the word. The second is the impression that the poser may not be *not* having sex. Describing the second impression in this convoluted way has its purpose: I am not refuting the possibility that the poser is, in fact, receiving a blow job, nor am I advocating that we must by all means seek empirical proof of this and that we must do so by consulting semiotics and anthropology. Rather, this formulation is used to articulate that this impression harbors two submerged antitheses and to point out that these antitheses may be experienced by one and the same viewer in a single viewing. In this sense, the viewer is disciplined by the film because the film subjects him or her to the play of competing suspicions. In addition, given Foster's analysis of the polysemic effects of Warhol's art, the wording is used to accommodate the claim that different viewers of *Blow Job* tend to view quite different films. Again, I don't mean to discredit claims that the poser is, in fact, being fellated, nor to dispute any effort to pinpoint the exact moment when he reaches orgasm. Rather, stating that the poser may not be *not* having sex (as opposed to simply saying that he is) enables me to refocus my analysis on the film's *simultaneous sponsoring and containment of sex and desire*—which, I believe, is central to disciplining *Blow Job*'s viewer. In addition, this formulation allows me to further analyze *Blow Job*'s relationship to myth.

Even as *Blow Job* produces the possibility of a sex act, it mitigates against this possibility via its set of aesthetic features, which help the poser screen the trauma he might also be said to index. In this way, *Blow Job*'s relation to those myths that regulate the discursive construction of sex and sexuality differs only superficially from pornography's relation to these myths. To this we must add that even though the poser's facial expressions put *Blow Job* in marked contrast to hard-core pornography, they are not entirely unrelated to a genre of sexual representation. That is, they are standard elements of soft-core erotica and, as such, also permeate the aesthetics of advertising. Yet, as MacCannell points out, the primary intent of soft-core erotica is not to trigger sexual arousal but to contain it: rather than circulating sexual desire, soft-core images substitute for it by promoting erotic self-sufficiency and ego-identification,[39] a dynamic *Blow Job* feeds into because of the poser's beauty and self-absorbed pose. Unlike hard-core porn, *Blow Job* thus simultaneously sponsors and contains sex. The film thereby attenuates its capacity to denaturalize the mythological regulation of sex—a capacity anthropologists value in hard-core porn. To the extent that the poser's face may, in fact, be said to express sexual activity unambiguously, it fleetingly and modestly displays the semiotic dynamic found in porn performers' facial expressions during sex. These expressions foreground the cultural "imperative" that interpreted and divided the fluid relation between sex and speech and that overdetermined the initially incidental relation between sex and procreation. Yet, *Blow Job* also "glosses over" precisely this display by its wholesale sublimation of sex: Whatever traces of porn are present in *Blow Job*, the film subordinates them to its overall aestheticism, which cites the soft-core tease as well as situations of nonsexual bodily impact, suffering, and pain. This overall equivocation, then, characterizes *Blow Job*'s relation to myth in general: On the one hand, the film displays on a sliding scale what are otherwise perceived as irreconcilable contradictions; on the other hand, it dissimulates this display and neutralizes its own analytic force by encouraging "easy," that is, conciliatory, explanations. *Blow Job* may, in this regard, be little more than a heuristic tool for the analysis of the rhetorical operations of mythic taboos. In fact, it functions much in the same manner as myth because of its refusal to cancel out the discursive regime that erects the taboo in the first place.

Of course, the simultaneous sponsoring and containment of sexual desire in *Blow Job* is also prominently reinforced through the film's politics of framing. I will discuss the implications of this framing in detail in the following section. Of interest at this point is how they relate to a phenomenon persuasively discussed by Art Simon in the broader context of Warhol's pop art—the characteristic triggering of spectatorial anxiety particularly with regard to the truth-bearing powers of the image.[40] With regard to *Blow Job*, this spectatorial anxiety indicates that it is very difficult to take the poser's face on its own terms. The not entirely unreasonable possibility emerges that the film's politics of framing also constitute a framing of its audience, which falls for a blow job that never took place. As discussed earlier, the film encourages audiences to trust as well as distrust the image; they may harbor the nagging suspicion that the poser may simply fake sexual stimulation and/or pain or may express nonsexual rapture that may be induced by drugs. Yet, how does one reconcile the possibility of fake with the fact that at least some of *Blow Job*'s viewers can legitimately claim sexual arousal during the film? MacCannell has persuasively argued that faking sexual arousal in pornography is semiotically irrelevant, because even a "mere" pretense of sexual arousal nonetheless indicates a person's sexual prowess and the fact that he or she is a capable sexual performer.[41] The faker's faking may thus arouse the partner, whose arousal may, in turn, eventually turn on the faker— a dynamic that leads to the ever-increasing expansion of the unconscious.

Yet, *Blow Job* once again presents a special case here, as the film splits this dynamic in half. On the one hand, the question of whether *Blow Job*'s poser is merely faking sexual arousal may, indeed, be completely irrelevant because, as MacCannell points out, the viewer's "good faith" is always on the side of sexual expressiveness. On the other hand, while spectatorial faith need not rest on the verification of the poser's sexual arousal, it *does* rest very much on the verification of the *sexual nature of the broader context* in which the arousal is performed. But since this verification fails, the nagging question of whether the poser is "faking it" slips back in and, in turn, may well increase the chances of spoiling viewers' attempts to "get off" on *Blow Job*. It certainly spoils a full application of MacCannell's argument to this context, and it also marks the limits of the comparison between *Blow Job* and pornography. Nonetheless, *Blow Job* does foreground just how deeply imbricated porn spectatorship is with issues of visual proof and documentary evidence (and, thus, just how phallogocentric porn can be): No matter how irrelevant the question of how authentic a male porn performer's sexual arousal is, sooner or later it will have to be backed up with proof of his erection.

While *Blow Job*'s foregrounding of the sliding scale between the nonsexual and the pornographic is articulated primarily through the poser's face, the film's mise-en-scène manipulates this sliding scale additionally with the help of several aesthetic features. In this respect, it is interesting how *Blow Job* appropriates and changes one of soft-core erotica's staples—the flat backdrop. While in soft-core erotica this backdrop isolates the individual from the outer world and articulates his or her disengagement from practical and social affairs,[42] *Blow Job* holds this formal aspect in tension with those aesthetic operations that do, in fact, emphasize the poser's relation to the outer world (and to a putative sex partner). We have already noted that the brick wall helps destabilize the figure/ground relationship in the image—it functions as a point of contrast as well as assimilation to the figure of the poser, suspending the image between flatness and depth. The brick wall's iconographic qualities signify transgressiveness and introduce the possibility of sex. The brick wall thus functions in analogy to the ambiguity of the poser's facial expressions to the extent that both may potentially provide a way out of the narcissistic self-containment of sexual pleasure so characteristic of soft-core erotica. *Blow Job* thus reflects the social division between sexual and nonsexual codes, but it also always potentially bridges this division. One notes as an interesting aside here that the brick wall, which is central to the film's display of these social divisions, was also a staple of postwar gay erotica, which negotiated very similar issues (see Chapter 5). Postwar gay erotica existed on the cusp of licit and illicit representation, which, according to Tom Waugh, also constituted a watershed between a displaced and an overt articulation of gay male desire.[43]

Another important way in which *Blow Job*'s mise-en-scène influences our perception of the sex act is the film's lack of sound. We have already discussed how facial expressions during sex hint at the paradoxical relationship between sex and language. Because the need to speak is functionally linked to the institution of exogamous marriage, a set of regulations has developed that links sex to linguistic capacity. However, linguistic capacity is measured not only by semiotic criteria but also in terms of a particular, prescriptive relation between the semantic and the acoustic. According to MacCannell, this relation dictates, for example, that sex should occur only between those who can and might speak and should not be practiced with, say, animals, infants, the incapacitated, or the dead. Furthermore, sex must be discussed only in strictly defined discursive paradigms and speech genres, such as science, psychoanalysis, ethnography, and jokes.[44] Yet, sexual activity tends to be associated with a minimization or even proscription of linguistic activity. Speech, if it does occur during sexual intercourse, more often than not makes no sense, nor does it need to, since, in most cases, it is not important to the sex act itself. Sex partners communicate via facial expressions, gestures, and what anthropologists have termed "prelinguistic vocalization."[45] MacCannell notes that the temporal trajectory of intercourse, at least in Western bourgeois society, is frequently modeled in reverse of the evolution of speech. It begins with elaborate discussions or flirting at social gatherings, parties, a bar, or a theater lobby and ends "in growls, grunts, and moans."[46]

As a silent film that disallows the phonetic expression of any kind of sexual activity, *Blow Job* provides an interesting commentary on this set of rules and regulations—

not the least because the relation in the film between linguistic activity and sex leads to ambiguous effects that come to form yet another instance of the film's double strategy of demythologization and remythologization. Just as the proscription of linguistic activity marks sexuality's own taboo status, the silence of *Blow Job*'s poser becomes a marker of suspicious goings-on. It is reminiscent of sexual cruising, which does not depend on speech and takes place in public. The effect of this silent speech is enhanced by the film's complete lack of sound and tends to produce a nervous self-consciousness among viewers in classrooms and movie houses. *Blow Job*'s silence may well enhance the impression that its sex act exists, and exists outside normative borders. Like hard-core porn, *Blow Job* demythologizes those disciplinary regimes that have attempted to make sex "speak" in prescriptive ways; the film debunks these prescriptions, as it refuses to model its sex act on the socially imposed regulations between sex and speech that define sexuality's position within the public sphere and make it acceptable to bourgeois society. But unlike hard-core porn, *Blow Job*'s refusal to endorse the blow job through "growls, grunts, and moans" is complicit with the social proscriptions bourgeois society has imposed. *Blow Job* thereby endorses the very paradigm it defies, but to which it also exists in contiguity, whereby it garners its own mythological currency as a transgressive underground film.

This double structure is replicated by the poser's ambiguous facial expressions. To the extent that these expressions signify sexual activity, they subversively identify the continuity of sex across the divide between preverbal and fully verbalized, discursively regulated human relations. But this set of facial expressions enables one to identify the sliding scale between acceptable and unacceptable sex *only* if one believes in the sex act in the first place. The poser's facial expressions are vague enough to make this sex act uncertain. Thereby they reference and, indeed, constitute *Blow Job*'s status as an underground film, as they reflect, according to Richard Dyer, the impulse to show a certain kind of sex and also the cultural proscription to do so.[47] In other words, underground films transform sexual transgressiveness into aesthetic transgression. Notwithstanding underground film's mythologized status as a naughty, rebellious, and semi-licit cinema that was often threatened by censorship, *Blow Job*'s self-imposed censorship marks the underground as a place in the public sphere where moral conventions were not simply heroically defied but were, both consciously and unconsciously, addressed and negotiated.[48] Even though the film's framing and the subtle nature of the facial expressions preempted further censorship, *Blow Job* foregrounds the impulse for sanctioning and for censoring on a basic semiolinguistic level as well as through its self-allegorizing politics of representation.

FRAMING THE MYTH—MYTHOLOGIZING THE FRAME

Blow Job's most famous feature is the prickling irony produced by the tension between on- and off-screen space. The film's self-conscious framing has made it the quintessential Warholian tease and to a great deal accounts for its status as enigmatic underground flick with a mythology of its own. This status rests on a certain paradox, as it seems to be constituted by two simultaneous yet somewhat antithetical operations: Having made us very much aware of its rhetoric, *Blow Job* recasts any "truth" it might be said to proffer into an assumption—but our opinionated speculations about the film nonetheless point to our desire to close the gap between assumption and truth. The particularity of

Blow Job's manipulative power lies in the fact that it can simultaneously heighten and numb our awareness if not of the image itself then of how we as viewers relate to the image. More accurately, *Blow Job* draws our attention to the thin line between what we see and what we fantasize and, in the process, makes us cross this line. There may be several reasons why one crosses this line: One cannot help being intrigued by the image's suggestive power; one may seek what is broadly known as visual pleasure; one may seek the more particular pleasure of having the image confirm one's own world view. In other words, even though we know all too well that we are the addressees of a certain "pitch," we willingly succumb to the game. What has been described here is, of course, also the dynamic produced by the rhetoric of advertising. While I will not further discuss advertising as such, the analogy between *Blow Job* and advertising is useful, as it allows me to draw on a particular set of qualities that may be characterized as the ideological aspects of *Blow Job*'s image.

Advertising has been a privileged object through which critics can show ideology at work: If ideology is, in Bill Nichols's words, "how the existing ensemble of social relations represents itself to individuals," if it is "the image a society gives of itself in order to perpetuate itself," the ideological use of representation in general and advertising visuals in particular may indicate how ideology persuades us "that how things are is how they ought to be and that the place provided for us is the place we ought to have."[49] *Blow Job* self-reflexively foregrounds the assignment of this place we ought to have as an ideological operation. Nonetheless, *Blow Job* seems to enhance one of ideology's key functions: to *seduce* the one who is addressed by its image. If *Blow Job* were merely a dry tool for the undoing of visual pleasure, it would have long been forgotten. The film's mythical status rests on its ability to seduce the viewer into its rhetorical play. Its aptitude for seduction is intrinsically bound up with its aptitude for (self-)mythologization. But if it is true, as I have been arguing, that *Blow Job* has a particular relation to myth, and if it is true, too, that *Blow Job*'s mythical status rests at least partly on its uncanny ability to manipulate its spectators in a way they find pleasurable, it is useful to explore how the rhetorical operations of myth itself exploit the potentials of pleasure for the goal of personal address. Therefore, we first need to consider *Blow Job*'s volatile and unstable visuals in terms of one very particular characterization of myth, though one observed in no less colloquial terms: Roland Barthes's treatment of myth as ideology. Issues of ideology will also inform the subsequent discussion of *Blow Job*'s framing, the particular reflexivity produced by this framing, and the limits of this reflexivity as they influence the film's demythologizing and remythologizing tendencies.

The inverse link between the overall sparse quality of *Blow Job*'s image and the amount of talk it has generated bears out Barthes's point that myth seizes on and works best with poor, incomplete images. *Blow Job*'s framing in particular exemplifies most flagrantly what Barthes describes as "the alibi"—a sign of myth. According to Barthes, "the ubiquity of the signifier in myth exactly reproduces the physique of the *alibi* (which is, as one realizes, a spatial term): in the alibi too, there is a place which is full and one which is empty, linked by a relation of negative identity ('I am not where you think I am; I am where you think I am not')."[50]

It is this alibi, as Barthes tells us, that enables myth to always have an "elsewhere" at its disposal;[51] the alibi helps myth fulfill its main function—to reconcile irreconcilable contradictions. And it is this alibi that is at the epicenter of *Blow Job*'s own mythical status. However, its function is more complex than it first appears. For if the alibi must, to

Chapter 1

a certain extent, be credited with mythologizing the film, it is only because the film first mythologized the alibi. More particularly, the film became a trendsetter for a kind of alibi known as the tease. Tom Waugh has pointed out that the tease, one of the signature features of 1960s visual culture, danced around two irreconcilable poles—the acceptable and the forbidden—and seemingly reconciled them.[52] In this regard, *Blow Job*'s framing demonstrates most clearly how myth springs from a paradox: Consistently pointing to the limits of the acceptable but never overstepping them, *Blow Job* gleefully flaunts its own transgressiveness precisely by censoring itself. This self-censorship contains no small amount of self-reflexive irony. While this irony has the effect of disguising that the tease is really a cop-out—a glorified alibi—*Blow Job*'s self-reflexive mise-en-scène lays bare a host of other alibis, cultural assumptions ranging from the truth of the image to the truth of sex, and invites us to ponder them.

But myth, one might object, never deconstructs; it always naturalizes, glosses over, placates. Barthes's characterization of myth as "nebula" is apposite here.[53] However, Barthes also points to the fact that myths do not suppress meaning—they simply impoverish it, reduce it to a pure signifying function, make it available for signification.[54] Like all myths, *Blow Job*'s myth has a parasitical relation to meaning: It can appear only through a given substance—an already constituted meaning—which it does not hide but exploits for its own purposes. In *Blow Job* this "purpose" can be characterized as the effort to distract from the film's own timidity by passing this timidity off as its opposite, something that might be characterized as "underground-ness."[55] Because this blanket term is vague (as myths tend to be), it has the advantage that it can suggest several sub-myths at the same time, such as "sexual transgressiveness" and "drugginess." Because myth transforms meaning into form, it becomes the parasite of meaning. It insinuates itself into meaning, becoming a "robbery by colonization."[56]

Note that what is being colonized by *Blow Job*'s "underground-ness" is no pure, innocent, or neutral substance. The denotative qualities of the image may simply signify the face of a young man, but because of the film's connotative force, this image would often *instantly* be invested with a set of connotations themselves imbued with certain myths: James Dean, the teenage rebel, the suffering martyr, and so on. More accurately, then, *Blow Job* represents both sides in the axiomatic recommendation Barthes made when he wrote, "Since myth robs language of something, why not rob myth?"[57] To produce the myth of "underground-ness," *Blow Job* actually robs other myths. In this sense, "underground-ness" is already derivative. It is what Barthes calls a "second-order myth,"[58] a myth that was able to thrive only because it robbed such first-order myths as "visual truth," "truth of sex," "manliness," "hero-ness," and "rebelliousness." On the one hand, the resignification of these first-order myths endows *Blow Job* with a certain analytical capacity. As the film foregrounds the rhetorical nature of myth, it offers itself to us as a heuristic tool for the study of myth. On the other hand, this robbing of first-order myths is, of course, the rhetorical move whereby *Blow Job* can then mythologize itself as a seemingly original dispatch from the underground. In sum, the given substance—or, if you wish, the "host"—for *Blow Job*'s own mythologization is myth itself.

Chapter 2 discusses *Blow Job*'s robbing of fairly recent myths found in mass culture. For the moment, let us remind ourselves that *Blow Job*'s mythologized boundaries also map the dynamics of a much older myth that the film appropriates. As discussed earlier in this chapter with regard to *Blow Job*'s framing, the film's self-censorship separates not only the visible from the invisible but also the acceptable from the taboo. Thus, the frame's function can be considered a conceptual analogy to a guard patrolling the (metaphorical) border between civilization and barbarity, rigorously regulating its permeability, ardently stemming the tide of unregulated eros on behalf of civilization's course: Only what passes for "advanced" may cross over. Not surprisingly, the section to be defended is the lower limn—the "southern" border—always considered most vulnerable, always guarded with utmost paranoia, always defended with blood. In *Blow Job*, this section is particularly contested, as the conflict between eros and civilization is flaring up as the tension between different discursive determinants of sexuality. Before we turn to the details of this local conflagration, let us focus briefly on the larger war.

Tales that describe human existence in relation to nature and culture and, perhaps more to the point, the naturalization of culture tend to figure prominently in the ways many civilizations throughout the world represent and narrate their own genealogies, histories, and traditions to themselves. Structural anthropology tells us that these civilizations, upon encountering the relationship between nature and culture as an irreconcilable contradiction, have availed themselves of myth to negotiate the rupture. What myth papers over, structuralist studies of myth have unearthed, organized, and condensed into binary opposites. And while structural anthropology, a subdiscipline of Western ethnography, focuses on what it calls "primitive civilizations," it is of course in the "civilized" West where such opposite conceptual pairs as nature/culture and logic/faith have wielded their most insidious, ideologically powerful influence, permeating such otherwise diverse discursive systems as science, popular culture, and religion. These systems typically assign to myth the task of presenting as a pure product of nature what is already passing through culture, what is articulated by discourse, and, as Barthes tells us, what exists within ideology. These systems are noted here for two reasons: First, because they all fall victim to *Blow Job*'s robbery; and second, because *Blow Job*, in the course of robbing them, foregrounds and spatializes their underlying binary opposites in the very process of mobilizing our desire to see them reconciled. An engagement with the ways in which *Blow Job* plays out this rhetoric will help us understand just how deeply and massively Western culture is pervaded by notions of sexuality determined by the course-of-nature argument.

Blow Job teases the spectator into constructing sexuality through a dialectic between the visual presence of the poser and the visual absence of his off-screen fellator. To do so, the image mobilizes a set of formal tensions—let us call them outward and inward movements—that define the relation between the image and the space beyond the frame,[59] or, more specifically, the relation between *Blow Job*'s poser and his putative sex partner. The tension between the individual and the outer world—to formulate it somewhat more broadly—is also what informs Western culture's truth discourse of sexuality. Its rhetorical operations—one universalizing, the other particularizing—correspond respectively to the outward and inward movements between the image and the space beyond. Both rhetorical moves accommodate the same procedure, which is so ingrained and pervasive that it is equally likely to surface in such diverse areas as, say, religious doxa and popular entertainment. These rhetorical moves are more particularly part of what Foucault termed *scientia sexualis*—a broad-based attempt at reading sexuality and sexual desire via such disciplinary discourses as natural science, ethnography, psychology, and psychoanalysis, all of which have constructed the body as a sexual body in their effort to make sex "speak."[60] To this effect, the procedure these rhetorical moves enact on

Blow Job consists of three compulsory steps: first, to find a "mate" for our poser; second, to fashion this mate in his image so that their relationship can be defined in terms of certain anthropological, sexological, and psychological truths; and third, to read back into the poser's image the blueprint of his phantasmatic partner. Thereby, what is really cultural appears natural, because it is "naturally so"—it has been naturalized.

In *Blow Job*, however, the image's simultaneous mobilization and frustration of these discursive operations foreground the many "ifs" that surface everywhere in the construction of the poser's sexuality, announcing the frisson between the image's seemingly authentic representation and the lack of information it yields. Yet, perhaps more significantly, the image thereby provokes a rhetorical dialectic in which the assumption about one element poses as proof for the factual status of another. Hence, if the poser were assumed to be a heterosexual male, the fellator would then have to be a woman; if he were assumed to be gay, the partner would be a gay man. The conclusion, the dialectical third element, acts as naturalizing in two ways: It presents as its logical result what is really the outcome of a rhetorical projection, and its dialectical structure *follows the copulative structure of procreative sexuality*. In this sense, the disciplinary production of *Blow Job*'s poser as a sexual subject reveals that the production of sexuality in general through disciplinary discourses and through whole discursive regimes has been a profoundly and gigantically heterosexualized project. Even if the poser's identity is constructed as homosexual, the modus operandi for the construction is that of heterosexuality. No matter what our own sexual persuasion is, *Blow Job* forces us to encounter its poser through the matrix of sexual difference. In addition, we can here observe again *Blow Job*'s double operation of demythologization and remythologization: While *Blow Job* reveals that sexuality is defined rhetorically (or more precisely, metaphorically), the film does so only by mobilizing the copulative logic that it arguably exposes. Because the dialectical third element is passed off as a natural corollary and not as what it is—a mental selection, a discursive choice—the pseudo-logic that subtends it comes to be an ideal tool for the naturalizing power of myth.

If *Blow Job* debunks its own syllogism by making clear that it requires a leap of faith from off-screen space to on-screen space and back, the film also mobilizes the desire for establishing empirical truth and the wish to put one's faith in the natural and the "real." *Blow Job* thus not only self-consciously acknowledges the impact of such binary opposites as nature/culture, science/faith, and logic/rhetoric but feeds into our desire to reconcile them. While this reconciliation is, as Barthes tells us, the stuff of myth as well as ideology, it is always only a discursive construct. Notwithstanding myth's powerful insinuating force, its rhetoric—as Barthes's brilliant essay shows—can be identified and analyzed.

While Barthes's approach has lost none of its validity, Foucault's approach to the order of things constitutes a different order of questioning of the axiom that "how things are is how they ought to be." To think of this axiom particularly with regard to sexuality as a disciplinary production of power constitutes what we call a paradigm shift. This shift has enabled us to supplement—and, where necessary, replace—the concept of ideology with an analysis of the stratified productions of power, which work against one another as much as they work in collusion. The virtues and limitations of this shift with regard to theories of white gay male identity are explored in Chapter 4. For the moment, let us simply note that this shift has enabled us to deconstruct rhetorics of naturalization in new ways. Among other things, it has enabled us to appropriate ideologically laden texts as points of departure for devising strategies that help us realize that the notorious "place provided for us" may, in fact, *not* be the place we ought to have and that also help us make tentative, provisional moves away from it. The discussion of *Blow Job* continues under this reformulated aegis. To continue to discuss the film's self-reflexive framing, we will not have to jettison Barthes's notion of myth as ideology. But we will now be able to explore more fully the theoretical implications especially of the slew of binaries (inside/outside; nature/culture; individual/outer world) produced by *Blow Job*'s framing.

For example, a structuralist reading of *Blow Job* would hold that the relation between nature and culture is stable and always clearly identifiable: The image, not unlike that of Warhol's silk screens, produces a relation of close reciprocity between "substantial" (physical, material) and "insubstantial" (aesthetic) realities. Such a reading would thus posit the representability of the physical and the aesthetic—of nature and culture, of an original and its counterfeit—within a totality of possibilities. To the extent that it can also be found within discourses of high art, such a reading, as Rosalind Krauss has pointed out, often tends to replay the very terms mapped out by civilization's grand myths.[61] Curiously, though, this structuralist relationality also found its way into postmodernism, where it reappears, as we know from Jean Baudrillard, as the choice between zero and one—the modus operandi of the digital dyad—only this relationality is no longer defined by *analogy* (by original to copy), but (having abjured the original) has become one of cold, indifferent *equivalence* between two terms. Finite production has been superceded by infinite *re*-producibility of identical beings whose *raison d'être* ultimately becomes their perpetual self-reproduction,[62] measured no longer in relation to a model but in terms of pure oppositions. Digitality has thus appropriated structuralism's dyadic modus operandi—only to ignore, as it shoots its codes into infinity, structuralism's function as the gatekeeper of the knowable world.

Baudrillard's bleak and, ultimately, totalizing vision is that digitality not only enables an infinitesimal proliferation of knowledge but also completely determines the processing of that knowledge and the individual's confrontation with knowledge. In other words, the world itself is now ruled by the dyad, which allows only for preordained questions and answers and has made science a discipline of self-fulfilling prophecies. And yet, even though it declares the world an either/or place, Baudrillard's theory offers some important insights. Most important, it enables Baudrillard to debunk science as a rhetorical construct that "accounts for things previously encircled and formalized so as to be sure to obey it." In Baudrillard's words, "'Objectivity' is nothing else than that, and the ethic which comes to sanction this objective knowledge is nothing less than a system of defense and imposed ignorance, whose goal is to preserve this vicious circle intact."[63] This new form of knowledge is emblematized by the rise to prominence of tests and polls as means to quantify and discursively regulate knowledge. As Baudrillard argues:

> Everywhere the test functions as a fundamental form of control, by means of the infinite divisibility of practices and responses. We live by the mode of *referendum* precisely because there is no longer any *referential*. Every sign, every message (objects of "functional" use as well as any item of fashion or televised news, poll or electoral consultation) is presented to us as question/answer. . . . Now tests and referenda are, we know, perfect forms of simulation: the answer is called forth by the question, it is designated in advance. *The referendum is always an ultimatum:* the unilateral nature of the question, that is no longer exactly an in-

Chapter 1

terrogation, but the immediate imposition of a sense whereby the cycle is suddenly completed.[64]

I quote Baudrillard at length partly because his characterization of the question/answer dyad offers another critical perspective on *Blow Job*'s spectatorial address. But there is another reason. Baudrillard chooses to illustrate what he perceives as our near-total domination by tests via an interesting example: Walter Benjamin's theory of our near-total domination by popular film images. According to Benjamin, the film actor's performance is relayed to a judging, evaluating audience by means of the camera—the medium the audience identifies with. Hence, the actor's performance is subjected to a series of optical tests that Benjamin likens to vocational aptitude tests in the capitalist workplace: "The film shot and the vocational aptitude test," he writes, "are taken before a committee of experts."[65] In this sense, *Blow Job* may be regarded as a vocational aptitude test taken before an audience of mass culture consumers, some of whom may also follow their own vocational call as psychologists, sexologists, or ethnographers. It seems that *Blow Job* thus offers itself as a useful interface between Benjamin's diacritics and Baudrillard's digitality. We must realize that for Baudrillard, Benjamin's vocational aptitude tests epitomize the postmodern extension of the viewer as a disciplined subject. He writes:

> No contemplation is possible. The images fragment perception into successive sequences, into stimuli toward which there can be only instantaneous response, yes or no—the limit of an abbreviated reaction. Film no longer allows you to question. It questions you, and directly. It is in this sense that the modern media call for, according to McLuhan, a greater degree of immediate participation, an incessant response, a total plasticity (Benjamin compares the work of the cameraman to that of the surgeon: tactility and manipulation). The role of the message is no longer information, but testing and polling, and finally control ("contra-role," in the sense that all your answers are already inscribed in the "role," on the anticipated registers of the code).[66]

Baudrillard's remarks are inspired by Benjamin's example of the tactility of dadaist cinema with its changing camera positions and angles that subject the viewer to a never ending series of shock and stimuli. However, the territory from which this example is chosen is not entirely unproblematic with regard to our analysis. If one were to discuss *Blow Job*'s simultaneous enactment of and divergence from the function of the test as outlined herein by Baudrillard's comment, it seems one would first have to emphasize the film's simultaneous enactment of and divergence from dadaist cinema as such. That is, one would have to emphasize *Blow Job*'s lack of editing and its use of the long take, for are these not precisely the features that would allow viewers a more contemplative stance? However, as we concluded earlier, notwithstanding *Blow Job*'s minimalist extension of time and space, the film does not produce a contemplative viewer but a viewer who is, indeed, both subject *and* object of technologies of vision (and knowledge), a viewer who *self-consciously* invests back into the film precisely what the film *foregrounds* as a false investment. In the theoretical landscape mapped thus far, *Blow Job* is then equally removed from Barthes and Baudrillard. On the one hand, if *Blow Job* confined itself to pretending that its image is true to the film's title, it would fulfill too neatly Barthes's characterization of myth as ideology; in fact, it would have long been canonized, not unlike Hollywood films, as a classic carrier of ideology. On the other hand, if *Blow Job* simply confined itself to the defamiliarization of those binary opposites that constitute testing and, thus, to the defamiliarization of testing as our way of life, it would have long been canonized into the long line of Barthes's demystifying agents, which, in the course of time, have themselves come to form a new mythology—the doxa of demystification.[67] But in an equally clever and immodest move, *Blow Job* shuns this doxa for a different enigma. The fascination with the larger picture, the folly of presuming the totality of possibilities, gives way to an acknowledgment of the partial, a concern with the contingent, and a celebration of the speculative.

No doubt, Baudrillard would be rather unfazed by these possibilities. In fact, he might be inclined to regard *Blow Job*'s delineation of contingent speculations as emblematic of his theories. Indeed, the film may well be the ultimate Baudrillardian kind of test, precisely because the contingency of its image to the outer world may be regarded as corresponding fairly accurately to what Baudrillard calls "the infinite divisibility of practices and responses." Baudrillard defines responses (to questions and to images) as either/or responses that at least appear heterogeneous because of the large degree of proliferation they ultimately obtain. Yet, is this heterogeneity actual—"real," if you wish—or is it virtual, that is, does it ultimately constitute homogeneity because of the dyadic mode by which it must necessarily operate and which is the basis for its own reproducibility? It would be impossible to answer this question in any single book-length study. Instead, we should perhaps explore how Baudrillard's theoretical framework can be put in productive relation to other ways of reading *Blow Job*'s framing. In this sense, we need to keep in mind that even though we are often forced to make either/or decisions, we manage ourselves in the social also by leaving things open; by remaining vague, irrational, and illogical; by giving two contradictory responses at the same time; by reversing decisions halfway and tentatively—all of which produce (and not merely reproduce) the social as a concrete living space whose unpredictable livelihood the dyadic model can, as of yet, neither account for nor completely simulate through, say, artificial intelligence.

Theories of the social impact of representation tend to resist Baudrillard's simulacrum of the third order because it atrophies the social and neutralizes even the germ of an impulse for discursive intervention, as if the practices and responses at issue (no matter how infinite their divisibility) are no longer even worthy of consideration. Given that the social is completely absorbed by simulacra, it is precisely our unpredictable and heterogeneous ways of reading and appropriating them that we must now explore with renewed focus, for it is in this manner that we will be able to establish meaningful relations between these practices and the heterogeneity of the social itself. Without losing sight of Baudrillard, it is thus time to switch registers and turn our attention back to the details that describe and, in fact, constitute the contiguous relation between image and outer world. It is time also to backtrack to the point where we began discussing the differential nature of *Blow Job*'s simulacrum in terms of the differential nature of reading.

While the import of cultural assumptions into the reading of *Blow Job*'s image *does* indicate a meaningful relation between image and outer world, these assumptions may be varied and even contradictory and thereby crucially affect the seemingly autonomous physical reality of the poser. At no point is there visual proof that the poser's convulsions are actually caused by fellatio. Yet, if the off-screen blow job does not exist, these convulsions, which appear to indicate a raw, physical materiality, suddenly switch categories and become subsumed under the grouping of the aesthetic—they become a performance. Not only do audiences have to negotiate the discontinuity between what they see and what they believe is taking place, but the latter hosts a number of heterogeneous and contradictory positions across the divide between subject and object, between identification and desire. Audiences invest the image simultaneously with fantasies and beliefs about the self and others, and with desires and identifications that the individual spectator may hold or might have held in the past—all of which may be displaced, replaced, or rotated within a single viewing.

From this perspective, the relation between image and outer world is thus rendered more fluid. *Blow Job* reinforces the impression that the relation between the physical and the aesthetic is one of contingency and differentiality, not reciprocity. In some sense, a shift has taken place in the ways in which we read visual imagery—a shift from conceptualizing the relation between art and outer world in terms of universality and totality toward understanding it in terms of the openness of signification. However, the question remains as to whether this post-structuralist play of differences can do more than infinitely displace the heterosexualized matrix on which it is based. For even though our approaches to *Blow Job* are now reasonably stratified, *difference as such* is still what fuels our curiosity about the film and what facilitates our inquiry.

2

SHADOWS AND MYTHS

.B *low Job* has a meta-discursive relation to myth. The film's self-reflexive features mobilize a double operation: They help demystify certain philosophical and cultural assumptions (the fixity of basic linguistic codes; the autonomy of the viewer; the apodicity of nature), but they also always feed into our continued investment in these assumptions. They deliver them back to myth in order for myth to harness them rhetorically. By enacting this exchange, *Blow Job* offers itself as both tool for and object of its own inquiry. In addition, the film's contiguity to the myths it engages is emblematic of underground cinema's contiguity to dominant culture. We can see this by examining how *Blow Job* seizes on certain elements of mass culture, whereby it comments on mass culture's own exploitation of icons, stars, and popular myths. *Blow Job* identifies these mass culture elements through its play of simulacra. It was argued earlier that the interplay of light and shadow in *Blow Job* produces a considerable variety of image fragments. Within *Blow Job*'s image, these fragments can be grouped into three categories—or visual constellations, as I call them—because they arguably always come out of and merge back into their basic coordinates in a subtle pattern of repetition and variation. In the first visual constellation, the poser's head is at a low angle position (Figures 2.1 and 2.2). His face is directed toward the area in front of him below his waistline but, at times, also points toward left or right frame. It is completely cast in shadow, so that we often cannot even see whether his eyes are open. The iconographic and mimetic aspects of this image evoke impressions of inwardness, sadness, and isolation. There is

Figure 2.1
Blow Job. Film still courtesy of the Andy Warhol Museum.

also a sinister aspect to this position. It triggers associations of the stereotype of the dark, troubled, and brooding juvenile delinquent.

In the second constellation, the poser's head is at a medium angle and his face is directed either toward the camera (Figures 2.3, 2.4, and 2.5) or, again, slightly left or right frame. His forehead is now evenly lit, but his nose, chin, and especially his eyebrows cast deep shadows. The shadows from his eyebrows all but completely obscure his eye sockets. The impression of a brooding teenager gives way to the impression of a somewhat demonic person or of a skull. Sometimes the poser tilts his head at an angle so that one of his eyes almost emerges from darkness (see Figure 2.5). When the poser more or less directly faces the camera, he sometimes gives the impression of oscillating between a willingness to meet the camera's gaze and an attempt to avoid it. Particularly with regard to its head-on range, this visual constellation invites comparison to the mug shots of criminals Warhol used in his mural for the 1964 World Fair, *Thirteen Most Wanted Men*. But the differences between the poser in *Blow Job* and the mug shots of the mural are as significant as their similarities. They tell us something further about the way Warhol put documentation in relation to mythologization.

Figure 2.2
Blow Job. Film still courtesy of the Andy Warhol Museum.

In the third constellation, the poser rapidly throws his head back, his face directed toward the top of the frame, his eyes either wide open or completely closed. This is the most striking visual, as the light that meets his face seems to proliferate, streaming across the whole frame and making his face almost blend in with the brick wall (Figures 2.6 and 2.7). This visual strongly invokes images of Christ and suffering martyrs.

These three basic variations of the mise-en-scène are clearly not the only ones *Blow Job*'s viewers read into the film. I have no doubt that others make different choices because, if ever there was a film that means different things to different viewers, it is *Blow Job*. Nonetheless, I want to offer, at this point, a particular reading of the film in these terms for two reasons: first, because the connotations triggered by these visuals invite further consideration of *Blow Job*'s capacity to "rob" and display particular myths; and second, because these visuals enable us to comment on how myth insinuates itself

into and influences the portrayal of popular icons, their mass appeal, their ideological function, and the imaging of their genders. I am not claiming that the symbolism I have chosen for consideration in the film's mise-en-scène is something Warhol intended to produce. That would, in fact, mythologize the film and the artist in rather unproductive ways. However, after having established certain links between my reading of the mise-en-scène and some of Warhol's larger thematic and visual concerns that recur throughout his career, I found it hard not to speculate that as Warhol looked at the finished film, he, too, might have recognized some of this

Figure 2.3
Blow Job. Film still courtesy of the Andy Warhol Museum.

Figure 2.4
Blow Job. Film still courtesy of the Andy Warhol Museum.

symbolism and might have appreciated the film the more for it. I understand, however, that this is, of course, a fancy on my part that is not entirely free of mythologization.

Before discussing in detail some of these visual associations, their mythological currency, and their insinuations of certain masculinities, let us briefly reconsider some more general aspects of myth. To begin, let us recall Roland Barthes's somewhat paradoxical characterization of myth. He states, first, that mythical speech is made of material that has already been worked on, constituted by a meaning that is already outlined. In the case of visual myth, this visual "substance" through which myth passes is multidimensional, allowing for an unusually flexible and richly suggestive array of elements in space. But Barthes also reminds us that myth works best with incomplete, impoverished, visually poor images, building what he calls "a kind of nebula, the condensation, more or less hazy, of a certain knowledge. Its elements are linked by associative relations: it is supported not by an extension but by a depth (although this metaphor is perhaps still too spatial): its mode of presence is memorial."[1] Knowledge, association, memory, presence: these are the key terms in how we understand myth to operate. In the present discussion, they occasion three clusters of questions that map the agenda and the contours of this analysis: First, in what form do we encounter the condensation of a certain (more or less hazy) knowledge with regard to *Blow Job*'s image, and, further, how does the image link knowledge to association? Second, what function does memory play in and around *Blow Job*'s image? And third, if the nebula that is myth articulates itself via memory, and if memory is, by definition,

Figure 2.5
Blow Job. Film still courtesy of the Andy Warhol Museum.

fugitive and elusive, how can we apprehend these memories for our analysis of the mythical currency of *Blow Job*'s image?

The characterization of *Blow Job*'s three main visual constellations described earlier involved associating these images with specific icons, symbols, and myths—such as James Dean, the teenage rebel, the demonic criminal, and the suffering martyr. To establish a link between the poser and these respective icons, it is necessary to put at least two texts in relation to one another. That is, it is necessary to read *Blow Job* intertextually. Traversing daily across various and diverse areas of culture and media, we all become intertextual readers, as we constantly put multiple texts in relation to one another. We practice intertextuality on different levels, across different cultural spheres, and between different historical periods—and we do so with varying degrees of intensity and intent. Intertextuality is thus a broad, mundane practice of reading texts. The details and dynamics of this practice have been specified and brilliantly analyzed by Mikhail Iampolski, whose work has influenced the discussion in these pages. According to Iampolski, some of the ways in which we read intertextually must be related to the tendency inherent in Western thought to conceive of

Figure 2.6
Blow Job. Film still courtesy of the Andy Warhol Museum.

texts primarily in genealogical terms—that is, by tracing texts back to prior sources. The prior source that fuels such textual investments is constituted by various knowledges. In *Blow Job* these range from, say, the awareness of fellatio as a sexual practice to a knowledge of the types of characters embodied by James Dean.

But there is another, closely related way in which *Blow Job* encourages intertextuality: The film occasions and fuels the act of remembering. If intertextual reading involves investing a text with prior knowledge, it connects the present text to a prior one by means of a trace back in time to the point where the knowledge about the prior text was first constituted. Thomas Crow has discussed this tracing as constituting the memorial capacity particular to Warhol's images. These images' concern with icons and themes more often than not linked to death creates the parameters within which we remember what is no longer there. Even more important for constituting memorial capacity is the particular visual quality of Warhol's images. Their visual instability suspends their content between presence and absence, which both reenacts and plays into our impulse to remember the star who is no longer with us. The mobilization of a prior knowledge is thus facilitated through the image functioning as a mnemonic trace. As noted by Crow, "The screened image, reproduced whole, has the character of an involuntary trace: it is memorial in the sense of resembling memory, which is sometimes vividly present, sometimes elusive, and always open to embellishment as well as loss."[2]

While Crow discusses the mnemonic trace with regard to Warhol's silk screens of Marilyn Monroe, the visual

Figure 2.7
Blow Job. Film still courtesy of the Andy Warhol Museum.

instability of *Blow Job*'s image demonstrates some of the same dynamics. *Blow Job*'s image is at times full, and at other times it evinces a very elusive, fugitive quality. The poser's shadowy face fragments are little more than chimera. Their signifiers materialize just long enough to claim a stable base for themselves and to consolidate *as* signifiers before they are replaced by new signifiers. They constitute their impact not by achieving visual autonomy but by way of a slightly vague recurrence, as the poser's repetitive movements call them forth briefly, but repeatedly, and with subtle variations. This contributes to the phenomenon that one's impressions of *Blow Job* may change quite radically during a single viewing. For example, a straightforward realist impression of what simply appears to be a young, handsome man may, at any moment, give way to the perception of a certain stylized allusiveness in any one of the three main visual constellations or any combination of them. Our processing of the image involves negotiating both of these aspects, whereby visual "fact" and mental association are already past the point of extrication. In this sense it becomes irrelevant that *Blow Job* falls short of tracing its image to an actual celebrity (such as, say, James Dean), which is something the Marilyn silk screens do, despite their own simulacral qualities.

In similar fashion to the Marilyn silk screens, *Blow Job*'s visual instability triggers the dynamics of memorialization by mapping a historically charged image onto its own lateral surface, whereby the fluctuation of spatial depth entails the reconceptualization of historical depth. *Blow Job*'s negotiation of both of these aspects hinges, again, on its dual qualities of inauthenticity and authenticity. The image's aspiration to authenticity lets it assume both the physical and temporal connotation of the term "present." By contrast, the image's sense of fabrication and manipulation may lead to a visual disjunction of both connotations: The image becomes physically distant or "absent" to the extent that it exists no longer fully in the present but has become the past—which is the point at which the transgressive, and hence original, act of having one's cock sucked in front of the camera is visually translated into a repository of historically accrued and clichéd masculinities. Or to put it the other way around, the moment in which the image adamantly recites the reified and outdated aspects of the poser's masculinity is also the moment of his most intense and authentic sexual pleasure.

Blow Job turns its viewers into intertextual readers by playing on the image's antithetical aspects—its originality and its derivative quality. This process becomes imbricated with another—the image's mobilization of memory—which is constituted by an intertextual investment of the image with knowledge of prior texts, often taken from commodity culture and equally often imbued with mythical qualities of their own. It is on this set of qualities that *Blow Job*'s relation to myth rests: The film mythologizes itself as an original, transgressive document from the underground, and it alludes to other myths that it has appropriated, or "robbed" in Barthes's sense. But if *Blow Job* appropriates these myths by mobilizing the volatility of memory, how can we visually apprehend them and compare them to one another? Barthes himself expressed a certain dissatisfaction with the use of spatial metaphors for a characterization of memory. The only way to negotiate this problem, I believe, is to select certain "visual moments" from the film, to quite literally arrest them, and to discuss them in terms of the memories and associations they trigger. To make these visual moments available for detailed discussion, I present them here as freeze-frames. This approach has a double function. First, it enables the apprehension of concrete visual moments for specific textual analysis. Their shadowy appearance may lend these images a subliminal quality, but their impact is also immediate and explicit. They simulate referents and supercede them, giving rise to multiple associations, prior knowledges, and metaphorical lineages. Second, the act of freezing these visual constellations is itself symbolically fraught. It reenacts *metaphorically* the dynamics of accessing memory and the processes of remembering that the image triggers. Freezing images from *Blow Job* is thus both a means to an end and an end in itself: It enables me to access a repository of American culture that contains a pool of images that began to circulate sometime during the postwar period; in addition, it allows me to treat the film itself as a sort of archeological site in which the myths of the era become visible all at once. This site is also where Roland Barthes, despite his very specific treatment of myth as ideology, meets with Claude Lévi-Strauss. Arguing in analogy to Lévi-Strauss, who claimed that all recollected experience is part of a synchronous totality, Barthes states that myth's meaning will be for its form an instantaneous reserve of history.[3]

By freezing *Blow Job*'s visual constellations in their spatial array and establishing comparisons between them, I am taking certain initial cues from structural anthropology, which also visualizes myths by "freezing" their multiple elements in organized patterns that we can hold before our eyes for scrutiny. The horizontal axes of these patterns trace the sequential narrative of any given myth, while their vertical columns compare a given element of a myth to that of another myth positioned directly above or beneath it. But whereas structural anthropology thus compares multiple pairs of vertically mapped mythemes, *Blow Job* proffers, at best, one such column—which by necessity would be purely *mentally* constructed (unless one regards the physical filmstrip itself as such a column, which, in *Blow Job*'s case, would almost be possible). The poser's repetitive rotation through the same three positions forces viewers to constantly *re*-encounter and memor(ial)ize these three visual constellations. Even then, of course, *Blow Job* still lacks any horizontal sequencing, which each of its myths would obtain if spatialized in stilled order. Whether the narratives of each of the myths *Blow Job* alludes to get completed depends entirely on the *connotative* activity and mythical literacy of the viewer.[4]

Yet, ultimately, the full sequencing of each of *Blow Job*'s myths is at best secondary, since the film deals with extremely well-known myths in a rather profane and insinuating way. More important, *Blow Job*, as it unfolds in time, inevitably *does* build a sequence of its own—however minimal and inconclusive. Instead of spatializing its discrete myths in their respective syntagmatic chains (which can be achieved only on a grid-like map), the film "snatches" them from their separate existences and, as it unspools, presents them as paradigmatic elements of the same syntagmatic sequence: The teenage rebel evolves into a full-fledged demon or, for that matter, a psychopathic gangster or even a skull, then into Christ, then back into one of the previous figures. Whereas structural anthropology, in order to *de*mystify myth (to study how myths negotiate cultural contradictions), thus seeks to separate myth's paradigmatic from its syntagmatic dimension, *Blow Job* enfolds the paradigmatic with the syntagmatic. Hence, when *Blow Job* displays its "loot"—when it spatializes the mass culture myths it has robbed—this display is not only *de*mystifying but also *re*mystifying. *Blow Job* thus mixes myths like metaphors, blending them into promiscuous cohabitation, and, as I shall argue, unfolds its own method of enabling us to detect certain similarities between these myths. In doing so, *Blow Job* finds yet another way of foregrounding the polemics of mythmaking.

Precisely because *Blow Job*'s myths can and should be regarded as forming a meaningful spatial array, a reading of the image will benefit from at least some of structuralism's underlying insights: the fact that we apprehend nature by way of culture and do so by redefining the space before us through opposite pairs and binarism; the fact that we abstract these binarisms into larger symbolic clusters; and the fact that we put these clusters in relation to one another.[5] One type of understanding can thus always be reduced to another, allowing for one phenomenon to be apprehended in multiple ways. Therefore, if myth, as Barthes claims, always outdistances its meaning, if its signifier always has an elsewhere at its disposal, a visual apprehension of myth goes not only through but *beyond* a perceived reality. The minimalist, visually "poor" quality of *Blow Job*'s image thus takes us far beyond the perception of a realist recording of the poser and makes us associate the poser with other images.

The spontaneity and insinuating force with which the film evokes other images points to myth's parasitical relation to culture in general. However, myth's uncanny tendency to feed off images that are easily recognizable also says something about these images: More often than not, they already have a high degree of circulation and are deeply immersed in the structures of popular memory and perception. Sometimes, these images stand in direct relation to individual and specific referents, such as a movie star, a celebrity, or a popular icon who may have popularized a certain type or style. Sometimes, they reflect a range of standardized or normative perceptions of certain social roles, behaviors, or appearances, as, for example, is the case with gender norms. Typically, myth seizes simultaneously on several of these categories, such as when it popularizes certain gender traits through the resignification of a star. While this is often the domain of dominant entertainment, *Blow Job*, like other films of the American underground cinema of the 1960s, is an interesting example of this form of cultural robbery, as it plundered popular styles for more subversive rearticulations of cultural stereotypes, gender roles, identifications, and desires.[6]

One icon *Blow Job* seizes on more or less conspicuously is James Dean. Since the mythical figures to be discussed in relation to *Blow Job*'s image—the teenage rebel, the demon/criminal, and the Christ figure—all constitute key elements of the star persona of James Dean, they can be read alternately via a projection of Dean onto the poser or as elements of the mythical figures that the poser invokes and that stars such as Dean also embodied during the 1950s. These elements are discussed at some length in the following pages, where attention is paid to their separate existences as autonomous myths (including their attending sociocultural stereotypes), to their functions as part myths within the overall myth of James Dean, and to their currency in Warhol's overall pool of images. One reason why James Dean's overall myth, in particular, is so resistant to analytical grasp is that it consists of a large number of such part myths that partly overlap and both complement and contradict one another. Needless to say, a structuring map of this myth would be hard to come by. Visual metaphors for it, however, do exist. Consider, for example, a particular publicity still of James Dean, shown in Figure 2.8, which illustrates not only the mythologizing features of Dean's star persona but also his status as a commodity item. The still's design consists of a mesh wire that spirals inward like a vortex, with Dean's face at its center. The visual design skillfully plays up Dean's romantic isolation as a psychologically deep, withdrawn misfit; the mesh wire specifically connotes imprisonment, an important element on which Dean's persona was constructed, as his star appeal rested on his attempts to negotiate various modes of confinement and privatization.[7]

Somewhat in accordance with 1950s Hollywood aesthetics, this publicity still of James Dean is also notable for its visual excess, which bears out the simulacral nature of mass culture images. Its strongly fetishistic quality reflects Dean's status as a commodity quite self-reflexively. The expression of depth in the still is so exaggerated, its centripetal force so pronounced, that it tilts over into its opposite and bears the trace of its own reification. The tunnel that narrows down at the end almost seems to become an inverted funnel from which the heavily psychologized individual pours out onto the market as a mass-produced public persona—a commodity item to be distributed in the circuits of mass culture. The same visual details that make this image a somewhat self-conscious sales pitch of Dean-as-commodity not only effectively summarize his persona but also become a metaphor for Dean-as-myth that is no less insinuating than myth itself. In this sense, the still's visual qualities represent one of myth's paradigmatic features: Form outdistances meaning. Paradoxically, then, the still's visual excess constitutes its very impoverishment: Nothing is hidden, everything is up for grabs, and the larger the number of interested grabbers the better. At center frame there is simply Dean; around him, the mesh-wire funnel carries and nurses the myth spawned by this central image as an outward moving spiral of proliferating part myths, a dense and ever growing fabric of intersecting partial narratives that have prompted and secured a myriad number of appropriations of the star across the world.

Figure 2.8
James Dean publicity shot from *East of Eden*.

Dean's three films are only fragments in this overall spiral, the particularities of their narrative and ideological closures constantly exceeded by the spiraling mesh of what viewers take away from them: images of Dean. It is these images, diverse in their nature as part myths of the overall Dean myth, that *Blow Job* shows us. *Blow Job* brings them back to life, flashing them before our eyes, generating them anew in the visual constellations through which the poser rotates. While the image in *Blow Job* strongly evokes Dean in particular, it shuns the star as a concrete referent. By merely alluding to Dean, *Blow Job* puts the onus of referencing on the audience. It "unties" itself, so to speak, by representing Dean through the simulacrum. In fact, the image's simulacral quality—the act of exceeding and, indeed, superceding the referent in representation—displays the operation of myth itself, as it works through and beyond a given substance. Hence, *Blow Job*'s visualization of Dean, of his stereotypes, and of his part myths is both demystifying and remystifying. On the one hand, it literally throws the star in a new light and defamiliarizes him. This enables us to identify and analyze some of the mythical roles he inhabited in and for postwar American culture. On the other hand, *Blow Job* also, of course, encourages us to simply celebrate Dean as "our" star, "our" object of identification and desire—but, again, as the object of *all* the identifications and desires implied by such terms as "our," "us," and "we." Going beyond any particular part myth and refusing to commit to any particular mythical type, *Blow Job* may be regarded as a very template of mythmaking. It represents yet another variation on Barthes's recommendation that since myth robs language of something, why not rob myth? In other words, *Blow Job* robs a myth for multiple (including deviant) acts of consumption—a myth that, itself, already consisted of nothing but the accrued fragments of various popular American myths. Visualizing the possibility of multiple, contradictory appropriations of the same image, type, or tale, *Blow Job* points to the fact that myths in general exist in multiple versions or, more accurately, in loosely constituted clusters of part myths. It is to these part myths that we now turn.

THE TEENAGE REBEL

The first of *Blow Job*'s mythical figures inhabited by Dean—the juvenile delinquent or teenage rebel—must be seen against the background of one of the central cultural and ideological battles of the 1950s: the conflict between the bourgeois family and sociocultural types of the Other. Dominant discourses during this period increasingly affirmed the nuclear family as the main building block of American society and defined against it newly emerging, socially or politically antagonistic formations. This dichotomization was achieved mainly through the rhetorical redefinition of masculinity—an operation that may be regarded as one of popular mythology's more recent rearticulations of a much older phenomenon—a deeply rooted nature/culture split that represented a binarism between myths of the biological reproduction of humankind and myths of social formations not based on sexual reproduction. Versions of this binarism, still operating in postwar American mythology, were becoming indexes of the cultural intelligibility of gender. In fact, the 1950s was a decade in American history that posited with renewed force the strictly reproductive function of sex as the underlying criterion for a seemingly transparent link between sex, gender, sex practice, and desire. The ascendant suburban ethos enshrined the sexualities of mainly white heterosexual men who embraced and actively protected the social contract: They were considered procreative or, at least, potentially procreative. By contrast, whether real or fictitious, whether social type or cultural stereotype, the beatnik, the sad young man of the fifties, the juvenile delinquent, and even the specter of the Communist were, more often than not, defined in terms of their rejection of the nuclear family. As 1950s ideology increasingly strove to render masculinity into a culturally intelligible, coherent ideal, procreative sexuality became linked with a "natural," "substantial," and, in any case, unquestionable masculinity, while proliferating sociocultural formations outside the nuclear family were ascribed an "insubstantial" masculinity and, more often than not, a suspect political or social identity.

During the 1950s, teenagers, homosexuals, and beatniks often received such labels as "insecure," "passive," "inward," "mysterious," "volatile," "impetuous" and "immature." The underlying conceptual framework of lack and excess not only implicitly posited the existence of a gender core whose "natural possession" was linked to the fulfillment of the social contract but also branded these various categories of outsiders as socially and culturally unproductive or even destructive, or as belonging to secret gangs or some other ominous and possibly sprawling network. Since these groups were, for the most part, phenomenologically indistinguishable from the mainstream but still needed to be made culturally intelligible, their deviant cultural livelihood became the operative stigma through which their political, social, and cultural threat could be articulated. *Blow Job*'s first visual constellation loosely evokes this range of types of the "Other" and exploits the fantasies projected onto them: their clandestine and suspicious existence as "creatures" of the underground; their sinister, latently menacing, and, in any case, unfathomable appearance; and the implication of transgressive sexuality, which was projected onto or actually came with their subcultures. As *Blow Job*'s stylish simulacrum invokes these types in close relation to their most prominent inhabiter, James Dean, it liberates Dean from some of the ideological constraints of his own Hollywood vehicles—but only from some of them. In keeping the blow job "we" give to James Dean off frame, the film also repeats what mainstream culture had done all along—that is, banish deviant appropriations of Dean from the realm of the denotative.

Male teenagers were only one group in the spectrum of suspicious sociopolitical "Others," but they are of special interest here because their emergence as a sociodemographic category is closely linked to the suburbanization of postwar America. Perceived as both a product of and a threat to his middle-class environment, the male teenager's mythological function rested on the fact that he stood both inside and outside the social contract. Defined by such concepts as transition, growth, and integration, the male teenager started out in ignorance or even defiance of society and grew into a fully fledged citizen, responsible husband, and patriarchal provider. His traversing of the mythological rift thereby also demonstrates the way in which a liberal society's dictum of procreative sexuality was constructed upon its Other. By assuming a subordinate function as "children of a lesser myth," male teenagers, by virtue of their teleology of transition, served to legitimize procreative sexuality and liberal society. In addition, such features as "rugged individuality," still celebrated by pop culture in the frontier myth, were grafted onto the male teenager as proof of his healthy ego. Even though 1950s consensus culture was ambivalent toward "rogue" qualities, these were tolerated and to a certain extent furthered because they provided liberal society with both a self-legitimizing alibi and the prospect of mentally and biologically "sound" future citizens. As Judith Butler notes in a different but somewhat related context,

> The prevailing assumption of the ontological integrity of the subject before the law might be understood as the contemporary trace of the state of nature hypothesis, that foundationalist fable constitutive of the juridical structures of classical liberalism. The performative invocation of a nonhistorical "before" becomes the foundational premise that guarantees a presocial ontology of persons who freely consent to be governed and, thereby, constitute the legitimacy of the social contract.[8]

The liberal ideology of James Dean's films, his star persona, and the myth they produced, all of which were targeted at teenagers as well as adult audiences, carefully elaborated and romanticized the details of this teleology. Dean's transition from romanticized rebel outlaw to responsible citizen posits him as *subject before the law* in two ways. His clash with parental and state authorities indicated an immaturity that, while fed by a potentially destructive impetuousness, already appeared to contain the core of a highly individual, "substantial" identity. In addition, when Dean's transgressiveness was articulated, for example, through his willingness to form homoerotic bonds, the violent elimination of these bonds from the narrative went hand in hand with Dean's heterosexualization.[9] The law thus subjected him to a process of engendering—the outcome of which is clear: Homoeroticism and any other forms of nonprocreative sexuality were necessarily transitory, as they constituted the rhetorical Other upon which the heterosexual subject was founded. The law thus legitimized itself via the mythological function of the teenage rebel: Precisely because he stood without the law, his embrace of it was equally free and overdetermined and thus ultimately functioned to validate the law.

The myth of the presocialized individual is also very much present in the utilization of spatial depth and perspective in the aforementioned publicity still of Dean. The still's spiraling mesh wire with Dean at its center reflects that, as far as 1950s mainstream popular culture was concerned, the new male adolescent was a subject in depth, and spatial depth was a means of expressing psychological depth. Yet, visual excess and ideological reconciliation are not always mutually exclusive. On the one hand, the publicity still geometrically defines Dean as the psychologized individual who is temporarily disconnected from the larger community—a rhetoric that is analogous to perceiving the image's mesh-wire lines as moving inward. On the other hand, Dean's edgy individuality also has considerable romantic appeal. This appeal is exploited by Dean's films, which, at one point or other, invariably emphasize that Dean's individuality is of value for the larger community. The star's communal value would be conveyed by reading the image's visual design as spiraling outward. The still thus harnesses both aspects of Dean's persona (however excessively) into a spatio-metaphorical transfer whose outcome is preordained—that is, that reintegration must take place and that conflict must be resolved. Centripetal and centrifugal forces extend in diametrically opposite directions but cohabit the image as a means to the same end.

The clash of Dean's characters with state and parental authorities not only was a recurring theme in his films but, in fact, determined Dean's erratic body movements and facial histrionics. The classic gangster's relationship to authority was very different: His nervy, linear energy (consider James Cagney and Edward G. Robinson) and the violent shoot-outs in which he would invariably die enacted what one may call the paradigm of the frontal clash, which defined the relation between gangster and society as inherently inimical. It expressed the gangster's outsider status even more than his specific crimes did, and it defined his Otherness as a constant, predictable type of Otherness. By contrast, as children who had been born *into* the social contract, Dean's teenagers had a different pedigree, and their performed insecurity and inwardness reflected a different utilization of space. The frontal clash became replaced by a kind of dodgy vacillation: Dean was among the first to cultivate a set of self-conscious movements that bespoke his ambivalence toward the options of rebellion and consent and, perhaps more important, toward the fact that in accordance with the myth he inhabited, there now were options.

Dean's ambivalence toward the law and his awareness that he existed within its confines, that he had acknowledged what had brought him into the world, is also evidenced by his facial expressions. Dean's studied authenticity and method histrionics articulated the individual's ambivalence toward leaving his psychological prison and communicating with the outer world.[10] Within the parameters of the myth of the romantic, presocialized individual, the need for communication stood in potential conflict with maintaining one's own integrity, for it was tantamount to adopting a vocabulary that was not one's own and, thus, to acknowledging (and indirectly validating) the social as the realm of convention. Dean's characteristic kinetic restlessness functioned as a metaphor for breaking out of society. But the star's function as a tool for ideological containment, epitomized by the visuals of the spiraling vortex of the standard-size publicity still, translated with equal precision onto the big screen of 1950s Hollywood. Hollywood's elongated cinemascope format was large enough to both contain and exploit Dean's kinetic energy for the open minds and vistas of the liberal nation-state. Both visual treatments reinscribed him into ideological coordinates that dictated his heterosexualization and reintegration into liberal mainstream society.[11]

Blow Job's second visual constellation also engages the Dean myth. It invokes the dual qualities of the Dean myth along with the ambivalence expressed by Dean's movie characters via the display of the poser's self-consciousness. Whereas *Blow Job*'s first visual constellation romanticizes the new type of outlaw quite literally as a "dark figure" (that is, romanticizes him for his indifference to and even contempt for the law), the second visual grasps the concept of subject-before-the-law even as it subjects him to the dynamics of visual objectification by Warhol's camera. Unlike the first constellation (and also, in another way, as we shall see, unlike the third one), in which the poser seems indifferent to and unaware of objectification, the second constellation attenuates his self-absorption. The shading of the poser's face alternately obscures and reveals his own gaze, although at least one of his eyes is always cast in shadow. This ambiguity is doubled by the poser's behavior as he oscillates between acknowledging the camera and denying its existence. He seems more self-conscious and aware of being filmed. For a few fleeting moments, the possibility arises of the camera's visual mastery of its object, the potential for penetration, which is heightened by the poser's ambivalence about being an object for the camera. But with the poser's acknowledgment of the camera's gaze and, thus, of the scenario as such, the link to the social is established explicitly; the existence of some kind of contract, indeed, of the very concept of contract, looms large.

In addition, the lighting in the second constellation makes the poser more desirable. Its presentation of the poser as an object of desire, which entails a certain effeminization, is reminiscent of the eroticizing quality of many Hollywood and soft-core porn images; it can be characterized, in accordance with Richard Dyer's analysis of presentations of the sad young man stereotype, as "romantic-pornographic."[12] While the sad young man will be discussed more extensively with regard to *Blow Job*'s third visual constellation, of interest here is that this stereotype overlaps to a certain extent with that of the teenage rebel. Whereas social integration into mainstream society is only one of several options for the sad young man, he, like the teenage rebel, is a figure of isolation, suffering, and transition. There is considerable anxiety over how he will turn out in the end (straight or gay), and his oscillation between the straight and the gay world analogizes the teenage rebel's oscillation between parental home and teenage gang.[13] The self-consciousness of *Blow Job*'s poser is also a defining feature of the sad young man. Captured by the camera, he is, in Richard Dyer's words, "always caught at the moment of exploration and discovery."[14]

None of this is to say that the film's first and third visual constellations, in comparison to the second, authenticate any more sincerely what Butler calls a "presocial ontology." The film's constantly changing mise-en-scène keeps the relation between artifice and authenticity in flux. But the poser's carefully authored attitude of indifference to the camera (and, by extension, to the law) may *appear* more authentic in the mise-en-scène's two opposite extremes, as these enhance the impression of self-absorption through the respective visual effects of shrouding the poser in darkness and, alternately, bathing him in light. They also express more stable, albeit oppositional, gender codings. The first constellation evokes masculinity in its dark, brooding intensity; the third constellation, in which the poser looks up into the light in masochistic self-abandon, effeminizes him. By contrast, the shading of the face in the second constellation brings with it the mixing of the sets of metaphors that subtend the two extremes this visual combines. Its patches of light link it to the third constellation, while its dark shadings reference the first constellation's literal and metaphorical darkness. The apprehension by some viewers of the poser in the second constellation being self-absorbed becomes solidified precisely because we see so little of his self-conscious gaze. His dark eye sockets are the stuff of fiction, even if that fiction is written by the film's "reader."

Visually, mythologically, and metaphorically, the second constellation is thus constituted by the two visual poles between which it is wedged. As much as *Blow Job* seduces viewers here with the illusion of the poser as a luridly lit referent, it also arguably "shines through" this referent and transforms it into a simulacrum or, more accurately, into several simulacra, which become the site of several part myths. The central binaries that subtend these part myths—good versus evil; life versus death; narcissistic self-absorption versus sacrifice for humanity—are all imbricated with, articulated by, and, significantly, *reduced to* the same visual substance of light and shadow. *Blow Job* identifies the constitutive elements of the subject before the law (constructed by the social, yet posing as presocial) as being authored by the same source and thus shows us the presocialized individual precisely as what he is—a myth.

The dual gender coding of the second constellation is also informed by *Blow Job*'s double operation of dissecting myth and partaking in it. The impression of the poser's unstable masculinity is complemented by his vacillation between resisting the camera and "receiving" its penetration. But with these metaphorical floodgates opened, the poser also, at once, becomes a figure of inversion. His only partially successful attempt to resist the camera's objectification/penetration effeminizes him and makes his masculinity more suspect, recasting him as a member of the demimonde. (Bluntly put, the shading of his face suggests that he is a shady character.) He is not only in between the sexes, but he can also be read as going back and forth between straight world and gay underworld. In addition, the poser's self-conscious enactment of sexual transgression *as* a reified pose (an enactment for the camera and, thus, an act coauthored by the camera) reminds us that the "alternative" masculinities that 1950s culture associated with types of the "Other" were really stereotypes—they were still compatible with, and to a certain extent produced by, the same dominant discourses that used them as a means of demarcation.

Yet, all of this demystification does not preclude the obvious: Stereotype or not, the film celebrates the poser's good looks even as it shows us that these looks are what subcultural slang would call "tired"—they had been "done" many times before. By the time of *Blow Job*'s release, the poser's masculine qualities had become somewhat of a stereotype. The film features them at a moment when the dominant concept of masculinity was about to undergo a crucial transition. Partly due to the influx of British culture in the United States, new masculine types such as the Beatles, Jim Morrison, Terence Stamp, David Bailey, and Mick Jagger emerged and pushed such older masculinities as featured in *Blow Job* to the margins, where they became appropriated by segments of the working class and by certain subcultures. In this period of transition, *Blow Job* is then both a record of historical masculinities and a trendsetting image. It represents postwar images of masculinity at the moment of their subordination to the multifarious spectrum of significations that constituted the 1960s. As myths of a second, third, or fourth order (which themselves have seized on other myths), films of the American underground cinema, and certainly films by trendsetting stylist Andy Warhol, robbed outmoded gender appearances and enabled them to continue their existence elsewhere, for example, in such urban subcultures as the New York gay male scene. Resignifying James Dean in these ways, *Blow Job*'s relation to the Dean myth is more complex than the deadpan image initially lets one believe. By regenerating certain associations through the poser's motions, the film metaphorizes the Dean spiral. It features myth itself in a defamiliarized, transformed light. Yet the film also partakes in the Dean myth by robbing its parts and remythologizing them. Its fragments are fed back into the myth and become part of the (probably further out) areas of the Dean spiral.

THE GANGSTER

Another icon already mentioned briefly with regard to the mise-en-scène's second constellation is the gangster. The head-on range of this visual puts it in certain relation to the mug shots of criminals and, more specifically, to the mural Warhol constructed of such mug shots, *Thirteen Most Wanted Men*, which was his contribution to the 1964 New York World Fair. Yet, a closer examination of the mural problematizes this comparison. The mug shots that constitute the mural clearly reflect the visual vocabulary of criminal photography: Whether the objects are photographed full front or in profile, the image is evenly lit and the objects' eyes are open and clearly visible to comply with maximum objectification. By contrast, *Blow Job*'s second visual constellation features the poser's face in chiaroscuro with at least one eye (often both) obscured by conspicuous shadows and with the shadows cast by his nose and chin contributing to a progressive darkening of the picture plane from top to bottom. Even though *Blow Job* does not invoke the "classic" gangster but his 1950s variant—the criminal psychopath, as a mug shot, this visual would simply be rejected as useless. Precisely because *Blow Job* cites the mug shot obliquely, it repositions the gangster from being the object of criminal photography to being the subject of myth. The dark eye sockets give the poser a demonic air, exploiting his dramatic appeal as a potential threat. Mediating between two visual and mythological opposites, the image may also be said to comment on the gangster's ideological containment—only this containment does not consist of reintegration but takes the form of death. Signifying the gangster as a doomed, moribund figure, the image visually anticipates the skull, which also is a mythical figure of containment and transition. It contains our fear of death by visualizing it, and it signifies life's transitoriness. The skull is as typical a Warholian icon as the gangster and the suffering martyr. Its presence in *Blow Job* is never outwardly manifest but is overlaid with other mythical figures (see Chapter 5).

In its evocation of the gangster, *Blow Job*'s second visual constellation is also linked thematically to a number of visual motifs in Warhol's work, from the silk screens of the electric chair to the print of James Cagney. Cagney's persona is, of course, as indissociable from the gangster as James Dean's is from the teenage rebel, and Cagney's characters had to negotiate their own set of seemingly irreconcilable contradictions—that is, the romantic raw appeal of the gangster's anarchic impulse and his deviant form of success had to be converted into failure and downfall.[15] By the late 1930s, however, the gangster's mythical appurtenances had become more elaborate, as can be seen, for example, in James Cagney's Rocky Sullivan in *Angels with Dirty Faces*. Similar to Dean in *Rebel Without a Cause*, Cagney, in *Angels*, had the dual role of outlaw and mentor (to a group of slum kids). However, while Dean's social reintegration in *Rebel* took effect through the betrayal of his protégé, Plato, who, not unlike a gangster, died in police gunfire (*Rebel*, in fact, achieves its ideological closure by invoking two myths), *Angels* cleverly subverted its compulsory self-censorship by making Cagney's preordained end synonymous with the ultimate form of mentorship—martyrdom. Dying "yellow" on the electric chair, Rocky kept the slum kids from admiring him. Then he is redeemed by saving their souls. The disillusioned but morally salvaged kids symbolically escape their own dead end by ascending a set of stairs that looks like the stairway to heaven. In addition, the film cleverly reduces Rocky's execution to a play of light and shadow reflected on the wall of the execution chamber, a technique that made audiences second-guess Rocky's "cowardice." In a double operation not unlike that of *Blow Job*, *Angels* obtained a certain amount of filmic and ideological reflexivity and still perpetuated the myth by entrusting it to moviegoers. Indeed, *Angels*' final scene not only shows the myth in operation but, in fact, sponsors its dissemination. *Blow Job*'s own play of light and shadow like that in *Angels*, may then be regarded as mapping broader mythical parameters—a set of basic spatio-metaphorical coordinates that also pertained to the gangster myth as modified in the wake of the implementation of the Hays code: Equal parts bad guy and savior, the gangster finds redemption in the very act of death, alluded to by the second constellation's subtending skull symbolism as well as by the third constellation's martyr theme.

By all accounts, then, the visual properties of *Blow Job*'s second visual constellation are a far cry from the forensic naturalism of mug shots. Yet, the juxtaposition of *Thirteen Most Wanted Men* with *Blow Job* in this way is not meant to suggest that there exists an essential divide in Warhol's work or elsewhere between an inherent, truth-bearing capacity of documentary photography and a subsequent aestheticization. We know that every image, whether mug shot, publicity still, or family portrait, is aesthetically manipulated. In fact, as argued earlier, the pop image combines documentation with aestheticization, foregrounding the aestheticizing features of the documentary genre. Instead, I submit that Warhol, when he made *Blow Job* and *Thirteen Most Wanted Men* within just a few months of each other, engaged the same set of mythical binaries but utilized two different visual vocabularies to create two different aestheticizing effects.

For the mural, Warhol used actual mug shots of criminals as source material. These images were drastically blown up for the mural's installation, expanding to twenty by twenty feet for the overall panel. But the images retained their graininess and more than a trace of their status as visual documents. The effect, as Richard Meyer points out, was a spectacularization of the traces of state power, "elevating a compulsory image of identification to the heroic status of a public mural."[16]

It is not so much that Warhol, aestheticizing the panel the way he did, did not also partake in the myth of the gangster. The mural certainly celebrates the grandeur of the felon, to borrow Meyer's phrase. But one must ask whether Warhol displayed the gangster *as* myth. The answer, I believe, would have to be no, for whereas the myth itself (like any myth) works to conceal ideological contradictions (the gangster as romanticized Other; the gangster as ordinary citizen), the mural presented these contradictions with unmitigated force. As the mural itself did not comment on whether some of the real-life criminals it elevated to star status were still at large, were still behind bars, or had by then been released from prison, anxiety arose that some of its outlaw stars might sue the fair organizers on grounds of libel.[17] The momentous impact of the mug shots' de facto criminalization stood in no stable relation to the current de facto status of their objects. While the mural is not devoid of aestheticization, it still presented the gangsters as real-life criminals. *Thirteen Most Wanted Men* refused to disguise or resolve a central dilemma—that the classic felon of ten-most-wanted caliber, who is usually perceived as "Other," does, in fact, partake in sameness. He is one of us. This is enhanced by the fact that the bottom three slots of the overall panel were left empty, implying that new felons will emerge from our midst. Warhol's mural tends to get discussed in terms of its objectifying features, but Meyer's close analysis emphasizes that some of the frontal photos are not only not complemented by the obligatory profile shot but feature its object in semi-profile, some even effusing a friendly smile. The effect of sameness is thus enhanced by the intrusion of the vocabulary of the candid photograph.[18]

Blow Job has, of course, its own tension between documentary and fiction, but it presents its mythological figures as stereotypes, and its aestheticization of these figures foregrounds their functions as myths. Warhol's mural, by contrast, confronted its public with a social reality that it did not help resolve but simply stated and actually enhanced. Given the fact that the mural's exhibition site was the New York State Pavilion, whose function was to demonstrate the "state government's desire to represent itself officially," in Benjamin Buchloh's words, it comes as no surprise that the mural's fate was as sealed as that of the mythical gangster.[19] The mythical resolution that Warhol's mural denied the fair organizers was subsequently provided by the organizers themselves, as they, in a very matter-of-fact way, ordered Warhol to eradicate the mural within twenty-four hours.

THE SUFFERING MARTYR

In *Blow Job*'s third visual constellation, the poser's head is tilted up at an extreme angle and his face is directed toward the ceiling. The light from the spotlight in the upper left corner beyond the frame meets his face and, as it is reflected, proliferates across much of the image. This is the film's most striking visual constellation, and its association with images of Christ are almost overdetermined. However, the deadpan character of this image belies the subtle and complex commentary it implies, especially if one examines this constellation with regard to the system of myths and metaphors suffusing the film and with regard to the thematic and iconographic concerns traceable across Warhol's oeuvre. As we shall see, in this oeuvre Christ "pops up" in multiple versions: as transgressive underground movie star, in the guise of the teenage rebel and the sad young man, and as centerpiece of Warhol's own renditions of *The Last Supper*.

Representations of Jesus are not uncommon in American underground cinema, and they are usually transgressive with regard to two aspects. First, they refuse to engage in high art's conventional veneration of Christ's singular spiritual nobility and his heightened individuality as God's son. Instead, they present him as a mythical figure who circulates in mass culture—a commodity. Second, they extend their notorious celebration of transgressive sexuality to Christ and often homoeroticize him. Kenneth Anger's 1947 underground film, *Fireworks*, utilizes Christ symbolism in this way. The film depicts the dreamlike nocturnal hazards and sufferings of a young man who is repeatedly depicted in what Richard Dyer has characterized as pietà-like positions[20] and who wears a Christmas tree as a headdress. The 1948 film *Images in the Snow*, which was made by avant-garde filmmaker Willard Maas, centers on a young man whose peripatetic wanderings are likened to the Passion of Christ. The film presents Christ as a picaresque antihero whose spiritual and, sometimes, erotically charged journey from an urban industrial wasteland to a suburban cemetery negotiates such binaries as past/present, life/death, and spirit/flesh.[21] The most elaborate treatment of Christ can be found in Kenneth Anger's 1963 film, *Scorpio Rising*, in which the filmmaker subversively edited footage from a biblical epic, *The Road to Jerusalem*, with images of skulls, crossbones, Nazis, Marlon Brando, and James Dean. To further the irony and to enhance the context of Christ as commodity, Anger underscored the Christ imagery with such pop songs as "He's a Rebel" (The Crystals), "Torture" (Kris Jensen), "Point of No Return" (Gene McDaniels), and "I Will Follow Him" (Little Peggy March).[22] By subversively citing Christ out of context, the film identifies Christianity, as Richard Dyer points out, as repressive and utilizes the theme of transubstantiation as a metaphor for the birth pangs of gay rebirth. It makes this very clear through its aggressive—many might say blasphemous—eroticization of Christ. For example, it insinuates that a man whose vision had been restored by Christ and who kneels in front of him to thank him is actually sucking him off.

While the eroticization of Christ in these films is a particular mark of modern culture's aggressively secular, even heretic, attitude toward Christ, the possibility of an erotic or sexual side to Jesus and of sexual episodes in Jesus' biography has been raised since the apostles. *Cassell's Encyclopedia of Queer Myth, Symbol, and Spirit* tells us that while mainstream Christianity has always defensively insisted on Christ's asexuality and asceticism, minor Christian traditions have long suggested that Christ may have been sexual like most other humans.[23] Others have surmised that he was transgendered or had bisexual characteristics and have linked him to homoeroticism and androgyny (the latter claim is echoed in high and low art depictions of Christ's long hair and by the interpretation of the wound in his side as an analogy to a vagina). Indeed, a long list of artists, literati, scholars, philosophers, and sovereigns from Christopher Marlowe and King James I to Denis Diderot, Jean Delville, Xavier Mayne, Andrew Lloyd Webber and Tim Rice, and lesbian feminist theologian Mary Daly, have pondered, from different perspectives and with varying degrees of sympathy, the possibility of Christ's homoerotic inclinations. According to *Cassell's*, these debates frequently draw on the same three events in Christ's life: He was said to have had a "special" love for Lazarus; during the last supper one of his disciples, "whom Jesus loved, was lying close to the breast of Jesus," giving rise to the presumption of the existence of homoeroticism in Jesus' inner circle; and he was betrayed by Judas with a kiss.[24] The Judas kiss has since become a potent metaphor especially for homophobic abjection. (One might see an analogy in the ritual of straight men raping a gay or androgynous man or sexual transgressor as a form of gay bashing—see, for example, the rape of Joe Buck in the 1969 film *Midnight Cowboy*.) While these three events figure few and far between in the totality of Christian tradition, the consistency with which they resurface over the centuries and the heated debates they have sparked give one pause.

Blow Job refers no more explicitly to Christ than to James Dean, the teenage rebel, the sad young man, or the gangster. Unlike *Scorpio Rising*, *Blow Job* does not use found representations of Christ from art and theology, nor does it place its Christ image in subversive dialogue with obscene iconography or pop music. Instead, the film's mise-en-scène, minimalist and expressive at the same time, evokes Christ through the simulacrum; the territory staked out for Christ—as for James Dean and his mythical stereotypes—is that of metaphor. In this way, *Blow Job* simultaneously falls short of and exceeds *Scorpio Rising*'s insinuating force. To the extent that it stops short of utilizing preexisting Christ imagery, *Blow Job* allegorizes mainstream Christianity's vehement withholding of its chief referent from any kind of erotic activity. However, on another level, the film may also be said to reflect the marginalized Christian discourses that eroticize Jesus, but this reflection is more like a refraction. Merely alluding to Christ, evoking him via the very act of connotation/interpretation, the film denies the referent its ontological status. Perhaps, *Blow Job*'s self-imposed distance to the referent is of minor importance within the context of American underground cinema. After all, one could argue that Anger's re-interpretation of Christ is so radical and offensive that it is tantamount to abjuring the referent altogether. Rather than overstating the case, I simply want to point out that *Blow Job* foregrounds what detractors as well as supporters of Christ's sexual side have in common—the claiming of the referent for their own respective truth discourses via representations that are always already interpretive.

Blow Job may then be understood not so much as an effort to claim Jesus as a de facto homosexual but rather as offering a rich, if subtle, commentary on Christianity's historically changing attitudes toward Jesus. Treating Christ as a myth, the mise-en-scène's third visual constellation is able to pull him into the broader mythological rift mentioned earlier—the struggle between competing mythologies of the genealogy of humankind, one of which seizes on the centrality of biological reproduction while the other insists on some kind of spiritual force or, in this case, on divine decree as the ultimate explanation. Christ's dual status as the product of an immaculate conception, as both human and divine, has spawned different attitudes at different historical moments toward Christ's sexuality and his sexual parts. Pre-Reformation discourses, which primarily emphasized Christ's function as a spiritual leader, steadfastly disavowed the existence of his penis, and visual representations sublimated any whiff of eroticism into celebrations of Christ's spiritual beauty and suffering. Post-Reformation discourses, by contrast, rearticulated Christ's sexuality by secularizing him as the model for the mundane paterfamilias, who has become Western bourgeois society's spiritual as well as material provider endowed with phallicized procreative power.[25] In this vein, artistic representations of Christ have, more often than not, referenced Christ's private parts even in the act of censoring them (consider the thin, barely concealing loin cloth). The Christlike pose of *Blow Job*'s poser and the image's self-censoring framing comment on both of these attitudes toward Christ's sexuality. *Blow Job* mocks the sanctity of Christ in Western culture because the poser, in the tradition of Baudelairean cinema, "becomes" Christ precisely through the use of his cock and the pleasure extracted from it. Yet, as much as the image subversively invokes Christ as an erotic being, this erotic, even priapic effect is, at once, sublimated into spiritual beauty, which is reminiscent particularly of pre-Reformation discourses. In addition, *Blow Job* simultaneously subjects the Christ image to and "saves" it from the reactionary implications of the post-Reformation tradition that secularized Christ in the first place—secularized middle-class culture. The film partakes in the taboo this culture has placed on the display of sex, but it does so ironically and, significantly, via the insinuation of a nonreproductive, transgressive sex act. Transporting this act into the public sphere (metaphorized by the brick wall behind the poser), *Blow Job* subverts the rigidly iconized private/public split. Although central to Lutheran mores, this split, it is safe to say, was unbeknownst to Jesus himself—whatever his sexual inclinations.

Blow Job's evocation of mythical types and iconographic stereotypes is richly suggestive and elusive at the same time. The same visual substance that helps carry the allusion to such referents as Christ and James Dean also facilitates their spatial overlap and mutual substitution. It is thus not only the figure of Christ that is worth discussing here, but his stand-ins—such postwar stereotypes as the sad young man of the fifties and the teenage rebel, who, to varying degrees, partook in the Christ myth. According to *Cassell's Encyclopedia of Queer Myth, Symbol, and Spirit*, the significance of the Christ story for modern homosexuals is hardly based only on the three notorious (but apocryphal) homoerotic episodes already discussed. Rather, Jesus preached a new, radically different version of Judaism that was regarded as heresy and that eventually led to the splitting of the faith. For his beliefs and teachings, he was crucified by the Romans, who, less than 300 years later, would, themselves, officially embrace Christianity. The myth of Christ, while earmarked by historical facts, remains a myth (and an archetypal Western myth at that) precisely because it combined in prototypical fashion an individual's outsider status with his messianic qualities and his passion—in both senses of the word. The overdetermined implications of this story have been (and still are) played out by homosexuals and homophobes alike: Gays, it is assumed, are taking over the world, and though many may perish in the act, they will win not through the sword but through gentle (or sneaky) subversion. Christ's combined features—his outsider status, his spirituality, his suffering, and his gentleness (indeed, *gentileness*), have condensed in high and low art representations into the adoration of the white, naked, stricken young man, whose suffering is always noble.

Richard Dyer has pointed out that it is exactly this image, which stresses the "moral worth and erotic beauty of white male flesh in agony"[26] and is embodied by such martyrs as Saint Sebastian, to which the iconography of the stereotype of the homosexual as sad young man can be traced. Dyer also finds this iconography in the Romantic poets' correlation between physical appearance, emotional capacity, and gender identity. The androgyny of the sad young man marks his appearance and heightens his passion; his body may be a mere cadaver, but it is not decaying—it is "cadaverously beautiful."[27] Dyer further points out that the sad young man is at the nexus of certain sexual truth discourses that pathologize sex and polemically conflate sex with gender. These discourses represent a cross between science and demagoguery. First, there were early twentieth century third sex theories (the homosexual as being between male and female or, specifically, a woman trapped in a man's body); second, there was vulgar Freudianism's postulations about the dangers of narcissism and an "unhealthy" closeness between mother and son; and third there was the mid–twentieth century social invention of adolescence as a distinct phase in the transition from boy to man, whose uncertain outcome in sexual terms gave rise to parental anxiety and moral panic. But Dyer also emphasizes that the popularity of the sad young man stemmed from the very contradictions he harbored as a stereotype. He notes,

> If at one extreme [the stereotype] represented a warning of misery, which a gay man could have laid at the door of his ineradicable pervertedness, at the other it offered an image of

holy sensitivity, stunning good looks, overwhelming erotic experience and escape from the dreariness of real manliness, for all of which a gay man may have felt that some unreasonable, socially induced suffering was a small price to pay.[28]

Blow Job's third visual constellation evokes many of the contradictory qualities of this stereotype, most notably the combination of spirituality and transgressive sex: The poser's own stunning good looks, articulated earlier through the image of a dark, earthy masculinity, are enhanced in the third constellation because it both effeminizes and spiritualizes him; he is clearly (and more than in the other two constellations) in a state of rapture (whose source could be either sexual pleasure or pain, or both). In addition, his self-absorption insinuates the impression of narcissism at least on the level of a clichéd pose, whereby his nature as a figure of transition is captured and arrested—indeed, captured *as* arrested—by the image's strongly fetishistic character.

That Warhol was personally fascinated by the stereotype of the sad young man—to the extent that he deliberately attempted to stylize himself in this manner—can be seen by two photographs of Warhol taken by his boyfriend from the 1950s, Ed Wallowitch. The first one (Figure 2.9) shows Warhol in a dark space under a bare lamp that illuminates his head. His tilted-up head, his serene facial expression, his closed eyes, and

Figure 2.9
Andy Warhol, 1958. B/w photograph/transparency. Courtesy of the
Edward Wallowitch Estate. Reproduction by the Andy Warhol Museum.

Figure 2.10
Andy Warhol, 1958. B/w photograph/transparency.
Courtesy of the Edward Wallowitch Estate. Reproduction by
the Andy Warhol Museum.

his right hand lifted up and opened to "catch" the light falling on it clearly signify a state of rapture, however performed it might have been. The second photograph (Figure 2.10) is a head-on close-up of this constellation, whose blurred visuals actually intensify the spiritual aspects of the sad young man stereotype that is being emulated. These photographs strongly suggest that Warhol was conversant with some of the qualities of the sad young man as a popular type, which he sought to appropriate for his own consumption and self-stylization. Warhol's sensibility and wit helped him reenact the type as a pose. In addition, his spiritual air in both of these images somewhat seeks to make up for his lack of beauty, and it enhances his own effeminacy. At least iconographically, both images display a similarity to *Blow Job*.[29]

Richard Dyer's description of the sad young man makes clear that stereotypes get appropriated by consumers from different strands of mainstream culture. Such cultural products as novels or Hollywood movies are always read against the grain, despite and beyond whatever narrative and ideological closures these presentations put in the way to regulate the stereotypes they serve up. Therefore, it is only fair to say that we do not need a film like *Blow Job* to help us appropriate an attractive icon, such as James Dean. Rather, *Blow Job* is significant for the way in which it lifts these stereotypes out of their naturalizing mainstream contexts and hyperbolizes their contradictions without resolving them on a denotative level. This can be illustrated, once more, by comparing *Blow Job* with a mainstream text that is particularly apposite here because, culturally, it combines the Christ myth with the figures of the sad young man and the teenage rebel. The text is James Dean's breakthrough film, *East of Eden*, which clearly reflects the function of the Dean myth as a vehicle for negotiating mainstream culture's growing awareness of the dual role of sex as procreative act and as transgressive pleasure or, in other words, as sin. James Dean plays Cal Trask, a dysfunctional teenager who is supposed to assume his "proper" place by the side of his God-fearing father but who takes after his mother (the source of his "badness"), who left the family and opened a brothel. In one of the film's key scenes, the father punishes Cal by making him read the Bible aloud, but Cal angers his father even further by reading deliberately too fast and, significantly, by reading out loud the numbers in front of every verse. Not only does Dean as Cal here assume the double function of bad son and Christ surrogate, but his transgressive act of explicitly announcing the individual verses defamiliarizes Christianity by transgressively foregrounding its discursive structure as a myth. While in this scene from *East of Eden* the "bad seed" wins the day, the film ultimately yanks its bad boy from his heretical course and brutally forces him to take his father's place. The paradoxical structure of myth is finally resolved through narrative—or, more accurately, the myth splits into textual resolution (enforced by the particular constraints of the film as text) and paratextual evolution (appropriations of Dean not dependent on the film but enabled by Dean publicity material, public appearances, gossip, etc.).

Blow Job's visualization of the teenage rebel as Christ figure is conceptually analogous to this scene from *East of Eden*, but its visuals pare down Dean's myth to its essential elements, which are otherwise scattered across texts and paratexts. The oppositional placeholders that compose the Dean myth not only overlap visually in *Blow Job* but, in the absence of narrative solution, remain interchangeable within the moving image. The image's ever new production of fragmented shadows arguably constitutes a kind of refusal not found in mainstream narratives: *Blow Job* refuses to "commit" to any one of these images permanently; it refuses to prioritize any one moment of appropriation over others. Instead, it commits equally strongly to all possible part myths. This sort of commitment then also constitutes a crucial functional analogy to the way structuralist anthropology studies myths by spatializing them in grids: In the grid, too, no myth is privileged against another. Instead, according to Rosalind Krauss, the grid holds the myths it spatializes in "para-logical suspension."[30] That is, it violates the temporal dimension of myth by refusing to sequence its story toward resolution. The structuralist utilization of the grid effects this paralogical suspension by spatializing the stories into vertical columns in order to display the features of their contradictions and their concealment through narrative. *Blow Job* produces a similar effect through its mise-en-scène, which repetitively displays its mythemes by rotating through the same set of images over and over again. None of the film's visual constellations provides resolution to any of the other ones. The constellations simply present their mythemes in ever new patterns of variation and repetition.[31] The poser moves from brooding outlaw and insecure teenager to enraptured saint and back. If anything, this effect is increased by the film's slowed-down projection speed and its overtly visible nine-roll structure, clearly apparent by the white flashes that mark the point at which two rolls are spliced together. These flashes may be regarded as an objective correlative to Dean's defiant enunciation of the Bible verse in *East of Eden*.

Whether one chooses to liken *Blow Job*'s visualization of mythical antinomies to a mentally produced vertical column of images is ultimately insignificant. More important is the effect afforded by the film, which is analogous to the one Krauss describes for the display of myths in grid-like structures: "The sequential progress of the story does not achieve resolution but rather repression. That is, for a given culture, the contradiction is a powerful one, one that will not go away, but will only go, so to speak, underground."[32] If, according to Krauss, the vertical columns of structuralist analysis are one way of unearthing the unmanageable opposition that drives myths, *Blow Job*'s rotating series of images is another one. As *Blow Job* visualizes its part myths in the form of such unmanageable oppositions as God/man, insider/outsider, saint/demon, authentic individual/reified clone, the film's underground status implies—or, at least, may help suggest—that their irreconcilable relations are usually repressed. By contrast, such durable popular genres as the mainstream gangster film, which also partake in these oppositions but invariably "resolve" them, merely indicate our "need" for texts that function, as Krauss states, to promote endless repetitions of the same conflict. It would perhaps not be too facetious to claim that the underground status of these repressed oppositions comes to be reflected in *Blow Job*'s status as an underground film. After all, underground cinema's transgressiveness was at least partly constituted by its films' subversive conflation of cultural paradigms and discourses that mainstream culture usually sought to demarcate from one another. However, if we acclaim *Blow Job*'s refusal to resolve these antinomies as the film's most prominent feature, we run the risk of reducing the film to the status of a demystifying agent. A perhaps more apposite way of defining *Blow Job*'s underground status is to focus on the film's production of pleasure. Whereas the grids of structural anthropology simply identify cultural oppositions in their repressed status, *Blow Job* celebrates them by eroticizing their placeholders. *Blow Job* may thus also be said to release them from repression in its own way.

The promiscuous cohabitation in one image of the sad young man, the teenage rebel, and Christ—indeed, their interchangeability—speaks to the fact that, in modern culture, they have become stand-ins for one another. *Blow Job*, as it moves through its three basic constellations, presents them as variants of the same myth complex. By showcasing them as reified stereotypes, the film also identifies them as mass culture commodities that have been severed from their respective cachets of sanctity, originality, and authenticity. Even though the teenage rebel is much more closely associated with pop culture, Christ, too, has been represented on film virtually since its inception (consider the turn-of-the-century staging of Passion plays by immigrants on New York rooftops—precursors to Hollywood's biblical epics) and entered the circuits of mass culture virtually at the moment when the mechanical reproduction of images became possible. Nineteenth century reproductions of various stages of the Christ tale may have been intended to provide spiritual succor, but their status as mass items (printed postcards, cheaply made paintings or prints) make them symptomatic of the same shift that would later determine the status of such new profane deities as James Dean. Walter Benjamin has characterized this shift as the loss of the aura: The spell of personality replaces the uniqueness of an individual, and the ritual function of a person (whether preacher or performer) is replaced by such notions as exhibition value and beauty.[33] Few have displayed this matrix of reproduction and commodification (and its attending aspects of profane respiritualization and sexualization) more blatantly than Andy Warhol. In the artist's overall oeuvre, *Blow Job* is but one example in which spiritual authenticity and profane exhibitionism meet on the level of the pose. Another example is Warhol's versions of *The Last Supper*, which can be usefully compared to *Blow Job* precisely with regard to these issues.

Warhol based his Last Supper paintings on Leonardo da Vinci's world-famous *The Last Supper* (1495–1497). However, Leonardo's work did not come to serve as the actual source for Warhol's paintings. Warhol used Leonardo's original merely as the parental motif but based his own series on a nineteenth century encyclopedia reproduction of the painting. Warhol's work, as art historians have noted, is thus the copy of a copy, a status openly celebrated by the artist's mechanical reproduction process and by his commitment to seriality (he used serigraphs with acrylic and transferred them to canvas[34]). The overall series of Warhol's Last Supper paintings consists of almost 100 works, some of which are hand-painted, others silk-screened. Some of these reproduce, as Carla Schulz-Hoffmann describes, the pictorial carriers of the encyclopedia drawing, which consisted only of outlines. Consider Corinna Thierolf's description of the overall effect:

> Warhol's bold mixture of elements of pictorial design appropriated from Leonardo (including the proportional relationship between the figures and the room) and those he altered (hanging the pictures lower, varying their size, repeating the scene or focusing on details,

"cutting the composition apart" and reassembling it, or—in the collages—using a "torn" background with complete detail printed on it, dispensing with local or natural colours in favour of a two-colour scheme) set a confusing perceptual game in motion, the effect of which is further heightened by the unusual, curving space, which prevents the viewer from establishing any kind of fixed orientation. Christ became present not only once but many times in numerous Last Supper scenes, and Leonardo's composition based upon a central perspective from the standpoint of the viewer was opposed by multiple versions by Warhol.[35]

One might add that the preservation of the outlines of the encyclopedia reproduction and the abstraction from the background of Leonardo's original give some versions of Warhol's Last Supper paintings the quality of unfinishedness, as can also be found, for example, in coloring books for children. Other versions of Warhol's Last Supper paintings feature outlines of Christ in various monochromes (Figure 2.11, for example).

The varying application of the ink gives the image of Christ shown in Figure 2.11 a chimera-like quality comparable to the one discussed for the image in *Blow Job*. Both images clearly flaunt their own simulacral features. To be sure, in his Last Supper series Warhol acknowledges a referent, as he uses a painting of Christ as a found image. But since the Christ myth is abstracted into the characteristic Warholian minimalism, which underscores its nature as an image several times removed, it enables the viewer to behold Christ *as* a myth and to fill in the blanks. A further functional analogy to *Blow Job* is offered by the cutting apart of the motif in some of Warhol's Last Supper paintings (Figure 2.12, for example), as described by Thierolf. Even though *Blow Job* counter-

balances the impression of fragmentation with the illusion of a unified image, the viewer has the option of focusing on the individual fragments within the overall image. In Warhol's Last Supper paintings as well as in *Blow Job*, the fragmentation of the image into part objects signifies the proliferation of the myth into what may be described as part myths or subnarratives.

With regard to the Last Supper silk screens, their nature as simulacra turns them into commentaries not only on the commodification of the Christ myth but also on the key role Leonardo's original played in this "slide" into low art—a shift that disseminated the referent to such a vast degree that the current scale of appropriations, ranging from the slightly subversive to the drastically perverse, seems but a natural result. Carla Schulz-Hoffmann notes that it was Warhol's awareness of his own celebrity status as the international mas-

Figure 2.11
Detail of *The Last Supper*, 1986. Screenprint on paper (31⅞ × 23¾ inches). © 2002 Andy Warhol Foundation for the Visual Arts/ARS, New York.

ter of silk-screening that caused him to handpick the silk screens over the hand-painted Last Suppers for the now famous 1987 Milan show.[36] But the fact that any famous artist exists as a figure watched by the public and the fact, too, that artists tend to have a heightened awareness of the exhibition context and reception of their work were already very much the case with Leonardo. Warhol's selection criteria for the Milan show may then also be regarded as an ironic comment designed to bring out the earlier master's need for flattery, just as Warhol's silk screens bring out Leonardo's homoerotic brush stroke. In fact, art historian Cornelia Syre cites one eyewitness to Leonardo painting *The Last Supper, novelle* writer and later bishop Matteo Bandello, who notes "the revealing fact" that Milan's art aficionados would gather in the refectory to observe the progress on the work, which the master himself did not mind at all. Bandello is quoted as saying, "The latter enjoyed it that anyone who saw his work should openly express their opinion of it."[37] While Leonardo's original may still be endowed with the aura described by Walter Benjamin, which indexes the integration of the artwork in the context of an organic tradition of experience (*Erfahrung*), its production history and background show signs of the vanishing of the aura in this particular historical context, as indicated by the artist's self-conscious consideration of external factors.

The simulacral quality of Warhol's Last Supper silk screens may also be read as a provocation targeted at the purists and pundits still obsessed with completing the epic project of restoring Leonardo's *The Last Supper* to its "original" version. Having gone into decay just decades after its completion, the painting has, over the centuries, been subjected to numerous "restorations," which are now lending it the status of one of the world's most famous palimpsests. Warhol signed a petition against the ongoing restoration and in an interview made his attitude very clear, saying, "All I know is that it is a mistake to restore *The Last Supper*. It is incredibly beautiful the way it is! The old things are always better and shouldn't be changed."[38] Warhol's opinion that all the restorations have not improved the painting's general condition reflects, as Thierolf notes, his insight that the perception of Leonardo's original is doubly mediated—once by the numerous restoration efforts, which have changed its looks, and a second time by the myriad of low art reproductions that, themselves, reflect the painting at its various stages of decay and restoration.[39] Warhol's comment should then not be interpreted as an effort to draw a direct comparison to his own versions of *The Last Supper*—Leonardo's work is, alas, still treated as a buried original, while Warhol's versions are a celebration of the ontological equality of all possible layers and the readings they spark. Warhol's anti-palimpsestual attitude, does, however, imply that his own paintings may have something deeper in common with Leonardo's original after all. That is, that at this point in time, both are indissociable from the mass mediation of Christ and also reflect the fact that, with the secularization of Western culture, the Last Supper motif as such has lost its traditional place; it has become an idiom of myth in Barthes's sense—that is, a robbed myth that has been made available for resignification through multiple plunderings. Both *Blow Job* and Warhol's version of *The Last Supper* constitute a robbing of the Christ myth and, as it were, also offer some suggestions for further plunderings.

In global capitalist culture, the activity of plundering is always in one way or another an index of the underlying system of capitalist exchange, whose rules and regulations are simultaneously undercut and hyperbolized by plundering. The plundering of myth is an index of the commodification and mass circulation of signs and images, which, as we have seen with regard to the myths Warhol plunders, leads to the proliferation and refraction of the myth into smaller part myths and narratives. The diverse narrative directions of these part myths and the equally diverse possibilities of their appropriation may even end up contradicting the broader myth, or they may foreground the contradictions that already exist in the broader myth in buried or concealed form. A typical example of this phenomenon is the figure of the halo, which allows further comparisons between *Blow Job* and Warhol's Last Supper series.

Comparing Leonardo's *The Last Supper* to some of its cheap reproductions, Corinna Thierolf notes that such mass culture items as prints and postcards significantly alter the vocabulary for conveying Christ's eminence as a religious figure. Whereas the sheer size of Leonardo's painting enabled the artist to inscribe Christ's spiritual distinction by naturalizing it (his head simply rises high in front of the window, which metaphorizes his aura of holiness rather than explicitly referencing it), this technique proved too subtle if reproduced en masse on small cards. So mass art introduced the halo instead—a "foreign body," as Thierolf notes,[40] which conveyed Christ's spirituality by external means. The halo is thus an aesthetic gesture intrinsically linked to low art that secularized Christ in the very act of expressing his spirituality. Substituting the uniqueness of a person, his original ritual or cult value, by the spell of the personality (his asset as an exhibition piece), the halo symptomatically identifies mass art's signification of the loss of the aura.

The iconography of the halo occasions an interesting comparison between the proliferation of light above the poser's head in *Blow Job's* third visual constellation and a subseries of the artist's Last Supper silk screens entitled *Be a Somebody with a Body* and *The Last Supper/Be a Somebody with a Body.* For this subseries Warhol isolated the Christ figure from his other silk screens and brought it together in several stages with the image of a young bodybuilder who bears a halo. The halo becomes yet another one of Warhol's floating signifiers that enable us to trace the proliferation of part myths from a broader

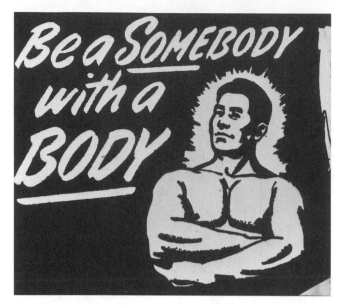

Figure 2.13
Source image for Warhol's *Be a Somebody with a Body* painting
(c. 1984–1986). Photostat (12 × 14 inches). Archives of the Andy
Warhol Museum, Pittsburgh Founding Collection. © 2002 Andy
Warhol Foundation for the Visual Arts/ARS (photo: Richard
Stoner, 3/26/01).

myth facilitated by the artist's cumulative plunderings. *Be a Somebody with a Body* is based on an unidentified newspaper ad for a gym that displays the bare-chested, smiling youth in simple outlines and richly saturated black-and-white ink, his youth, health, and self-confidence accentuated by the halo and the slogan "Be a Somebody with a Body" printed to the left above his head (Figure 2.13).

The aestheticization of this ad in Warhol's reproductions varies according to the ways it is set in dialogue with the Christ figure from the silk screens. In the subseries' first installment, Warhol simply restates the ad without using the Christ image (Figure 2.14); in the second version, he places it side by side with the Christ figure (Figure 2.15); in the third one, he superimposes the Christ figure onto the ad (Figure 2.16).

The aestheticization of the ad in the first installment, titled *Be a Somebody with a Body*, is minimal: The slogan is retained in the same place, and the dark areas of the ad are slightly less filled in, which makes the image look like a quickly and casually produced copy and, if anything, enhances the impression of the image's mercantile nature. In accord with the utopian agenda of advertising, the ad further secularizes the already mundane function of the halo by transforming it from a symbol of spirituality into a signifier of physical glamour that complements the youth's body. This rhetoric is underscored by the metonymic slippage in the slogan between "a Somebody" and "a Body," which promises individual distinction through building one's body. However, of more interest here is another reading that is prompted by the particular historical context, if not of the ad itself, then of Warhol's plundering of it in *The Last Supper*. Its production context places the image squarely in the mid to late 1980s and, thus, at the moment when urban gym culture was at its peak and when the horrific dimensions of AIDS as a mass epidemic had become fully apparent. The image's celebration of physical

Figure 2.14
Be a Somebody with a Body (c. 1985–1986). Synthetic polymer
paint and silk-screen ink on canvas. © 2002 Andy Warhol
Foundation for the Visual Arts/ARS, New York.

glamour as the new form of man-made saintliness partakes in the commercially motivated rhetoric of utopia, which targeted a large segment of male consumers; yet, to the extent that this image celebrates both personal agency in and control over shaping one's body, it is not far removed from (perhaps even produced by or for) a smaller demographic segment—urban, mostly white, gay men. This segment succeeded in appropriating and redefining this utopia as a significant part of their own particular reality. In his characterization of gay male gym culture, D. A. Miller argues that while gay bodybuilders do not exactly signify a radical renunciation of the privileges of the male in our society, they resignify the male body dramatically enough to put themselves at odds with patriarchy and, thus, to put themselves in harm's way. This suggests that there is something heroic, perhaps even saintly, about gay male bodybuilders. As Miller sees it,

Figure 2.15
The Last Supper/Be a Somebody with a Body (1986). Synthetic polymer paint on canvas (23 × 23 inches). © 2002 Andy Warhol Foundation for the Visual Arts/ARS, New York.

> The men of the Muscle System or the Chelsea Gym, who valuing tone and definition over mass give as much attention to abs and glutes as to pecs and lats; who array their bodies in tanks and polos, purchased when necessary in the boys' department, in Spandex and Speedos, in preshrunk, reshrunk, and, with artisanal care, perhaps even sandpapered 501s— let us hail these men (why not by the name given during the Directoire to the women who dampened their that much more dramatically clinging gowns: *les merveilleuses*?).[41]

Miller's description suggests a shift in gay sensibility away from self-defining discourses of defeat and martyrdom. But the very need for this sort of affirmation reflects the fact that gay men's sexual transgressiveness and self-stylizations make them threatening outsiders while also comprising all connotations of the term "marvelous." Seen from this perspective, the halo may not be completely outmoded after all.

I have no way of determining whether the gym ad appealed to Warhol for this particular reason—that is, as a tribute to a social group that succeeded in redefining its bodies for purposes clearly beyond the mundane achievement of what is commonly called "physical fitness." Characteristic of Warhol's visual rhetoric across the contexts in

Figure 2.16
Detail of *The Last Supper/Be a Somebody with a Body* (c. 1985–1986). Synthetic polymer paint and silk-screen ink on canvas (50 × 60 inches). © 2002 Andy Warhol Foundation for the Visual Arts/ARS, New York.

which we have encountered it, the ad refuses to turn images into agitprop. Partisanship is not a quality associated with Warhol's art; it needs to be brought to the image by the reader who must keep in mind that other readers will produce different readings. Warhol's minimalism notoriously enables the images' "kidnappability," to borrow a term from Robert Stam. *Be a Somebody with a Body* can thus function, among other ways, as "proof" for detractors as well as supporters of gay gym culture. It can be said to celebrate gay body pleasure, gay agency, and gay survival in the age of AIDS just as much as it may be read as visualizing the body cult as a form of false consciousness and an escapist reaction against AIDS. In other words, even as a part myth extracted from the broader myth, it bears the possibility for contradictory appropriations.

The second installment, as announced in its title, *The Last Supper/Be a Somebody with a Body*, places the copy of the ad in dialogue (side by side) with the figure of Christ abstracted from the Last Supper silk screens. The two sides of the image translate such contradictions as anonymity versus individuality, which are characteristic of some of the myths discussed, into more specific binarisms (Jesus as God's son and figure of identification for all humankind; the bodybuilder as glamorous individual and clone). The two sides also complement each other in displaying more specific part myths. Taken together, the binary visual may, for example, be read as constituting the range of metaphors that have sought to stereotype gay men in past decades and that are also evoked by *Blow Job*, but it also bespeaks the historical distance between the images: The gym ad transforms the tragic air of suffering of earlier decades into a kind of self-imposed work ethic for physical improvement. The sad young man has turned into a happy young man, whose halo and spatial isolation in the image no longer reflect a morbid, if glamorous, self-hatred but the beaming self-sufficiency of the post-Stonewall clone, one of the key figures in the evolution of gay identity between *Blow Job* and Warhol's Last Supper paintings. These two sets of metaphors now come back together in a new context, and it is all the more interesting that Warhol decides to reintroduce Christ here, which is, of course, symptomatic of the respiritualization of 1980s culture in the face of AIDS (be it in the form of liberal humanist blanket discourses of sympathy or pity, or in the form of period-specific gay mystical self-help groups). Thus, the image represents another turn in the evolution of gay types and the way they were perceived by the outside world. It filters these types into more specific AIDS narratives and commentaries as to what AIDS bodies look like, what attitude one should adopt with regard to AIDS, how the gay community should recompose itself, and so on. While Warhol's own attitude toward AIDS was not always flattering, it is as unimportant in this context as is the question of whether Warhol took a fancy for the bodybuilder as beefcake or saint. (Yet, unable to repress my own fancy, I am indulging in the fantasy that Warhol likened his own and Leonardo's artmaking to the equally artistic acts of self-stylization and the closely linked exhibitionist glee of the gay men of the Muscle Gym: The latter enjoyed it that anyone who saw their "work" should openly express their opinion of it.)

The image is made more complex by two important figures that throw its apparent symmetry off balance. The image of Christ cropped from *The Last Supper* also contains a disciple's arm extending toward Christ, but this arm is now spatially and metaphorically associated with the bodybuilder. In addition, it is the bodybuilder who possesses the halo and, via the principle of the speech bubbles in cartoons, seems to address Christ with the image's slogan. The image thus assigns agency, address, and authority to the bodybuilder. What some may read as an expression of condescension and pity for the era's victims or as a mocking criticism of panicky escapism into the body cult can also be reinterpreted as an articulation of gay male survival strategies. If Jesus is read as a stand-in for the sad young man in the age of AIDS, the bodybuilder's ironic, cocky advice for him is to overcome defeatism and learn a lesson from the "new gay man," who is sex-positive, body-conscious, and, as the halo signifies, in every respect marvelous. Here, as in other Warhol works, the openness of the image translates some of the era's signature discourses into mythical shorthand. Even in its display of more particular myths, the image remains sufficiently equivocal to enable contrasting readings that nonetheless partake in the same sets of metaphors.

The third version of this subseries, also titled *Details of the Last Supper/Be a Somebody with a Body*, superimposes the figure of Christ onto the copy of the ad. This version is particularly interesting with regard to *Blow Job*, as the visual overlap of both figures in the image could be read as a stilled correlative to the film's capacity for identifying its diverse mythical types as *evolving* within one and the same myth complex. Yet, there are important differences that, again, point to Warhol's shifting use of simulacrum and illusory referent. In this particular instance, *Details of the Last Supper/Be a Somebody with a Body* appears to undermine Warhol's own anti-palimpsestual attitude. While the medium-specific quality of *Blow Job*'s simulacrum blurs not only the spatial positions of the poser but also the subtending metaphors (Christ, the teenage outlaw, and the gangster constitute one another and are figments of the same myth complex who lend themselves to a seemingly unlimited number of appropriations), this particular installment of *The Last Supper/Be a Somebody with a Body* acts like a palimpsest. Here, Christ is clearly superimposed over the bodybuilder—an effect that keeps both figures ontologically separate and thereby consolidates the very binaries that *Blow Job*'s image subversively blurs. The fact that the silk screen reverses some of *Blow Job*'s visual details (for example, Christ now looks down) is of minor importance here. Rather, the superimposed quality of the image in the silk screen redistributes address and authority away from the bodybuilder to Christ. Christ holds his head at a low angle and looks down past the bodybuilder, but the overdetermined dialogic between the figures makes Christ metaphorically look down on the young man, who seems to have his face directed toward heaven. In addition, in this version the image's slogan appears to be assigned to Christ rather than to the youth. If one reads this image as confirming rather than subverting received cultural notions of spiritual authority and mentorship, Christ either seems to bless the bodybuilder and confirm him in his agenda to be a somebody with a body or, alternately, may be read as wanting to punish the bodybuilder for his cocky sense of entitlement. While the image thus still displays a certain variability, the ontologization of its figures points to a delimitation of possible readings, which, in turn, reflect an increasingly charged historical context in which responses to the crisis at hand were more and more overdetermined by either/or scenarios. The part myth that has spiraled out from the larger myth has narrowed here into a much more specific set of narratives. As such, it remains an interesting commentary on its historical moment, but its similarities to *Blow Job*'s image are limited.

As critics have noted, what makes the Warholian canon one of the more fascinating ones to explore is that many of Warhol's images double as referent and simulacrum. Even our limited review of a small number of Warhol images has shown that this double function pans out differently from image to image, resulting in nuanced reconfigurations of visual rhetoric and spectatorial address. In *Blow Job*, for example, the visual impoverishment of an already apocryphal referent seems to stand in direct relation to the heightened productive power of the film's simulacra. Oscillating between a unified image and a series of semiabstract chimera, *Blow Job* becomes richly suggestive, as it exploits our tendency to invest its chiaroscuro patterns with symbolic meaning. Like most images, really, Warhol's images address the reader as a socially inflected being, but they are of special interest because of the particular ways in which they foreground processes of visual association and, hence, because they make us aware of the ways in which we have been acculturated.

The territory on which this double address is played out is that of myth. Warhol's images are heightened, self-conscious metonyms of myth. Their double address of working through and beyond a given visual substance reenacts myth's capacity for insinuation, but Warhol's choice of themes and their aesthetic relay as simulacra also foreground this insinuation as a rhetoric. The overall display that results—in *Blow Job* as well as in Warhol's Last Supper silk screens—may best be described as a kind of spiral, its central theme spinning out in a potentially endless series of part myths, particular narratives, and appropriations. As *Blow Job* in particular visualizes different mythical types through the same set of images, it calls upon diverse areas of our mythical literacy. It sharpens our awareness of the tools and conventions of myth without abrogating myth altogether. On the one hand, *Blow Job* demystifies myth by making us privy to myth's modus operandi. On the other hand, it also remystifies its display and, in fact, remythologizes the icons it draws on by enhancing their mythical qualities. Yet, myth is not quite the same once it has passed through *Blow Job*. The film has done to myth what myth does to culture in general, that is, it has perpetrated acts of plundering. *Blow Job* becomes the parasite of a parasite, a third-, forth-, or fifth-order myth in Barthes's sense.

I am thus proposing two ways by which we may examine *Blow Job*'s method of appropriation. We have already explored the specifics of this robbery as a form of cultural resignification that transforms a range of stereotypes and other commodity items it has appropriated from a broad cultural field. The next step is to focus on particular sexual and gender identities inscribed in the image. Our discussion, thus far, of *Blow Job*'s iconography with regard to gay culture indicates the direction in which this study is moving: It will increasingly be concerned with the ways in which the film functions in relation to white gay men. However, at issue will not be a revisionist reading of the image that insists on the existence of a gay male fellator at the poser's cock. The doubt that *Blow Job*'s image infuses in our reading of the poser's identity frustrates not merely the construction of a meaningful heterosexual totality but also its replacement by an equally meaningful homosexual totality. In fact, despite its politically important appropriation by the gay male subculture and by gay male historians, the image casts doubt on the very concept of meaningful totality—if only in the process of mobilizing our desire for it.

3

WHITE GAY MALE IDENTITY
BETWEEN PASSING AND POSING

If audiences view images not simply as entities unto themselves but as parts connected to one another and to the cultural hemisphere to which these audiences belong, viewing images means, more often than not, viewing them intertextually. *Blow Job* is a particularly apposite case in point. Precisely because of its minimalism, *Blow Job* can be viewed and appropriated by a whole range of spectators who inscribe multiple meanings into the film. To read *Blow Job* intertextually can mean treating the film and the icons and myths it alludes to as a kind of archeological site of fragments of postwar American culture. To read *Blow Job* intertextually can also mean reading homosexuality into the film in a number of ways, all of which, however, involve negotiating the tension between the manifest and the latent, between what one sees and what one imagines as present in the image. For example, it involves investing the image with diverse prior knowledges about sex practices or sexual significations—the awareness, say, that fellatio is a sex practice particularly widespread among gay men; the interpretation that the film's poser is what Richard Dyer has termed "a sad young man" or a gay martyr; the fantasy that the poser is James Dean who, one might remember, had a "suspect" gender identity even when he was alive.

As Mikhail Iampolski has argued, our intertextual construction of knowledge is based on a certain archival work, as we tend to trace texts to prior sources and read them against already well-established facts, wisdoms, and opinions. Iampolski's concept of intertextuality, to which I am indebted, is informed by Michel Foucault's argument that the production of meaning in manifest discourse is always based on a silent, unspoken discourse, a "never-said."[1] This never-said is, in fact, an "already-said." It is never said not because it may simply be tautological but because the polemical impact of reading into a text rests on the imported text's incorporeal makeup and on its taciturn apprehension and incorporation. Among other things, this way of investing texts with meaning is pleasurable. However specious the effort to infuse the manifest content of *Blow Job*'s image with a latent prior discourse, it is also titillating, because *Blow Job*, rather than confirming one's assumptions, suspends both hypothesis and purported confirmation in perpetual circularity.

The current chapter continues the activity of reading into the text and continues, too, to pay attention to the implications of that activity. However, the focus is more narrow than in previous chapters: I will discuss *Blow Job* mainly with regard to the signification of homosexuality, and describe the relevance of *Blow Job*'s icons and myths with regard to a specific subgroup of homosexual spectators, white gay men. I will further discuss the film as a repository of a particular era in the history of white gay men, the immediate postwar period and the 1950s. Of course, the history of black gay men is part of this period, too, but black gay men also have their own, similarly specific past, the analysis of which requires a different focus.[2] This is not to say that *Blow Job* begs no further analysis with regard to certain race discourses it helps produce. In fact, these discourses are discussed in Chapter 6, where they are described as belonging to a larger terrain of white hegemonic signifying practices the film is part of, no matter the extent of its transgressive aspects.

If *Blow Job* mobilizes what Iampolski terms a "genealogical curiosity," the film arguably reenacts the process by which white gay male identity reconstituted itself in the postwar period by searching and reclaiming past icons and mythologies for its own cultural makeup. However, this reading only partly accounts for the *dynamic* evolution of white gay male identity during those years, as it considers only one of two axes—the diachronic axis, which, taken by itself, would seem to explain the evolution of white gay male identity as simply the cumulative total of gradually incorporated fragments of culture. While this accumulation and incorporation certainly took place, psychoanalytic discourses of identity formation have shown that identity often needs to negotiate impulses that are highly contradictory or even inimical to one another, such as the subject's desire to assert the self in imaginary fullness versus the subject's impulse for self-dissolution. Indeed, the discussion in later chapters of this book will incorporate the fact that white gay male identity also shaped itself via the repression and/or conversion of certain "antisocial" impulses in its desire to partake in standard forms of sociality. These conversions are as momentous as they are compulsory. The diachronic is thus consistently affected by the synchronic.

Because *Blow Job* arguably reenacts some crucial aspects of identity formation, our analysis of the film in this chapter considers the image not only as an archeological dig but also as a psychoanalytic dig—a site for the active, momentous conversion of the latent into the manifest, a metaphor for a kind of psychosexual veil that must shelter its subject from the latent danger of unraveling. To trace the full implications of latency in this context entails not merely "digging deeper" but also going against the teleology of manifestation itself; in other words, it entails dealing with the question of why it is that even though the motions and facial expressions of *Blow Job*'s poser may produce a range of contradictory yet equivalent significations, these significations—to the extent that they may be regarded as reenacting certain aspects of identity formation—will ultimately not remain equivalent but will undergo a process of hierarchization and prioritization equally rigorous as that of identity formation itself.

George Chauncey's research into gay history has, once and for all, abolished any assumption that Stonewall alone put homosexuals on the American cultural map. While Chauncey delivers incontrovertible evidence of the visibility of homosexuals in urban centers in the first few decades of the twentieth century, his findings also indicate a gradual diminution of this visibility by the 1930s through the ascendancy of white middle-class gay men. Their lifestyle was more subtle, more integrated into the mainstream, and thus less visible than earlier forms of gay signification, which were constituted more by ethnic and working-class cultures and which then became largely marginalized into isolated subcultural pockets.[3] The current chapter tracks how this decrease of overtly visible homosexuality became enhanced and modified through the massive sociocultural and demographic reorientation caused by World War II and how it persisted through the immediate postwar period until homosexuality became gradually more visible again in the 1950s, its precarious position still marked by a tension between invisibility and visibility.

Any charting of such a sweeping trajectory would hope to support itself through recourse to the kind of sociological data Chauncey provides for the prewar period. Alas, as of this writing, the second part of Chauncey's study, which is to deal with the postwar years, is not yet available. Once it is, it will no doubt throw into relief the lacunae of the arguments made in this chapter. With that said, the plan of this chapter is to analyze the various postwar attempts to construct homosexuality and gay identity as textual operations. I will treat the end products of these operations—certain attitudes and statements, images, types and stereotypes—as texts and relate them to one another to allow inferences about the dynamics that arguably determined their authoring. Thus, I will analyze the situation of white gay men in the postwar period by considering certain acts of signification imposed on them as well as authored by them. Even though the 1950s is a period still much in need of illumination, some important work has been done in this regard by a number of scholars, and it is their studies that inform the discussion in this chapter.

An intertextual comparison between mundane gay signification and such gay-authored texts as postwar gay erotica, such hegemonic texts as the Hollywood film *Tea and Sympathy*, and a text such as *Blow Job*, which, I argue, reenacts many of the dynamics that inform the production of these other texts, involves a certain leveling process. Because there is a potential danger in glossing over the differences between these texts and the actual everyday lives of white gay men in the 1950s, my argument will by no means lay claim to a comprehensive illumination of contemporaneous gay culture. Rather, I hope to show just how much of gay culture of this period was influenced by the tension between visibility and invisibility, and how much of the decade's overall textual production, whether authored by dominant or subaltern forces, required "reading into" a text for the figuration of homosexuality. This tension between visibility and invisibility must be seen as the overall effect of the fact that homosexuality in the postwar period became something that was both produced and repressed, something that was made manifest but also remained latent—in fact, something that manifested itself, more often than not, via its latency.

As I argue that these forces were crucial to dominant constructions of homosexuality in the period, I also hope to demonstrate that postwar homosexuals themselves very consciously operated with and through the manifest and the latent. Rather than categorizing postwar gay performance as an index of a transhistorical closet, this and Chapter 4 discuss how the logic of the evolution of gay performance—the reasons for why it took some paths and not others—must be understood as a historical dynamic in which latency and manifestation are feeding off one another. In the current chapter, the analysis of *Blow Job* recedes into the background, serving to merely puncture and accentuate the discussion. Because the film was made in 1964, when the period under investigation was coming to an end, *Blow Job* obviously had no active part in the formation of gay identity in the 1950s. However, it arguably reenacts many of the dynamics of gay male self-assertion in various areas of the American public sphere through the cinematic evocation of social and symbolic contexts. Thus, for the remainder of this chapter, *Blow Job* serves primarily as a metatext on the intricacies and problematics of gay performance during this time.

To understand the special status of homosexuality between visibility and invisibility during the war and postwar years, one must consider the context of 1940s America, in which discourses on homosexuality became reformulated. The 1948 Kinsey report is of special importance here. The Kinsey scale, which argued the continuity of gradations between hetero- and homosexual histories in male sexual behavior, not only somewhat depathologized homosexuality[4] but also located it firmly within the public sphere. This relocation of homosexuality was facilitated by Kinsey's notorious assertion that ten percent of the total male population are more or less exclusively homosexual between the ages of sixteen and fifty-five.[5] But while ten percent was an unprecedented and shocking figure for 1948, it would hardly have produced such paranoia had it not been for the fact that the ten percent he cited were a subgroup of a much larger number—thirty-seven percent of the total male population of the United States, who, according to Kinsey, must have had at least some overt homosexual experience in their lives. To put it the other way around, more than one third of American males had some involvement in or recourse to a sexuality that was still commonly conceived of as embodying abomination and the monstrosity of Otherness. Worse still, Kinsey concluded that the individual homosexual by no means differed *in essence* from one fourth or even one third of the total male population in the United States. Thus de-essentializing homosexuality as a category, Kinsey bluntly stated the options Americans might ponder when forced to face homosexuality: mass institutionalization or the acceptance of homosexuality as a mundane, that is, essentially invisible and widespread form of sexuality.[6]

The sliding nature of the Kinsey scale and the prospect of being forced to acknowledge a mundane and pervasive homosexuality helped trigger a set of tensions between which homosexuality was caught during the 1950s—the tension between the wish to "Other" homosexuality and the inability to do so fully and, correspondingly, the urge to see and show homosexuality and the failure and even the refusal to detect it. A rereading of Kinsey is rewarding especially with regard to this second tension, since it helps us understand the contradictory forces at work in the relationship of the dominant homophobic culture to the invisibility/visibility of homosexuality. Ever the fetishizer of statistics, Kinsey laments that the U.S. armed forces during World War II missed a unique opportunity to secure statistical data on the incidence of homosexuality.[7] Many draftees were keeping their homosexuality a secret for fear of being excluded from the war effort. In addition, a draft rejection, under certain classifications directly indicating or "smacking of" homosexuality, could potentially have made them subject to persecution in civilian life. According to Kinsey, this closetedness resulted in legions of military psychologists and physicians coming to realize that the incidence of homosexuality in the armed forces during the war must have been considerably above the official numbers and, more important, that homosexuality could not be made manifest on medical or on phenomenological terms.

Perhaps even more interesting in this context is the military's own reluctance to acknowledge the homosexual once he had actually been detected. In an interesting passage, Kinsey writes:

> Many psychiatrists in the armed forces were aware of the great social damage done to an individual who was discharged for such reasons, and they considered it desirable to help him

by showing flat feet, stomach ulcers, shock, or some other non-sexual item as the immediate cause of the discharge. Consequently, no one anywhere in official circles in the Army and the Navy will ever be able to obtain any adequate estimate of the number of men with homosexual activity who were identified and discharged from the services during the war.[8]

Whatever the circumstances that enabled army medical staff to "read" and identify the homosexual, this reading, then, more often than not, resulted in a kind of rewriting: Homosexuality, at the very moment of its discursive manifestation, became once again relegated to latency. It reassumed its unspeakable status. This latency was pre-ordained by the armed forces' official announcement *at the beginning of the war* that the military would exclude any person with a homosexual history.[9] While this statement reflected and further consolidated the stigmatized status of homosexuality in civilian as well as military life, it also reveals a considerable paranoia about the presence of homosexuality *before* the fact. This official a priori rejection of homosexuality by the armed forces is a clear indication that the military was ahead of Kinsey in its insight that it might be rather difficult to demarcate oneself from what is so close and so widespread. Yet, because the military's declared policy on homosexuals on the eve of the war bespeaks both a prior "knowledge" and a fear of homosexuality, it also constitutes a prophylactic device against *re*-encountering homosexuality, that is, against having to identify officially what and who one is already well aware of but whose mention, once the war is under way, one wants to avoid at all cost. Army physicians may thus have helped protect homosexuals not simply because they took pity on them—or because they may themselves have been homosexual—but because sustaining the homosexual as a phantom rather than making homosexuality manifest was congruous with the overall logic established by the armed forces in anticipation of the "problem." Thus, the military's double impulse to identify/abject the homosexual and to pretend that there simply were no gay soldiers resulted in the logistic quandary of naming/not naming. Because neither the military nor the bulk of gay draftees had any interest in filling the category of homosexuality with empirical evidence, the homosexual became produced as abstract Other outside the military as well—a phantom whose abjectness disavowed its presence prior to its abjection, a phantom category that was defined by its nonapplicability. The concrete, mundane homosexual became produced as culturally unthinkable.

Although he initially assumed that the military might simply have failed to identify homosexuality on a broad basis, Kinsey came to realize that the armed forces had, in fact, deliberately produced a low incidence of homosexuality; the military had downright refused to produce the kind of taxonomy of homosexuality that would have spared Kinsey a considerable amount of legwork.[10] Kinsey's remarks on the military thus illustrate those aspects of the repressive hypothesis that Foucault—instead of rejecting the possibility of repression altogether—thought in need of being complemented by aspects of production: While homosexuality certainly *did* become produced as a category in the armed services' draft regulations, it is evident that these procedures were designed to yield little evidence of concrete incidences of homosexuality. Repression and production became almost synonymous. Their synergetic operation helped suspend homosexuality between visibility and invisibility during the postwar period and into the 1960s— a tension that became evident on different levels and in different areas of American culture.

Competing strategies of repressing and/or manifesting homosexuality can be identified by briefly juxtaposing two texts from the war and immediate postwar years—the 1945 novel *The Brick Foxhole* (which, in 1947, was adapted into the Hollywood film *Crossfire*), and Kenneth Anger's gay underground film *Fireworks* from the same year. Written by Richard Brooks, who would become one of the most prominent liberal Hollywood directors of the 1950s and 1960s, *The Brick Foxhole* tells the story of an antigay hate crime: During World War II, several Washington, D.C.–based soldiers who suffer from an inferiority complex toward fellow soldiers heroically fighting overseas vent their alienation and insecurities by killing a gay interior decorator who had picked them up on their night out and had brought them to his apartment. Brooks's political liberalism is indicated by his characterization of two of the soldiers not only as homophobes but also as white supremacists. Robert J. Corber rightly interprets the novel as Brooks's attack on the Popular Front's concept of "the common man," which began to unravel even during the war. Corber notes that the novel showed that the concept's equating of "common man" with "white heterosexual" had inequality inscribed into it from the beginning.[11] It was this "message" that attracted liberal and soon-to-be blacklisted Hollywood producer Adrian Scott to adapt the novel into a film. To eschew censorship, *Crossfire* replaced the homosexual victim with a Jewish victim and thus, as Corber argues, made gay men invisible in two ways: First, the suppression of the theme of homophobia is congruous with the efforts of the national security state to make gay men invisible; and second, implicit in this elimination is the false assumption that minoritized groups and their respective oppressions are interchangeable.[12] Corber further argues that *Crossfire*'s depiction of murder as an impulsive act is indicative of the tendency within the postwar genre of the "social problem film" to displace political, socioeconomic, and institutional ills onto the level of individual psychology. By contrast, as Corber notes, one of the points the novel makes is that the military simultaneously furthers and prohibits homoeroticism: The soldiers can express their desire for the homosexual only through violence, which makes the military itself responsible for their crime.[13]

One may add that Brooks's stereotyping of homosexuality assumes a certain importance here. By constructing the interior decorator, Edwards (the victim), as a draft reject and a "fairy," Brooks's novel feeds into the belief prevalent during the war and immediate postwar years that the mundane (masculine-identified, "normal") homosexual was culturally unthinkable. In addition, the novel suggests that the army was devoid of homosexuals. However, the novel's plot effectively utilizes the gay man's effeminacy to illustrate servicemen's hostility toward men whose draft rejections furthered suspicions about their sexuality. When Edwards is unforthcoming about the reasons for his exemption from service, one of the soldiers smirks: "Bad arches?" The novel makes clear that these hostile suspicions were expressions of U.S.-based soldiers' fears of being associated more closely with "useless" (nonfighting) young men such as Edwards than with their "active" front-based fellows. In addition, the novel describes the nation's capital as a "meat market" in which the cohabitation of multiple sexual identities and pursuits would also lead to encounters triggering such fears of association. In this sense, one of the novel's more interesting insinuations is that, from the perspective of one of the novel's homophobes, Monty Crawford, the mere fact of being home-based could, in certain cases, already constitute a potential effeminization and homosexualization.

However, notwithstanding its liberal agenda, *The Brick Foxhole* is by no means a defense of homophilia. Like most examples of heterosexual liberalism, it evinces a simultaneous identification with and rejection/abjection of homosexuality not all that removed from the soldier Monty's homophobic attraction/repulsion to Edwards. To begin with, the novel is heterocentric: Its two gay characters (Edwards and his lover) have no existence outside the novel's description of the crime and one brief scene at the police precinct. Brooks uses exactly ten pages to describe the scenario leading up to the crime and another seven pages to suggest what actually happened. In contrast to the novel's lengthy and arguably interesting exploration of racism and alienated heterosexual masculinity, *The Brick Foxhole*'s remaining two hundred twenty pages are, plain and simple, as devoid of homosexuality as *Crossfire* is. In other words, homosexuality itself is contained by the very act of utilizing it as a "hook."[14]

So much for gay visibility. Now what about its visualization? While it is clear that *The Brick Foxhole* constructs Monty as Edwards's homophobic and lethal double, Edwards's more interesting double is arguably Jeff Mitchell, liberalism's classic "straight but sensitive good guy" whose point of view overlaps with that of the narrator at crucial moments. The novel uses Jeff's sympathetic eyes to construct Edwards as a gay stereotype with pale skin, full red lips, delicate wrists, impeccable grooming and taste, and a "strange" expression on his face.[15] But even while labeling Edwards a "fairy" and a "sexual pervert," Jeff has a problem—he likes Edwards and, suspecting what his fellow soldiers are up to, wants to warn Edwards but nonetheless agrees to go along to Edwards's place. Heterosexual liberalism thus uses its main figure of identification as a vehicle to mediate between homosexuality and its straight liberal readers. The novel's four-page chapter during which the plot takes place in Edwards's apartment and places Jeff at the threshold of homosexual encounter is a veritable primer for what one might call "liberal homophobia." This homophobia is evidenced by Brooks's utilization of intoxication as a central rhetorical device. When Jeff gets drunk at Edwards's place, intoxication simultaneously reinforces and attenuates the protagonist's encounter with homosexuality; it becomes a metaphor for the protagonist's seeking of "danger," and it also lets him off the hook, as it ascribes limited accountability to his curiosities and actions. Jeff's relation to homosexuality in Edwards's apartment is suspended between identification and denial. He perceives Monty's gay-baiting in the kind of hazy way that is similar to the artistic depiction of a nude woman and a nude male archer hanging on Edwards's wall.[16] When he finally decides to leave the group, Jeff is too drunk to remember to take his furlough bag. Even though Jeff leaves before the murder, his bag allows Monty to blame him for the crime. Jeff spends the night at a female prostitute's place and only later learns about the murder and the fact that he is the prime suspect. For Jeff, the bag comes to function as a kind of "hangover"—a residual yet fateful proof of his encounter with homosexuality. Therefore, this sequence of events from Jeff's point of view gives the novel the classic structure of a homosexual/homophobic nightmare—the gay version of a contemporaneous, fairly standard heterosexual phantasmagoria (such as that found in the plots of crime writer Cornell Woolrich's potboilers) that has the heterosexual protagonist encounter abysmally threatening sexual difference and, for a while, suspends him between identification and abjection, as evidenced in his comment, "Jeff was sorry for Eddie. Through the fumes in his mind he thought he knew now why Eddie was hungry and for what."[17]

Phantasmagoria as a textual device enables a *masochistic* (read: submissive but pleasurable) encounter with homosexuality and the obligatory "rescue" from it. Notwithstanding that this rescue is, of course, synonymous with the reconsolidation of the protagonist's heterosexuality and masculinity, *The Brick Foxhole* somewhat qualifies the saying, "one man's dream, another man's nightmare." A much more ardent, much less hypocritical qualification of this saying—and one dressed in a more stylish and arousing phantasmagoria—can be found in Kenneth Anger's underground film *Fireworks*. Richard Dyer, whose important and detailed analysis of the film I am using here, points out that this short, black-and-white film is not a literal visualization of a dream but is, "in its use of sexual symbolism and handling of space and time, dream-like."[18] *Fireworks* consists of several scenarios loosely strung together that show a young man picking up a sailor, being gay-bashed by a group of sailors, and then having sex with the initial sailor, who jerks off over him, which makes the young man come, too. While this makes the film sound like a hard-core porn flick, Anger uses symbolism to convey sexual activity, such as a burning candle for the sailor's dick and milk poured over the young man to represent cum. Dyer, who has also written at length about gay male pornography, points out that *Fireworks* is original and provocative in its intent to visualize male orgasm in its plenitude, but he also notes that Anger censors himself by symbolizing sex rather than showing it.[19]

What puts *Fireworks* in sharp contrast to *The Brick Foxhole* is the fact that its phantasmagoric qualities overtly bespeak gay male desire. It is made from the perspective of the gay man who is gay-bashed. While I do not know whether Anger was familiar with Brooks's novel, *Fireworks* must be seen as a response to *The Brick Foxhole*'s conventional if liberal negotiation of homosexuality. The film's dreamlike quality (which, as Dyer has pointed out, visually merges the young man's bedroom with a public bathroom, whereby it suggests that the private and the public are equally sexually charged) recasts homophobia as wish fulfillment, and it does so quite literally. As Dyer writes, "Gay men are beaten up and/or arrested in these sexual spaces but *Fireworks* neither documents nor protests this. Rather, it turns it into a part of sexual pleasure."[20] Dyer notes that this has been interpreted by critics as masochism. However, if juxtaposed to *The Brick Foxhole*, it becomes clear that Anger's version of masochism is very different from Brooks's. In *The Brick Foxhole*, Brooks utilizes masochism for a straight encounter with heterosexuality's double, which is hypocritical not only for its mobilization of homophobia but in its very structure. This structure enables the novel's straight readers to fantasize that the gay protagonist's seeking of the pleasures of masochism brought him face-to-face with death, while they (the straight readers) themselves seek these pleasures in being brought face-to-face with homosexuality. In addition, in the novel, masochism is given a tremendous "use value": It is the very mode that produces a "cure" to the temptation of crossing sexual boundaries.

By contrast, Anger "outs" masochism's potential for sexual pleasure by inverting its causality. Its "reward" is not *the relief from* the temptation to seek sex and/or pain via an identification of or with homosexuality; instead, masochism becomes the result of this identification. Unlike *The Brick Foxhole*, in which the homosexual's masochism kills him, *Fireworks*, as Dyer notes, parodies "the masochistic ecstasy of death" and reveals it as a put-on.[21] In sum, *Fireworks* brings out what remains submerged and deliberately masked (but nonetheless operative) in *The Brick Foxhole*—that the encounter with one's own or someone else's homosexuality (and the encounter with homosexuality as a general phenomenon) is both fearful and pleasurable. The stratified significations of desire and fear in these texts indicate the various ways in which homosexuality became suspended between invisibility and visibility.

These texts are symptomatic of the discursive territory of homosexuality in the postwar period. The modes by which homosexuality was produced/repressed in visual and literary terms in these texts indicates much about the positions through and into which homosexuality would evolve in the 1950s. If homosexuality during much of the 1940s was strictly defined by latency, in the wake of Kinsey this latency showed its full productive potential. No longer simply marking an unspoken knowledge, it began to assume a key function in the production and proliferation of "qualitative" attributes that were meant to manifest homosexuality. If homosexuality shortly after the war was still characterized by invisibility—that is, if it was in some ways an empty discursive category—the 1950s and 1960s saw a frenzy of efforts to fill this void. Dominant culture, of course, continued to pathologize homosexuality through a host of medico-scientific discourses (especially in the service of classifying the homosexual as a threat to national security[22]), but it also gradually supplemented these discourses with an increasing ethnographic interest in homosexuality. By the early 1960s, mainstream publications were running features on gay subcultures and "the gay life style," indicating that mainstream society had not exactly lost its interest in containing and demarcating homosexuality as the Other but that this containment was now increasingly conducted via studying the homosexual as a member of an exotic tribe. In their efforts to displace and/or to (re)figure homosexuality textually, both dominant heterosexual culture and the gay subculture partook in some of the same tropes, discourses, and stereotypes, albeit with very different goals. For example, during the 1950s, both sides became increasingly concerned with, for example, possible interpretations of bachelorhood and of cultural sophistication, which indicates that during the postwar period questions of sexual identity became increasingly displaced onto issues of gender and the way gender is performed.

What was at stake in the figuration of sexual identity via gender identity? For heterosexual men, bachelorhood became the award of postwar prosperity, epitomized in the new cultural figure of the playboy, whose compulsive heterosexuality became a bulwark against possible suspicions of homosexuality in light of his urban sophistication and his refusal to commit (to women).[23] Gay men themselves began to negotiate issues of visibility during the postwar years through an increasing network of gay subcultures complete with bars, gossip networks, cruising grounds, and proliferating licit and illicit publications and films with homoerotic content. Tom Waugh has shown that these texts involved the gaying of mainstream icons, the (re)articulation of gay mythologies (for example, through the figure of the misunderstood outsider, the sad young man, or the martyr), and the investment of traditional homosocial scenarios (the prison, the army) with homoeroticism.[24] The gaying of heterosexual scenarios involved the appropriation of mainstream texts for gay-specific practices and led to the gradually increasing visibility of gayness in mainstream culture. Whether straight- or gay-authored, 1950s discourses on male sexuality were compelled to negotiate homosexuality's suspension in the tension between latency and manifestation, between invisibility and visibility.

It is here that *Blow Job*, again, deserves consideration, because its minimalist features can be regarded as an aesthetic response to the quandary of "invisibility." *Blow Job* can accommodate numerous historical as well as contemporary (re)evaluations of gay identity during the cold war era. First, the film may reflect the total camouflage of 1950s homosexuals who depended on a clandestine mode of intimacy and communication. Second, it may be viewed as overtly expressing an iconographically distinct subculture in opposition to the dominant. Yet *Blow Job* can also be read as foreshadowing the increasing acceptance of homosexuals during the second half of the 1960s, especially if the film's refusal to show the actual sex act is read as an allegory of the partial visibility and growing acceptance of homosexuality, if only on straight terms. And finally, one may read this partial visibility even more specifically as referencing the iconography of the hustler, whose involvement with male clients depended on the performance of straightness.[25]

HYPOCHONDRIA AND GAY PERFORMANCE
BETWEEN PASSING AND POSING

To explore in greater detail the fluidity between the invisible and the visible, the latent and the manifest, let us consider a figure that exists in broader cultural discourses as well as in more specific psychoanalytic debates and that, in some ways, can be seen as symptomatic of the postwar period: the figure of hypochondria. Hypochondria may appear to be an odd choice because the connotations it evokes are mainly negative. However, this negative valence somewhat belies the term's broad and flexible applicability as a metaphor and its pervasive significance for issues of the formation of identity, the performance of the self, and the production and perception of texts that figure homosexuality.

Webster's Third New International Dictionary defines hypochondria as an "extreme depression of mind or spirits often centered on imaginary physical ailments." One subsequent sample citation characterizes a hypochondriac as someone who "lives in a world of sick imagination." This is, in fact, largely the state of the male protagonist of one of the key texts to negotiate homosexuality during the 1950s, the Hollywood film *Tea and Sympathy*. This film has been read as constructing an alternative masculinity for its protagonist (giving the impression that he is not a "real" man and stands outside normative heterosexuality).[26] I argue that his peculiar state, which comes to be figured as a malaise that is, however, only imagined, was emblematic of much of 1950s culture—a culture of hypochondria.

Psychoanalytic theory characterizes hypochondria more specifically as the imaginary investment that substitutes the psychic for the physical and vice versa. Investing body parts with libido, hypochondria makes the body epistemologically accessible to the subject as it brings these body parts to the attention of the bodily ego. In this sense, hypochondria is analogous to erotogenicity, the psyche's designation of body parts that are sexually excitable. Both processes make the body "knowable" to the one who inhabits it; both also help psychoanalytic discourses account for the process by which body parts become central to the formation of psychosexual identity.[27] Significantly, in helping establish a meaningful relationship between the subject's identity and the subject's body parts, both processes vacillate between real and imagined body parts. Hypochondria and erotogenicity thus help account for the fact that the imaginary always maintains its influence on the ways in which even a fully matured subject knows, feels, "experiences," and performs his body, for example, when pursuing sexual interests in an often frustrating, adverse, or even hostile social environment.

Because hypochondria and erotogenicity constitute intersecting modes of producing knowledge about the body as a sexual body, they may be regarded as partaking in much larger epistemological projects of making the body "speak" its sexuality. These projects are essentially disciplinary processes that "produce" the sexualized body in the act of making it accessible as a knowable body. While these knowledges often constituted hegemonic attempts at classifying sexuality into empirically verifiable "truth" categories, the production of knowledge seems to be motivated not only by a will to control the sexual but also by a range of pleasures that come with the production of sexual knowledge. This must at least partly account for appropriations of the tangible sexualities thus produced by the very groups who were supposed to be controlled by them. Therefore, while I will argue that hypochondria is basically a pathologizing discourse and was utilized as such by much of 1950s mainstream culture, I will also discuss how hypochondria's positing of a sliding scale of what is imagined and what is perceived was appropriated by white gay men—the very subjects whose presence helped prompt its deployment by dominant, homophobic society. In addition, I will discuss the ambiguity of 1950s gay performance with regard to the tension between invisibility and visibility in which gay men found themselves during the period and to which they responded with two practices—passing and posing. As gay subcultural practices, passing and posing were marked by a certain fluidity between the imagined and the perceived and significantly influenced the evolution of gay identity. Because the relationship between passing and posing involves, among other things, issues of spectatorship (passing and posing for someone), and because, as subcultural forms of communication, they blur the line between onlooker and participant, it seems only apposite to relate these practices to an analysis of spectatorship in *Blow Job*, which, as I have been arguing, reenacts some of these dynamics. Signifying aspects of passing as well as posing, *Blow Job*'s minimalist mise-en-scène—immensely open to various interpretations—would thus enable gay readings while at the same time protecting the fledgling gay subculture from what Juan Suarez calls "the fixity of medico-journalistic objectification."[28] In other words, the film references the practice of passing and gay camouflage's strategies of doing so while it also articulates the desire for and practice of posing, which gay men deployed, among other things, to identify themselves to other gay men.

The tension between invisibility and visibility, in which homosexuality was located, pervaded 1950s culture in general. While gay themes began to become more visible in certain, somewhat marginal, areas of cultural production, their signifying force became attenuated at the moment they were beginning to attract the interest of the mainstream and of mass culture. A good example can be found in Robert Anderson's 1953 play, *Tea and Sympathy*, and its 1955 Hollywood adaptation, as will be described shortly. The play is part of a long tradition in American drama to investigate such controversial issues as rape and homosexuality. Despite, but also because of, its interest in risqué subject matter, the American stage—less mainstream than movies, imbued with more cultural prestige, and seen by a far smaller, predominantly urban and well-educated audience—has always provided Hollywood studios with ample material for its bourgeois "quality" productions. The studios produced this relatively small line of high-end product, so to speak, in addition to its output of popcorn fare not only to boost box office differently but to garner cultural cachet. To be sure, for the first sixty or so years of the twentieth century, much of American drama also relied on realism and audience identification for dramatic thrust. But American drama was never identical with pop culture, and when it was turned into the latter, it fell victim to sometimes drastic modifications and alterations. Hence, the long line of Hollywood's adaptations of such postwar dramas as *A Streetcar Named Desire* and *Who's Afraid of Virginia Woolf* invariably bespeak the difference between American drama and American film by foregrounding their very own drama—the drama of censorship enacted to make the plays' controversial issues compatible with the demands of the Hollywood Production Code.

Staged for the first time in 1953, when Hollywood was still either refusing to acknowledge explicitly the existence of homosexuality or displacing/transposing it with symmetrical consistency onto such figures as the Communist and the psychopathological killer,[29] Anderson's *Tea and Sympathy* tackled the possibility of homosexuality head-on. The play tells the story of Tom, a student at a small college, who comes to be terrorized by his fellow students and his headmaster because he does not conform to their standards of masculinity, sexual behavior, and sexual identity. He is considered "queer" not only because of his refusal to behave in the red-blooded, hypermasculine fashion of his fellow students but because he was reportedly seen socializing in the nude on the beach with an allegedly homosexual teacher.[30] Critics have stressed that while the idea of a sexual liaison between Tom and Laura, the headmaster's wife, was created by Anderson, the play's ending need not be read as indicating Tom's final decision on sexual object choice. The fact that the stage version makes explicit that Tom's homosexuality is, at least, a possibility somewhat counterbalances its heterosexualizing ending.[31]

Tea and Sympathy soon gained the attention of several Hollywood producers who, ever on the lookout for new material that is both "spicy" and "artistic," read the play's considerable success on the New York stage as a portent for movie box office appeal. It seems that Hollywood found it hard to pass up an opportunity to bring to celluloid the next *A Streetcar Named Desire*, even though the censorship battles Warner Brothers had with the Breen Office and the Catholic Legion of Decency with regard to *Streetcar* were well known. However, George Custen's research on the film adaptation of *Tea and Sympathy* has shown that most moguls ogling the play soon became discouraged because of the staunch, uncompromising stand of the Production Code Administration (PCA) on the issue of homosexuality. The only movie mogul remaining in dogged pursuit of the material was MGM's Dore Shary, a self-professed liberal, who sought to salvage the adaptation for the studio by replacing the issue of Tom's homosexuality with a more general nonconformity linked to Tom's gender traits (his sensitive nature; his "unmanly" body movements) and "alternative" proclivities (his love for the arts; his yearning to socialize with women for nonromantic purposes). The fact that Shary, defending these changes before the PCA, cited an article from *Look* magazine entitled "How Much Do We Know About Men?" indicates how keenly aware he was that 1950s culture had become very conscious of the fluid nature of masculinity and that masculinity had become a way for American culture to deal with issues of (homo)sexuality in displaced fashion. According to Custen, when the PCA still would not budge, Shary went so far as to entertain the plan to make Tom's problem one of unbridled hypermasculinity and rampant heterosexuality—a sign that *any* indication of an "excessive" sexual identity during the 1950s, whether homosexual or heterosexual, was deemed exploitable for its suspect straying from anxiously guarded, though constantly redefined, norms.

Temporarily deliberating and discarding a number of more or less preposterous designs to defuse *Tea and Sympathy*, MGM and the PCA finally came up with a solution: Not only would the film delete any explicit hint at the existence of homosexuality, but it would frame the play's main dramatic plot as a flashback. The film version begins and ends with Tom's visit to the college for a ten-year reunion during which he is handed a letter written by Laura (who has gone into exile as punishment for their affair) in which she responds to the events that Tom had put on paper as a roman à clef. The film's plot is then relayed to the audience as Tom's memories triggered by reading the letter. Custen and Gerstner have argued that the letter thus has several functions: First, by ending with Laura commending Tom for now being married, it heterosexualized Tom beyond their affair; second, the letter indirectly reemphasizes that Tom had mastered his sexual identity crisis without resorting to the "wrong" object choice; and third, Laura invokes Tom's marital status to rationalize his crisis as simply imagined. According to Custen, this reflects the PCA's perception of homosexuality as a physical category (rather than an emotional condition) which, if removed from the film, simply ceased to exist. While the psychologization of homosexuality was still controversial, making homosexuality intangible in this manner helped avoid an otherwise inevitable clash with moralizers. Custen summarizes: "Long before Jacques Lacan's usage of the term 'imaginary' came to be linked with the process of identity formation, MGM's negotiations with the PCA used the term to connote denial. There might always be the fertile imagination to lead one astray (particularly in artists). But in the film's new world, there were *neither* actual homosexual acts nor, as it turns out, actual psychologically constituted homosexual people."[32] The rewriting of *Tea and Sympathy* is thus an example of how mainstream culture used the imaginary and the narrative past to deny the existence of homosexuality. While the film reenacts and critiques moral and ethnographic discourses for their obsession with gender "aberration" and, thereby, engages in liberal fashion the cold war culture's phobic response to homosexuality, and while it sets out to question dominant culture's investment in the transparent and causal link between sex, gender, and gender identity, it ultimately performs a compulsory denial of homosexuality.

Tea and Sympathy reflects a compatibility between the medico-pathological conceptualization of homosexuality and an ethnographic discourse. On one level, the film actually remains consistent with the paradigm of defining sexuality in terms of illness: It is not simply that the protagonist's classmates are ignorant bullies; by positing a strange malaise—a veritable ailment—as the root cause of Tom's oppression, by insinuating that his search for identity, acceptance, and peace of mind is really a search for a cure, *Tea and Sympathy* partakes in the myth that social ills evolve from medico-psychological illnesses and not vice versa. Yet, this illness is now clearly a kind of hypochondria, for the heterosexualization of the film's protagonist "cures" him of a disease he never had to begin with. The masculinity of the sissy, redefined as straight but alternative from an ethnographic perspective, was but one manifestation of a larger trend by which 1950s culture negotiated gender difference both through increased attention to body movements and manners and through heavy, often pathologizing, psychologization.

In this sense, such heavily psychologized mainstream stars as James Dean and Montgomery Clift also can be seen as basic figures of a pervasive hypochondria insofar as they emblematized the process in which physical, medico-pathological difference becomes substituted by the psychic and vice versa. Such stereotypes as the sissy, the sad young man, and the suffering martyr, which, to varying degrees, marked both Clift's and Dean's film roles and star personae, were thus indications of a more general hypochondria that characterized the period. Their "inappropriate" masculinities buffered the threats to the culture's still prevailing model of a normative, natural, and "healthy" masculinity by offering alternatives that were different but not really different[33]—that is, they posed alternative masculinity that, itself, posed as an illness that was really only imagined. Correlatively, if the alternative masculinity at issue alluded to homosexuality, the homosexual was soon outed as a heterosexual. If it was that of a generally unstable and volatile teenager, the teenager became "cured" through his rite of passage to adulthood.

The deeper rhetoric of postwar liberal discourses on masculinity and sexual deviance was still modeled on both medico-pathological and ethnographic representations of homosexuality, but these discourses were also beginning to criticize these paradigms. Steven Cohan has pointed out that *Tea and Sympathy*, for example, with its message that straight boys can be sissies, too, was questioning more or less directly the tendency of defining gender performance in terms of sexual object choice.[34] As such, it must also be regarded as broadly reflecting Kinsey's findings that de-essentialized homosexuality. The film's hypochondriacal alibi pointed to dominant culture's slow and still hesitant acknowledgment that gender identity may be more fluid than hitherto assumed.

Given hypochondria's propensity to assume alibi functions, it may not be particularly surprising that hypochondria came to figure prominently within and for discourses of passing—and here I am thinking of passing as initiated by not only the gay-identified subject but also the non–gay-identified subject. Before focusing on how white gay men appropriated hypochondria for what Juan Suarez terms a "decentered subjectivity"[35] (the gay subject constituted by a kind of mimetic bricolage), let us consider the possibility that this decenteredness may pertain at least initially also to the potentially homophobic subject. In this regard, I propose that the fear of sexual alterity is produced not only upon the direct encounter of, say, a heterosexual with a gay person but that it also exists dormant within the heterosexual and is sometimes frighteningly awakened. Hypochondria, in this context, may not simply hide the gay person from the straight one, but it also may hide from the non–gay-identified subject his own identification with and, in some cases, desire for the homosexual. The non–gay-identified subject can then simultaneously read homosexuality and "misread" it; or he can sublimate it into such guises as sympathy, empathy, and friendship, which act as fetishes that buffer the real threat and help rationalize the subject's affect toward the homosexual. It is not that homosexuality is not there. Paradoxically (as is the case with fetishes), the subject can find these identifications desirable without having to identify homosexuality explicitly and, perhaps even more important, without having to identify with homosexuality as such, which is precisely what secures his status as non–gay-identified subject. This particular type of passing, then, does not make the one who encounters homosexuality completely oblivious to the presence of homosexuals, but it offers him the option of an *alternative* reading of gayness. Hypochondria positions homosexuality in a tension between simultaneous acknowledgment and disavowal, whereby it becomes but one possible—or passable—interpretation among a host of others. For those who entertain it as but one possibility, the fear of association is diffused.

To the extent that the existence of homosexuality on the level of the imaginary is characterized by transience and by phantasmatic identification and desire, the non–gay-identifed subject misperceives gay performance as a private imagination on his part, an imagination that is fleeting, transient, and thus itself determined by hypochondria. We have observed this with regard to *Tea and Sympathy*, but—as with *The Brick Foxhole*— even an encounter with an explicitly identified homosexual is often phobically cast and contained in terms of a transient nightmare or phantasmagoria. Nonetheless, hypochondria does inscribe homosexuality into the symbolic. Acts governed by it are read and interpreted "concretely," if not unambiguously. No longer exclusively subjected to those irrational aspects of cathexis and abjection that produce the well-known homophobic gut reactions, homosexuality can now also be dealt with "rationally." This rationalization of homosexuality should, of course, by no means be confused with an elimination of homophobia in the public sphere. Rather, it helps us understand the residual, yet persistent, homophobia especially in liberal efforts to "understand" the homosexual, and it must be seen as central to dominant culture's attempts to ethnicize homosexuality in the pre- and even post-Stonewall period. Judith Butler points out that in such efforts "homosexuality is not fully repudiated, because it is entertained, but it will always remain 'entertainment,' cast as the figure of the symbolic's 'failure' to constitute its sexed subjects fully or finally, but also and always a subordinate rebellion with no power to rearticulate the terms of the governing law."[36] The invocation of "homosexual entertainment" suggests the well-known classification of gays and particularly drag queens as figures who possess a "lesser" symbolic currency. Hypochondria in its dominant form relegates homosexual signification to the psychosexual basement and allows its reentry into the parlor only as a phobically recast figure of the monstrous or the grotesque. In its particular function as a reactionary defense mechanism, hypochondria may also—sometimes—protect gay men against gay-bashing. However, in a hegemonic context it functions invariably to contain gay culture and homosexuality in general.

Considering how much hypochondria has helped shape many psycho- and medico-pathological discourses, and given hypochondria's teleology of transitoriness (it articulates and "proves" its existence through the figure of the cure), it may seem odd that such a figure could be invoked usefully to understand gay men's move away from invisibility and passing and toward visibility and posing. But even though hypochondria was typically mobilized by such dominant texts as *Tea and Sympathy* to relinquish the concrete phenomenon of homosexuality, it arguably carried at least the potential of becoming a structuring paradigm of gender performance and its fluid relation to sexual identity. The positing of a continuum of manners, behaviors, and habits across the divide between hetero- and homosexuality bore out what gay men had known all along—that body movements, mannerisms, and certain cultural practices and lifestyles can always be read in more than one way. While gay performance of the period surely availed itself of a complex mix of diverse strategies and paradigms, not all of which can or should be linked to hypochondria, there was one figure—the popular stereotype of the sad young man—that embodied this paradigm.

As Richard Dyer notes, the sad young man was, for the most part, a construct of dominant culture, too (we find a variant of him in *Tea and Sympathy*'s hero, Tom).[37] However, unlike such more one-dimensionally insidious stereotypes as the Hollywood Indian or the (early) Hollywood Negro, the sad young man was a privileged object of appropriation for the very group he was supposed to stereotype. Comparable in function to the femme noir's relation to postwar female spectators, the sad young man was produced, at least as far as twentieth century popular culture is concerned, not only *as* a gay man but also, at least partly, *for* gay men. The subject of a long series of pulp novels published from the late 1940s to the mid-1960s, the sad young man signified the existence of a barely-acknowledged niche market of gay readers whose existence as gay consumers it helped keep closeted. Dyer notes that most of these novels simultaneously denied and acknowledged their gay readership: They pretended to address straight readers to inform these readers about "them," but their tales were often surprisingly upbeat, suggesting ecstatic homosexual love, unfair social attitudes, and much camp.[38] In addition, while these novels often conveyed an air of social passivity, isolation, fatefulness, and doom, they also constructed their protagonists as figures of both identification and desire. It was precisely because these gay icons were so troubled, haunted, unfulfilled, suffering, yearning, and stricken by melancholia and malaise that they became so appealing and were able to turn their ordinary good looks into what Dyer terms "cadaverous beauty."[39] In fact, as the discussion in Chapter 2 of Warhol's attempts to stylize himself as a sad young man sought to demonstrate, not even ordinary good looks are needed for cadaverous beauty—just "ordinary" will do.

Particularly with regard to being a hypochondriac, the sad young man thus possessed certain qualities that reflected some of the larger culture's prejudices. But these qualities also spoke to his prospective audience. As a figure of multiple transitions, the sad young man was suspended between straight and gay worlds, between arrested and "properly" completed development, between isolation and physical consummation, between eternal sadness and the hope for happiness. These features bore out dominant culture's greatest fears and anxieties and thus fulfilled the scapegoat function of the stereotype, but their very balance—the absence of resolution—made the sad young man a durable fetish object to be consumed by gay readers. In addition, the sad young man qualified the position and function of the imaginary in hypochondria. While dominant concepts deploy the imaginary to present homosexuality as a phantom of the mind that will leave as a result of the cure, the sad young man literally embodies the imaginary. Most of his efforts of connecting to other men are based on the fluid relation between social observation, imagination, and projection. He is a phantom character who is placed into a twilight world in which nothing is clear-cut and everything could potentially happen. Precisely because this "half-world" is, from the perspective of dominant culture, in between the sexes, less than self-sufficient, and, to quote Dyer, "without the connectives that make normal society so rich and satisfying,"[40] it puts notions of the latent and the manifest and of the imaginary and the symbolic in new, potentially productive relation.

This "homosexual half-world" becomes the setting of a practice that will be dealt with in more detail in Chapter 4: the collapse of desire and identification. This practice existed not only around the figure of the sad young man but, as Dyer points out, structures the texts of gay and lesbian fantasy in general and 1950s gay male self-stylizations in particular. Suffice it to say for the moment that the fluidity of gay signification comes about in two ways: First, "wanting" becomes inscribed on the body, manifesting what is usually deemed "latent," "intangible," and prior to signification, and second, the split, seemingly contradictory nature of "wanting" (wanting to be/wanting to have) becomes inscribed on the same body in endlessly modifiable combinations. What this underlying sensibility abhors is attempts to fix meaning in the symbolic and raise it to the level of standard—such as normal masculinity, which, as Dyer points out, is a far from attractive prospect for the sad young man despite his own misery. However, the inscription of more fluid and, indeed, contradictory signifiers on the body of the sad young man did not always automatically identify him as gay. Like most gay performance types of the 1950s that were broadly operating within the parameters of the masculine, the sad young man was also a figure of passing or, more accurately, positioned himself between passing and posing. Dyer's characterization of the sad young man in this regard indicates that the sad young man passes and poses with the same set of gestures. He notes that "in relation to visibility, he both is and is not knowable from appearance" and that "as is most usual with sad young men, you can't tell one (queer) from the other (normal) and yet there are always tell-tale signs—the fear over our invisibility is stated simultaneously with the reassurance that we are not invisible."[41]

A typical indicator of the prominence of hypochondria within postwar Anglo-American culture, the sad young man's complex deployment of illness, imagination, passing, and posing significantly modifies hypochondria's oppressive aspects and gives it new potential as a figure of gay performance. As such, the sad young man's deployment of hypochondria must be viewed as harboring the seeds for the development of a counterstrategy in the maze of strategic productions that contributed to postwar gay men's self-assertion in their homophobic environment. Because the sad young man thrives on, rather than suffers from, the fluid relation between the psychic and the physical, he can continue to act on what he imagines without having to be cured (i.e., returned to "the real"). While formerly paraphrased by the twin terms of "sick, but not really sick," hypochondria now no longer needs the latter of these terms to undo the former, since it has transvalued the former. Furthermore, because the sad young man is placed between discrete worlds, he cannot be harnessed easily and without losing his appeal as a stereotype into teleologies of stable, normative sexual identity. While formerly invoked to analogize "queer, but ultimately not really queer," hypochondria now reconfigures the latter to a figure of *passing for straight* rather than *being/becoming straight.* In addition, because his type is, as Dyer argues, both romantic and pornographic, the sad young man ends up presenting gay malaise and melancholia as something chic and desirable. While formerly considered a combination of ethnographic and medico-pathological discourses, hypochondria subsumes the latter set of discourses under the former and transforms it into a style or, if you wish, a self-reflexive performance genre. Finally, implicit in these three aspects of the transvaluation of hypochondria is the redesignation of pleasure. Dominant constructs of hypochondria suggested the attainment of pleasure merely as a distant possibility. Indeed, hypochondria was the figure that stood between the subject and pleasure. By contrast, hypochondria reconfigured through the potentials of the sad young man shifts the emphasis from longing for pleasure toward all the pleasures involved in longing. Hypochondria is then no longer entirely about deferral or complete denial; it also includes consummation—at least the consummation of a literary/pop cultural idol who is "eaten up" by a group of readers. This eating up spells the beginnings of identity and community, as it produces pleasure through the positing of recognizable, repetitive, and reified scenarios.

As a "cultural sensibility" (rather than a psychosexual phenomenon) with a unifying impulse, hypochondria thus arguably also had very important functions for and within gay culture, as it helped gay performance to enlarge its spectrum of social codes and gestures of sexual expression and erotic communication. The more subtle these codes, the greater was their impact on gay performance in the postwar period, when the criteria for detecting and classifying homosexuality increasingly revolved around phenomenological discourses. While hypochondria became one way of diffusing homophobia, it persistently, if moderately, helped assert the possibility of homosexuality in the public sphere. When appropriated by homosexuals, hypochondria, especially when it helps facilitate gay cruising, can function in a way that is similar to the fake performance of sexual arousal in porn: If one follows Dean MacCannell's argument that the audience's good faith is on the side of the performer, even (or especially) a pose may eventually succeed in engaging and possibly arousing the one who encounters and observes it. Precisely because it enfolds the sliding scale between sexual and nonsexual behavior with another sliding scale between the latent and the manifest, hypochondria socializes sex and facilitates its passage from the imaginary into the symbolic and back. Its modus operandi negates the notion that passing and posing are ontologically separate and, indeed, contradictory concepts. Instead, hypochondria presents them as a continuum, indicating how gay performance was, at one point, forced to negotiate its position between invisibility and visibility by recognizing (perhaps both intuitively and rationally) the significance of the latent and the manifest and the gain that lies in manipulating their relation for acts of passing and posing.

However, just as Richard Dyer cautions us not to overrate the subversive or liberatory potential of the sad young man, we should be equally careful not to overstate the potentials of hypochondria as, say, a reverse discourse. Reverse discourses have traditionally been discussed as being authored by medically scrutinized and ethnographically objectified minorities who transform the discourse of and knowledge implied in their objectification into a self-affirming, self-legitimating political position, oftentimes using the very vocabulary with which they have been disqualified.[42] Pre-Stonewall gay activists, for example, attempted to legitimate homosexuality by claiming that homosexuals were, on the one hand, "normal, not sick" and, on the other hand, still a minority in need of protection.[43] While reverse discourses sooner or later become linked to the explicit manifestation and transformation of minorities in the social, hypochondria—the performance of illness—has, understandably, not been used as a political tool, and its relation to sociosymbolic manifestation assumed, at least during the 1950s, a kind of complexity different from that of politicized minoritarian discourses.[44] Yet, as a strategically deployed cultural practice negotiating the relationship between passing and posing, hypochondria helped white gay men (many of whom still had negative feelings about their homosexuality and were, for the most part, very indifferent to 1950s gay activists and their ideas) to insert themselves in the social via a certain performance genre and lifestyle. In addition, the sad young man's articulation of gayness as a malaise did, in fact, succeed in inverting the negative signifiers on which gayness was originally founded. Identifying himself as an index of contradictory social constructs, the gay man as hypochondriac reverses the cause and effect of signifying illness—it is society that is ill in blaming him for its inability to reconcile its own highly constructed and deeply contradictory dictums and rules, which he, in turn, embraces and celebrates instead of attempting to naturalize and resolve them. Yet, this insight did not become a political slogan until Stonewall and such post-Stonewall manifestos as Rosa von Praunheim's film, *It Is Not the Homosexual Who Is Perverse, But the Situation in Which He Finds Himself.* Thus, hypochondria should not be viewed as a reverse discourse proper. Rather, it was one among several structuring paradigms of gender performance of which gay men availed themselves in the 1950s. It was firmly bound up with fairly narrow notions of class, race, and ethnicity, and rather than becoming defunct as a political tool, it simply went out of style sometime in the 1960s or early 1970s. (Rainer Werner Fassbinder's *Fox and His Friends* [1972] and John Schlesinger's *Sunday Bloody Sunday* [1971] still contained traces.)

From the late 1940s to the mid-1960s hypochondria arguably held some importance not only because it informed a gay stereotype—the sad young man—but also because it designated a set of dynamics that helped determine the relationship between passing and posing during a specific historical phase in the evolution of gay identity. Positioned at the nexus between passing and posing, hypochondria continues to deserve our attention because of the impact passing and posing have had on degrees of gay visibility, on their strategic implications, and, thus, on the political viability and the evolving historical and sociocultural situation of at least parts of what has come to be known as "the gay community." Posing, for example, undeniably helped build this community (whatever its current forms), and it contributed to the evolution of gay identities at the very least by producing a host of styles and signifying a number of practices that an increasing number of gays and lesbians could find desirable and with which they could engage. This stratification of styles and practices has led to the stratification of gay and lesbian identities themselves. That is, it has produced what theorists have characterized as sexual pluralism—itself an index for the broader project of re-theorizing the body as a source of multiple sexual practices and pleasures that, one might want to note, are noticed, discussed, and emulated by both gays and nongays. In short, posing and its attendant practice of collapsing desire and identification not only have helped gays go public; they have also served the argument that there may be an intrinsic link between homosexuality and political intervention, perhaps even political radicalism.[45] In Chapter 4 I will discuss certain theoretical perspectives that may allow us to posit such a link. These perspectives will then be juxtaposed with critiques that have argued that the inhabitation of oppressed sexualities in and of itself does not result in political action and social change but that it can serve as a point of departure for an exploration between sexuality and a whole range of political affinities.

4

GAY MASCULINITY BETWEEN
(DE)CONSTRUCTION AND *DEMONTAGE*

From the 1940s to the late 1960s, passing and posing were central to the ways that helped gay men position themselves in homophobic public places and often even in private spaces. Passing and posing influenced gay male signifying practices, gay styles, and aspects of gay sensibility and gay community. Thus, their impact on variants of what is termed gay male identity merits further discussion with regard to theoretical approaches to identity. This chapter is concerned with passing and posing in relation to a range of ways in which white gay male identity, in particular, can be theorized.

Identity theories are as numerous as the philosophical perspectives that feed them and, one might add, as numerous as the identities they trace, characterize, and, indeed, help produce. Even an already fairly specific minority group such as gay men diversifies further into several sub-identities, the theorization of which needs to take into account the complex interplay of aspects of class, race, ethnic background, membership to other minorities, and historical context. Given the variety and variability of these vectors, it is perhaps not surprising that over the past two decades, the critical-methodological perspective that has come to dominate theorizations of sexuality, gender, and gender identity is one that may broadly be called constructionist. Significantly, it has been feminist discourse that has most vehemently refused to regard sex and gender as reducible to "the natural" or to static "essentials" and that has significantly been rethinking sex and gender as *indissociable from their particular historical, political, and sociocultural contexts.* Over the past five decades, feminist discourse has gradually but systematically honed in on the term "woman," arguing that this term is itself constructed by patriarchy as a category of the Other on which phallocentrism erects itself. Far from denying the specificity of female anatomy or from ignoring the convergence of medico-biological and scientific vectors that mark women as "Other" and that amplify the oppression of women, feminist constructionists from Simone de Beauvoir to Monique Wittig have, from different angles and to different degrees, come to reject the concept of a putative female essence or a "core identity" and have argued instead that gender is socially constructed.

In the late 1980s and early 1990s, this discourse reached a peak particularly in the postmodern American academy with Judith Butler's work on gender as performance, so far the most eloquent, systematic, and influential theoretical refutation of gender essentialism. Butler rejects and debunks as traditionally humanist the view that our sexual and gender identities are mere surface reflections of an "essence" underneath, a stable gender core, "worked upon from above," as it were, by scientific, sexological, juridical, ethnographic, and cultural discourses. Instead, according to Butler, gendered subjects *perform* their gender by producing on their bodies—indeed, *as* their bodies—a host of diverse, even contradictory, gender styles.[1] Whether complying with or transgressing the cultural norms of gender, the gendered subject always performs gender in relation to a set of more or less established norms, traditions, and conventions. The gendered subject thus becomes an index of the complex interplay between power and pleasure, which, in their combination, make the subject adhere to gender norms in the first place. There is, for example, the power operative in "rewarding" or, by contrast, punishing certain gender performances, and there is also the pleasure of complying with or defying established gender norms. (But, it should be added, even outright defiance of norms never produces completely new genders. Gender always carries over a traditional element; it always thrives on partial recognition.)

Arguing that gender is a set of fabricated if normative concepts of femininity and masculinity, Butler's theory complements that of another attacker of essences, Michel Foucault, and his characterization of *scientia sexualis*—that is, enlightenment culture's apprehension, disciplinization, and production of the human body as a fully eroticized, fully sexualized body. Feminist-influenced gay, lesbian, and queer constructionist theorists have drawn on these and other theories to argue the inherently discursive and inherently political nature of sex and gender. Their close collaboration with lawyers and activists has led to the overall politicization of lesbian, gay, bisexual, transgendered, and queer positions in numerous heavily embattled politico-legal, socioeconomic, and cultural arenas, such as same-sex marriage, same-sex partnership benefits, gays in the military, the medical, political, and media discrimination against persons with AIDS, and the homophobic and heterosexist stereotyping of gender, sex, and sex practices by mainstream media in general. In fact, in the early 1990s, when ACT UP demonstrations were mass operations that made national television news, when Queer Nation organized kiss-ins in rampantly straight bars and clubs, when drag went mainstream and S/M came to be featured on cable television, there was a moment in which it seemed widely assumed that if gender is socially constructed, then gender can be *de*constructed as well as *re*constructed in new, creative, and less oppressive ways. And even though this moment has clearly passed, it lastingly demonstrated, at least to large numbers of North American lesbians, gays, bisexuals, transgendered, and queer people, the key position of the concept of *agency* in their politico-legal actions *and* their day-to-day lives. In addition, as gay historians Richard Dyer, Tom Waugh, and George Chauncey have shown, and as the remarks on hypochondria in Chapter 3 were meant to show, gays and lesbians assumed agency long before Stonewall through strategic community formations and through mundane acts of (re-)performing their genders.

And yet, the concept of agency has inhabited a far from unproblematic place in gender theory and politics. There are theoretical blind spots, as well as the sobering realization that lived history rarely conforms to the programmatics of activism. With regard to theory, we note that the concept of agency becomes a challenge, for example, to Judith Butler's theorization of gender as performance. On the one hand, any performance requires an active performer, and gender performances are often highly individualistic, creative, and deliberately defiant of normative gender codes. Butler's theory succeeds in that it makes plausible how punishment from without functions as "proof" that gender performance is always thought of in terms of a "perpetrator" who becomes singled out and targeted for "reformation" or plain punishment (the severity of which is often a measure of the severity of the gender transgression at issue). On the other hand, because gender is, as Butler persuasively argues, a grand script that precedes and succeeds any individual performer (Butler is at her most structuralist here in treating gender like genre), and because gender is punitive also *from within*, its inhabitation propelled by deep-seated, perhaps subconscious impulses of phobia and desire, abjection and identification, Butler has felt compelled to point out that gender performance as a philosophical concept involves much more than the sort of direct, confrontational strategic-creative revamping that is commonly associated with female and male drag. One of gender's dicta is coherence. But gender coherence is not only compulsory, it is also desired. The sense of inhabiting one's gender coherently is integral to the psycholinguistic subject who, despite its reiteration of the law, always already assumes that what it is trying to "fulfill" is something it already possesses, that is, something it deems "natural."[2] In this sense, Butler's concept of agency, which, it would seem, is integral to the notion that gender is fabricated and can be performed, keeps running up against the essentialist residue of the Lacanian and Althusserian models she so powerfully appropriates.

Butler's theory helps us recognize the performative nature of gender both in thoroughly strategic "acts" and in certain embodiments of the heavily coerced subject of gender, who is driven by the specters of Otherness, prohibition, and phobia. Or, to put it crudely, Butler's theory is genuinely helpful in making us understand why both drag and beating up drag queens are instances of gender performance. Yet, how does one fully theorize the vast and complex middle ground between these two extremes with regard to gender performance as a mundane, everyday act and as a broad-based social and theoretical phenomenon?

Precisely because phobia, abjection, desire, and identification are so central to notions of gender and sexual identity, they complicate questions of agency also with regard to gay politics and the history of gay identity and community formation. Here, the gay ethics of inclusiveness have been punctured by tales of gay racism, classism, and misogyny. Echoing on a sociological level Butler's psychoanalytic observation that any identity (including the oppressed, marginalized one) constructs itself against that which is abject and Other, Geoffrey Escoffier has argued that while community building confers on its members a shared recognition of common interests, characteristics, and values and a shared sense of identity ("it is a group of significant others"), it also produces new moral codes and norms of behavior that invariably lead to the exclusion of other "Others" who are not part of this community.[3] In addition, while having agency is no guarantee for obtaining power, it seems always suffused with the ambiguities of power and power play. It has been remarked that the formation of alternative communities does not automatically abolish the reactionary deployment of power within these communities; neither does their emergence as communities guarantee their members an increase in actual power in the overall political structure. Finally, if agency has helped the subcultural subject emerge into specific visible forms, it is always a double-edged sword in that it also puts the subject on the radar of the dominant and, thus, marks it for inclusion.

What is white gay men's position in this complex system of forces and counterforces? The discussion in the next section focuses on the function of agency in white gay men's efforts to negotiate (read: engage as well as resist) assimilation. A central point raised is that an understanding of agency may influence an understanding of what "white gay male" means in sociohistorical, psychosexual, and phenomenological terms.

THE GAY SIMULACRUM, THE GAY COCK, AND THE GAY PHALLUS

To explore some of the implications of agency during certain historically specific phases of white gay male identity, let us return to *Blow Job* and the figure of hypochondria. *Blow Job* reenacts the 1950s tension between passing and posing through its visual alibi, the structure of which is analogous to that of hypochondria. *Blow Job* is part of the adjoining pantheons of underground and gay folklore, even though (but also because) the film provides proof neither of gay sex nor of sex in general. Even when focusing on the face work of *Blow Job*'s poser, we note that facial expressions suggesting sexual activity can hardly be distinguished from those also associated with nonsexual excitation (such as pain). The tension between a real and an imagined injury complements the tension between a real and an imagined (playacted) sexual arousal. The fluidity of the poser's face work between sexual and nonsexual expressions, between the proliferation and the containment of eroticism, leads us to wonder whether a blow job is really taking place. But the film's anti-positivism does not altogether erase the possibility of a gay sex act. It posits its existence as but one explanation for what the poser's face registers, with other possibilities including a straight sex act, the possibility of pain, the possibility of a drug high, and the possibility of faking all of the above. Thus, the film can pass as both fiction and documentation. This double rhetorical structure also characterizes the modus operandi of hypochondria, whose mimetic overlap between such multiple, contradictory, and fleeting signals as ill/non-ill, sexual/nonsexual, and drugged/nondrugged never provides an unambiguous declaration of the hypochondriac's status and intent. *Blow Job* can then also be said to identify hypochondria as part and parcel of a broader paradigm of postwar white gay male gender performance that potentially enables gay communication but that never forecloses the interpretation of these codes as basically "innocuous" and devoid of sexual intent. By inviting and juxtaposing various readings of its mise-en-scène, by presenting them as "passable," *Blow Job* becomes an idiom of the structure of passing in general. Not every viewer of *Blow Job* necessarily feels cruised by its image, yet even those who claim they feel "sexually untouched" by or even indifferent to the film would not necessarily remain completely unaware of its sexual, and thus also of its possible gay, discourse. However, at the very moment in which one takes up and champions one specific reading, the moment one becomes invested in a specific reading's plausibility in terms of the cultural assumptions that one has imported into *Blow Job*'s image, passing turns to posing. Hence, the theoretical implications of posing are of interest, too, for a discussion of white gay male identity, as they help us understand the link between white gay male sexuality and self-assertion in the social.

Gay theorists have discussed posing in terms of gay performance's characteristic practice of collapsing identification with desire. Probably central to gay performance since the beginning of the modern era, this phenomenon assumed particular modes during the postwar period with regard to signifying masculinity. As noted earlier, gay men's experiences in the military during the war, with its unprecedented opportunities for same-sex encounters, had confirmed to them that while masculinity might commonly have been modeled on straight terms, it was no indication of sexual orientation. Obviously, gay men's looks and manners were not necessarily different from those of straight men, and, as Richard Dyer notes, gay servicemen not only desired but also identified with the man in the bunk next to their own.[4] The phenomenological likeness between subject and object of desire significantly determined the formation of gay male identity and the production of gay subcultural art during the period. Tom Waugh's research on male physique magazines and films of the postwar period has produced especially cogent evidence of this new sensibility. Licit mail-order images were populated with masculine types such as Greek wrestlers, sailors, soldiers, bikers, and cowboys, whose hyperbolized masculinities narrativized and theatricalized gay male identity between censorship and the display of gay sexuality. The absence of same-sex sexual acts or even so much as a kiss between two models safeguarded the licit status of those images. But they nevertheless had gayness inscribed into them through displaced narratives of wrestling matches or other highly theatricalized homoerotic interactions.[5] Most important, however, they inscribed gayness on the bodies of their models by subversively appropriating those aspects of masculinity usually taken to be an expression of heterosexuality. Postwar gay erotica displayed male models as objects of the gaze and articulated their masculinities as expressions of the libidinal investment in the cock as an object of both desire and identification.

The collapse of desire and identification leads to a certain mimetic self-consciousness: One sees oneself as an object as much as a subject; one wants to look and be looked at; one wants to cruise and be cruised by other gay men. At work is what Leo Bersani describes for the gay macho—"a fuckable set of pecs"[6]—but which has existed in various forms across a range of gay types. The duality that inheres in signifying subject and object of desire—the desire *for* and identification *with* the cock—contributes to the particularity of white gay male gender performance.

The gender performance of *Blow Job*'s poser, too, shows signs of the collapse of desire and identification. Like the simulacral qualities of 1950s gay performance, *Blow Job* engages gay style and partakes in gay genre. The self-conscious display of the poser feminizes him and enhances his object status. The fact that he is featured only in an extended reaction shot subverts dominant representations of the macho heterosexual. In Hollywood, this mode of representing men is usually a signifier for masculinity in crisis (consider film noir; the male "weepie"). In *Blow Job* it signals the poser's ambiguous pleasure in being objectified by the camera. Beyond the poser's feminization, *Blow Job* is notable here for its invocation of style marked by hypochondria. As the film progresses, the poser's face suggests a certain masochistic pleasure in the undulating waves of impact on his body. At some points, he simply seems to abandon himself to bliss (Figure 4.1) and/or pain (Figure 4.2). Toward the end of the film, the poser briefly throws his hands up to the sides of his head and bends over backwards, purportedly writhing under the full impact of sexual pleasure (Figure 4.3).

At other moments, his gestures appear to be more overtly melodra-

Figure 4.1
Blow Job. Film still courtesy of the Andy Warhol Museum.

matic, such as when he lifts either hand to stroke his forehead (Figure 4.4), to press his temple (Figure 4.5), or to touch his mouth and chin in a somewhat uncontrolled way (Figure 4.6). At one point, he even lifts both hands to rub his eyes and eyebrows in a histrionic gesture of exhaustion (Figure 4.7).

To the extent that these images index the performance of the masochistic self, they are also broadly comparable to images of the suffering or hystericized body in religion and art. The raising of the poser's brows, the lowering of his eyelids, the biting of his lip, and the wave-like expressions of heightened sensitivity are complemented by the undulating play of light and darkness that streams across the screen. In fact, since the flow of light is largely determined by the movements of the poser's head, one could argue that the masochistic body and the melodramatic mise-en-scène mutually reinforce each other.[7] In addition, the poser's handsome features are, particularly in the historical context of the 1950s and early 1960s, in and of themselves telltale signs of gayness— indicated both through his referencing of the frail beauty of the sad young man and the clean-cut but often too "pretty" trade of postwar gay erotica.

Blow Job foregrounds that a reading of its poser as a gay man engages conventional views on gender substantiality and sexual orientation, both of which the film forces us to question, qualify, and reformulate via the concept of the simulacrum. If during World War II and the immediate postwar years, homosexuality's epithet of "insubstantiality" had been defined initially through such stereotypical qualities as timid physique and effeminacy, by the mid-1950s gay performance, as Waugh has shown with regard to gay erotica, was subverting these notions.

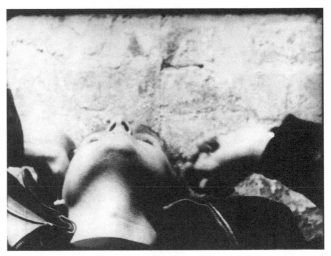

Figure 4.2 (top)
Figure 4.3 (middle)
Figure 4.4 (bottom)
Blow Job. Film stills courtesy of the Andy Warhol Museum.

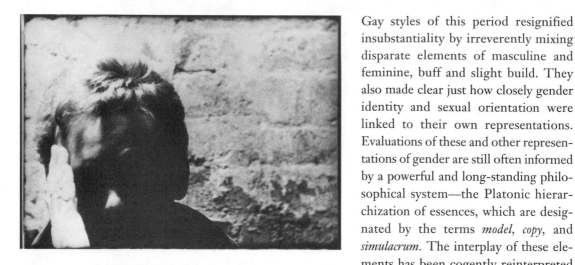

Figure 4.5 (top)
Figure 4.6 (middle)
Figure 4.7 (bottom)
Blow Job. Film stills courtesy of the Andy Warhol Museum.

Gay styles of this period resignified insubstantiality by irreverently mixing disparate elements of masculine and feminine, buff and slight build. They also made clear just how closely gender identity and sexual orientation were linked to their own representations. Evaluations of these and other representations of gender are still often informed by a powerful and long-standing philosophical system—the Platonic hierarchization of essences, which are designated by the terms *model*, *copy*, and *simulacrum*. The interplay of these elements has been cogently reinterpreted by Gilles Deleuze: Short of being able to ever be the godlike, mythic *model*, the *copy* attempts to assert "substance" and "authenticity" by claiming proximity to the model or, more accurately, the Idea of it. The *simulacrum* incurs the label "inauthentic" or "insubstantial" by laying claim to the same model without passing through its Idea, or essence. The copy depends on the simulacrum's lack of substance, the comparison to which the copy needs to place itself closer to the model. The simulacrum, in turn, "contaminates" or "debunks" the copy, since it seems to achieve what the copy aims for without having to go through what the copy goes through. The simulacrum thereby reveals that the copy is closer to it than to the model. Deleuze calls this "subversive mimesis" and characterizes this regime as one built on absolute and objective standards for authenticity.[8] As we saw in the discussion of *Tea and Sympathy*, gender wars tend to partake in this system: Macho men often attempt but ultimately fail to boast their gender "substance" by singling out and picking on "sissy boys."

Blow Job, too, situates gender performance in relation to culturally received notions of essence and fabrication, substance and appearance. The way the film signifies these terms may be related to the subversion of the mimetic field through the simulacrum. The film repetitively displays the various masculine types and stereotypes in a way that accords them the status of cultural citations that hold visual and ontological equality. If these overt and incongruous citations of masculinity are to Plato's simulacrum what an impression of the poser's gender as "natural" is to the concept of the "eligible" copy, the film would seem to disturb an essential distinction between simulacrum and copy. In other words, the film blurs the line between the documentary-like impression of a specific masculine subject, a "real man," so to speak, and a host of artificial male stereotypes mainly taken from pop culture. In addition, the masculine if somewhat suspect styles of some of the icons *Blow Job* evokes (consider Dean) are amplified by the film's allusion to prohibitive sexuality, posing, and cruising. *Blow Job*'s image thus homosexualizes a spectrum of masculinities that ranges from alternative to mainstream, from butch to introvert, and from macho to sensitive.

As an idiom of gay performance, *Blow Job*'s simulacrum subversively rearticulates masculinity. However, one might ask whether the film's gender simulacrum subsumes all aspects of the poser under its politics of representation, or whether parts of this young man's appearance exceed its mimicking reach. For example, while the simulacrum questions the authenticity of the copy, it is not at all clear whether it questions the model, which, in this case, might be described as the overarching category of maleness. Part of *Blow Job*'s irony lies in the fact that it represents the poser's masculinity and his maleness through the same image, forcing those who desire the poser's cock to make do with his face, which at least *looks* like the face of a male. But if spectatorial investment in the image is played out across a whole range of positions, what is the relation between face and cock? Is the cock a biologically constituted referent that generates both a kind of ur-desire and a kind of ur-meaning that predetermine a range of fantasies and interpretations of gender and sex? Or is the cock conceived and reconceived in these "readings," assuming different valences for different spectators but, significantly, losing its status as anchor for the phallus?

Of course, feminist constructionists have consistently debunked patriarchal culture's attempts at collapsing penis and phallus. Judith Butler, for example, has argued that psychoanalysis, one of Western culture's prominent models for understanding human sexuality, also actually constructs that sexuality, but its phallocentric narratives project this construction as natural. For Butler, sexual identity can be unfettered from phallocentric discourse only by rendering genital sexuality itself discursive: If the penis is not naturally owned by men, male heterosexuality must lose its status as the dominant episteme by which to understand *all* identities. This thesis also pertains to an investigation of gay male identity. Unmasking the psychoanalytic phallus means understanding the dynamics behind the Othering not only of women but also of gay men. A constructionist line of inquiry is thus useful also because it helps us understand whether gay men are, ultimately, simply men or whether they differ from straight men with regard not only to their sexual desire and behavior but also to their psychosexual identity. Yet, for constructionists who are engaged in reimagining sex and the body's capacity for pleasure, gay men pose a certain challenge. While gay men have made their relation to their penises more visible than straight men have, what exactly are the terms of this relation and how does it affect any discussion of the ways gay men have positioned themselves in the social?

These questions revolve around issues of agency and identity: They call for exploring how identity is claimed (for example, at the expense of other identities) and how it is defended on both a mundane, everyday level and a psychoanalytic, psychosexual level; they suggest the need to consider modes of male socialization and ways of engaging in and reformulating traditional male privileges. But because gay men also desire the penis, these inquiries also have to engage with the penis itself: Does the gay desire to suck cock—a desire at the heart of gay male gender performance—affect the phallus in such a way that one might speak of a politically subversive synergy between cock and phallus? On a more general level, the debate revolves around what gives shape to the body, what meanings can be drawn from these shapes, and whether those meanings inhere in the "purely" physical aspects of these shapes or whether they, too, need to be extracted from the same social field in which gender is constructed. To continue this line of inquiry, let us return to the figure of hypochondria, which, I believe, marks a discursive territory in which gay identity literally takes shape.

As noted earlier, in psychoanalytic discourses, hypochondria's and erotogenicity's vacillation between real and imagined body parts are important to the psychosexual formation of the subject. They make the subject knowable to itself as a libidinal and erotic entity. However, constructionist theorists such as Judith Butler have critiqued the Lacanian narrative of subject formation for positing an *overdetermined* metonymic relationship between the genitals and other body parts (such as the erotogenic zones) and for projecting these into a unified whole, enabling the narrator to naturalize what is, in fact, constructed.[9] By fantasizing a causal and transparent link between his penis, his masculinity, and his sexual orientation, the heterosexual man thus misrecognizes himself as naturally male, masculine, and straight. While radically questioning this genital overdetermination, Butler nevertheless holds on to certain Freudian insights about hypochondria and erotogenicity. For example, if both are marked by the vacillation between real and imagined body parts, this vacillation makes it impossible to speak about a body part that would "exist" prior to its idea. An example of both hypochondria and erotogenicity would be the penis in a state of excitation, when it is particularly vulnerable and sensitive to external impact (such as pain) but not, in fact, afflicted.[10] If the penis does not exist prior to its idea, Butler argues, there is no longer a reason to see the metonymic relation between the penis, other body parts (such as the face), and psychosexual identity as a whole as being overdetermined.

A case in point would be the penis of *Blow Job*'s poser: Because its utilization and stimulation are questionable, and because it exists only by virtue of being metonymically substituted by the poser's face, the film becomes an overdetermined metaphor in its own right for the social construction of gender and its impact on the perception of sex. For if the poser's cock does not exist prior to its idea, in the dynamics of gay spectatorial desire its hardness is not encountered as a prediscursive materiality that is subsequently chosen as something desirable. Instead, it is produced *as* hardness, as substance in the act of desiring it. This specific production of substance is still a production of identity. But it is also, and more clearly than ever, an act of projection, in which the gay male viewer no longer simply presupposes the poser's cock. Rather, he always also produces it in various shapes and sizes. Since the poser's cock exists only in metonymic relation to other body parts, which make it accessible in the first place, it can be imagined only in terms of these body parts. But these body parts, to the extent that they are visible on the screen, may exist without it. The cock is thereby no longer necessarily involved in the image's metonymic chain of associations.

This chain is radically expanded by the postmodern drag queen, whose relation to the penis is much more fluid. The penis exists as body matter but is divested from reactionary cultural meanings. The drag queen articulates discourses of sex and gender via a combination of penile and vaginal discourses. In many ways the ultimate simulacrum, she produces the model of a "real" woman in new ways and thereby redefines gender reality as gender "realness."[11] If "realness" means that the simulacrum actually replaces the model, the drag queen is a privileged signifier, as she disturbs semiolinguistic fixity most effectively. In other words, she mixes metaphors, and she mixes them in subversive ways (consider the range of butch and femme drag queens). But can something comparable also be said of masculine-identified gay men? The penis, having been an overdetermined metaphor of maleness and remaining the object of desire and identification for gay men, retains its prominent position within masculine-identified gay male performance. However, the fact that the masculine-identified gay male simulacrum, in contrast to the drag queen, always ends up reproducing the model does not necessarily mean that he does not also produce it "from scratch." In addition, the masculine-identified gay simulacrum signifies the vaginal metaphor, too, if through further displacement, such as the desire to be anally penetrated by the penis. A constructionist perspective may thus argue that while the gay male simulacrum never completely replaces the model, at least he still constantly displaces it.

If one wanted to be catty about queer theory's relation to masculine-identified gay men, one might remark that constructionists—no matter how much they may try to salvage gay male identity from the political baggage of the penis—have yet to succeed in deconstructing the penis away. However, what has emerged in the theorization of gay male identity is the need to focus on the relation between the penis and the phallus. How do gay men's relation to their cocks influence other aspects of their sexual, social, and racial/ethnic identities? If one claims, as I do, that the gay male simulacrum at the very least qualifies and stratifies the desire for the cock into multiple relationalities, but if one must also recognize that the patriarchal phallus seeks recourse to the penis as proof and originator of its erectile identity, is it possible—or even worth the effort—to develop a concept of the "gay phallus" as a politically productive signifier of variants of gay male identity and gay male agency?[12] How—if at all—would the possibility of displacing the penis negate the concept of phallic identification? I believe the phallus is worth retaining as a concept for theoretical reasons, as it describes psychic processes of identification in terms of specular relations, which have been central not only to the general investigation of cinema as a medium but also to my focus on gay visualizations during the postwar era. In addition, some of the accounts of gay culture and history discussed earlier in this book have described a significantly qualified phallicism—which also implicitly questions the significance of the penis as ontologically privileged originator of the narrative of psychosexual identity formation. Finally, if it is true, as Judith Butler argues, that even gay and lesbian identities adhere to psychoanalytic master narratives to the extent that, like all identities, they are based on exclusion,[13] a reconceptualization of phallic identification may help us gain insight into how gay male identities produce abjection and what exactly it is that is cast as prohibitive in the process of their erection.

Blow Job consolidates the phallic identity of its young man by keeping his penis invisible. The poser's face metonymically substitutes for the penis and becomes an index for the penis as a source of pleasure. This observation leads us down two lines of inquiry, which will now be explored for the ways in which they attribute different valences to gay men's positions in the social based on the relationship between penis and phallus.

The first line reads the cock's hiddenness as indicating that gay men are simply men and, as such, are socialized as patriarchal males. The image is phallicized in the sense that the poser seems to derive his power and pleasure from an *invisible, generative* source that leads to conventional heterosexual male (self-)positioning and implies (however illusorily) the assumption of male power, untouchability, self-sufficiency, and autonomy. To the extent that the phallus is a metaphor that delineates the formation of identity in the social field, it configures the phallic gay male subject always at least partly as a conventionally socialized subject of patriarchy. In this function, the gay phallus identifies gays not apart from but in relation to heterosexual males; it defines the gay subject as a subject of ideology, as a subject of power relations, and, particularly in the case of white gay men, as a hegemonic subject.

A brief example illustrates this point: The gay beefcake of male physique magazines of the 1950s resignified heterosexual macho masculinity, because the particular performativity of his body (his self-objectification and effeminization) subverted conventional phallicism. Yet, while the beefcake thus introjected gay specificity into dominant culture, its mode of production and presentation also replicated traditional heterosexual models of capitalist consumption and fetishization. Tom Waugh describes the postwar genre of the homoerotic posing film as "the most naked, frontal enactment of the sexual pleasure of looking at the male body, the most unquestioning assumption of our socialization as males, gay or straight, within a culture that privileges the male sexual regard."[14] Hence, the dynamics of gay male and straight male identification are not as mutually exclusive as are their objects of desire. Gay-bashing and homophobia notwithstanding, what gay men had in common with heterosexual bachelors and stags was the freedom to celebrate their socialization as males. For example, just as straight bachelors began to enjoy *Playboy* magazine and its various imitators, gay men, too, quickly came to control the production and consumption of their own soft-core porn industry. Unlike straight men, of course, gay men reveled in self-objectification. However, looking at the example of the gay posing film, Waugh points out that this self-objectification often actually refuted specifically gay and queer aspects by articulating an attitude and aesthetics of conventional phallic hardness. As Waugh notes, "[The posing film] was also a denial of all of this, the most explicit embodiment of the physique alibi. It disavowed the cult of homoerotic desire through the profession of a cult in some ways every bit as marginal, the cult of the hyperdeveloped muscle. It was predicated on the masking of the phallus not only by the posing strap but also by the bicep, the doctrine of 'Look but don't touch.'"[15] This look-but-don't-touch attitude in some ways sums up the situation of gay men in the postwar era: The pose and the hyperdeveloped muscle contained gay male desire as much as it contributed to its expansion. Significantly, this strategy may have warded off gay men who did not have such hyperdeveloped muscles or otherwise failed to meet the general standards of masculine beauty propagated by physique culture. If gay identity, like any identity, is erected partly on prohibition and abjection, the gay phallus of physique culture may be based on the prohibition of such stereotypes as the effeminate fag and the drag queen.

Of course, the very concept of alternative masculinity was an invention of patriarchal culture. Corresponding to its own (initially) marginal position, *Playboy* magazine, for example, which emerged in 1955, could concern itself with everything hip and alternative as long as it supplied its bachelor readership with female pinups. Part of the hipness was an image of alternative masculinity, of nonconformism, individuality, independence, and anti–nuclear family attitudes.[16] Predictably, giving up male privileges was not part of this hipness. In this sense, alternative masculinity in and of itself guarantees neither the end of heterosexism nor the end of male sociocultural dominance. This, of course, holds true also for white gay men.

However, several points suggest that white gay men at this point also significantly differed from straight, upwardly mobile male singles. Barbara Ehrenreich notes that the playboy's rampant heterosexuality easily dispelled suspicions of homosexuality.[17] His conspicuousness, however, may have been founded on his fear of the latent presence of homosexual signifiers. While the playboy might have conceived of himself as a sexual libertarian heroically attempting to loosen the rigid postwar sexual mores, it is just as reasonable that he would have welcomed mainstream efforts to contain homosexuality ethnographically, since they helped him demarcate himself from his double.[18] This double, in turn, made every effort to play up the very elements of 1950s masculinity that his heterosexual counterpart attempted to minimize or disavow. In addition, the fact that gay erotic magazines and films met with even more censorship than *Playboy* magazine— a form of censorship primarily based not on middle-class moralism but on a form of psychosexual abjection termed "homophobia"—strongly suggests that the differences between the gay phallus and the straight male phallus weigh at least as heavily as their similarities. Therefore, we need to consider the second line of inquiry suggested by the phallicized image of *Blow Job*'s poser.

While the poser's face becomes a metonymic substitute for the pleasures of the cock, *Blow Job* also reverses the process of metonymic substitution. It constitutes the poser's penis not only as the imaginary origin, but also as the imaginary end result, of the poser's facial expressions. Viewers may ponder the poser's face for some time before they actually arrive at imagining the penis, and this fantasy may have to compete with other fantasies, also possibly both source and effect of the poser's facial expressions. Some viewers may not imagine the poser's penis at all. Engrossed by the image's aesthetic impact, they may import their own cultural assumptions and libidinal fantasies into the image that are not overdetermined by genital sexuality. In other words, the penis is dislodged from its position as originator of the metonymic chain of substitutions. One could even go so far as to claim, as Callie Angell has, that the poser may be brought to orgasm not through direct genital stimulation but by the act of being filmed.[19] To the extent that the fetish is usually defined as a placeholder for the real conditions of existence, *Blow Job* illustrates how these conditions are themselves as fluid and diverse as the functions of the fetish itself. They can be known only through the libidinal investment that constitutes the fetish. Thus these conditions can be thought of as just an infinite number of fetishes.

A gay male perspective recognizes the duality of *Blow Job*'s phallicized image: The poser identifies (with) his cock as a tool to be served by other men, while his face also conveys a desire to serve other men's cocks. Gay men denaturalize the relationship between penis and phallus by straddling both sides of the phallus: They have the phallus (they desire to possess other objects) and they are the phallus (they want to be possessed as an object by others). In fact, it is from the joy of being possessed by others—by other gay men and by the viewers who possess the image—that *Blow Job*'s poser derives his prowess. In patriarchal mainstream North American culture, a gay man's ability to be possessed by other gay men depends on the visibility of his body. In *Bringing Out Roland Barthes*, D. A. Miller explains how gay men's inclination to flaunt the outlines of their genitals in briefs constitutes their expropriation of the heterosexual phallus. Lending contours to one's private parts flies in the face of patriarchy's prohibition of male objectification. According to Miller, this prohibition results in "an immodest practice of hiding the penis, which disappears into a cool rectangularity that (already anticipating the suit that is such underwear's 'logical' and ethical extension) only apotheosizes it as the phallus. In boxer shorts, a man no longer has a dick; he becomes one."[20] By attaining muscular bodies, gay men do not run risk of being confused with straight machos. The straight body is a mercenary *tool for* labor and for the domination of others; the gay body an openly flaunted *site of* labor and of transgressive desire. According to Miller, "Even the most macho gay image tends to modify cultural fantasy about the male body if only by suspending the main response that the armored body seems developed to induce: if this is still *the body that can fuck you, etc.*, it is no longer—quite the contrary—*the body you don't fuck with*."[21]

It is this paradoxical idealization of the self as a submissive (subjected) subject and as a dominant, assertive object that constitutes the gay phallus. As a theoretical concept, the gay phallus introduces novel possibilities with regard to understanding gay identity. It has helped shape gayness as a sexuality and an identity, and it is crucial to gay self-assertion, which is indispensable in the fight against anti-gay oppression. Perhaps it is not the gay phallus's semiotic makeup that is its most important feature, but its capacity for celebrating the gay self—the gleeful embrace of the *necessity* for idealizing the self—that has been a strategy of gay survival under, for example, AIDS-related discrimination by government, media, and fundamentalists. Twenty years before the beginning of the AIDS epidemic in the United States, *Blow Job* constructed a self-reflexive image of phallic objectification, as it objectified our culture's deep desire to collapse penis and phallus. Obviously, neither the film nor psychoanalytic narratives of identity formation honor this desire. Yet, while traditional psychoanalytic discourses would read *Blow Job*'s configuration of desire in terms of lack, a historical perspective on *Blow Job* might redefine lack as concrete, external prohibition and censorship—censorship that necessitated a *displaced* signification and produced elaborate systems of gay-specific performances and styles. Allegories of their own conditions of censorship, images of 1950s physique culture theatricalized gay identity in relation to its own prohibitions, for it was through prohibition that homosexuality first became defined. Thus, gay identity makes visible the formation of identity in general: Identity formation involves fetishism and disavowal, substitution and displacement. But unlike heterosexuality, whose dominant status has allowed it to sediment into an array of naturalized identities, homosexuality never had the option to consistently disavow the status of abjectness itself. Historically, it has always been formulated in close relation to abjectness. It is to this relation that we now turn.

MASCULINITY, MASOCHISM, AND MELODRAMA—
OR, BERSANI'S RANT

The gay phallus was arguably central to the evolution of gay male identity from the 1940s to the 1960s, as it guided gay men's forays into the homophobic public sphere and influenced their public and private self-presentations. The aesthetic and utilitarian aspects of gay male self-stylizations during the postwar period and beyond suggest that the gay phallus has enabled a range of performance strategies—indeed, that gay male performance may be largely strategic to begin with. Yet, gay performance is also a good example of how strategizing vis-à-vis and within hegemonic systems makes it extremely difficult to resist or even so much as question and qualify the basic elements that make up these systems, such as the concepts of production and productivity, the telos of prosperity and success, the ethics of communitarianism, certain deeply ingrained values still projected onto various identities, and, indeed, the indispensability of the very concept of identity. Leo Bersani has made a number of more detailed observations in this regard. First, he finds that while gays and lesbians may have more visibility and cultural acceptance today than ever before, these forms of empowerment have yet to translate into the legislative/executive areas of federal and state politics. To effect political change, gays and lesbians are as dependent as ever on the political patronage of liberal heterosexuals. In addition, while gay and lesbian agency may well have resulted in the triumphant claim "We are everywhere," it can also come to mean "We are nowhere." In focusing on what they can contribute to dominant society, as Bersani notes, "gays have been de-gaying themselves in the very process of making themselves visible."[22] According to Bersani, this new invisibility is more damaging than the earlier one because it threatens to make gays largely tautologous with mainstream America.

Concerned with the definitional dilemmas of gay identity, Bersani argues that homosexuality be returned to what he believes are its "fundamentals"—sex between men that entails an ecstatic, antisocial loss of self. According to Bersani, homosexuality is a desire for the same, and "homo-specificity" is the radical inaptitude to fetishize (and thus, of course, to fear) difference, an inaptitude that entails and evinces a proclivity for *passivity* and *self-abdication*.[23] In the words of David Halperin (one of Bersani's targets and subsequent critics), this manner of defining homosexuality amounts to reducing homosexuality "to its specificity as a sexual practice, to treat it not as either central or marginal but rather as a crime against civilisation, an attack on the foundations of social life as we know it."[24]

Much of this section is devoted to Bersani's arguments, not so much because some of these have flown in the face of constructionist theorists but because his notion of "homo-specificity," while conceptually rocky and idealist, has a certain heuristic value for my own thinking about gay male identity and, significantly, for theorizing gay male agency in new ways. No doubt, Bersani's argument foregoes applicability to the North American queer-activism–queer-theory complex. But to the extent that this argument concerns itself with the loss of agency, it may from a reverse (his critics would say, adverse) angle throw more light on the ways in which gay men are forced to deal with the loss of agency every day—as caused, for example, by homophobia.

As noted earlier, the postwar gay male posing film is an example of how homophobia—inflicted from without *and* from within—not only inspires agency but clearly deprives gay men of it. Even though the posing genre's semiotics of masculinity, forged under external censorship, arguably effected a temporary crisis in representation and thus denaturalized the falsely essentialist nature of gender and sexuality, it continued to partake in deeply ingrained norms, dicta, and prohibitions. Gender reconstructed, no matter how subversively, is still gender constructed against cultural anathema and psychosexual taboo, which can be so resilient to change that their power appears *substantive*, not functional. Bersani reaffirms constructionism's tenet that power is not prior to but imbricated with the social and psychosexual construction of the self. But he claims that constructionists are deeply beholden to the concept of power that comes to be reflected in what he perceives as constructionism's "de-genitalization" of the body: the expansion of the concept of sexuality to one of erotogenicity, which affects all parts of the body, which defines the sexual body as a disciplined body, and which designates the body as a site of power struggles.

Since the concepts of power and the self are braided, for Bersani a more radical displacement of power must entail an equally radical displacement—or even negation— of the self. Exploring this idea with regard to gay male identity, Bersani draws on psychoanalytic concepts of masochism and, particularly, on masochism's provocative embracing of pain and passivity as evident, for example, in S/M. If pain signals us to flee from anything threatening the body and, on a psychoanalytic level, the integrity of the ego, to embrace pain means to ignore this warning and to enable—even court—the dissolution of one's ego. This favoring of pain is taboo and constitutes masochism as a psychological and cultural perversion,[25] a status enhanced by masochism's designation of pain (which is never fully desexualized to begin with) in close proximity to pleasure. S/M's conspicuous display of sex as both hyperbolic self-assertion and self-dissolution evidently points to the twin forces and dual needs central to human sexuality—exercising power *and* abdicating power for the obtainment of pleasure.[26] Yet, Bersani sees S/M's true potential not in the neutralization of power through role switching but rather in the perverse pleasure masochists take in pain, passivity, and the abdication of power. If the seeking of pleasure is basically ego-building, and if pain, by contrast, is the protection mechanism against the ego's self-dissolution, masochism's ignoring of pain helps S/M subvert "larger coercive designs" more radically, that is, beyond strategic resignification. Encapsulating his particular interest in masochism, Bersani writes, "If there is anything that needs to be accounted for in masochism, it is not a supposed identity of pain and pleasure, but rather a passion for the pleasure so intense that extreme pain is momentarily tolerated (rather than loved for its own sake) as necessary to bring the masochist to that biochemical threshold where painful stimuli begin to produce pleasurable internal substances."[27] S/M can thus potentially make pleasure flourish, not in complete independence from but alongside the erotic disciplining of sexuality.[28] When pleasure becomes so strong as to overwhelm the conventions that have facilitated it, it also becomes profoundly anti-communitarian. Once a certain threshold of intensity is reached, sexual pleasure becomes indifferent to the object in sex[29] and threatens to erode a whole set of functions and forces that oppressively control our sexualities: the compulsion to conquer and dominate the sex partner(s); the compulsion to psychologize the sex partner for the sake of knowledge; and the compulsion to *gender* the sex partner, which recasts into sexual difference the shared recognition and celebration of what, according to Bersani, *could* be a fundamental sameness or "homo-ness."[30] It comes as no surprise that for Bersani a disengagement of sex from relationality remains officially taboo: It could teach a growing community of practitioners the values of powerlessness (and, by extension, the value of recognizing a fundamental sameness). Phallocentrism, as Bersani rightly points out, is ultimately the denial of the value of powerlessness.[31]

Bersani's writing is interesting in that it attempts to link the loss of agency to an area of gay men's lives—illicit sexual behavior—that other theories of gay identity would rather like to ignore, as it fails to fit into strategies of courting acceptability. Examples of the persecution of illicit sex abound on a daily level. Consider the gay school teacher who recently was entrapped and arrested for cruising at a rest stop off a Florida highway and had to fear that his job might be taken away and his life ruined.[32] Consider also the case of eighteen-year-old Matthew Limon, who was arrested for having consensual oral sex with a boy one month shy of his fifteenth birthday and who, under the Kansas sodomy law, was sentenced to seventeen years in prison, a sentence upheld by the Kansas Court of Appeals on February 5, 2002. Had Limon's friend been female, he would have been sentenced to thirteen to fifteen months. These examples illustrate the ferociously violent and intractable pattern of anti-gay oppression. They are also particularly violent instances of gay men's loss of agency, where the violence of this loss resides not only in the randomness and gratuitousness of the persecution but in the abjection of its subject as unworthy and perverted.

There is probably no one who takes the concept of sex outside the law as literally as Bersani, who attempts to theorize it past culturally conventional heroism toward the area of the abject. He argues that gay sex per se is inimical to phallocentrism as a psycholinguistic, social, and legal phenomenon, which implies that the law without which illicit gay sex falls is so fundamental that any particular state law of, say, statutory rape (Limon's case) is but its most superficial manifestation. Yet even though statistics, if they existed, would probably be on Bersani's side in identifying the bulk of illicit sexual behavior as gay male, gay men are certainly not the only ones to practice sex outside the law and to suffer the loss of agency as a result. Are gay men unique here only because some of them have, at certain times, demanded the right to have the kind of sex they want? But if so, does not Bersani, in positing the gay outlaw who constantly flirts with disaster, conflate homo-specificity with a minority group which has, in particular historical contexts, protested the legal classification of "sex offender?" Or does homo-specificity refer to something altogether more basic than the disaster gay men flirt with? Does homo-specificity enable us to draw a distinction between two kinds of loss of agency, only the first of which would be violent abjection by the state apparatus?

The disaster of incarceration, the knee-jerk nature and reprehensibility of which are matched only by the havoc it wreaks on those detained, would have to be regarded as a response to the profound threat posed to the patriarchal fabric by another loss of agency, a form of abjectness deeply desired and persistently courted by gay men. Gay men actively bring about this abjectness by actively seeking out sexual scenarios that, in turn, subject them to a spectrum of object positions ranging from the happenstance character of illicit cruising to the dissolution of the self in anal penetration. It is of course true that the pleasure in transgressive sex is defined by the very boundary transgressed. Yet it simply makes no sense to assume that the ultimate kick gay men get out of illicit sex is that, if caught, they could go to jail and lose their jobs. One may perhaps concur with Bersani's characterization of S/M—that the lure of the loss of agency and the taste for adventure are so appealing to gay men that the potential consequences of getting caught (which are different from the actual moment of getting caught that may be imagined as a turn-on) are considered only in the abstract, if at all. Certainly the dynamics of and stakes in transgression are ripe for a much closer (possibly book-length) investigation.

Patriarchal society severely punishes gay men for pursuing the loss of agency; yet probably because this loss of agency is so irredeemable, so transgressive, and so prohibitive on the basic levels of language and law, gay men have not been able to utilize the reverse-discourse model on their behalf and have thus failed to politicize their pursuit as worthy of legal-political protection. In addition, white gay men in particular frequently incur the charge from parts of both the gay and straight communities that they have taken white male privilege to a new extreme by successfully capitalizing on their whiteness *and* their maleness. In light of all these factors, the concept of homo-specificity as formulated by Bersani (a white gay man himself) must be considered, above all, as a symptomatic response to a larger dilemma, which can be formulated as the question, What are the terms and conditions that, on the one hand, produce white gay men as abject Other and that, on the other hand, prevent white gay men's very distinction as something other than what they are usually taken for—white men? While Bersani fails to answer this question on the level of theory, his discourse consistently amplifies it as a dilemma. On this level, it is worth reading his work heuristically for the frustrations he runs up against and for the homo-specificity that he ultimately *fails* to establish.

How, then, do these frustrations and failures surface? When Bersani discusses the radical dissolution of the self, he is forced to acknowledge that this dissolution is temporally limited and can be measured only in terms of certain effects. He juxtaposes these to strategic productions of power, characterizing them as "the non-strategic effects of the body's exercises in power."[33] No doubt these effects have a pervasive existence, but can they be systematically cultivated within the broader field of power without being turned into yet another regime of power? Bersani acknowledges that it may be all but impossible to render a description of pain not tied to its function as a protection mechanism. When he then nonetheless charges that S/M, rather than exploring its radical potential, makes itself special for the wrong reasons, it seems he is really reproaching S/M for not being a more orthodox subgenre of abject art. The matured subject who practices S/M, in Bersani's view, seems biochemically and culturally compelled to instantly transform or transvalue pain into pleasure; masochists, far from enjoying pain, have devised strategies to bypass pain; the chemicals released through S/M suppress pain and also produce euphoric pleasure—a process complemented by a highly ritualized, even melodramatic histrionics. Hailed by some as destabilizing representations of sex and power, for Bersani these theatricalizations are not a blessing but a curse. They instantly recast pain *as* pleasure, whereby S/M becomes little more than a conventional utterance that is object-oriented and that constructs the illusion of an enunciating subject—it becomes a strategic production of power, melodramatic theater played for an audience.

The problematic presence of melodrama as a "performing arts" genre then points to a larger problem: Even if Western culture were to succeed in "hollowing out" its power structures, in demoting them to an empty framework or completely neutral forum in which pleasures could be cultivated in gradually growing independence from power itself, these power structures are intricately intertwined—in many cases absolutely identical with—their *representation*. Even if they became reduced to bare grids, they would still stake out the terms and parameters for the visualization of pleasure, although this pleasure may be connected to them only tenuously. For example, the frenzy of power that pornography displays is always a frenzy of the visible, as it is produced entirely for and within the visual. But pornography is merely the most drastic example of the fact that the primacy of the visual produces oppressively universalist parameters for the apprehension of pleasure: Pleasure exists and can be measured as long as it can be seen—and what cannot be seen is nonetheless assumed to register "indirectly" visually. It is subsumed under the same set of parameters that mark the boundaries within which we define what is pleasurable. Hence, the criteria and constructs that define pleasure, criteria in and of themselves human-made and, thus, ultimately delimited, can pass themselves off as universal. This is precisely also what enables S/M as a "performing art" to lie to itself, as it were, and pretend that it partakes in pain for its own teleology: S/M claims that it pursues pain *as* pleasure, whereas pain is really only put up with to get to a pleasure that has little to do with pain. This teleology is enacted through the visual field of S/M's histrionics, in which pain is made to *pass* as pleasure. According to Bersani, the practice as a whole becomes glossed and falsified: Pain is falsely and retroactively characterized as pleasure, and all we are left with is melodrama.

Within Bersani's theory, S/M's pleasurable melodramatic histrionics come to function as a veil, an instance of subversive mimesis in the Deleuzian sense. Its simulacrum conquers and universalizes the mimetic field, proffering a range of pleasures which, in their theatricality, seem to surpass or subvert a whole range of far less flamboyant copies of the Idea of sexual pleasure (for example, sex without Prince Alberts and nipple clamps), but it nonetheless upholds sexual pleasure *as* the Idea. The simulacrum renders sexual pleasures into one more touchstone for the pervasive teleologization of Western society. Even if superficially transgressive, sex can be rendered redeemable. Even S/M can ultimately be communitarian, ego-building, individualizing, in short, empowering. The simulacrum prevents the identification of the mimetic field as a *delimited* field and, thus, as yet another (if hegemonic) fabrication. S/M's superficial transgressiveness disguises the fact that it still stands in relation to the model: It could be a radical *practice* (if it undid the regime that sets the parameters for the discursive codification of pleasure), but all it amounts to is yet another pseudo-original *disciplinary production.*

One may object that it is really Bersani's notion of pleasure, and not S/M's, that courts the model in the Platonic regime of essences. In fact, Bersani's notion of masochism as the key to "authentic" sexual pleasure in a sea of inauthentic disciplinary erotic productions is very similar to the notion of high art (in a sea of mass culture) proffered by Theodor Adorno and Max Horkheimer, whose critique of the Enlightenment is also anchored in a discussion of the Platonic system of essences and substances.[34] But Bersani's objections against S/M's facetious investment in pain as pleasure are still useful, as they help us to understand dialectically how taboos tend to get produced and negotiated. We can conclude from Bersani's caveat about S/M that S/M's rhetorical subsumption of pain under a teleology of pleasure is analogous to the similarly rhetorical subsumption of sex under the teleology of heterosexual reproduction. And melodrama comes to function structurally within S/M much like the incest taboo functions within foundation myths of civilization in that it *masks* the fact that there is a sliding scale between what has come to be artificially divided into two regimes (in this case, two kinds of masochism). Just as the incest taboo reinscribes the teleology of civilized sex into the preverbal (by labeling nonreproductive sex "primitive" and by placing it on the other side of utilitarian, language-related, reproductive sex), melodrama reinscribes the teleology of ego formation into its concept of masochism and recasts masochism's radical potential (which might be characterized as the *jouissance* of self-dissolution) as the great bugaboo of theories of psychosexual formation—the death drive. On this side of the great divide stands the only acceptable form of masochism—the one that is saintly, self-sacrificial, and performed for the greater good. In other words, melodrama is to masochism what pro-creative sex is to sex. As a deliberate performance of pain for an audience —whether in certain stage acts that theatricalize the performer's calamities or in such mainstream examples as the famous filibuster in Frank Capra's *Mr. Smith Goes to Washington*—melodrama instantly transvalues self-annihilation into unilateral and teleological self-assertion and thereby renders more radical forms of self-dissolution taboo.

To refocus this theorization of agency on gay male identity, we can note that *Blow Job*, for example, also exemplifies key aspects of Bersani's argument and the challenges he encounters in attempting to link the loss of agency to transgressive gay sex and gay masculinity. The rigid duality that marks *Blow Job*'s simultaneous signifying and masking of illicit sexual activity makes the film both index and allegory of the framework within which gay male identity has come to be accepted for assimilation. This framework designates not only mainstream society's attitude toward the sexualization of the male body but also what Bersani laments about the queer academy—that is, the disciplinary sexualization of all parts of the body via the concept of erotogenicity, which has led to the displacement of genital sexuality. Having to make do with the poser's face, we observe that this face, although possibly eroticized, disallows us to qualitatively distinguish what Bersani calls the "non-strategic effects of the body's exercise of power" from the strategic productions of power. *Blow Job* becomes an example for our inability to determine whether and on what terms it might be possible to visualize humans' desire for self-abdication as a momentous truth—an unexpected paroxysm that nonetheless happens within a contractual framework, a truth unsolicited yet "confessable." After all, this framework introduces the important vector of consensus and, thus, immediately blurs the line between strategies and effects, between artifice and authenticity. The perverse impulses in *Blow Job*'s poser's face that mark the pleasures of passivity and self-abdication are absorbed in the apocryphal quality of the overall display. Even if these impulses register visually, they ultimately may not be dissociated from strategic performance. If they indicate the poser's flirt with transgressing the law of masculinity, his potential recourse to strategy keeps all of his expressions within reach of the psycholinguistic *system* that issues these laws in the first place.

Consider, for example, the earlier discussion of the display of masochism in the poser's face: I selected two groups of stills from *Blow Job* that I presented as symptomatic of the way in which the poser signifies masochism—one set of frames indicating the poser's broadly masochistic abandon to the act (see Figures 4.1, 4.2, and 4.3) and another set showing the poser in more "flamboyantly" melodramatic poses (see Figures 4.4, 4.5, 4.6, and 4.7). Ultimately, a distinction between these impressions is difficult and highly specious because of the impossibility of distinguishing visually between a substantive and a strategic definition of pain. However, the flamboyance of the second set of stills seduces me into making this distinction and prompts me to designate (however falsely) the first set as showing a more "authentic" masochism. This impression hails from the infectious presence of melodrama—a powerful master text that seeks to authenticate its overall teleology of ego formation by polemically recasting some of its elements as authentic masochistic expressions (again, see Figures 4.1 to 4.3). It also corresponds to the Platonic system's competing concepts of essences and (dis)simulations as outlined by Deleuze: While the simulacrum subversively shows that the copy is closer to it than to the model (whereby the model is upheld as essentially different from all copies), it always helps divide the world into good and bad imitations and always implicitly authenticates the good copy. What the good copy has to show for itself are those nonstrategic bodily effects (uncontrolled twitches of the poser's eyebrows, cheeks, and mouth area). They puncture the screen in a way that is comparable to Barthes's punctum, registering as visual irregularities, hitting spectators in a manner Hal Foster has described as the "return of the real." But since the punctum is no more real than its visual environment, the return of the real is an *effect* produced by the interplay of punctum and overall mise-en-scène. The artifice in Figures 4.4 to 4.7, then, does not subvert the effect of an authentic masochism. On the contrary, it produces it precisely *as* an effect, which then enhances the overall impression of the performative prowess of the fully developed, fully strategic, if melodramatic ego.

Melodrama in this context assumes a paradoxical function: *Culturally* assigned to women, melodrama here *structurally* designates masculinity. It produces a frisson that is characteristic of straight masculine-identified masochism and that finds its perhaps best known and "classic" variant in straight male travesty. The inclusion of elements of femininity supports the ontologization of the performer's gender as masculine (as can be found in such temporary transvestite narratives as *Tootsie* and *Mrs. Doubtfire*,[35] but also in nontransvestite contexts, such as depictions of the male protagonist in film noir). *Blow Job*'s poser's masochism, while destabilizing gender to a certain extent, always maintains recourse to gender's renaturalization. Paradoxically, elements conventionally assigned to femininity are harnessed into the overall impression that the poser looks and feels like a natural, "real" man, if a masochistic one.[36]

Much of Bersani's argument against constructionist and postmodern psychoanalytic theories seems motivated by the dilemmas he encounters in theorizing masochism—dilemmas that, as we have seen, are also apparent in *Blow Job*'s production of the "healthy" melodramatic ego. Because outlaw sex makes many gay men fall outside phallocentrically motivated juridical laws, Bersani aims to develop a concept of gay male sex, gay male desire, and gay male identity that would, as it were, cement this outlaw status with psychosexual findings. In this way, he hopes to point to new ways by which to theorize gay men's oppression and gay men's status as a minority. He persuasively argues that gay men subversively appropriate dominant models of macho masculinity not because these models become resignified on the surface of the gay male body but because of the particular way in which these models become "killed," so to speak, and *buried* in the gay man's anus. While gay men may internalize the butch model by aping it, they also lethally violate it by having themselves anally penetrated, which goes against everything this model stands for.[37] To the extent that gay hypervirility connotes femininity and female sexuality, it terrifies straight men with the specter of anal penetration. According to Bersani, the real reason that gay sex incites such public phobia is not because of what gay men look like but because of what the homophobic mind-set imagines that gay men do. The phallocentric imaginary associates gay male sex and gay male identity with passivity, promiscuity, and contamination—in other words, with performing a form of sexuality that has been associated primarily with women and particularly with prostitutes and that represents a cluster of stereotypical features that may be termed abject femininity.[38]

When Bersani argues that "what passes for the real thing self-destructs from within its theatricalized replication" and "the imaginary negates the real to which it purportedly adheres,"[39] he is emphasizing that gay male signification has a dual potential that enables gay men to explore certain implications of abjectness precisely without killing themselves. (In this sense, the mass decimation of gay men through AIDS is seen *not* as a result of gay male desire but, emphatically, as a symptom of gay men's medical-political oppression). Gay men are deeply invested in masculinity and, at the same time, never cease to destroy it, which enables them to kill the masculine without killing themselves. Even though Bersani's valorization of gay men's seeking out the abnegation of agency during anal sex is marked by a certain essentialism and has a certain teleology of its own, it constitutes an important intervention in the debate about masochism, repetition/compulsion, and the death drive. If it is not pain that gay men seek but the pleasures that lie beyond it, pain may be ruled out as the central vector in the logic of repetition/compulsion. Pain is then neither the means nor the end of repetition/compulsion, and repetition/compulsion does not aim at self-destruction. In other words, Bersani's claim that gay men put up with pain rather than seek it out during sex importantly dissociates gay sex from the death drive. Death is dissociated from sex and desire and, instead, defined as the consequence of socio-political oppression from without. Bersani thus seeks to depathologize gay sex without resorting to claiming any sort of redemptive qualities for it.

Gay men thus constitute a vanguard in Bersani's theory for two reasons: First, homosexuality, gay sex, and gay desire harbor at least the potential for the negation of power and the negation of the self; and, second, to the extent that these elements, notwithstanding the AIDS catastrophe, have evidently functioned to *support* rather than eradicate a certain sexual and cultural livelihood, gay desire marks a viable alternative to suicidal *jouissance*. This alternative explodes the overdetermined binary between phallocentrism and the death drive. Gay men can "kill" the phallocentric self and still go on living because they seize on phallocentrism's nonsuicidal double—a set of features that have been associated (however insidiously) with abject femininity. In this sense, homosexual desire is desire for the same (the cock) from a perspective of the self (male) already different from itself (non-male).[40]

In this sense, the hyperbolic set of gay muscles in the gay resignification of machismo conveys not only, not even primarily, playful alternative phallicism but its opposite—penetration, passivity, and pain. However, at this point, the dilemma of a universalized mimesis threatens to catch up with Bersani. It is not easy to distinguish between the effects of postmodern play and painful poking, as both partake in the same set of signifiers. Since the vast majority of constructionist theories of gender and sexuality are based on the assumption that the subject is constructed firmly within discourse (of psycholinguistics, of science, of institutions), and since we live in a culture in which the discursive more often than not takes the form of visual representation, the authentication of the gay outlaw and of his transgressive desires escapes neither the parameters of the semiolinguistic nor those of phenomenology. The challenges faced by Bersani's argument illustrate the dilemma of theorizing sex and gender identity based on the elusive nature of desire: To apprehend desire for theoretical and political purposes, one is forced to deal with the concrete shapes in which desire manifests itself. And because desire is given form only through disciplinary productions and their representations, it is not easily apprehended outside these channels. This does not bother constructionists, who view these channels as potentially infinitely expandable and sufficiently heterogeneous for the construction of equally heterogeneous counterstrategies, and who, as I attempted to demonstrate in the earlier discussion of some of these strategies, have gotten a lot of mileage out of this approach. However, for such theorists as Bersani, who advocate focusing on the subject as a site of the *effects* of power and who engage phallocentrism via some of its opposite signifiers—such as passivity, the loss of the self, and explorations of the limits of the discursive (concepts of the abject)—strategic productions are little more than window dressing. While Bersani does not engage Warhol's work, the discussion in this book particularly of the discursive limitations of *Blow Job* illustrates that these productions are epitomized by the Warholian tease, which, from a Bersanian perspective, is to equivocation what mutton is to lamb. *Blow Job*'s textual limitations disallow us to do anything more than hypothesize that the loss of control in the poser's performance, visible as it may be, would ultimately enable that performance to "defect" from the realm into which it is locked—the performing arts.

As one may have gleaned, the central problem here goes deeper: One can deconstruct gender as something that is not essentially determined by nature, but how can one negotiate the challenge posed by the powerful continuum of scientific, legal, and institutional discourses and their visual representations? Particularly with regard to Bersani's argument, which seeks to apprehend and comprehend (the former being the greater challenge) the subject's dissolution of the self, indeed, its fleeting flirt with the abject, would one not have to speak of a different order of the deconstruction of gender, a kind of *demontage?* Hal Foster has pinpointed the challenges of this type of project with regard to how contemporary abject art illustrates the aporia around the problem of signifying abjection. According to Foster, this aporia is brought to a point by a slippage in Julia Kristeva's discourse between "the operation *to abject* and the condition *to be abject*."[41] While the former produces the subject and society as coherent entities and products of sublimation/abjection, the latter is the negation of the self and the social, but it is not clear whether it threatens or helps constitute the former. More particularly, Foster asks:

> Can the abject be represented at all? If it is opposed *to* culture, can it be exposed *in* culture? If it is unconscious, can it [be] made conscious and remain abject? In other words, can there be a *conscientious abjection*, or is this all there can be? Can abject art ever escape an instrumental, indeed moralistic, use of the abject? (In a sense this is the other part of the question: can there be an evocation of the obscene that is *not* pornographic?) . . . If a subject or a society abjects the alien within, is abjection not a regulatory operation? . . . Or can the *condition* of abjection be mimed in a way that calls out, in order to disturb, the *operation* of abjection?[42]

Miming the condition of abjection in this particular way seems to be precisely the goal Bersani strives toward in his theory of an anarchic gay male desire. If one could somehow cultivate gay men's desire for self-dissolution and their frenzied enjoyment of passivity, it could be the beginning of this kind of miming, a less-than-strategic but nonetheless survivalist move with the potential of exposing in culture what is opposed to culture and what poses the only alternative to what a Freudian such as Bersani believes to be behind abjection's self-destructive version—the death drive. Because Bersani's gay outlaw is an internal outlaw, one might polemically describe him, as Marcos Becquer has, as someone who is forced to pass as a man.[43] Although Bersani does not use passing this way, it is not clear whether this is because he is unaware of the radical implications and possibilities of the idea or whether he is disinclined to attempt to reconcile it as an idea with the reality of the socioeconomic and cultural privileges white gay men in particular have enjoyed *as men*. However, Bersani's reticence in this regard has not kept critics from pointing out certain blind spots in his argument: For example, his theorization of the dissolution of the self has been deemed idealistic and schematic. Critics have contended that his confidence in the subversive power of self-abdication rests on his conflation of ego and subject, whereby he ultimately obfuscates what a dissolution of "the self" might consist of concretely.[44] This lacuna gives rise to his schematic proposal to overcome power by erasing power instead of by negotiating power's more localized manifestations.[45] Further, if one measures the value of a theory by its applicability, Bersani's theory is largely useless because, as noted by David Halperin, the totalizing implications he attaches to sexual *jouissance* mute political agency.[46]

But if Bersani's theory is weak as theory, is it of use at all? Recent readings of Bersani's discourse argue that despite the important interplay between queer theory and activism, a programmatic assumption of the integration of theory and practice threatens to subordinate theory to the field of activism and to the inherently compromised (in the sense of strategic) context in which activism must move. To avoid the containment of the flow of ideas, it may be just as important to posit a more complicated relation between theory and practice, one that may even be characterized by mutual resistance.

In this sense, then, while proposals of the abdication of gay male agency seem removed from political intervention, they may be able to trace and to *performatively honor* what pragmatist, activist-oriented queer theory must suppress or discard, so as not to crack under the burden of contradiction—that is, gay men's need to experience, even to embody, passivity. The main area in which Bersani's argument locates this passivity is ecstatic anal sex, but Bersani's concept of the gay outlaw suggests that falling outside the law can be facilitated through self-abjection as well as abjection by others—and here I have in mind those others who may seize gay men in the act of self-abjection and criminalize them, whereby the state of passivity gay men seek on one level (*jouissance*) they end up getting "treated to" on quite another (complete shock triggered by the trauma of humiliation). In this regard, it is Bersani's thinking, not that of most of his constructionist colleagues and perhaps no longer even to be called "theory," that addresses that very first instance when anyone experiences the full violence of his loss of agency. Significantly, this moment is not identical with the moment when this loss gets recounted in outrage to the world (which, again, is queer activism's moment)—it is the moment when the gay man *embodies* this loss because he must; because it is the only way by which he can "catch" himself in the act of being abjected, the only way he can embody his own "I" as a hated, ruined, unworthy mess, before he picks himself up and becomes, once again, outraged. One might even argue that the moment when gay men decide to seek out a situation that might jeopardize them in this way, that may or may not lead to this moment, constitutes a latent acceptance of the possibility of the loss of agency—it is the "flirting-with-disaster" phenomenon, a desire for abjection that, again, no theory can reduce to gay men but which is, perhaps, predominantly experienced by gay men.

With the exception, perhaps, of Lee Edelman, Bersani stands alone among gay male theorists with his interest in the area of abjectness and abjection, which also complicates the way his work must be positioned within the academy. On the one hand, historians such as Halperin have every reason to feel insulted by Bersani's potshots at constructionism and queer theory, particularly since the psychoanalytic work Bersani engages runs risk, as psychoanalytic approaches do, to ignore historical factors. On the other hand, Halperin's criticism of Bersani emphasizing gay men's wishes to be recognized as a sexual minority is not unproblematic either. Halperin states that "the history of miscegenation laws makes this wish less gay-specific than Bersani claims, and in any case does not begin to describe what it is that gay men want. What I want at the moment, for example, includes at least four other things besides sex with impunity."[47] It is certainly true that anxiety about miscegenation still plays itself out in American culture, even though miscegenation laws were drawn up only in part to prevent interracial sex acts. However, unlike the history of anti-sodomy statutes and the closely related prosecution of many areas of gay sexual culture, the history of miscegenation *laws* is precisely that—history. Who is more likely to become the target of police stings—interracial heterosexual couples or gay men?

Halperin is of course right in pointing out that anti-gay oppression takes many forms and necessitates action on many fronts. Yet his claim that he can think of at least four other things besides sex with impunity rings a bit too familiar. While most queer theorists can—and should—think this way, many (including myself) have, at one point or another, been all too willing to swap the "besides sex" for an "instead of sex." It is much easier and potentially more productive to confront the citizens of liberal pluralist America (many of whom look forward to an evening with *Ellen* and *Will & Grace*) with such issues as anti-gay marriage motions or anti-gay adoption laws than trying to get them fired up against the latest police raid on a highway rest area. Whom would one expect to listen, much less to understand? This problem suggests that, three and a half decades after Stonewall, there are still certain areas of gay male identity that are politically unassimilable and that, more often than not, force the theorist-activist's resignation before the issue.

The illicit nature of gay male sexuality is one of the central contexts in which *Blow Job* must be placed. While *Blow Job*'s image opens up a range of interesting readings that, in turn, invite a slew of creative (re)contextualizations, one is always brought back to (and up against) the film's self-censoring framing. And while homosexuality is not the only thing *Blow Job* may be regarded to censor, the context in which we have just discussed illicit gay sex instantly makes clear how *Blow Job* most poignantly allegorizes liberal pluralism's discursive regulation of homosexuality. It is not that liberal pluralism simply acknowledges a range of positions of which homosexuality is but one, or a range of aspects of homosexuality of which sex is but one. In fact, if liberal pluralism thought of "four other things besides sex" the way Halperin does, gay activism would have a powerful ally. It is rather that liberal pluralism has its own strongly centrifugal force that tends to displace or even fully replace sex in its attempt to speak on behalf of gays. From popular movies like *Philadelphia* (1993) to public defenses of George Michael, what is invariably stressed in liberal defenses of homosexuality is its redemptive aspects. There is no question that these defenses have, at times, been the only ones that have come to the aid of gay causes and that gays could count on. And yet the sobering truth is that liberal pluralism has depoliticized homosexuality by turning it into a lifestyle or a personal choice, and many homosexuals have fully complied with this process.

Public gay sex equals illicit gay sex and apparently cannot be incorporated into the agenda of a liberal pro–gay and lesbian culture, a growing white gay and lesbian middle class, or even a coalition of queer activists. Efforts at politicization are quickly crushed, as was recently the case with the New York group *Sex Panic!*, which quickly failed in its efforts to mobilize against the Giuliani administration's closing of public sex places and cruising spots. Because illicit gay sex cannot be assimilated to gay and lesbian politics, it is relegated to the area of "culture" or to the dustbin of history. In this sense, Guy Hocquenghem's *Homosexual Desire*, if it is taught at all, is prefaced with the label "pre-Foucauldian" (read: obsolete), and John Rechy's *The Sexual Outlaw* and Andrew Holleran's *Dancer from the Dance*, whatever else their qualities and merits, are now first and foremost identified as "pre-AIDS fictions." Even the story of a sex/gender transgressor such as Brandon Teena seems ultimately more assimilable to liberal mainstream culture than the idea of a gay man cruising adult movie theaters and parks. To so much as wonder aloud why it is that there is no Academy Award–winning movie about Paul Reubens being arrested in a porno movie theater in Florida is to invite ridicule, for such a question seems to defy common sense. And yet if the appeal of *Boys Don't Cry*, Hollywood's version of the Brandon Teena story, can be explained because it is, more or less, about "four other things besides sex," do not these four other things boil down to one thing, a fine line that constitutes the great divide between what makes one pathetic or heroic—one's redemptive potential? Redemption means everything, not only to liberals. It is largely responsible for the fact that, at least on the level of popular myth, even the most transgressive outlaw can be transformed into his opposite: an inlaw.

Given the unassimilable nature of outlaw sex, Bersani's argument gathers new significance. But even Bersani, in the act of theorizing the gay outlaw, cannot escape the larger challenges and contradictions that befall all of those who attempt to side with the gay outlaw. If one considers Bersani's polemical promotion of sex as "anti-communal, anti-egalitarian, anti-nurturing, anti-loving," if one further considers the general thrust of *Homos* as what is really a book-length *rant*, and, finally, if one considers recent discussions of Bersani that read his discourse as moving "towards an impoverished and dispersed self," enacted through "textual self-dismissal,"[48] it becomes clearer that Bersani may not only not have any answers for the theoretical and political problems he raises but also does not consider the seeking of answers a part of his intellectual agenda. In fact, it becomes clear that Bersani's rant bears certain similarities to a specific subgenre of feminist discourse—abject art—which dramatizes and explores the possibilities of showing the abject/Other. It may not be surprising that Bersani's *discursive mode* ultimately redoubles some of the theoretical challenges and underpinnings of his theory. It seems that Bersani, by enacting his own authorial "self-delegitimation," to borrow one of James S. Williams's terms, transforms himself, if not into an abject artist, then into an abject theorist. This intellectual and emotional pose helps seal his withdrawal into aestheticism and away from any pragmatically or constructively oriented politics, albeit with the provision that anything abject, because it is shocking and controversial, remains latently political.

The postmodern American academy—which, for all its playfulness and radical aspirations, is deeply paranoid, homophobic, and erotophobic—needs Bersani for two reasons: first, for the screaming nature of his rant, and, second, for the heuristic value of his argument. Taking interest in abjectness as a symptom of the great insecurity and fear of phallocentric society, Bersani treats the abject not as a condition in which he wants us all to wallow, but as an *episteme* that centrally leads to the deconstruction and, ideally, the destruction of phallocentric society. In this sense, Bersani's argument may, perhaps, best be glossed in analogy to his own writing on S/M that was quoted earlier: If there is anything that needs to be accounted for in Bersani's theory, it is not a supposed identity of abjectness and anti-phallocentrism, but rather a passion against phallocentrism so intense that the concept of the abject is momentarily tolerated (rather than embraced for its own sake) as a necessary analogy to bring us to that epistemological threshold where we begin to realize that abject impulses begin to produce anti-phallocentric results.

HYPOCHONDRIA AND GAY PERFORMANCE REVISITED— OR, FLIRTING WITH DISASTER

Bersani's attempt to theoretically link masochism, abject femininity, and white gay male identity is of heuristic value because it helps to clarify the contradictory impulses in gay male signification, which are also present in many of the gay representations discussed thus far. We may now better understand why Kenneth Anger's *Fireworks* presented masochism as something that postwar, predominantly white gay male subcultures celebrated as one of its indigenous idioms. In sharp contrast to *The Brick Foxhole*'s characterization of masochism as suicidal, these subcultures regarded masochism as intrinsic to their cultural and sexual livelihood. It helped them negotiate the binary between self-assertion and self-abnegation—and here it is important to bear in mind that during the postwar period the range of implications of the second term was even wider and more horrific than it is now. Bersani's theory also gives new urgency to an analysis of the deeper phobias at work in mainstream culture's association of gay men with femininity —as evidenced, for example, in the film adaptation of *Tea and Sympathy* with its recoding of Tom's putative homosexuality via the female homosocial. (The play's utilization of male homosocial and homoerotic nudity is replaced in the film by the female homosocial, that is, by Tom's seeking out of the faculty wives' sewing circle.) Conservative mainstream culture in the 1950s may have used the category of effeminacy to simultaneously connote and displace the issue of homosexuality, which was still taboo. To escape the socially constructed category of woman to which he fears he is being misassigned, Tom disciplines himself and strategically subjects himself to a training that may help him (ful)fill more effectively the gender he is deeply convinced is his own— after all, by all accounts, he *looks* like a man. However, this same culture may have been on target in a much more profound sense in its skepticism about Tom being a "man to the core."

While Tom, as a product of the mainstream imagination, is invested in having the script of gender expand only to the point that would safely encompass his alternative heterosexuality and rescue him from punishment, Tom's real-life gay male contemporaries may well have been dealing with a different dilemma. Their investment in masculinity was—and if one is to believe Bersani, still is—determined by a deep duality. On one level, they are very invested in masculinity and take it very seriously. After all, they desire sexually what is masculine (although the concept at once begs qualification by such terms as "stylistically" or "hyper-"); their upbringing and cultural environment make them identify with what, for lack of a better term, must *broadly* be called masculine (a range of styles more defined by what they are not than by what their variety may loosely constitute); and they partake in the range of economic, educational, and sociocultural privileges that white masculinity, in particular, has had to offer (some of which, to the present day, can be revoked if the codes of masculinity are transgressed). On another level, their investment in masculinity must be qualified. Notwithstanding the factors just mentioned, and notwithstanding postmodern culture's sponsoring of straight male forays into androgyny and "experimentation," Bersani is absolutely right in arguing that gay men take masculinity far less seriously *on a mundane level* than straight men do—their desires and sexual practices draw them to an area where straight men do not go of their own free will, an area that makes them abjure such key elements of masculinity as power, domination, and self-assertiveness. And while these renunciations happen in secrecy, gay men know all too well that the practices that trigger these renunciations are so taboo that the moment of their public discovery is the moment when psychosexual self-abnegation is instantly externalized as institutional abjection and criminalization. Therefore, while many white gay men today seem to move with a fair amount of ease within the framework in which they have been "accepted" by Euro-American culture, their desires, their sex practices, and the very sense of being framed have imposed certain limits on a substantial identification with this framework. These limits merit further discussion, in which *Blow Job* can be instrumental, since its framing so heavily allegorizes the parameters at issue.

The duality in *Blow Job*'s framing (the simultaneous signifying and masking of illicit sexual activity) may also be described as a duality between the film's titillating approach toward and distancing protection from illicit sex. On this level, *Blow Job* indexes the modes gay men adopt to this day when they negotiate the duality of their lives with regard to the parameters of acceptability staked out by homophobic society. To be sure, anal penetration is generally not considered among the range of pleasures *Blow Job* possibly signifies, but as Matthew Limon's case has shown, neither is it the only sex practice through which gay men can criminalize themselves. Whatever capacity gay men assume when they involve themselves in the act of giving face, even though they know all too well they could lose face altogether, they continue to seek out the act, and not always in the privacy of their bedrooms. But David Halperin has a point when he questions Bersani's claim that gay men demand the sex they want. With few exceptions, gay men don't make this demand, and this may well be because gay men believe gay sex *is* outside the law. It is not that gay men simply agree or disagree with the law that labels gay sex illicit (that is, criminal, endangering, unethical); if the law were this palpable, the gay movement would have by now made greater strides in fighting the criminalization of gay sex. More likely, as subjects of straight society, gay men internalize and/or intuit a certain abjectness that Old Testamentarian law, for example, describes as an "abomination" and that modern secular law fails to even adequately reflect. But gay men also desire this abjectness. In this sense, gay men frequently flirt with disaster. They court the status of being outside a law that is more fundamental than the laws of the state of Kansas.

If *Blow Job*, too, is marked by a duality that can be characterized as flirting with disaster, does this disaster correspond to, or even designate, the act of transgressing the psycholinguistic law that constitutes masculinity proper? And if this were the case, can we apprehend this flirt, this playing with plunging outside the law of gender, as in any way registering in the poser's face?

If postmodern theories of gender as performance are correct in arguing that the subject performs its gender by realizing its deep impulses for gender coherence through strategic operations that produce the subject as "man" or "woman," do any nonstrategic bodily effects in *Blow Job*'s poser's face identify these operations and, thereby, the psychosexual law of masculinity "from without," so to speak? The price of answering this question in the affirmative is considerable, of course, for if one were to claim that their "inadvertence" makes these effects in any way autonomous, one would incur that notorious charge that Bersani only barely escapes—the charge of having placed these effects outside discourse. This is why my earlier discussion in this book related *Blow Job*'s signification of a certain authenticity to Barthes's notion of the punctum, which, in strict contingency on its visual environment, produces a "bedrock reality" precisely as a textual *effect*. The production of this effect was then related to what Hal Foster has described as traumatic realism, a shock effect characteristic of certain Warhol images produced through aesthetic irregularities and blemishes, which thus designates the spectator as the subject of traumatic realism. In *Blow Job*, however, it is the pro-filmic subject, the poser, who is the site of shock and who indexes this shock through punctum-like visual irregularities. Does he simply perform traumatic realism strategically, or do his rhythmic motions and the purported purity of his sensations suggest that he can in any way be characterized as the subject of trauma, becoming, as it were, trauma's embodied canvas? And if this were the case, how could it further our understanding of the dynamics at work when gay men flirt with disaster? No matter whether gender bedrock or bedrock effect, these dynamics are enigmatic. For in the Platonic regime's synergetic play of elements, the signs of self-dissolution that purportedly mark the moment when disaster strikes paradoxically end up ontologizing the poser's gender as anything *but* feminine and, thus, as anything *but* disastrous.

My analysis of the poser's face work in Chapter 1 cited arguments that claim that facial expressions in (pornographic) sexual representation register obscenity because they become a trace to the moment when sex became colonized by culture. This regulation of sex by culture may be understood as a traumatic imposition analogous to the subject's traumatic plunge into the symbolic, as it is understood by psychoanalysis. And to the extent that the regulation of sex also entails the imposition (and constant reimposition) of discursive heterosexuality and thus, ultimately, the imposition and continued safeguarding of fixed gender positions, gender itself may be understood as traumatic. The structural symmetry of trauma is such that trauma can discursively manifest itself because of the subject's compulsive, dysfunctional effort of integration and because of the however minuscule opposite signifier, which is *apprehended* as the "breaking-through" of what trauma means to screen and which takes the *effect* of a prediscursive referent. However, the fact that the subject's gender performance serves to screen that the subject is at a traumatic distance from the gender to which it is assigned and the fact, too, that the subject tries to integrate this trauma through compulsive repetition should not lead us to believe that the gendered subject simply responds to an ur-trauma. Rather, as Butler has argued, gender is a script that exists before and after the gendered subject. It is modified, expanded, amplified in its punitive status, and constantly rehearsed. Indeed, it is amplified only through constant and continuous rehearsal.

As *Blow Job*'s poser consensually partakes in a visual production that he knows his audience will be encouraged to read as the act of having one's cock sucked, this young man's manliness is eminently on display even as his anatomy is hidden from view. As with most subjects dealing with the challenges of performing in front of Warhol's camera, the performance to which *Blow Job* treats us reveals more about its subject than the subject means to convey. Left to his own devices in a context in which gender intersects with sex in highly charged manner, the poser's assignment to perform on camera merely occasions and foregrounds his more basic assignment—to act like a man, to be a man. In other words, even though he stages his masculinity strategically, the self-consciousness of his repetitive motions (the area where action and reaction, strategy and effect, exist in close proximity) helps us read him as the subject traumatized by the assignment of gender—a subject whose repetitive attempts at emplacing himself as a man reveal, in their very effort to conceal, that he is at a traumatic distance from that place. *Blow Job* functions like a screen also by subsuming the display of unexpected bodily effects under the overall act. In those moments when the poser's inadvertent facial twitches are apprehended, the screen of his performance of masculinity is punctured—but these moments only seem to increase the impression that the poser's masculinity is supported, as it were, by a hard, natural, essential core of "maleness." The signification and visual apprehension of trauma as "the real" here correspond to the Platonic system's concept of the *model/Idea* and to the argument made by Butler's postmodern gender theory that the subject's desire for coherence leads to the displacement of the sum total of elements that constitute gender—acts, gestures, and enactments of desire—onto an *illusory core*.

In *Blow Job*, the poser's particular kind of male masochism constitutes the effect of an essential "core" masculinity. The moments of visual "tremor" in the poser's performance, which seem to enable brief, privileged glimpses to the gender "bedrock," are then by no means instances when the poser falls apart as a man but, conversely, are instances when he "falls together"—that is, when his true designation as a "man" is produced as an illusory effect. In other words, the moment when the poser is man-to-the-core is also gender performance's high moment of illusion, when effect wins out over cause, artifice over authenticity, and surface effect over substance. Because in *Blow Job* the poser's facial twitches constitute the punctum of Warhol's screen, they become the link, the interface, between traumatic realism as a theory of aesthetics/perception and trauma as a way of understanding the performing self—that is, of understanding the psychosexual aspects of gender performance. In this sense, trauma is far from placing the subject outside the symbolic and far from silencing the subject. Rather than stopping the subject from generating meaning, trauma can be counted among the great civilizational motors that produce ever new partial meanings.

This reading of *Blow Job* understands the poser's gender performance as always striving toward coherence and "fullness," as always seeking what the poser has not obtained but assumes is his natural possession. As such, this argument runs counter to Bersani's, but only as long as one ignores that what Bersani calls "inadvertent effects of the body's exercise in power" are *textual* effects. In addition, this reading of *Blow Job* seeks to argue the traumatic nature of gender. It uses the film to illustrate that gender is based on sexual difference, that it may be inhabited, but not naturally so, not without effort, and never to natural perfection. This argument also runs counter to Bersani's. If trauma constitutes a privileged trace to the cruel imposition of sexual difference, it is clear why Bersani would argue that "homo-specificity," which he perceives as the recognition of a much more fundamental sameness from a perspective already internally differentiated, does not recognize the significance of trauma. In addition, since sexual difference predominantly refers to gender, a theorization of trauma does not seem to further a discussion of the implications of sexual orientation—that is, of gay desire, gay sex, and "homo-specificity." For example, if *Blow Job*'s image functions like a screen that indirectly tells us that the subject is at a traumatic distance from the gender it is assigned to, this distance, in and of itself, tells us nothing about the subject's sexual orientation. If gender must be conceived of as a traumatic imposition on *any kind of subject*, a straight man may be no less traumatized by his distance from masculinity than a gay man. Indeed, if *Blow Job*'s traumatic realism disallows us, as it were, to identify the universalizing designation of masculinity as something that is, in fact, *delimited*, the film merely bears out the not altogether surprising fact that trauma, in its guise as a classic psychoanalytic discourse, is profoundly heterosexualizing.

However, one doesn't have to leave it at that. I believe that both the concept of trauma and the concept of homo-specificity can be read against the grain. These idioms may offer at least a starting point from which to rethink gender-as-trauma specifically for a theorization of male homosexuality. Gay men's *contradictory* investment in masculinity is of interest here: Gay men qualify an understanding of the traumatic nature of gender because they attempt to fulfill their gender assignment in not quite the same manner as straight men do. And, as Bersani rightly observes, because gay men, apart from being invested in masculinity, also happen to be particularly drawn to the opposite signifier of phallocentrically constructed masculinity—the desire for self-dissolution—they may be said to have *incorporated* into their gender performance their psychosexually and historically specific proximity to abjectness. These polar opposites then constitute the highly contradictory nature of their socialization as males. In other words, gay male gender performance becomes specific through the hyperbolic oscillation between both of these extremes, with gay men's internalization of their frequent and characteristic proximity to abjectness possibly even enhancing their urge to fulfill phallocentric-heteronormative masculinity.

The hyperbolic oscillation between fulfillment of and abjection from the norm of gender arguably determines the very rhythmicality of the motions of *Blow Job*'s poser. Like the visual irregularities that interrupt these motions, their rhythmicality does not escape Warhol's camera. These rhythms assume their overall place in the film's signification of binaries and polar opposites—light/dark, masculine/feminine, copy/simulacrum—that mutually constitute one another. *Blow Job* may well be a privileged example of visualizing both hyperbolic self-assertion and the desire for the dissolution of the self as opposite poles (even though the latter can never be signified unambiguously but can only be inferred). In addition, the poser's writhing under the undulating waves of bodily impact also foregrounds his refusal to commit to any particular type of masculinity. Thus, on the one hand, the poser's rotation through the visual constellations (which were identified earlier as key masculine stereotypes of the postwar period) indicates that he excels in "hitting all the marks" of normative masculinity with a kind of performative prowess that is characteristic of gay performance, whereby he literally "over-fulfills" the norm. On the other hand, the fact that the poser never comes to rest in any of these positions, that he does not linger long enough to "settle down" and inhabit any of them permanently, may be read as the poser "under-fulfilling" the norm or, to be more accurate, as the poser not taking this norm seriously. He visits these positions briefly, rhythmically, and without the slightest expression of any commitment. In this sense, the term "flirting" appositely characterizes gay men's attraction not only to disaster but also to disaster's safe and proper opposite. Because *Blow Job*'s poser inhabits these positions with self-indulgent promiscuity, we may hypothesize that he indulges in them not—or, at least, not primarily—for the sake of their illusory coherence but simply for the sake of infinitely and pleasurably sequencing them, reexperiencing both their assumption and his abjection from them.

Reading *Blow Job* in this way entails particular appropriations both of the concept of trauma and of Bersani's argument. Perhaps in contrast to straight male responses to trauma, which are marked by a compulsive effort to fulfill the gender norm by "coming to rest in what is natural," gay male responses to trauma may fulfill gender much more superficially. Refusing to rest on any one gender position for long, gay men invalidate gender's false cachet of the natural. They become natural gender's final resting place. This altered impression of trauma encourages me to hypothesize that *Blow Job*'s poser is a gay man in the sense of Bersani's argument, but not without altering his argument. My reading of the poser's performance of masculinity suggests that if gay men are not traumatized by sexual difference in the same way as straight men are, gay male gender performance nonetheless acknowledges sexual difference. Homo-specificity does not steer clear of trauma; it engages trauma and, to a certain extent, seems to neutralize it. Repetition does not indicate the repetitive attempts at fleeing from what one must not become and, synonymously, attempting to reach what one thinks one is, but the repetitive attempts at engaging both these poles *in a much more uninterested manner*. In other words, to the extent that gay male gender performance is homo-specific, coming from a position of the self already different from itself, it may, to a certain extent, take the traumatic (the fear of difference) out of trauma. But its repetitive motions also suggest that it preserves the framework of trauma—however hollowed out it may be—that provides the parameters for the oscillation between gender assumption and abjection.

Since this discussion has developed from my historicization of post–World War II white gay male gender performance, its implications should be brought back to bear on some of the idioms I discussed earlier as being attached to this type of performance. In this regard, then, my analysis of gay male gender performance's hollowing out of the structure of trauma also complexifies the role of hypochondria, a figure appropriated particularly by white gay men in the postwar period. As noted earlier, one of hypochondria's gay-specific functions during the postwar years was to signify an alternative masculinity, but for the purpose of alternately camouflaging and communicating one's sexual orientation. Now, however, hypochondria may be taken up on a territory perhaps even closer to its makeup: It may be the key idiom by which to characterize the differential relation between the gay man and his masculinity. If, for example, *Blow Job*'s poser strives to fulfill the gender norm, if gender performance is, in fact, the striving toward coherence and fullness, gender itself has the status of an unfulfillable telos. Yet this is an insight in which gender performance does not luxuriate. The subject goes right on to strive toward gender fullness, compulsively, because it must. But if compulsive repetition indicates that this norm can never be fulfilled, if the teleological nature of gender is rendered utopian, the specificity of gay male gender performance may lie in its potential for becoming uninterested in this utopia. In gay gender performance's hollowing out of the structure of trauma there inheres an element of performed dysfunction, even performed sickness, in the *celebration* of the very frustration that comes with failed attempts at fulfilling the telos. And since this particular sickness does not manifest itself in pathology, it does not become the reverse of teleology—that is, deterioration and death. In fact, for all its compulsory aspects, gay male gender performance does not have a root cause that can be isolated and modified. To compare it to sickness means putting sickness in quotation marks. It means having to forego *scientia sexualis*'s frenzied investment in the etiologies of diseases.[49] With its *appearance* of sickness, yet with neither cause nor resolve, this disease is, in fact, most appositely termed "hypochondria."

Chapter 5 investigates in greater detail and with specific reference to a selection of Warhol images how the evolution of white gay male identity involved not only the triumphs of reverse discourses and strategic productions but also a series of repressions, exclusions, and compromises that mark the curious position that exists to this day: White gay men have been ethnicized by others, have ethnicized themselves, and have ethnicized others; white gay men are, as Bersani has pointed out, both visible and invisible; white gay men remain society's (possibly last authentic) Other and, at the same time, constitute one of the most staggering "success" stories of assimilation since World War II. In addition to mapping this dual status of white gay men in postwar American society, the chapter discusses how this duality may be regarded from a different angle, that is, as a differential status in which white gay men inhabit certain norms and commodified types and stereotypes in a way that foregrounds the emptiness of masculinity as a framework, its bankruptcy as a category bestowed on us by *scientia sexualis*.

5

ANDY WARHOL, JAMES DEAN, AND WHITE GAY MEN

eginning in the 1950s and peaking during the 1960s, the American public viewed homosexuals as members of an exotic tribe. For example, the years from 1962 to 1966 can be seen as the period in which the press "discovered" the homosexual community. Major newspapers and magazines such as the *Washington Post*, the *Denver Post*, *Life*, *Look*, *Time*, and *Harper's* ran features on gay communities, gay meeting places, and gay lifestyle. The number of books on various aspects of homosexuality published from the perspectives of sociology, psychology, and their popular counterparts increased markedly.[1] Yet, the fact that psychiatrists, lawmakers, journalists, and the larger public started to perceive homosexuals as a social entity with such communitarian features as bars, restaurants, and social and sexual networks did put an end to the designation of the homosexual as Other.

If one considers Foucault's qualification of the repressive hypothesis, one may view the increasing scrutiny of homosexuals in the 1960s along with the proliferation of discourses on homosexuality as constituting less homosexuality's liberation from repressive silence than its consistently refined discursive management by the dominant.[2] The various discourses in the mainstream media echoed a spectrum of reactions ranging from fearful recognition to genuine interest, but they all had in common a rhetoric of ethnographic objectification, which either still regarded the homosexual as Other or was beginning to see him as proximate and less-than-exotic and marked him out for various forms of integration and containment.[3] The proliferation of studies in the mid-1960s with such sensationalist titles as *The Homosexual Revolution*, *The Homosexual Explosion*, and *The Homosexual Uprising* strongly suggest that the public's reaction created a demand for further classification. Psychoanalysts joined ranks with sociologists in advocating behaviorist theory and adaptational models and in debating the appropriate method of sampling homosexual objects for their studies.[4] Homosexuality thus emerged not only as a knowable social entity but as a tangible cultural identity with minutely defined features.

The definition of homosexuality as a distinct cultural and psychosexual identity was gradually embraced by the homophile movement itself, becoming an overdetermined aspect of the movement's struggle. In the specific context of the 1960s, this definition was the only basis from which homosexuals could simultaneously exploit their emerging visibility as a social group and organize an antidiscrimination rhetoric. In addition, the strong urge to refute the medical sickness theory forced the radical wing of the small homophile movement into putting forth the image of the "wholesome homosexual." Espousing this viewpoint, gay rights activist Franklin Kameny stated in July

1964, in a speech before the New York Mattachine Society, "We cannot ask for our rights from a position of inferiority, or from a position, shall I say, as less than *whole* human beings."[5] In 1965 the New York Mattachine Society and the Daughters of Bilitis demanded the movement's unequivocal stand against sickness theory and urged homophile activists to picket government offices. While this was the decisive step in fighting the concept of homosexual identity as pathological, it was also a further step toward unifying identity under the aegis of a gradually nationalizing movement.

The propagation of the image of the healthy, strong homosexual assumed a special function in the education of the general public. In this regard, radical homophile activist Randy Wicker became the most visible conveyor of homosexual propaganda in a way that helps us understand the increasingly central function of the public self-authoring of one's homosexuality into a *coherent* identity.[6] Wicker, who had successfully fought his expulsion from college when he was denounced as a homosexual, wanted to see the gay movement modeled on the civil rights struggle. Among 1960s homophile activists, his greatest achievement was to win the interest and, to a certain extent, support of large sections of the press with respect to educating the public about homosexuals and their communities and support systems. As early as 1962, he convinced a radio station to broadcast a program in which men spoke about their homosexuality.[7] When a conservative columnist lambasted the show and denounced Wicker as an "arrogant card-carrying swish," the program received a barrage of inquiries from the public and triggered gay-friendly features in *Newsweek* and the *New York Times*. Wicker subsequently persuaded other publications, such as the *Village Voice*, to run features on aspects of gay life. As the decade wore on, novels, magazines, and news reports from inside the gay community also were gradually beginning to tell their readers that their situation was widely shared. Ultimately, by the mid- to late 1960s, gay-authored as well as straight-authored discourses were intermingling in the public production of homosexuality in radio shows, TV programs, and print press—all to the effect of increasing homosexual visibility and meeting the public's growing ethnographic interest in homosexuality.[8]

The putatively "exotic" qualities of white gay male identity would gradually become diminished by a kind of cultural work that pulled the Other into the sphere of the same to prep and prime it for assimilation. Increasingly defining themselves in relation to mainstream society (to which, as they claimed, they were both same and Other), white gay men enabled dominant society to apprehend and classify them and, ultimately, to assimilate them into the social stratum of the liberal nation-state. Judging this historical development in hindsight, we recognize that assimilation is thus premised on ethnicization, but we also need to qualify this observation in certain ways. First, we need to note that, in the early 1960s, the kinds of gay self-ethnicization described earlier were still being authored by a small minority of activists and fearless "exhibitionists," to which the overwhelming majority of white gay men had a distant, indifferent relation. This insight has important implications for the treatment of Warhol's images in this chapter. Warhol neither associated himself with any particular politics nor became a figurehead particularly of gay activism. All wishes to the contrary, these factors do have their advantages, at least for the way we can treat Warhol's images as reflections of their historical context. It may be exactly because Warhol was not interested in activism that his images may be said to reflect the "mundane" homosexual more than any pro-gay activist efforts at gay self-ethnicization. Yet, we also need to be clear that even if mainstream culture's interest in white gay men may have caught them by surprise in the early 1960s, before white gay men were pushed into the dialectic of ethnicization and self-ethnicization of *gayness*, they were already deeply imbricated with disciplinary structures that produced their *whiteness* and *maleness*. However, as we shall see in this chapter, Warhol's minimalist images were foregrounding these structures for what they were—frameworks that facilitate the disciplinary production of sexual and gender identities. The stark duality in these images between their bare frames and the emptiness inside does not abolish the basic discursive grid of, say, masculinity, whiteness, American-ness, and so on. But the minimal assertion of these contours on their visual environment and the very barrenness of this environment suggest that the sensibility of the up-and-coming gay artist differed from that of the fledgling gay activist. Unlike someone like Wicker, Warhol still saw—and represented—a certain indifference on the part of white gay men to fill these frames and thus, as it were, to "embody" the homosexual.

The observation that the assimilation of white gay male identity follows a common pattern of ethnicizing Otherness (as discussed, for example, by postcolonial theory) must be qualified further. One needs to note that a comparison between the ethnicization of white gay men as Other and the ethnicization of non-Western Others is not unproblematic. Most obviously, the power relations between white gay men and dominant society have been very different from those attending classical colonialist attempts to control the Other through ethnographic scrutiny and ethnological classification. Even though white gay men became objects of a particular ethnographic discourse, they would still always be white, male, capitalist Western subjects. Yet precisely because of this clear-cut diacritical opposition to the non-Western Other, it must initially seem striking that the ethnographic lens, when focusing on white gay men, has time and again portrayed the homosexual as the Other of Western civilization (where "Western civilization" is used as an epistemological construct referring to space, culture, and psyche) —that is, as a savage and a psychopath. Even though the production of knowledge about white gay male Americans in the 1950s and 1960s became increasingly clad in terms of contemporaneous "progressive" psychology and sociology, these professions were themselves deeply indebted to the two intrinsically Western disciplines concerned with the discovery of the Other both deep down within oneself and way out in a distant, exotic place: psychoanalysis and ethnography. Both of these disciplines began to flourish at the same time as—and in the case of the latter, as a direct result of—colonialism.

The perception of gay sexuality as a deeply eruptive, savage spectacle constitutes the flip side of an increasingly public, increasingly accepted white gay male identity. Homosexuality's "savage" aspects need to be distinguished from the kinds of gay (self-) ethnicizations discussed earlier by way of a conceptual-terminological juxtaposition: The efforts of 1960s gay activists to claim acceptability of homosexuals in the mainstream went by the rhetoric that gay men were really just like the rest of America with the exception of their object choice—an argument that had evolved from the 1950s notion of "sick, but not really sick." While the 1960s' stance irreversibly corrected the 1950s' assumption that homosexuality was just imagined, it nonetheless partook in a decidedly *inward* move that was very similar to the one from which it had evolved: As the 1960s wore on, white gay men may have been increasingly called upon to officially describe their "homosexual lives," but only on condition that they kept any testimonials to or display of same-sex affection (and especially gay sex) out of the public sphere. In other words, the growing acceptance of homosexuals on mainstream terms during the 1960s was still based on a mentality of introversion—the public acknowledgment and toleration of homosexuality had as a condition that the consummation of homosexuality remain private and undetectable. In contrast to this model stands one of extroversion—the mainstream characterization of the homosexual as a psychopath and of homosexuality as a widely visible spectacle of savage, precivilized sex. Needless to say, at issue here is not the admission of white gay men into the club of otherwise respectable middle-class citizens but the fetishization of the homosexual as monster or, at best, as exotic performer. Predictably, mainstream society never assimilated the gay psychopath/savage into any kind of dialectic of official political inclusion; instead, this figure returns every once in a while as a repressed force, simultaneously admired and feared, holding audiences in thrall yet invariably denigrated by them as "mere entertainment."

It is these two sides of homosexuality that concern the analysis of several of Warhol's images in this chapter. These images are considered here, first, as markers of a fairly linear and perhaps necessarily idealizing erection of white gay male identity in (and, to a certain extent, for) the public sphere. This discussion draws on earlier discourses on the phallus but focuses on an idiom that was arguably central to the evolution of this identity and, one might add, to the imaginary production of "collective" identities (such as "community," "nation," and "the public"): the figure of mourning. The focus then shifts toward certain aspects of homosexuality that, by contrast, remained submerged or even repressed in the process of identity formation. Their unassimilated (indeed, unassimilable) qualities are discussed with regard to an idiom that is juxtaposed to mourning—the dynamics of trauma. But I shall argue that Warhol's particular aestheticization of trauma does not simply display trauma's symptomatology but suggests white gay male gender performance's rearticulation of trauma, which ultimately produces white gay men's idiosyncratically differential relation to masculinity.

JAMES DEAN, MOURNING, AND THE FORMATION OF WHITE GAY MALE IDENTITY

As noted in Chapter 4, to the extent that the gay phallus is "just" a phallus, it must be seen as constituting an idealization of the self, a process not particular to gay men. Phallic idealization appears to be central to the constitution of the subject as we know it through one of the few paradigms of theorizing sexuality available to us in Western culture—psychoanalysis. But to the extent that this phallus is erected particularly by gay men, it foregrounds the rhetorical character of phallic assertion, potentially severing the subject's narcissistic predispositions from a false concept of natural entitlement—that is, from naturalized membership. If the gay phallus is primarily a metaphor of specular relations that describes the idealization of one's identity as signified through the surface of the body, it renders the link between the penis and the phallus metaphoric. Thus denaturalized, the phallus becomes autonomous. It can be figured as an object and/or utilized in the figuration of other objects; and it can be appropriated by groups other than (indeed, the Others of) white heterosexual men. However, it is also true that positing the denaturalization of the phallus and its appropriability by others easily threatens to gloss over the specificity of the respective terms and conditions on which these others appropriate the phallus. We have noted, for example, that white gay men's relation to the phallus remains problematic because they have always had the option of retaining a more direct and, at least superficially, more seamless access to the broader hegemonic categories of whiteness and maleness.[9] While the gay male phallus as a denaturalized phallus may be sufficiently malleable to be worked into certain political alliances between white gay men and, say, phallic lesbians, its link to the penis still harbors potentially hegemonic implications—no matter how displaced or denaturalized this link may be.

Having discussed the questionable terms on which white gay men have been admitted to the homophobic social, and having placed white gay male self-assertion in the more particular context of postwar anti-gay repression and paranoia, we may now, perhaps, suggest one way by which to characterize the specific kind of tenuousness that marks white gay men's relation to their penises: The phallic resignification of the body as a white gay male body may be explained psychoanalytically through the claim that the penis is always already lost. But traditional psychoanalysis does not explain how this loss could possibly inspire the kinds of gay self-stylizations discussed earlier. After all, a gay man wants to lose his penis no more than a straight man does. Rather, loss in the historical context of postwar gay culture means, among other things, *inaccessibility* of the penis, which was signaled by its absence in censored gay erotica, constantly enforced by police raids on gay meeting places, and generally ensured by the oppressively homophobic climate. If the penis as an object of gay identification and desire became displaced in 1950s gay subculture onto other body parts and phallic poses, one could perhaps say that for homosexuals in general, *it never had a proper place to begin with.* Our society puts the penis in a position of legal liability differently for gay than for straight men. For straight men, liability is concerned mainly with the penis as an instrument for rape. By contrast, for gay men, liability has, more often than not, zoomed in on the penis as a device for obscenity and indecent exposure. In this regard, the propriety that sanctions the penis—its use, effect, display, and desirability—lends it a somewhat different status for homosexuals than for heterosexuals, and this may affect its status as property, too. This does not mean that gay men never experience fear of castration. Yet, while men in general secretly ensure that their penises are still attached to them, gay men openly rejoice in being attached to the penis. And while straight male culture treats the penis as a secret possession, gay male culture treats it as a gift that one receives and gives away—and as the fantasies of gay hard-core porn show, the greater the fluctuation (indeed, the bigger the trade), the better. Even (or especially) within repressive contexts that, to this day, deny visibility of the gay cock and demand its displacement, gay performance is a ritualized enactment of this joy that is simultaneously an act of mourning (the lost penis) and one of celebrating (its substitution). Within the performativity of the gay phallus, lack is then redefined as excess and mourning becomes a central aspect to the phallic erection of gay identity.

But how does mourning function for the historical white gay male subject? How did mourning figure into the evolution of white gay male identity during the 1950s? More particularly, how did the need for and the practice of mourning affect such aspects as identification and desire, which are themselves central to the development of identity in general? In her study of the complex role of identification in Freudian psychoanalysis, Diana Fuss has pointed out that identification, though often a private, secret, or subconscious process, is of necessity relational. Even its broadest and most basic textbook characterizations, which describe identification as "an act or process of becoming like someone or something in one or several aspects of thought or behavior"[10] (often through basic acts of mimicking and imitation), indicate identification's operation through and subjugation to a classic set of binarisms of self/other, subject/object, inside/outside, and so on. Fuss writes that identification is basically "the detour through the other that defines a self." She quotes Maurice Blanchot, who states that "it is the other who exposes me to unity, causing me to believe in an irreplaceable singularity [while at the same time] he withdraws me from what would make me unique."[11] In other words, the subject becomes a seemingly unified subject through a series of (not always deliberate or pleasant) identifications that define the subject through, and individuate it within, the social. But while identity provides a sense of the unique self, it also makes one realize that one is not at all indispensable. Fuss mentions that the problem of alterity in western culture is determined by the tension within identity between specificity and substitutability, between singularity and anonymity. Affecting intellect as well as libido, identifications have a lasting impact on the development of the ego and, hence, on the way the self produces itself in the social as a public self.

Identity, as Fuss emphasizes, is constituted by a mosaic of (often contradictory) identifications that "show through" across a variety of identities. Identification is thus a mode by which we can understand ourselves as social beings. As Fuss puts it, "Identification names the entry of history and culture into the subject, a subject that must bear the traces of each and every encounter with the external world."[12] This definition is important to keep in mind when considering the concept of mourning as one key aspect of identification. Mourning functions as a defense mechanism when one's love object is lost (through death, through a long separation, or through the subject's fantasy/anticipation/anxiety of the death of or separation from the love object). The subject defends itself against this loss by identifying with the lost object. Freud describes this process as the subject replacing the object internally through identification;[13] Lacan, who translated Freudian thought into linguistic concepts, characterizes this replacement as the production of an image or a facsimile of the love object.[14] Both characterizations indicate how mourning, the psychosexually "healthy" response to object loss, is a crucial vector in the evolution of selfhood: The self that is able to mourn the objects it has lost by taking them inside and incorporating them into the ongoing production of itself then also becomes an index of those objects; these lost love objects are part of the mosaic that becomes the self.

The theoretical discourse on mourning helps us understand how a gay icon such as James Dean and, more important, James Dean's death constituted a milestone in the evolution of white gay male identity in the second half of the 1950s and first half of the 1960s. As a first step, let us briefly recall some of the findings from Chapter 2 to remind ourselves why James Dean would be somewhat overdetermined to become a figure of identification for white gay men. To begin with, Dean's dramatization of outsider qualities—his alienation from middle-class society, his refusal to be a patriarchal provider, his search for alternative families and peer groups, and his "alternative" masculinity—were all discourses produced by society to negotiate its contradictions, such as the urge, in the wake of the publication of the Kinsey reports, to identify and Other homosexuality and the inability to do so. Thus, Dean's rebelliousness came to be romanticized and exploited for the image of what may be one of Hollywood's most archetypal anti-heroes. As Hollywood defined the existence of the teenager by narrative transition, the characters played by Dean produced a space of an albeit temporary sexual ambiguity that strongly spoke to postwar gays and lesbians. In addition to his alternative masculinity, Dean's handsome features made him an object of identification *and* desire for gay men. But even the star's gay-specific appeal was broad enough to accommodate a range of identifications. He combined elements of the volatile outlaw with those of the sensitive, misunderstood, and insecure youth. More particularly, Dean's embodiment of the wistful melancholy of the martyr made him one of the prototypes of the sad young man of the fifties—an epithet by which the decade's homosexuals became known as a stereotype. Within Dean's persona, Christ merged with the teenage rebel.

As a second step, however, we need to clarify exactly how and what white gay men gained from identifying with James Dean as a public person and celebrity, as someone prominently positioned in the public sphere and indelibly ingrained in memory. Jonathan Flatley has claimed that ethnic and sexual minorities and outsiders, in particular, have the need to see themselves represented in public, to feel they are part of a public body into which they can abstract themselves but to which they may nonetheless maintain a critically self-conscious relation.[15] The appropriation of movie stars and other public figures and their transformation into minority and subcultural icons enable the marginalized subject to access the public sphere and, thus, to become, as Michael Warner puts it, "subjects of publicity—its 'hearers,' 'speakers,' 'viewers,' and 'doers.'"[16] Drawing on Warner's work, Flatley argues that this enables minorities such as homosexuals at least "to *imagine* that one is representable—in order to feel like one *is* at all."[17] Flatley argues further that Warhol was particularly apt at enacting what Flatley terms "the poetics of publicity," and these, as he argues, were also closely related to mourning. In Flatley's words, "To become public or feel public was in many ways to acquire the sort of distance from oneself that comes with imagining oneself dead. The 'self-negativity' that we experience by imagining ourselves as 'public' might be seen as something like attending your own funeral."[18] While Warhol, in the course of his career, turned himself into such a public body, visible yet mysterious, alive yet displaying the ghoulish veneer of death, it is particularly the artist's portraits that, according to Flatley, reenact processes of mourning. What Fuss observes from a Freudian perspective Flatley finds in Lacanian discourse—that the basically phantasmatic nature of identification is exemplified by processes of mourning: "Warhol's portraits remind us that *recognition*—of the famous and the everyday alike—is contingent on our ability to *remember* the image of a person in the same way as if we were mourning her. There is no recognition, indeed no face, as it were, before the portrait."[19]

To explore the phantasmatic processes of identification and mourning (identification through mourning) in Warhol's work, let us now analyze the significance of James Dean and some of the mythical and pop-cultural types he embodied—the teenage rebel, the suffering martyr, the misunderstood son, the son-turned-father—in a series of images that range from the mid-1950s to the 1964 *Blow Job*. That the suffering martyr and the teenage rebel are two of the central figures invoked by both James Dean and by *Blow Job*'s simulacrum has made the film a site for retrieving and understanding gay men's relation to James Dean. But *Blow Job* is not the only instance by which Dean came to figure in Warhol's work—in fact, it is one of the more remote instances. In the mid- to late 1950s, Warhol artistically engaged with Dean's image, persona, and myth at least twice the first time via a ballpoint pen drawing, the second time via a blotted line image. In an analysis of these images we find not only how one particular white gay man made his private obsessions with Dean public but, as I shall argue, that some of these images have a self-reflexive relation to gay desire and identification. They not only reenact the appropriation of the star by gay men but also self-consciously foreground the function of certain acts of appropriation for identity formation as such. Taken together, these images form a trajectory that marks the formation of gay identity in analogy to classic psychoanalytic narratives of identity formation, and, in doing so, they also give us significant clues as to the frictions necessarily incurred in processes of identification and identity formation—certain alienations, repressions, and compulsory conversions at the heart of this process.

Let us now turn to the first and, in many respects, most interesting of these images. In 1955, Warhol produced *James Dean* (Figure 5.1), an elegiac drawing that depicts the star's death by car accident and that arguably represents one of Warhol's first death and disaster works. While this drawing is early evidence of Warhol's obsession with celebrity and death in general, the array of pictorial elements and their meanings also clearly articulate the special appeal of the tragic rebel particularly to white gay men. The drawing arguably constitutes Warhol's first work of gay mourning—a tribute to Dean as a gay hero and a lost love object for white gay men. In contrast to, say, melancholia (one of mourning's dysfunctional doubles, which is often characterized as paralyzing the subject), mourning is considered a "healthy" way of parting from the love object; mourning enables the subject to "work through" the loss by converting the incorporated lost object into new enunciations and narratives, which not only memorialize the object, but reshape and "enrich" the enunciating subject. In this sense, the various pictorial elements of *James Dean* are meant to be incorporated by the mourning subject. They offer points from which to initiate narratives of transference between the idol and his gay following. As such, they may be regarded as becoming incorporated into

and helping shape several aspects specifically of the identity of the white gay male mourner. For example, the depiction of Dean's head and the cross underneath strongly link the star to the stereotypes of suffering martyr and sad young man through which postwar white gay culture so strongly articulated itself. Further, while the car in the postwar context is traditionally associated with male heterosexual mobility, recent studies have also confirmed its significance for gay male culture during the 1950s and 1960s.[20] However, the most important indicator of Warhol's gaying of James Dean in this drawing is the brick wall, which is posited as a sign of gay men's hazardous claim to public space. All of these elements also work in synergy to help articulate an elegy or, if you wish, to prompt a more or less coherent mourning narrative.

Figure 5.1

James Dean (c. 1955). Ballpoint pen on paper (17⅝ × 11¾ inches).
© 2002 Andy Warhol Foundation for the Visual Arts/ARS, New York.

The mythologizing function of the brick wall in this drawing will be discussed shortly. (The wall was "invented" by Warhol for the specific purpose of misrepresenting the circumstances of the car crash.) But let us note first, with regard to mourning, that the brick wall becomes an expression of unfulfilled gay male desire and a symbol of a certain bleakness, perhaps even a fatalist sensibility, within white gay male culture. In *James Dean* Warhol tells us that the most famous sad young man of the fifties had died by crashing his car into a brick wall, leaving all the other sad young men grieving over his loss. Functioning as a key conduit of gay mourning and as a symbol of gay martyrdom, the brick wall in *James Dean* still conveyed gay specificity mostly in negative terms; but since martyrdom is predominantly associated with the triumph of spirituality and the transcendence of bodily pain (*James Dean* clearly emphasizes the psychic appeal of the star over his physical aspects), the drawing proffers and preps these negative signifiers for instant conversion into building blocks of gay identity. *James Dean* may then be considered an important early testimony to the postwar gay male subject's ability and will to mourn and a testimony, too, to this subject's desire for a certain degree of public visibility and for identity. The impression that *James Dean*'s pictorial elements are arrayed fairly loosely somewhat belies the drawing's rhetorical power to coerce a gay reading. For it seems that such a reading is more or less compelled to respond to the drawing's "call" to process, harness, and condense its parts into a more unified narrative of and for the emerging postwar white gay male subject.

It is interesting to trace this narrative along the trajectory that *James Dean* forms with later renditions of the teenage rebel, such as the one from Warhol's *A Gold Book* and also, ultimately, the image from *Blow Job*. While *James Dean* suggests the white gay male subject's desire for coherence and the process he was undergoing of developing a more unified and tangible identity, these later examples acknowledge and address this process more explicitly by depicting it as an already partly accomplished act—even though their unstable visuals also reflect the precarious and rhetorical nature of the process of unification and condensation. The portrait of a juvenile delinquent from the 1957 *A Gold Book* (Figure 5.2) is based on the photograph of a street youth (see Figure 6.1), but modified by Warhol in such a way as to resemble Dean's pose in the poster from *Rebel Without a Cause* (see Figure 5.4). Warhol gives us the image of a Dean look-alike depicted in a pose of relaxed cockiness—one hand on his belt buckle, the other one putting a cigarette into his mouth—but the image is striking also for the extreme thinness of the lines by which Warhol suggests the figure's contours.[21]

The evolution of pictorial elements from *James Dean* to *A Gold Book*, that is, from a loose assemblage of signifiers to an already somewhat more unified if minimalist image, reenacts the process of identity formation. It harbors the beginnings of a process of identification of the self via the Other, which Jacques Lacan has characterized as an act of misrecognition whereby the scattered parts unify in front of the mirror and give the false appearance of a seemingly unified subject.[22] This unified subject bears the markers of certain exclusionary and repressive processes at the heart of identity formation—the pose itself becomes an indicator of the subject's perception of itself as a coherent speaking subject (in the psychoanalytic/linguistic sense of the word), and taken together with the macho iconography, it is the strongest indicator for white gay men's participation in a new and somewhat alternative, yet still mainstream, masculinity and for the prowess they were taking in their transgressive, subcultural identities.

Yet, the image from *A Gold Book* also shows the unstable, vulnerable aspects of the fledgling postwar gay subject. The Dean look-alike, like all drawings from *A Gold Book*, is a minimalist figure, faintly indicated by single lines that produce the figure only via bare contours. The tentativity of the shapes can be compared to the tentativity of gay performance (as understood, for example, by the figure of hypochondria) in its act of lending tenuous, chimerical contours to the gay body and forming a still tentative and somewhat camouflaged gay identity. The figure speaks to different viewers differently, accommodating gay as well as heterosexual identifications. The theme and mode of this depiction can be traced back in Warhol's work to the early 1950s collection of drawings, *a is an alphabet*, which preceded the emergence of gay idols such as James Dean but which contains the image of two men, *S Was a Snake* (Figure 5.3), or to *Two Girls Hand in Hand*—both of which depict same-sex pairs with a certain minimalism that suggests their intimate relationships through the very emptiness and proximity of the silhouettes.[23] Inscribed into the thin contours of these images is both the minimalism of passing and the potential for gay self-stylization. As Trevor Fairbrother has pointed out in his important essay on Warhol's pre-pop art, reading these images as gay literally amounted to reading between the lines.[24]

One could even go so far as to claim that the technique used by Warhol for *A Gold Book* in and of itself relates to gay performativity. At issue here is the so-called blotted

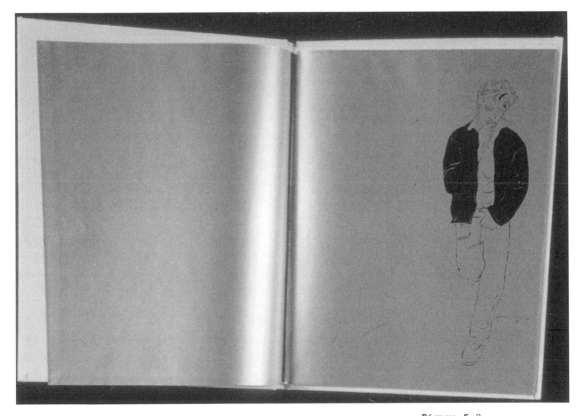

Figure 5.2
A Gold Book (1957) with illustrations by Andy Warhol. © Archives of the Andy Warhol Museum, Pittsburgh Founding Collection.
© 2002 Andy Warhol Foundation for the Visual Arts/ARS (copy photo: Robert P. Ruschak).

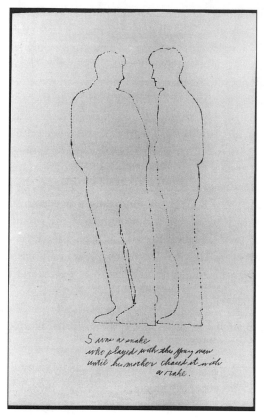

Figure 5.3

S Was a Snake, 1953. Page from unpublished book. Ink and pencil on paper (10⅜ × 6⅜ inches). © Archives of the Andy Warhol Museum, Pittsburgh Founding Collection. © 2002 Andy Warhol Foundation for the Visual Arts/ARS (photo: Richard Stoner, 3/26/01).

line technique, by which Warhol would trace the contours of a pre-existing image and make a print from the ink line. According to Rainer Crone, this technique de-ontologizes the process of artistic creation. It differs from techniques used by Picasso and Matisse, in which the single line served not simply as a contour, but its very thickness and intensity were significant features that in one way or another would suffer in the reproduction process. That is, in Picasso's and Matisse's works, any copies would have had the status of traditional (somewhat inefficacious) simulacra in relation to the original drawing. By contrast, according to Crone, "Warhol's very style of drawing . . . was so close to the final result of a printing process, namely offset printing, that we may refer in his case to a reciprocal relationship between style and technique, in fact a relationship in which the one neutralizes the other."[25] The simulacral qualities of Warhol's early drawings thus correspond, in their collapse of style and technique (which can be substituted by one another), to the gay male simulacrum's tenuous relation to his penis (which is also based on substitution).

In this trajectory of the evolution of white gay male identity, *Blow Job* may be regarded as constituting the next step. The film's unstable visuals continue to express the visual tentativity of the drawing in *A Gold Book*, but in two ways *Blow Job* must also be regarded as indicating a definite advancement in the consolidation of white gay male identity. First, *Blow Job*'s spectatorial address casts with greater rhetorical force the act of identifying (with) the poser as a white gay man in terms of an investment in fullness and coherence. As we shall see, this act is based on three aspects that are deemed central to identity formation in general: ambivalence, violence, and repetition/remembrance.[26] Second, the film's display of gender, even though fluid and complexly aestheticized, nonetheless remains firmly anchored within and beholden to the basic phenomenological terms that, as discussed in Chapter 4, limit the ways in which gender can appear and that dictate the terms on which gender can be apprehended and categorized. *Blow Job* links this phenomenological anchoring of gender to the anchoring of the white gay male subject within the social. This becomes clearer if we reconsider the trajectory of images from *James Dean* to *Blow Job* as one that charts gay men's increasing claims to a public space that—even though it had been shaped by dominant culture—could never be controlled by dominant culture completely. These two aspects deserve further discussion

Figure 5.4
Detail of poster art from
Rebel Without a Cause.

now, as they help us understand the complexity of the mech-anisms that underscore gay identification with James Dean. Ultimately, Dean serves not only as a privileged object through which white gay male identity constructed itself but also as an idiom of the contradictions the white gay male imaginary had to negotiate with regard to the inhabitation of gender.

Let us deal with the second aspect first, simply because it can be discussed concisely via an iconological tracing, which then forms the sociohistorical background for a more detailed discussion of psychosexual aspects of identity formation. Warhol's 1955 drawing of the death of James Dean (see Figure 5.1) already harbors the impulse for converting the loss of the gay love object into a statement that signals gay men's claim to public space. For this statement, Warhol seizes on the brick wall as an iconographic element central to the larger iconographic pool of Dean's persona as well as to gay men's self-assertion in the public sphere. In Hollywood publicity material for Dean, walls of any kind—but especially the brick wall chosen for one of the posters for *Rebel Without a Cause*—were used as a backdrop against which Dean's film characters were depicted as loitering in characteristic poses. These poses simultaneously communicated cocky defiance and alienation (Figures 5.4 and 5.5), and given the fact that these walls signified public space, they identified Dean's teenage characters as urban cowboys of sorts, who took to the streets and public areas of cities to escape the stifling confines of the parental domestic sphere.

When one compares the 1955 *James Dean* to the 1964 *Blow Job*, one realizes that the brick wall's function as both icon and metaphor had evolved in relation to the other elements within each artwork. Interest-ingly, *James Dean* deliberately falsifies the circumstances of Dean's death by positing the brick wall as the cause of the hero's fatal car accident.[27] Its inclusion by Warhol into the picture clearly evidences Warhol's intent to mythologize Dean's death and to spark a gay-specific version of the larger Dean myth that developed instantly in the wake of the crash. Warhol's drawing thus privileges myth over fact and myth-making over documentation. Warhol's decision to include the brick wall in the image must be read as reflecting gay men's desire to claim access to the social *as* gay men. In *Blow Job*, some of the drawing's other elements, such as the cross and the name "James Dean," have been eliminated as denotative icons and have, instead, been incorporated into

Figure 5.5
James Dean publicity shot.

the connotative spectrum of the film's minimalist symbolism. Only the brick wall remains, and it figures even more prominently than in the 1955 drawing.

The brick wall in *Blow Job* becomes a symbol of the triumphant assertion of white gay male identity within the public sphere, as it now conveys gay male vitality rather than gay death. The film celebrates the kind of public space in which white gay men move about and find one another, even though in this way they subjected themselves to playing hide-and-seek with dominant homophobic elements. (The poser at times seems to blend in with the brick wall just like a guerrilla fighter blends in with his natural environment; his sometimes strained expressions speak to any gay man who has experienced sex in public as both a risk and a thrill.) Yet, with gay sex banished off-screen, *Blow Job* not merely allegorizes but, in fact, more or less accurately *indexes* the price white gay men were paying for claiming access to public America. The brick wall, then, sustains its original connotation of a basically hostile public sphere, a realm by which white gay men were alienated but to which they still needed to obtain access. It is against this background that we may now further discuss the relation between Warhol's imaging of James Dean and the three figures Fuss has identified as salient to identification: ambivalence, violence, and repetition/remembrance.

If identification and desire are by nature very primal processes, they are also very complex, as they harbor strong ambivalences. Consider, for example, the following comment that Warhol made with regard to the proliferation of popular icons and their functions, which was cited by Richard Meyer in this article "Warhol's Clones": "So today if you see a person who looks like your teenage fantasy walking down the street, it's probably not your fantasy but someone who had the same fantasy as you and decided instead of getting it or being it, to look like it, and so he went and bought that look you both like. So forget it. Just think of all the James Deans and what it means."[28] This comment gives us an impression of the artist's perception of James Dean's significance for postwar teenagers—and it aptly characterizes what Meyer, in a gay reading of the quote, calls a "scenario of mass desire," whereby "a loosely organized subculture is generated through the collective fashioning of the self upon an ideal image of (in this case same-sex) desire, through the mirroring of parallel fantasies played out upon the surface of the body."[29] Warhol's comment on teenage consumers' relation to James Dean is of special interest here for the way it suggests the pressures and challenges involved in appropriating particularly a popular icon such as James Dean.

Of course, gay males were not the only consumers of mass culture to feel these pressures. Warhol's comment of "Just think of all the James Deans and what it means" and, we should add, much of Warhol's artistic output during the 1950s and 1960s point to a more general tension between individuality and anonymity or, in the more particular context of artistic/visual representation, between individuation and reification.[30] The publicity still of Dean surrounded by the spiraling mesh wire, discussed in Chapter 2, articulates this tension in what may be described as *the paradox of the mass appeal of the individual*. It involves a set of discursive tensions that, in Western culture, have determined the representations of political figureheads, religious leaders, and popular stars. Hollywood, too, has traditionally exploited this paradox for the construction of its mythological stereotypes, such as the gangster and the westerner. But Hollywood's version of the 1950s teenager, who also retained aspects of both civilization and "savagery" as well as conformity and rebellion, was symptomatically related (in very timely manner) to one of the decade's signature debates. Proponents of consensus management argued that the postwar economic growth and military strength would ensure opportunity for all, and that the nation as a whole had, in fact, already superceded sociopolitical conflict.[31] On the other side of the debate, the proponents of individualism warned that the individual American (male) was paying a steep price in autonomy and meaning for the security and comfort he was reaping from the bureaucratically organized and managed society. In this context, the "average" teenage mass consumer's effort to appropriate Dean in his or her own, original way for the purpose of enhancing his or her own individuality was potentially undermined by the very terms that made consumerism a mass phenomenon. Appropriating and consuming Dean could threaten to take a teenager's individuality away from him or her as much as the act was meant to bestow it; ironically, this consumption potentially made the Dean fan a teen version of his or her own father—the man in the grey flannel suit. For white gay male consumers of Dean, this dilemma was compounded by the additional challenge of appropriating Dean for their own prohibited desires and identifications.

If Dean's star persona, perhaps more than any other star's, embodied the paradox of the mass appeal of the individual, it also lent itself to—and was, in fact, very deliberately and shrewdly exploited by—the studio for the kinds of multiple significations that also included (and even spoke directly to) gay consumers. The studio's intention to produce a field of open signification around Dean and the thrills and anxieties this strategy must have triggered in consumers can be gleaned with regard to a publicity still from Dean's first big success, *East of Eden* (Figure 5.6).

The shot features Dean sitting on a bed in the right-hand corner of a room, half naked, playing a flute. The flute effeminizes him. Not normally associated with men, Dean's instrument is an expression of his spirituality and the alternative masculinity that the star came to embody during the period. In the bed behind him lies another man whose naked torso is only partly covered with a sheet and whose arms are under the sheet. The man looks at Dean. Dean does not return the look, but his facial expressions basically leave open whether he is aware that he is being watched. The man is Dean's fictional brother in the film, but that is not evident from the still. In fact, the still is so suggestive that one wonders whether this is an instance of a studio in-joke of the kind so often played on Rock Hudson. In any case, queering the scenario of homosocial intimacy was meant to ensure that the still would be noticed by 1950s gay moviegoers, who may have read it as a blow job of sorts. The unreturned gaze and Dean's expression, simultaneously self-conscious and self-absorbed, evoke the scenario of cruising but also, quite specifically, evoke the melancholy and isolation of the sad young man. Highly suggestive but also quite innocuous, this still is a real teaser particularly for gay male moviegoers. It strongly encourages gay narrativizations of its visual scenario and gay identifications of and with its star. While these phantasmatic narratives and identifications were the bread and butter of the 1950s gay consumer of mass culture, they also, of course, constantly operated at a certain level of frustration, as a result of Hollywood's publicity departments' refusal to confirm any such fantasies.

This mixture of desire, anxiety, and frustration constituted the ambivalence with which the gay consumer appropriated Dean for himself and to which Warhol's 1955 drawing of the death of James Dean arguably responded. The particularly assertive nature of this response leads us to the second aspect so important to identification—violence. Falsifying and mythologizing the circumstances of Dean's car crash, Warhol's drawing is far from being a simple expression of sympathy and it is far from merely be-

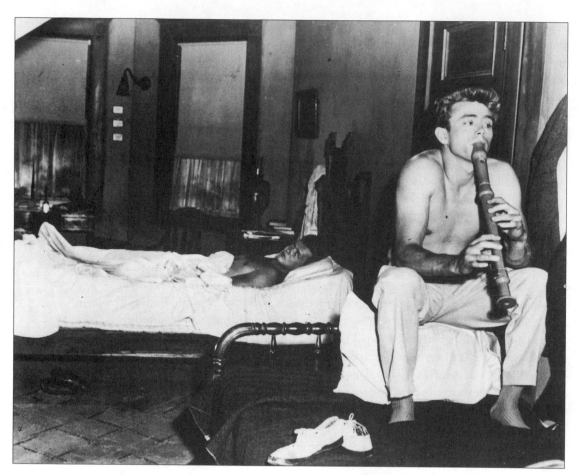

Figure 5.6
Publicity shot from *East of Eden.*

ing an attempt to depict Dean's death-by-accident: It creatively reenacts the tragedy with considerable but perfectly understandable liberty. In other words, *James Dean* testifies to the fact that Warhol, in this image, sought to assassinate Dean in a highly specific manner and for his own specific gay purposes. For in order to safeguard one's appropriation of the love object, to ensure that this object has passed into one's possession, and to demonstrate to the world that this object is not owned by anyone else but is part of one's own unique individuality, simply reenacting the death of the love object may not be sufficient. James Dean's death, in particular, triggered a myriad of elegies and nongay mourning narratives, with which Warhol's and those of other gay men had to compete. To appropriate Dean for himself as a gay man, Warhol, first of all, had to "make" Dean gay, and he did so by working, however subtly, the signifiers of gayness into the star's death. The "gay assassination" of Dean and the erection of white gay male identity thus mutually constitute each other in Warhol's drawing.

James Dean's seemingly primitive visuals belie its complexity. On the one hand, the drawing constitutes a very *strategic* gay-specific appropriation. In their combination, the pictorial elements may well reflect Warhol's recognition of the transgressive status of homosexuality, his desire to make homosexuality visible in subtle ways, and his urge to redeem it as a general condition through the killing/resurrection of a gay messiah.

(We should remember that Warhol here merely operates within a 2,000-year-long tradition of articulating a taboo spiritual conviction through compensatory narratives.) On the other hand, the drawing is also quite unself-conscious in the sense that it kills the star off in the most resolute, matter-of-fact way, reflecting, as it were, the "utilitarian necessities" that dictate processes of self-empowerment—Dean's assassination is also underscored here by a certain despair. But, as I shall argue shortly, the killing itself is not without a trace of remorse. Indeed, this act of appropriating Dean via a gay-authored "assassination" must be closely related to the prohibited nature of homosexuality and the punitive nature of gender. In this sense, Warhol's images tell us something about the taboos involved in inserting oneself into the public sphere as both *gay* and a *man*.

After ambivalence and violence, repetition/remembrance is the third aspect Diana Fuss has designated as salient to processes of identification. This aspect is particularly evident in *Blow Job*, but the film also harbors the first two aspects. With regard to the first aspect described by Fuss, the image's minimalism, with its attending conceptual and aesthetic tensions, creates spectatorial ambivalence and even anxiety as to how to confirm the possibility that the poser may be gay. The dynamics *Blow Job* mobilizes in gay male spectators are not that far from those mobilized by the queer publicity still from *East of Eden* discussed earlier. *Blow Job* retraces the anxiety over Dean's sexuality by subjecting the identity of its poser to similar interpretations. The burden and the thrill of speculating about the sexual identity of one's object of desire has special significance for homosexuals, who cannot expect to find their own sexuality confirmed in public images and discourses. To claim gay identity thus means to negotiate the constraints involved in appropriating and reformulating whatever limited cultural material is available for a production of the self. This activity of speculating, and the anxieties and desires that it involves, have had a long history in gay discourses. Since modern homosexuality is essentially a highly attributive and highly punitive category, its emergence is intrinsically linked to the act of speculation (on the part of courts of law, for example, but also in the postwar context of gay hypochondria).

The appropriation by gay audiences of *Blow Job*'s poser reflects the sort of anxiety that can be traced to characters as far back as Erskine, Oscar Wilde's protagonist in *The Portrait of Mr. W. H.*, who wants to confirm his homosexuality by proving that the boy in the portrait he desires was Shakespeare's lover.[32] To ascribe any identity to their respective objects/sitters, both Erskine and the spectator of *Blow Job* have to put the model's identity under erasure, which means subjecting it to their own respective projections, interpretations, and needs. This process makes clear how *any* construction of identity is carried out at the expense of the other person involved. *Blow Job*'s image, more than many we have encountered in contemporary culture, then also reflects the violence (Fuss's second aspect) of such acts of identification, since any projection of identity onto the poser necessarily "assassinates" him. What links Wilde's Erskine with *Blow Job*'s (gay) spectator is the (often painful) insight that placeholders are not inherent properties but signify relative positions that, in the violent game of identification and identity formation, become veritable beachheads to be occupied by some and besieged by others.

Finally, with regard to repetition/remembrance (Fuss's third aspect), *Blow Job*'s oblique referencing of seriality through its spliced-together rolls of film and, more important, through the poser's rhythmic and recurrent motions arguably commemorate James Dean via repetitive display. In this context, Warhol's serial paintings from the 1960s come to mind. The artist's silk screen panel *Jackie*, which features Jacqueline

Kennedy in mourning, most explicitly enfolds discourses of mourning and identification with those of memorialization and repetition.[33] But the fact that mourning processes are rendered iconographically explicit in *Jackie* is perhaps secondary here. In fact, much of Warhol's work of the period bespeaks the artist's fascination with death and commemoration, and it does so less through content than through technique. Commemoration in Warhol is typically expressed through seriality and fragmentation, the latter being evidenced in *Blow Job*, too, through the film's chiaroscuro patterns, which divide the picture plane in changing patterns of light and dark. Diana Fuss points out that in identification the subject paradoxically destroys the love object only to better preserve it. Or, as Julia Kristeva (whom Fuss cites) put it: "Better fragmented, torn, cut up, swallowed, digested . . . than lost."[34]

GENDER, TRAUMA, AND THE "CONSERVATIVE" ASPECTS IN WARHOL'S IMAGES

On one level, *Blow Job*'s mise-en-scène is clearly aligned with the practice of remembrance. But as we shall see, *Blow Job* also articulates another relation to James Dean, which differs from the white postwar gay male mourner's "orderly" divestment from the lost love object and which has to do with a certain taboo around the "killing" of Dean in Warhol's 1955 drawing. The implications of this taboo are complex. A first step in defining these implications may be to note that within the trajectory of images up until and including *Blow Job*, one can identify a certain duality: On the one hand, there is the impulse to assemble disparate elements and to construct a complete image. However tentative the contours of the figure in *A Gold Book*, however chimerical the appearance of the poser in *Blow Job*, these images evince certain unifying tendencies—they prompt us to construct their subject as a "whole" subject. On the other hand, we find that these images deindividualize this subject. They make him impenetrable even as they prompt us to penetrate him; they expand his qualities to the realm of typology, even as they offer him for appropriation as vehicle and medium for the appropriator's individuation. In addition, the 1955 drawing *James Dean* is the first—and last—instance of Warhol unambiguously declaring the referent. The 1957 figure from *A Gold Book*, which is strongly likened to James Dean, constitutes a displacement precisely to the extent that Dean is not explicitly named. This displacement anticipates the 1964 *Blow Job*, which fully resurrects Dean on the level of "James Dean-ness" or, to be more exact, on the level of myth.

Now, in and of itself, Warhol's mythologization of Dean, which begins with the 1955 drawing, does not necessarily indicate an "unhealthy" divestment from the love object. In fact, it seems to bear a certain analogy to the myth Sigmund Freud concerns himself with in *Totem and Taboo* of the primordial horde of sons who cannibalize their father and who, Freud hypothesizes tentatively, may have mustered the gumption to collude against their father because of "homosexual feelings and acts."[35] In her persuasive reading of Freud's analysis of this myth, Diana Fuss argues that in Freud's eyes, it is the sons' post-parricidal guilt that makes their assassination into one of the central foundational myths of Western culture: The sons' relation to their father is marked by both love and hate, fear and envy, which, in combination lead them to kill and devour him.[36] But as Fuss rightly notes, the dead father is even more powerful than the living father, as his sons' guilt causes them to attempt to "make up" for their crime by instating a set of socially and sexually proscriptive laws *in the name of the father* that were meant to prohibit an actual repetition of the crime.[37] Fuss asserts that at the heart of this paradigmatic parricide is the complex territory of identification, which registers and results in the building of civilization. The latter is thus founded on the ritualistic killing of the father and his reinstallment at the level of the law.

Warhol's reenactment of the killing of James Dean in *James Dean*—an assassination of sorts—and the artist's subsequent negation of the referent arguably constitute a queering of this myth: The dead icon (that is, James Dean) whose killing, as argued earlier, was also preceded by feelings of ambivalence toward him is resurrected indirectly but paradigmatically through a set of terms that outline an alternative, queer society in his name. It should be noted again that the feelings of ambivalence at the heart of this queer killing are indexed by a number of uncertainties and anxieties, which, in turn, reflect the existence of a range of obstacles and implicit as well as explicit interdictions any such queering has to overcome. Consider, for example, the speculations and doubt as to Dean's "true" sexual orientation, society's prohibition of homosexuality, mainstream culture's attempts to regulate and narrate the Dean myth particularly with regard to his sexuality (i.e., whose object is he?), and so on. In this light, the queering of the Dean myth in these images appears all the more radical in that it would seem to release and then perpetuate precisely what is repressed in the construction of Dean's persona as well as in the original myth Freud investigates—homosexuality, gender fluidity, queerness.

On one level, the analysis earlier in this chapter of Warhol's images of Dean in terms of a gay mourning narrative thus seems to confirm the analogy to the myth of the original parricide. But things are not that clear-cut—or, more accurately, even in Warhol's images of James Dean there is a notable ambivalence about the gay mourning of the icon. This ambivalence is conveyed by the images' minimalism and by the fact that they somewhat qualify their respective inscriptions of queerness. Indeed, a quality within Warhol's minimalism arguably neutralizes and rearticulates certain etiological aspects in discourses of psychosexual identity formation. I will elaborate on this later. At this point, however, my discussion focuses on the "conservative qualitites" of these images.

While Warhol's images of James Dean, in their respective ways, display, appropriate, and sexualize what we have called "James Dean-ness," they also mute certain less assimilable aspects of sex and gender. The implications of a quite literally crushed self in *James Dean* are eclipsed by the drawing's overdetermined function of "jump-starting" the Dean myth; the androgynous touch of the figure in *A Gold Book* is counterbalanced by the display of masculine cockiness; in *Blow Job* the promise of a graphic depiction of taboo sex is foiled by the self-censoring framing; in addition, as discussed in Chapter 4, the image functions as a screen/buffer in more than one way. How does this conservatism stand in relation to the fact that each of these images must be regarded as a key step in the increasingly open celebration of an identity, whose evolution must be attributed in no small measure to successfully claiming its icons by mourning them? One answer is that these images take on a quality quite apart from the act of mourning: Indeed, they seem to follow a trajectory somewhat inverse to normative and often idealizing clinical "progress" narratives of coping with loss. On a certain level, their relation to Dean also remains unresolved. It bears signs of trauma, and this despite the fact that these post-1955 works can be read as way stations marking the increasingly palpable speaking position called white/gay/male. But what could possibly be so traumatic about giving a blow job to James Dean? To answer this question, we must first explore certain links between gay male orality and the traumatic aspects of white gay male identity.

To the extent that identification through mourning involves the act of incorporating the lost love object, it is often modeled on the physical act of eating, tearing apart, devouring, and swallowing.[38] And to the extent that one may think of identity as being constituted through a series of identifications, identification thus also appears to be linked to the concept of oral incorporation. In addition, Diana Fuss has argued that the concept of oral incorporation has taken on an even more potent function in dominant homophobic views of homosexuality. Fuss traces the link between mourning, oral incorporation, and same-sex desire to Sigmund Freud, who in *Totem and Taboo: Some Points of Agreement Between the Mental Lives of Savages and Neurotics* relied on temporality and space to collapse notions of the racial Other with those of the sexual Other.[39] This collapse is then instanced for the first time and most prominently in the myth of the primordial homoerotically inclined horde of sons who cannibalize their father. Considering that both psychoanalysis and ethnography emerged as quasi-scientific disciplines at approximately the same time and were either determined by or more or less directly modeled on discourses of colonialism, it may not be surprising that Freud finds same-sex acts among the colonial Other perfectly complementary with his observation of a "primitive psychology" in homosexuals. As Fuss puts it, Freud places both "within a static ontology that constructs each figure as representative of a primordial phase of human development."[40] Fuss suggests that the cultural mythologization of the savage and the invert—whom she aptly describes as "modernity's two great figures of mimetic prowess"[41]—often projected the figures of sodomy and cannibalism onto each other. In other words, a discourse of anal sex became rearticulated as an excessive, savage orality and vice versa. It was precisely the apocryphal, mythical nature of the notorious parricide through cannibalism that made it neatly fit Freud's teleological theory that civilization is based on the repression of homosexuality and the taboo against cannibalism. In addition, the cannibalistic act is permanently enshrined and prepped for reenactment in the sublimated form of the totem meal.

Freud's grand scenario of the building of civilization through a series of complex, tortuous identifications harbors two aspects that are of interest here: first, that identifications are not always rational and premeditated (indeed, they can be subconscious and, in fact, very primal acts); and second, that it is precisely homosexuality's presence-as-absence in this scenario that helps us understand why broader processes of identity formation also partake in identifications that are not readily apparent, not easily traceable, and, in fact, repressed. These two aspects reverberate in Andy Warhol's perspicacious and, as usual, notoriously deadpan comment on how the suggestive powers of the cinema deeply inform and enhance the way we relate to popular actors, stars, and celebrities—a relationship that Warhol claims to honor with his early, minimalist portrait films. As quoted by Gretchen Berg, Warhol says: "I made my earliest films using, for several hours, just one actor on the screen doing the same thing: eating or sleeping or smoking; I did this because people usually just go to the movies to see only the star, to eat him up, so here at last is a chance to look only at the star for as long as you like, no matter what he does and to eat him up all you want to. It was also easier to make."[42] This comment suggests how the fetishistic nature of modern visual culture is particularly conducive to the primal and, as I will argue later, traumatic nature of a broad spectrum of identifications (made across the board of homosexual and heterosexual identities and often erasing the tenuous boundary between identification and desire). It takes on an even more specific, more potent connotation with regard to the role of homosexuality in identification, crystallizing the context in which *Blow Job* must, indeed, be seen as nothing less than a queer totem meal for James Dean. While the film serves up its poser for consumption to all kinds of spectators, its catering to gay men in particular points to a cultural territory in which gay male desire in general and the primal, transgressive nature of anal and oral sex in particular have, more often than not, come to be associated with certain forms of "savagery," such as cannibalism. However, in *Blow Job*, oral incorporation becomes not only articulated but also displaced, reflecting, among other things, the complexity of gay men's relation to a primal gay sexuality and the complexity, too, of gay identity's murderous relation to James Dean. If Warhol, by 1964, was no longer content with expressing his white gay male fascination with James Dean entirely in terms of martyrdom, transcendence, and spirituality, he still conceptualized *Blow Job* in a way that banishes its visceral elements off-screen—eating and sex, identification and desire, are more clearly than ever displaced onto the viewer. In some ways, this seems congruous with *Blow Job* being a metaphor for the ways we as spectators "eat up" the stars on the screen. But the fact that *Blow Job*—beyond the grace of clever irony—*represses* fellatio in the act of producing it puts it in more complex relation to mythic and psychoanalytic tales of orality.

If it is true that, as Diana Fuss points out, identification is also always about what cannot be taken inside, what resists incorporation, we may argue that trauma and mourning are not two completely discrete responses to loss but, are, in fact, closely linked. What becomes marked as the ultimate loss is the loss that is irrecoverable, that cannot be assimilated[43]—and, as the myth of the cannibalistic, guilt-ridden sons who resurrect their father via the law would indicate, the loss that does become assimilated through mourning produces a sign or a set of terms that covers up the unassimilable, irreducible, and traumatic residue of that loss. In this sense, trauma seems to precede and exist alongside mourning as a failure to fully resolve and "work through" loss. And in this sense, too, *Blow Job*'s compulsive pointing toward the absent referent seems to function in ways that partly overlap with but also go *against* the act of mourning Dean, of revoking the killing, and, as it were, of constructing a gay identity in his image.

To the extent that *Blow Job* may be regarded specifically as a queer totem meal for James Dean, it is notably the first work in the trajectory of Warhol's commemorations of the star that links his death to the act of oral incorporation. We ought to acknowledge here that while the 1955 *James Dean* constitutes a gay appropriation of the star arguably by means of assassination, this assassination is not exactly an act of cannibalism other than perhaps in the broadest metaphorical sense of a subculture cannibalizing and feeding on the dominant culture for appropriations, identifications, and identity formation. It is not until *Blow Job* that gay male culture's relation to Dean can be understood not only as murderous but as cannibalistic: The imagined eating of the poser's cock by a gay man, which constitutes an erasure of the poser's identity—his murder—becomes synonymous with eating him up "all we want to." However, we should take *Blow Job*'s insinuation here for what it is—that is, not as the belated revelation of a secret truth (a killing that happened nine years earlier) but as a kind of retroactive renegotiation. This retroactive renegotiation can be thought of as but one symptom of a shift in white gay male identity and white gay male sensibility of the late 1950s/early 1960s, a response to the widening rift between the proliferation of a sexualized gay subculture and a roughly contemporaneous effort on the part of activists to obtain public respectability for gay men. Even if, by the early 1960s, many gay men were still feeling distant from gay activists' strategic responses to the mainstream's ethnographic scrutiny of "the gay tribe" (that is, the activists' strategic imaging of the "healthy," masculine-identified homosexual), the burgeoning market of gay beefcake glossies indicates that a large number of gay men were internalizing this masculine-identified image on another level. It was not the queerness of these images that stood in contrast to gay activist politics of masculinity (Tom Waugh has shown that these images had come out of the homosocial space of World War II culture and remained broadly within the parameters of masculine identification); it was their increasingly explicit sexualization, which helps us understand the rift between a publicly propagated image of respectability and a private and subcultural pursuit of gay sex. From the 1950s until fairly late into the 1960s, this rift, with its unbearable contradictions for this tribe with regard to masculinity and sexuality, was increasing rather than subsiding. In addition, while the subculture was the traditional outlet for gay sex censored from the public eye, Bersani's work (see Chapter 4) suggests that subcultures, too, have to negotiate the potential contradiction between sexual pleasure and masculinity. In this regard, queerness itself may be regarded as one of several disciplinary productions to negotiate this contradiction within and for the subculture.

Warhol's images reflected these contradictions between public gayness and subcultural gayness and between sex and masculinity in different ways. It is not that these contradictions are altogether absent from the 1955 *James Dean;* they are simply somewhat more submerged than in *Blow Job.* While *James Dean* successfully queers the original myth of the cannibalistic horde of sons who kill their father, it also still partakes in the myth and residually references its oppressive implications. We must not forget that the central figure of the mode of mourning and identity formation in which *James Dean* partakes—the founding father, who has lost none of his patriarchal qualities in the twentieth century—is inimical to the sustained flourishing of gayness. Consider that in *Rebel Without a Cause* Dean was at least as much a father/lover to Sal Mineo as he might have been a brother; in addition, the filial aspects of Dean's persona, as displayed, for example, in *East of Eden*, eventually become eclipsed by paternal ones. He becomes associated with the misunderstood saint and, more particularly, with Christ, who also starts out as a son (of God) and brother (to mankind), but whose martyrdom makes him a leader of disciples and imbues him with classically paternalistic features. Dean's films, then, may be thought of as strong reflections of patriarchy less because of their status as mass culture products but rather because they must be regarded as fairly symptomatic of Western culture's inability to conceive of rebels in terms other than patriarchal.

So, although Warhol's 1955 drawing—which is, after all, a barely known, fledgling artist's extremely marginal and fairly private attempt at queering a star—depicts Dean as boyish and effeminate (which is what constitutes its queering of patriarchy), it complies with this symptomaticity: It recasts what one might characterize as the potentially radical abjectness of Dean—the submerged implications of masculinity lying prostrate, powerless, and passive—as a conventional abjection of alternative yet still broadly mainstream masculinity. As a strategic appropriation of the saint/martyr figure, *James Dean* is an example of pleasure facilitated by the disciplinary productions of power. In Warhol's drawing, James Dean has already gone to heaven as a gay martyr. Spirituality here has the crucial, far from incidental function of instantly converting the condition of abjectness into heroic, sacrificial, and ultimately very conventional abjection—which is precisely how patriarchy defines the figure of the martyr and which is also, as noted earlier, how gay masculinity constructs itself as a coherent identity—that is, by instantly recasting a more radical abjectness. The very framework that safeguards the subject's coherence (for even abjection yields such assurance) and produces pleasure also constitutes the limits of a white gay male queering of patriarchy. The paterfamilias is queered, but his residual structure begins to produce friction in and for the queer identity emerging from it. *James Dean* was part and parcel of an era in which the white-homosexual-as-suffering-martyr was one of the few images available to gay men to strategize against the negative image the homophobic mainstream had constructed of them.

By availing itself of conventional discourses of abjection, suffering, and transcendence, the 1955 *James Dean* averted (and thereby indirectly acknowledged) gay male proximity to abjectness. *Blow Job* emblematizes an aesthetic era very different from that emblematized by *James Dean*, as it produces spirituality, suffering, and transcendence as a style, a pop citation, or a myth fragment. On this level, *Blow Job* indicates that these qualities were being divested from their once overdetermined function of constructing a white gay self-image. However, *Blow Job* indicates as well that this evolving self-image, even though now clearly more "secular" and sexual than in the 1950s, was not free from elements of repression, which can be inferred not only in the poser's gender performance but also in the film's simultaneous production and repression of gay orality. In other words, on one level, *Blow Job*'s aesthetic transgression may rightfully be regarded as a visual analogue to an increasingly assertive gay male culture whose relation to the mainstream was gradually becoming more self-confident; in fact, at first glance, *Blow Job* does not seem terribly concerned at all with the publicly performed self-image of the "normal" and wholesome homosexual. On another level, however, the film also latently indicates a certain trauma produced by the contradictions between white gay men's relation to their publicly performed masculinity and their sex practices. It is, of course, true that fellatio has always had the appeal of being "cool" among males of any sexual persuasion—provided one is the one being fellated and not the cocksucker. But this is different from the concept of a primal gay orality—and, for that matter, from the concept of a primal, unbridled gay sexuality. For this sexuality is indissociable from a freewheeling reciprocity and exchange of roles (those who have their cock sucked also like sucking cock; those who fuck others also like getting fucked) and, ultimately, from connotations of passivity. For these reasons, gay sex is not only transgressive but may, in fact, be inimical to an image of "normal" masculinity and, therefore, taboo.

However, despite the fact that the film's repression of a primal gay orality certainly marks the limits of gay men's identification with their own public self-image, it would be wrong to assign the trauma that surfaces in *Blow Job* only to gay men. Precisely because *Blow Job* is so closety, because the film constructs homosexuality mainly on heterosexual terms, it appears more apposite to analyze this trauma within the framework of heteronormativity, which it haunts and punctures—a heteronormativity that is, in fact, at the heart of the production of trauma. As argued earlier, the heteronormative field was negotiated by both heterosexuals and homosexuals through the same figure, hypochondria—a mode of negotiating Otherness that actually comprises a whole spectrum of strategies and rhetorics, gay- and straight-authored, such as the sublimation of homosexuality, its homophobic (but also homo-strategic) rearticulation into malaise, world weariness, or purported bisexuality, and its recasting into a homophobic spectacle of "mere" entertainment. Notwithstanding my provisional attempt at transvaluing hypochondria for a Bersanian homo-specificity, the utilization of hypochondria as a strategy indicates that it remains a child of *scientia sexualis* and, thus, a mode of constructing homosexuality within the binary framework of self and other.

To read *Blow Job* within a heteronormative framework may by no means result in wholeheartedly denying the existence of homosexuality; neither does it result in the exclusion of gay male readers. The division of the scenario into what is depicted inside the frame (which, in and of itself, is highly polysemic) and what is left altogether to the imagination enables such a reading to simultaneously deny and entertain the possibility of homosexuality, to produce it as one's own fantasy but also to dissociate it from one's own act of production. Especially when brought to bear on the late 1950s/early 1960s context of white gay male identity, in which subcultural assertion coexisted with internalized homophobia, it may merely be *the result* of this reading, and not *the mode* by which this reading proceeds, that pans out very differently for gay and straight readers. In this sense, if trauma may, in fact, be read as registering in the film's on-/off-screen division, it does so both as the failure to deny homosexuality fully and as the phantasmatic production of homosexuality as a fearful and/or alluring spectacle to which this division is, of course, highly conducive. We find trauma surfacing in the interstices between the set of heteronormative/homophobic rules and blockages and the deeply troubling knowledge that homosexuality nonetheless exists and, worse, that an identification with it has been made and continues to be made. The attempt, however futile and repetitive, to resolve this trauma is constituted by the simultaneous distancing from and narrating of this traumatic identification. Following recent art historical discourses on Warhol, I shall argue in the following section that one of the specificities and, indeed, peculiarities of Warhol's work lies in the fact that he pays attention to both.

INSIDE OUT: THE AESTHETICIZATION OF TRAUMA

As the analysis of Warhol's Dean images earlier in this chapter has argued, Warhol himself had an ambivalent relation to identification. This ambivalence sometimes becomes falsely spectacularized in the artist's notorious statements, such as "I still care about people but it would be so much easier not to care . . . it's too hard to care . . . I don't want to get too involved in other people's lives . . . I don't want to get too close . . ."[44] Yet historians of art, film, and culture, such as Thomas Crow and Art Simon, have also noted the emotional saturation of Warhol's celebrity silk screens and death and disaster paintings, which gives them a decidedly noncynical quality. And while Crow in particular reads the loss of the referent (for example, Kennedy) as an event that "galvanizes Warhol into a sustained act of remembrance,"[45] others such as Hal Foster have, without refuting the thesis that Warhol's art enables and enacts mourning, begun to read his images in terms of trauma. In this enhanced analytical framework, a silk screen such as the 1963 *Tunafish Disaster* can now be read as mobilizing the full gamut of discourses on and around identification—from mourning to the phobic refusal to mourn, from incorporation of the Other to what Fuss calls "a *withdrawal* of the Other"[46] that makes incorporation impossible. Crow reads *Tunafish Disaster*—a silk-screened tabloid front page reporting the death of two Detroit women from food poisoning—as Warhol's subtle foray into investigating the circuits of mass consumption that extend from the (sometimes lethal) ingestion of food to the (always frenzied) intake of death and misfortune as public spectacles. Crow asks, "Does Warhol's rendition of the disaster leave it safely neutralized?" The answer is no, as the silk screen creates a frisson between the tabloid tawdriness it cites and the empathy it enables despite the banality of the accident. Hal Foster's analysis of Warhol's death and disaster series then prompts us to redefine this frisson as creating a space not only of a trace tracking out to the referent but also, conversely, of the referent (or more accurately, the referential realm, the real) puncturing the screen (which is also the screen*ing* of the traumatic event) as it is being read and processed in the mind of artist and viewer.[47] With equal validity and respective aptitude, both readings wrest Warhol's imagery away from charges of cynicism and indifference, and if I, in this particular case, follow Foster's, it is only to argue that for Warhol *the whole broad process of identification as such was traumatic.*

This becomes strikingly clear if one considers an image outside the Warhol canon, an image that Warhol neither created nor processed in the strict auteurial sense of the term (always problematic especially with regard to Warhol's work). But Warhol's co-authorship of this image, however limited its nature, is as inevitable as it is interesting for the particular context that concerns us here. The image is a photograph taken by Warhol's then boyfriend, photographer Ed Wallowitch, of Warhol posing in front of a wall next to a skull with crossbones painted on its bricks (Figure 5.7).

Wallowitch took this and three similar photos during a break Warhol was taking from silk-screening *Tunafish Disaster* at his old Manhattan studio, Firehouse 13 (located on 87th Street), which preceded the Factory.[48] One can easily link this photo with Warhol's then ongoing work on *Tunafish Disaster*, noting that Warhol chose to place himself next to the official symbol designated to warn people about the deadly consequences of oral ingestion (of, say, hazardous chemicals)—a linkage that testifies to Warhol's wry sense of humor. However, of greater interest here is another warning, inscribed in the photograph, about the always hazardous process of identification in general, whether it is with the victims of food poisoning, or with the fatally wounded James Dean, or with the assassinated president and his widow. If an artistic commemoration of the dead is never just a neutral relay of a fatal event but, in fact, constitutes the latter's reenactment—an assassination in its own right—identification may become unbearable to the point of becoming taboo. This taboo, the photo seems to suggest, causes the artist/assassin to distance himself from the referent/victim, to revoke the crime by reenacting it with a stand-in that has the function of a fetish. For what else is the skull than a totem that erects a taboo around the referent as well as the crime, both of which it thereby simultaneously shields and confesses?

Since, as Diana Fuss has noted, trauma is always part of the process of

Figure 5.7

Edward Wallowitch, photo of Andy Warhol with a skull drawing, 1963. B/w photograph (8⅛ × 10 inches). Courtesy of the Estate of Edward Wallowitch. Archives of the Andy Warhol Museum, Pittsburgh Founding Collection, Contribution The Andy Warhol Foundation for the Visual Arts, Inc. (photo: Richard Stoner, 3/19/01).

mourning, the skull as a general idiom of identification indicates that mourning can only ever be partly successful. While the skull's traditional status as a vanity may be said to suggest, among other things, a successful parting with the lost love object, a mastery over the trauma of loss itself, it is also a memento mori and, as such, a reminder that life is transitory and loss is painful. Hence its fetish function, which is meant to defuse the traumatic aspects of identification.

While the particular skull Warhol associates himself with in the photograph was apparently painted by Wallowitch and not Warhol,[49] the skull as a visual motif became one of Warhol's popular images in the later part of his career. Painting the skull is, as one of Warhol's assistants once remarked, *like doing the portrait of everybody in the world.*[50] The skull is thus the perfect allegory for Warhol's fame and success as a portraitist. But it is important to distinguish here between the mid-1970s skulls created by Warhol and the skull as a general idiom, which visualizes certain aspects of identification and which has a slightly more particular meaning for Warhol. That Warhol invites comparison between himself and the skull by posing with it has a logic apart from the joke that this pose may have been intended to be. The skull functions as a buffer enabling Warhol to "safely" engage in the process of identification. This pertains not only to Warhol's engagement with death in general, and with death and disaster victims in particular, but also to his own homosexuality. Whatever the circumstances behind Warhol choosing a brick wall as the backdrop against which to pose with the skull, this choice, when placed in the context of the brick wall's iconographic significance for postwar gay male identity, speaks volumes about Warhol's traumatic identification with his own homosexuality and with his effeminacy.[51]

Thus the skull disguises the fact that one has identified with one's Other; but it is also the most extreme idiom of identification in Warhol's canon. As a substitute referent, it is the very placeholder through which identity formation literally takes place. But apart from the banal fact that every human has a skull, what enables the skull's universalizing modus operandi of incorporating the Other? How is it that no Other can potentially resist the skull's aggressively expansive reach? To the extent that incorporating the Other is phantasmatic, it actually *produces* Otherness. Rather than taking the Other inside, a copy is made of what is being feared and/or desired about the Other. The skull's dark hollow inside is then merely an internalized *copy* of the Other, indeed, of Otherness *as* a copy. The cavernous space actually excludes the Other and blocks knowledge about it and communication with it, whereas the skull's outside surface, the shell that defines its overall shape and appearance, stands as a reminder that what has been taken inside did, at least initially, have a referent. Maintaining a link to the (to any) original referent, while keeping it at bay, the skull shows that identification is as necessary (indeed, ineluctable) as it is traumatic.

It has been pointed out that the universalizing and minimalist starkness of the skull makes it an apt idiom for pinpointing and visualizing basic thematic opposites.[52] However, if one reads the skull more particularly as a meta-commentary on what psychoanalytic discourses have characterized as the split subject and on that subject's traumatic relation to Otherness, two things become apparent. On the one hand, the skull appears to rigidly hierarchize the position of self and Other; on the other hand, the skull's fetish character disguises the impossibility of such a hierarchization. In other words, the skull's dark eye sockets signify Otherness as empty and insubstantial; darkness's only function is to conceptually support the whiteness that engulfs it, a whiteness whose bone mass stands for *conceptual* fullness—the conceit of sheer presence. I use the word "conceit" here because this presence (the presence of the self) is phantasmatic. Even though the self conceives of itself as full and of the Other as empty, the self nonetheless incorporates the Other—which testifies to the self's emptiness, that is, to the fact that its fullness is a conceit. The incorporated Other's fullness is imagined, too, but since the subject is split into self and Other, this imagined fullness (of the incorporated Other) threatens to enable the traumatic possibility that the subject also sees itself as full(y) Other. This trauma becomes the driving engine for the split subject's continued striving to become, in turn, the self.

The skull thus shows that identity forms via the Other, but it also denies the fact that Otherness is always part of our identities. As an idiom for the split subject's traumatic relation to identification, the skull inverts the terms of fullness and emptiness and collapses them onto each other—but it also conceals this collapse in its fetishistic surface engulfment of Otherness. The skull's binary features, then, also seem to address the two sides of Warhol's ambivalent relation to identification. On the one hand, Warhol's association, in the Wallowitch photograph, with the skull as a fetish buffering him from what or whom he is asked to identify with can be said to reflect his impulse that it is so hard to care and that he would much rather not care. As such, the skull has a unique status in the Warhol canon, conceptually linking the artist's successful career as a pop art portraitist directly with his relation to identification. The skull's appeal as a motif of choice for the artist may well indicate most poignantly that, for Warhol, it would be much easier to care if one could care *for everyone in a similar way.*

On the other hand, Warhol's own skull renditions from the 1970s do not quite conform to the dynamics just described. They slightly alter the visual-metaphorical terms that we have outlined for designating the function of the skull. Because they are depicted at an angle that produces a shadow (Figure 5.8), the distribution of dark fields on the picture plane somewhat opens up the play between darkness and other colors (Warhol's skulls came in several colors). This greater fluidity, especially around the eye sockets and the teeth, amplifies the skull's already "sensitive" and unstable areas with regard to its engulfment of Otherness. The darkness in these areas remains not fully contained by the shell; it bleeds out into the skull's environment. To be sure, this liquidity can be read as simply confirming that the associative chain of metaphors these images produce deploys darkness-as-Otherness in such a way that it can always, among other things, be reduced to something that is more tangible than whiteness (it bleeds out) and, yet, less firm, less substantial—that is, ultimately expendable, nonexistent in relation to whiteness.

However, the shell's inability to contain what is inside may also furnish the impression of the Other's "unruli-

Figure 5.8
Skull, 1976. synthetic polymer paint and silk-screen ink on canvas (15 × 19 inches). © 2002 Andy Warhol Foundation for the Visual Arts/ARS, New York

ness." The Other constantly threatens to "take over," to escape its status as copy and to debunk incorporation as a conceit. While these Warhol images render their particular skulls less effective tools to simply ward off trauma, they also suggest that the dynamics of the phantasmatic incorporation of Otherness may be less stable than the skull as an idiom for the split subject makes them appear. Warhol's appropriation of the skull keeps the boundaries between inside and outside more fluid, suggesting, at the very least, that the skull's conceit of sheer presence is precarious and its effectiveness in regulating self–Other relations is far from guaranteed. In this sense, Warhol's highly idiosyncratic skull renditions suggest that he did identify and care, even though caring was hard and traumatic, and that he was willing to visualize and to explore, however subtly, those precarious regions in which identification is a constant struggle. Perhaps more important, Warhol's exploration of self–Other relations suggests that we are *imperfect* indices of the self–Other binary that constructs us. It may be the very inadequacy of our efforts to fully comply with and "live" this binary that may eventually point to new directions for theorizing identity away from binary models.

If Warhol's work bespeaks, as Hal Foster argues, a double relation to trauma, "a warding away of traumatic significance *and* an opening out to it, a defending against traumatic affect *and* a producing of it,"[53] Warhol's association with the spray-painted skull in Wallowitch's photograph is at least symptomatic of this sensibility, even if this particular skull may not be Warhol's own creation. The skull is a copy of Warhol himself, Warhol's own Other, Warhol-as-Other. Unlike Warhol's own skull renditions, in which Warhol explores the traumatic relation between self and Other by inscribing it upon one and the same object, Warhol ends up exploring trauma in the Wallowitch photo by willed association of self (Warhol) with Other (the spray-painted skull). In other words, the parameters of Warhol's collaboration in the photograph were such that self and Other became externalized into two spatially separate entities.[54] So, while the skull as a general motif designates the split subject's relation between self and Other as traumatic (the harsh black-and-white contrast around the eye sockets and the jaw being the very site where trauma manifests itself as the incommensurable contrast between self and Other), and while the destabilization of this harsh contrast by Warhol's skulls of the 1970s arguably opens out to trauma and explores it upon the skull itself, Warhol's association with the minimalist spray-painted skull some thirteen years earlier constitutes another such exploration. As can be gleaned from Wallowitch's photograph, this association asks us to compare fullness and emptiness across the visual "substance" that acts as a defining vector for both—whiteness.

Eve Sedgwick has written eloquently about Warhol's whiteness, a whiteness that she describes as "inhuman" in its "intractable literality," a whiteness that does not admit to whiteness's partiality (Warhol's whiteness is not the whiteness that blushes). So Warhol's displacement of shame, any kind of shame, onto shyness can be read, as Sedgwick suggests, as a symptom of the double bind Warhol faced: "What it may mean to be a (white) queer in a queer-hating world, what it may mean to be a white (queer) in a white-supremacist one, are two of the explorations that, for Warhol, this shyness embodied."[55] According to the Wallowitch photograph, this double bind means existing in close overlap, even synonymity, with the very structures that construct and privilege one as a white man, but it also means existing as one of whiteness's Others (dark, dirty, nonwhite sexuality), marked in value by nonwhiteness, positioned vis-à-vis whiteness, or, as the spray-painted skull suggests, defined as whiteness's empty inside.

To discuss whiteness at this point, however, can be misleading because of the overdetermined way whiteness functions hermeneutically. There is a danger in talking about whiteness that homogenizes and levels all of whiteness's Others. I am thus concerned here only with parts of the problem Sedgwick points to in her characterization of Warhol's "*un*blushing white skin" that, "in its very allegorical excessiveness, resists being normalized or universalized." I should also mention that Chapter 6 discusses the history of whiteness as an imperialist-racist force and its aspiration to being a transcendental signifier for self–Other relations. Right now, with regard to the spray-painted skull, it is particularly the hermeneutics of desire, sex, and perversion, called *scientia sexualis*, that interests me. In this context, the skull's outlines, which are the same white matter as the eye sockets and mouth opening, constitute not simply a particular instance of an Other produced by *scientia sexualis;* rather, they function as a template of Otherness itself. This particular spray-painted skull may be read as a minimalist allegory of the discursive regime that engenders self and Other through one and the same disciplinary production, and because the white line's minimalism accentuates rather than attenuates a sense of the skull's *conceit* of sheer presence, foregrounds the contiguity of self and Other.

Warhol made this particular skull his own not by drawing it but by posing next to it, and if his authorship by association creates a particularized instance of the self–Other dichotomy, it also appears that Warhol's minimalist drawings from the period and the skull's minimalist lines inspired one another, as it were, in the way they tend to allegorize the discursive grid and disciplinary nature of identity production. The minimalism of *James Dean* and *A Gold Book* may thus also be regarded as crucial to the way these drawings comment on the construction of gender and sexuality especially with regard to white gay men. The thin lines are the framework of the basic set of norms that designate the category "white man." The conceptual contiguity of the lines with the emptiness inside them signifies that white gay men's (ful)filling of these norms is compulsory yet superficial: This (ful)filling—especially in the historical context at issue in which the category of "white gay man" only gradually came to be fleshed out—appears to partake in heteronormative white masculinity, but it is based on this masculinity's opposite signifier—emptiness. White gay men's differential relation to the norms producing them leads to the result that, for white gay men, fullness equals emptiness, the self is Other.

One might argue with some justification that this self–Other relation is not particular to white gay men. However, what may be particular to white gay men is, first, that they amplify the self–Other relation as a conflict between two opposite signifiers, both of which white gay men are invested in, and, second, that the reason gay male gender performance resulting from this conflict evinces "performative prowess" may be because it signifies this conflict not as classically traumatic but as bearable, even pleasurable. In *Blow Job*, this pleasure may be evidenced by the poser's repetitive motions that make him inhabit various masculinities not as "end positions" but superficially, mechanically, and without commitment. While these positions all reside broadly within the masculine (they are reified masculine stereotypes), and while masculinity's opposite signifiers (antiphallocentric impulses, radical passivity, abjectness) are difficult or impossible to signify, the poser's indifference to these positions suggests that neither they nor their opposite signifiers that may be inferred have retained their conventional etiological nature based on gender as traumatic imposition of difference. However, as far as this self–Other relation is visualized in some of Warhol's noncinematic works (particularly his drawings), we note that Warhol signifies homo-specific appropriations of the structure of trauma by making their visual contours "vibrate."

This quality is particularly prominent in the drawing of the two men featured in *A Gold Book* (Figure 5.3). The tenuousness of the thin contours of the two figures is compounded by the fact that the line itself is discontinuous. For the most part, it is a line of tiny dots, which aesthetically accentuates not only the tenuousness of the form but the tenuous relation *to* the form, indeed, to form as such. In other words, in contrasting the tiny dots with the emptiness they produce by becoming a line, this drawing celebrates the fact that the process of assuming shape, of settling into (and for) form and thus into identity and the conditions for identification, is highly unstable. These dotted contours literalize the dual relation the white gay male subject evinces to committing to form as such; they suggest the distance to the very parameters that enabled white gay men to take shape—registering, as it were, in the tremulous oscillation between a compulsory subsumption under the dominant and an indifferent, noncommittal inhabitation of it.

The details of this visual tremor are particularly interesting with regard to another Warhol image (Figure 5.9). The image is a jacket cover Warhol designed for a novel entitled *The Desire and Pursuit of the Whole*, which was written by an epigone of Oscar

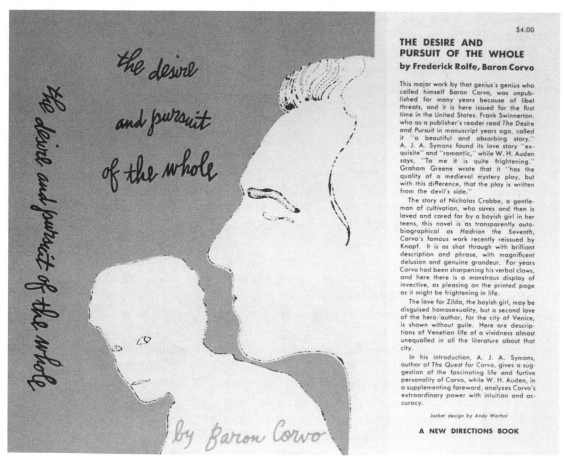

Figure 5.9
Book cover for *The Desire and Pursuit of the Whole* (1934) by Baron Corvo, 1950s (8¼ × 10¼ inches), published by New Directions. © Archives of the Andy Warhol Museum, Pittsburgh Founding Collection. © 2002 Andy Warhol Foundation for the Visual Arts/ARS (copy photo: Robert P. Ruschak).

Wilde, Frederick Rolfe, whose pen name was "Baron Corvo."[56] The summary on the jacket informs the reader that this is "the story of Nicholas Crabbe, a gentlemen of cultivation, who saves and then is loved and cared for by a boyish girl in her teens." Announcing that the novel is full of "magnificent delusion and genuine grandeur," the summary further indicates that the story of its protagonist may have homosexual aspects: "The love for Zilda, the boyish girl, may be disguised homosexuality, but a second love of the hero/author, for the city of Venice, is shown without guile." While this sounds like a conventional story of homosexual sublimation, the novel's foreword, written by W. H. Auden, says the following:

> In writing it, Rolfe certainly expected that his readers would see life as Crabbe sees it, that they would take his side, agree that he was the innocent genius victim of a gang of malicious boobies. . . . Thanks to Rolfe's remarkable talent, however, the reader has the very different and, for him, more interesting experience of knowing that he is looking at the world through the eyes of a homosexual paranoid. . . . As we read the extraordinary and magnificent twenty-fifth and twenty-sixth chapters of this book, in which Crabbe, friendless, homeless, penniless, delirious for lack of food, wanders day and night through the streets, we cease to laugh at or pity him and begin to admire. Faced with the choice of going home, or dying in the place he loves, he will choose to die, and behind all his suffering there is a note of exultation.[57]

While the first part of this description ("the genius victim of a gang of malicious boobies") makes the novel sound like a vague yet ominous precursor of Tennessee Williams's *Suddenly Last Summer*, the later part actually suggests striking parallels to André Gide's *The Immoralist*, which Bersani discusses as one of the prime examples of the homo-specific desire for self-dissolution within the framework of conventional masculinity.[58]

It seems very much that the second aspect of Auden's description is brought out by Warhol's cover design for the novel. Warhol visually adapted the novel's turn-of-the-century sensibility to the post–World War II sensibility of white gay men, and his visuals notably identify what is at stake in different kinds of gender performance. The two figures, the boyish girl Zilda and the novel's protagonist, are rendered in the same minimalist style as Warhol's other 1950s work: Their heads are outlined through thin contours, only indicating outer silhouette and mouth and eye area, leaving any further detail to the imagination. If this is the story of two friends who come from opposite ends of the sex/gender spectrum and whose friendship would seem to lead, as it were, to a queering of gender, to a mutual rubbing off of identity traits, there are two different but related dramas that unfold here. Zilda, the tomboyish girl, is depicted as seeing the man as the model for her own gender performance, which she successfully articulates as passing-for-a-man. (I use the word "successfully" because it is, in fact, impossible to tell whether Zilda is a boy or a girl.) The minimalist semiotics of this jacket cover drawing thus identify her differential position as a successful assumption of the speaking position of the opposite sex.[59] Crabbe, by contrast, is portrayed with enough detail (his head in profile, his prominent nose, and, most notably, his masculine eyebrow) to identify him unambiguously as male. Yet, to the extent that he sees his friendship with Zilda as formative of his own identity as a white gay man, Zilda's influence significantly complicates a reading of this identity, leading to multiple combinations and refractions. Zilda can be incorporated as a girl, as a girl passing for a boy, or as a boy. Each of these incorporations constitutes in its own respective way an opposite signifier to the speaking position with which Crabbe is officially aligned, that is, heterosexual masculinity. Yet, whatever the refractions of his identity produced by the range of Crabbe's possible identifications with Zilda, he is still forced to inhabit his masculinity at least superficially.

The minimalism in Warhol's drawing also has another effect. The dotted texture of the lines and the space between the darker outside and the white inside the lines create an area of friction, pointing to the kinds of frictions these characters signify in their respective gender performances. If Zilda can be characterized as successfully passing for male, this success belies the punitive aspects that her passing entails. In addition to the psychosexual friction that may be incurred by women passing for men, Brandon Teena's story, among others, has taught us that this friction is also always one between the passer and a predominantly hostile, even lethal, environment. White gay men certainly also have to negotiate this environment, but the friction they incur may be of a different order due to the fact that their distance to gender seems more like an internal one. If one applies Warhol's ironic visualization of the already campy homonymic pun of the novel's title to its male protagonist, it becomes clear that the differential position of white gay men is based on overlapping but deeply contradictory signifiers. If, with regard to Zilda, the homonymic Other most likely refers to object choice (that is, if her tomboyish looks indicate her desire for women), with regard to Crabbe it designates also *the Other of his assigned gender*. Through the dotted line of Crabbe's silhouette Warhol points to a frisson in the otherwise compulsory overlap of self and Other that contributes to a vague impression of the protagonist's wistfulness. There is a sense that Crabbe's contradictory investment in masculinity is something from which pleasure can be derived—the kind of pleasure that comes with fully but superficially living out the contradictions of inhabiting the disciplinary framework of gender, the kind of pleasure that leads to the draining of what is inside this framework.

Similarly, a reading of the James Dean look-alike from *A Gold Book* may find that the thinness of the figure's contours not only expresses tenuous and playful phallic self-assertion but also harbors at least the trace of its opposite signifier: the gay male subject's desire for self-dissolution. In this sense, the figure's bare contours may characterize homosexuality as chimerical and, in addition, may describe masculinity as an empty category, a bare grid that white gay men inhabit only superficially. So, despite and alongside what I have called "the conservative qualities" of Warhol's 1950s images, there is a sense in some of these images that, for white gay men, to explore the traumatic implications of masculinity means both to ward off trauma and to live with it, indeed, to live it by virtue of being drawn to both self and Other, and to do so in a particular way that does not necessarily foreclose pleasure.

In sum, all of these images not only formulate their appropriation of alternative masculinity as a strategic subversion of gender norms into something new, queer, and different, but they also indicate a more deeply felt, intuitive sense of a gender disparity within white gay men. This sense may be profound in that it always frames these images' strategic efforts (and, quite possibly, any strategic effort) at gender redefinition. Perhaps I need to emphasize here that I do not mean to ignore or deny the significant impact of James Dean as a figure for subversive gay, lesbian, and queer appropriations, resistances, and empowerments. Dean has been and will continue to be appropriated as a gayly perverse brother and a queer sister. To the extent that Warhol's Dean images strategically heighten Dean's androgyny and sexual difference, they cultivate queer deviation from the norm and inscribe a number of queer subject positions—adult white gay men, gay teens, transgendered and transsexual people, butch lesbians, and baby dykes—as appropriations of Dean-ness. To the extent, however, that these images ultimately identify, as they do, with the masculine, they make clear that there is something quite specific at stake in white gay men's appropriation of James Dean. Because of white gay men's differential position to the category of "men," white gay male counterstrategies within *scientia sexualis* invariably run into the same dilemma. Their contradictory investment in masculinity, which leads to a kind of "internal" distance from it, makes masculine-identified white gay male performance always superficially synonymous with the disciplinary structures that enable its production but from which it is alienated. The visual "tremor" around Warhol's minimalist lines marks this alienation as the site of trauma and, rather than only warding off trauma, also signifies a rearticulation of trauma as the mark of a possibly highly specific (homo-specific) gay male desire. Of course, it may be in the nature of this "different," homo-specific exploration of trauma that the particular set of images discussed here achieve little more than a denaturalizing effect. They make us infer more than identify this homo-specific pleasure. They suggest with great subtlety that the pleasure of strategic resignification may not be the only pleasure involved in gender performance.

6

DARKNESS AS METAPHOR

ndy Warhol's use of white male iconology from the 1950s into the 1960s engages discourses of sex and gender in ways that suggest a certain duality at the
heart of white gay male gender performance. White gay men's investment in
masculinity causes them to partake in discursive productions of white masculinity and to inhabit the disciplinary framework that enables these productions. But to the
extent that this framework is maintained in the name of heteronormativity and phallocentrism, the anti-phallocentric aspects of gay male desire and gay male sexuality alien-
ate white gay men from the very masculinities they produce and in which they are invested. This combination of a desire for and alienation from masculinity arguably
constitutes the "homo-specific" aspects of white gay male gender performance—a dual
yet disaffected engagement of masculinity and its opposite signifier, which forecloses a
more serious and substantive relation to masculinity and which "drains" masculinity of
its substance, making visible the bare structures of the framework itself. We have already
investigated Warhol's white male iconology with regard to certain "homo-specific" textual clues—empty spaces, barren contours, visual "tremors," and other minimalist markers of the special frisson between white gay men and white masculinity. However, since
the basic framework within which our society constructs masculinity appears to persist,
the roles of heteronormativity and phallocentrism need to be investigated. Guarding the
boundaries of gender, they do not simply constitute the discursive limits of white gay
masculinity but help produce it as transgressor, as Other.

Of concern in this final chapter is how a phallocentric, heteronormative white
male speaking position produces a whole range of Others by mobilizing discourses of
difference and playing out these Others against one another. The key strategy at issue is
to *champion* the Other at its own expense, to privilege some Others over other Others,
to use the Otherness of one Other to tell another Other that it is not so other after all—
all this to incorporate the Other and use Otherness as a tool against the Other itself.

Blow Job is part of this interrogation of white heteronormativity, because rereading *Blow Job* in this regard may help us understand how in the late 1950s and early 1960s
heteronormative constructions of gender and sex intersected with those of race. Most
constructs of sexual Otherness—whether targeting certain sex practices such as fellatio
or anal intercourse, marking the position of commodified sex, or stereotyping gender
and sexual identity—also bear connotations of ethnic Otherness. To the extent that the
sexual savage is a phobic construct, he or she cannot be imagined as completely white.
However, as we shall see, whiteness in this particular context is not a quality that effaces
itself before blackness or becomes diminished, taken away, or exchanged for blackness—
whiteness is that which conquers blackness and, despite all claims to the opposite, inscribes blackness as a variation of itself. In this way, the concept of a universal white-

ness is strengthened and enriched, whereby whiteness, in the final instance, comes to be ontologically prior to blackness.

In the late 1950s, the articulation of whiteness "through" blackness was performed most ostentatiously by an urban intellectual as a gesture of rebellion against white, square, middle-class America. More than four decades later, Norman Mailer's essay "The White Negro" still stands as whiteness's most notorious attempt at seizing on racial and sexual Others via a particular figure—the psychopath. Standing at the crossroads between criminology, mythology, and pop culture, the psychopath functioned as a response to consensus culture's social and sexual anxieties. He overlaps to a certain degree with the figure of the teenage rebel, whose ideological and mythological function was discussed in Chapter 2. The present discussion draws on some of these earlier findings but reads the psychopath's broader typology mainly through Mailer's essay to investigate how racial and sexual attributes intersected with popular discourses of psychopathy. My discussion will also read the psychopath into *Blow Job*. To the extent that a reading of *Blow Job* is partly constituted by what is fantasized to be below the frame, and to the extent that such fantasies may carry elements of "primitive," "savage," taboo sex, what is within *Blow Job*'s frame may perhaps be read as a register of the kinds of visual metaphors our culture uses to convey notions of the primitive, the savage, and the taboo. As we shall see, these metaphors are not restricted to sex and gender but link sex and gender to race. *Blow Job*'s mise-en-scène constructs these metaphors through the spectrum of shades that range from light at the top to dark at the bottom. The film's lighting links taboo sex to darkness in all its connotations, whereas lightness—indeed, light itself—is linked with whiteness and whiteness's triumph over and transcendence of sex and desire. Thus while *Blow Job* subverts this value system it retains the terms on which this system operates. After discussing this dynamic in detail, the last part of the chapter then investigates how *Blow Job*'s deployment of lightness and darkness may be said to comment on white gay men's relations to sexual and racial Otherness.

SHADES OF WHITENESS: THE PSYCHOPATH

In his study of the construction of masculinity in 1950s popular culture, Steven Cohan has pointed out that the cinematic psychopath was deemed uncontrollable and sadistic, with a violent contempt for family and property. These attributes functioned to establish psychopathy as a category that described antisocial male behavior.[1] Referencing Estelle B. Freedman, Cohan notes that while the term "psychopath" was initially used to classify women as a means of controlling prostitution, during the depression era it increasingly came to be applied to men to link "abnormal" male sexuality to male criminality.[2] The 1940s then saw a more systematic investigation of the type, especially furnished through Robert Lindner's 1944 study, *Rebel Without a Cause—The Hypnoanalysis of a Criminal Psychopath*. In the 1950s, discourses of both popular culture and popular science and sociology applied the term specifically to the 1950s teenager. Further citing Freedman, Cohan stresses that the concept's regulatory function also resurfaced during this period, "first, as a means of repealing, in the interests of normalization, the official valorization of hypermasculine aggression which had occurred during the war; second, as an articulation of anxieties about the violence of returning veterans; and third, as a representation of abnormality working to enforce heterosexual conformity for men as well as women."[3]

Due to the military's wartime shift away from defining homosexuality via effeminacy toward defining it via psychopathology, the 1950s homosexual was lumped in with the broader category of the psychopath. The terms "psychopath," "sex criminal," "pervert," and "homosexual" became virtually synonymous.[4] Nonetheless, presumably because of censorship, at least Hollywood representations of the psychopath during the 1950s remained predominantly hetero-identified (with some latent bisexual, homosexual, and pedophile facets). The fact that the psychopath was mostly a white stereotype during this time indicates the function of social regulation also with regard to race. Citing sociohistorical data on the racial bias of 1950s legal terms and practices, Cohan states that "courts repeatedly differentiated 'mental illness' from 'willful violence' according to an offender's race."[5] In other words, the category of "mental illness" was reserved for white criminals because, especially with regard to sex crimes, violence in whites was deemed an aberration so horrific that it violated deeply held assumptions about whiteness itself and had to be accounted for via the model of mental pathology. It was not until the late 1950s that the white psychopath as a type became overtly inflected with racial—and racist—discourses. These were a building block of Norman Mailer's aggressive romanticization of black masculinity as anarchic. Mailer helped boost such types as the urban white hipster and the beatnik strictly as masculine styles, but, as we shall see, his attempt to cleave fantasies of white and black anarchy by no means abolished the ideological division between what was regarded as incidental, "aberrant" white violence and what was perceived as the "natural" and mundane black predisposition for crime. In popular culture, too, the depiction of psychopathology remained a predominantly white affair for much of the decade not the least because, as Cohan argues, Hollywood films such as *Blackboard Jungle* shied away from addressing any sociocultural and race-related causes for the white delinquent's behavior and for teen violence in general.[6]

Vic Morrow's knife-wielding junior heavy, Artie West, in *Blackboard Jungle* may be regarded as a more violent, more explicitly psychopathic double of James Dean's Jim Stark in *Rebel Without a Cause. Rebel* milks its "troubled" and "misunderstood" protagonist's posturing for what it is worth but never releases him from the claws of its integrationist ideology. Dean's knack for performing nervy, restless, and deeply troubled characters made his public image sufficiently flexible to invoke, somewhat disingenuously, the full gamut of facets associated with violent white male teens (disingenuously, because apart from a few isolated outbursts, Dean's movie characters were for the most part nonviolent, gentle, and peace loving, and two of the three Dean vehicles at least superficially resolved their oedipal conflicts by domesticating the rebel). In addition to the double-edged nature of Dean's persona, it was, of course, the star's sudden, spectacular death that helped propel Dean to mythical proportions. It was Dean's almost instant larger-than-life status, not his fairly conservative Hollywood vehicles, that helped him become synonymous with the juvenile delinquent as both social type and pop culture stereotype, as a dangerous, psychologically disturbed young man and as a romantic hero. The blanket nature of the Dean myth proved a perfect match for the term "juvenile delinquency," which, according to James Gilbert, itself contained "a large measure of subsurface meaning."[7]

Because of the discrepancy between the Dean myth and Dean's films, we have to consider Dean's most famous vehicle, *Rebel Without a Cause*, both in relation to that myth and also on its own terms. *Rebel* is a problematic rather than an emblematic instance of popular culture's attitude toward juvenile delinquency. As discussed earlier, for the film to achieve its integrationist agenda, it has to perform a set of transferences, which also make it a less easily identifiable example of the division of mental illness and willful violence along race lines that Cohan identifies as typical of 1950s legal and cultural discourses around the psychopath. To (however self-reflexively) assimilate Dean's character, the film places all unassimilable qualities on Sal Mineo's Plato. In the film's ideological designation of stereotypical traits, Plato's ethnicity becomes a bizarre last-minute "umbrella" of sorts for his homosexuality and his violence. His attempt to shoot his way past the police reproduces the stereotypical 1950s classification of black violence as "willful"—and this occurs despite the film's implications, on another level, that Plato's violence is the result of a number of "white" psychological challenges, such as those that seemingly caused his white friend's erratic behavior (not to speak of the great fear and sense of threat Plato feels at the film's climactic ending). The film's superficial racialization of violence at the end (which merely reflects *white* middle-class society's legal attitudes toward *nonwhite* criminals) is meant to gloss over the "white"-inflected causes of Plato's violence. This comes as a "corrective" response to the earlier need to whitewash Plato's impulse for crime to assimilate him to the other characters and to a white middle-class audience by making his family background conform to the standard of the white family melodrama, which privileges individual oedipal dysfunction over social issues. In other words, while *Rebel* requires Plato to pass as white for much of its plot by making him live and suffer as a white person, the film's ending requires him to die "black," with blackness in this instance being a white construct.[8] In the film, then, race *and* homosexuality are respectively reduced to skin color and longing glances—they exist as structuring absences. Plato is exploited in two directions: for the color he adds to Jim's social life and for his need to be "calmed down" and tutored. But Plato is denied Jim as a white father/lover and his death then rids Jim of all specters that haunted him by association (homosexuality, blackness, and violence). The transferential scheme *Rebel* enacts makes clear how white consensus culture first endowed the white rebel with attributes of "primitive," "noncivilized" Otherness only to eventually rescue him from these attributes.

Citing the work of Toni Morrison, Edward Saïd, Sander Gilman, and others, Richard Dyer in his analysis of whiteness as a Western construct has pointed out that African Americans, Arabs, Asians, and a range of other non-white peoples have been recruited by white culture not only for the construction but also for the naturalization of whiteness.[9] And since whiteness refers not only to skin color but to numerous other ideologically constructed qualities (such as racial and ethnic superiority, moral purity and virtuousness, cleanliness of the body, and the ability to control bodily instincts and sexual drives), any aspects not associated with whiteness tend to become whiteness's Others, the negative instantiation of these features, or what whiteness supposedly masters and transcends.[10] In this sense, through his association with and ultimate dissociation from Plato, Jim in *Rebel Without a Cause* is made even more white at the end than he was through much of the film: He is no longer violent or erratic, his links to homosexuality have been dispelled, and his association with corporeal, ethnic darkness has been terminated because the latter, too, has been excised from the narrative, even as it was produced, first and foremost, in the act of excision.

This reading of *Rebel* reflects many of the findings of recent critical discourses on the construction of whiteness via nonwhite races and ethnicities. However, Richard Dyer reminds us that the act of tracing and analyzing how certain texts use blackness for the construction of whiteness tends to redouble the work these texts themselves do—that is, to subordinate blackness as a concept for the purpose of analyzing whiteness. Whiteness is then denaturalized only when directly set against blackness, whereas whiteness is really a construct of its own and in all texts.[11] In this sense, while it is worth pointing out that Plato functions in *Rebel* as a screen for the projection of sexuality and violence "on to dark races [as] a means for whites to represent yet dissociate themselves from their own desires,"[12] it is equally worth pointing out that whiteness itself—the whiteness of Dean's Jim Stark and of his adversaries, the teenage gang—has all along been informed by aspects of darkness *that strictly originate within white culture* and that reflect, as it were, white culture's attempts to designate its Others also within itself. Whiteness itself, then, evinces these dark qualities to a much larger extent than does Sal Mineo's Plato, embodying all those stereotypical qualities that whiteness deems "dark" and unassimilable: overly developed narcissism, impetuousness, erraticism, psychopathic violence, homosexual tendencies, and an all-around perverse sexual predisposition.

Rebel Without a Cause is complicated because it represents an interesting duality with regard to whiteness's appropriation of darkness. On the one hand, the temporary deployment and ultimate abjection of corporeal darkness represents a typical instance of Hollywood attempting to consolidate integration and assimilation via narrative closure. On the other hand, despite this whitening of Dean's fictional character, Jim Stark, in *Rebel*, darkness, far from being eliminated, actually became perpetuated in the overall Dean myth—as a *metaphor*. Certain instantiations and facets of the Dean myth (such as Dean's Hollywood vehicles) may, at times, avail themselves of corporeal darkness; however, as a sprawling spiral-like construct, the myth no longer depends on it and, given Dean's whiteness and the white genealogy of the psychopath, probably never did. It is precisely because, as Dyer emphasizes, "there need not be explicit or even implied racial reference, it is enough that there is darkness"[13] that vast and multifaceted myths such as the white teenage rebel absorb and accumulate a plethora of darknesses with rather disparate genealogies. Corporeal darkness is but one of these darknesses—however, in those instances where it is actually deemed important enough to be brought into play, it is absorbed in the most imperialist kinds of ways. White myths recruit corporeal darkness as but one aid for the construction of darkness as metaphor, which they may or may not fashion into a tool for the critique of the white aspects of whiteness, all the while depriving dark races of equanimity. In other words, they take more from corporeal darkness than they give back to it. Indeed, corporeal darkness is subjected to a white makeover; it is demoted to an irreducible residue to which even certain white-authored *attacks* on whiteness tend to seek recourse—however falsely, polemically, and unsuccessfully.

Therefore, while the darkness operative in such myths as James Dean, the teenage rebel, and the psychopath must be analyzed with regard to its white genealogy, within the parameters of the present study we cannot afford to lose sight of white-authored constructions of nonwhite races completely. Three things merit analysis in the particular context of this argument. The first is the possibility that a certain text's featuring of a nonwhite race for the construction of its whiteness does not preclude the fact that this text's whiteness may have its own anatomy and genealogy—which may, in fact, be eclipsed deliberately by the text's engagement with corporeal darkness. Second, even white-authored attacks on whiteness may continue to seize on—in fact, may *particularly* seize on—nonwhite races and ethnicities as mere objects, as grist to their mill of metaphors. And third, how whiteness seizes on its ethnic Others should be compared with the ways it seizes on its sexual Others, which overlap only partly and which may well suffer different fates in this appropriation. All three aspects become especially clear in Norman Mailer's essay, "The White Negro."

DELUSIONS OF BLACKNESS: "THE WHITE NEGRO"

Mailer's "The White Negro" was published in 1957 in the journal *Dissent*, a relatively small but influential publication. His thoughts on the white hipster, equally poetic and polemic, quickly gained impact from the instant notoriety the essay garnered in urban circles and also within the Beat movement, which, although a very small, marginal movement, was itself increasingly becoming the target of much popular interest. Critics and historians have pointed out that Beat as a movement, although romanticizing black culture, had little in common with Mailer's ideas. In fact, these came to be an embarrassment to many Beats who felt their art had been hijacked by someone who was not Beat but had made a diabolical—and successful—attempt at gaining attention. In addition, Mailer's essay was, in fact, separating Beat from hipsterism by creating what is essentially a gender stereotype that had little to do with the heterogeneous spectrum of actual Beat males and their masculinities.[14]

Whatever the essay's philosophical ambitions, "The White Negro," which carries the subheading, "Superficial Reflections on the Hipster," became a catechism and manual for white middle-class masculine self-stylization. In this regard, Mailer's essay was merely part of a historical moment in which white mainstream American society began to take interest in its margins, turning the spotlight on homosexuals, Beats, and—in several different ways—African Americans. Especially in the late 1950s and early 1960s, marginal movements and marginalized identities were separated from their cultures' and subcultures' organic values and implications and reproduced as commodifiable styles, typically triggering such conversions as the move from Hip to "hip" and from Beat to beatnik. The moment that saw the commodification of a whole spectrum of alternative masculinities was also the high moment of the white hipster. Although Mailer's essay was attacked almost instantly upon publication by white as well as black critics, today its misguided rhetoric tends to get attributed to a certain "impulsiveness" and naïveté on the part of its author and a whole intellectual set disenchanted with the consensus climate of the Eisenhower years. In other words, for many critics today, Norman Mailer and his white negro are "old hat." This chapter nevertheless accords a fair amount of space to discussing "The White Negro" because Mailer's impulsiveness does, in fact, bear a certain systematicity that merits investigation, for it can give us insight into the larger dynamics that guide appropriations of racial and sexual Otherness in a white heteronormative field.

Before we engage with the race discourse of Mailer's "The White Negro," it needs to be pointed out just how little historical evaluation—indeed, how little space—the essay actually accords to black men and black culture. Mailer describes the hipster as a white American existentialist, whose nihilism is a response to the totalitarianism of society and the death threat of the atomic age. In the face of apocalypse, Mailer argues, one needs to encourage the psychopath in oneself and join an "avant-garde generation" of white young urban people whose intellectual fathers are D. H. Lawrence, Henry Miller, Wilhelm Reich, and Ernest Hemingway.[15] The essay is prefaced by a gloss on the hipster taken from *Harper's Bazaar*, which describes the hipster as a white marijuana-smoking rebel who finds a prominent embodiment in James Dean and whose infantilism is a sign of the times.[16] While Norman Mailer may not have had primarily James Dean in mind when he began writing "The White Negro"—indeed, while Mailer's notorious literary creation could be said to by far supercede Dean's fictional characters with regard to disaffected cool—the very eagerness with which the type of the white hipster was received and reenacted by droves of urbanites and suburbanites can be explained most appositely by invoking the outer areas of the Dean myth. Some, but certainly not all, of these areas reflected an appeal that was as old as *white* America itself—notably the vision of the ruggedly individual, priapic male who traverses the continent from east to west in complete freedom from civilizational restraints and in touch with the larger spiritual forces of the land. In addition, Mailer saw it perfectly fit to support this image with Robert Lindner's 1944 characterization of the "rebel without a cause" and to invoke a movie star whose rebel image by no means suffered from the fact that his most notable film took from Lindner's study little more than the title. That Mailer could skim so effortlessly the long line of lone American heroes testifies to the fact that even by the mid-1950s, the American frontier had lost none of its appeal for the construction of American masculinity. Even in the decade of alternative masculine styles, male freedom, individualism, and entitlement still underscored a panoply of more recent types and stereotypes, generated within and without Hollywood. As Mailer writes:

> The psychopath is a rebel without a cause, an agitator without a slogan, a revolutionary without a program: in other words, his rebelliousness is aimed to achieve goals satisfactory to himself alone; he is incapable of exertions for the sake of others. All his efforts, hidden under no matter what disguise, represent investments designed to satisfy his immediate wishes and desires. . . . He cannot wait upon erotic gratification which convention demands should be preceded by the chase before the kill: he must rape. He cannot wait upon the development of prestige in society.[17]

It takes Mailer almost a complete section in his essay to trace the genealogy of the psychopath as a strictly white character. While Mailer seeks to qualify contemporaneous American society's attempts at juxtaposing white and black criminality via attribution of mental illness and, correspondingly, willful violence, he nonetheless accepts the broader parameters of this division. Although Mailer goes to some length to distinguish the psychopath from the psychotic and from the neurotic, and although he slams psychoanalysis for its lack of effectiveness, Mailer never leaves the territory of mental and psychological disturbance—except that for him, this disturbance has an effect worthy of affirmation and cultivation. He writes, "The psychopath is ordinately ambitious, too ambitious ever to trade his warped brilliant conception of his possible victories in life for the grim if peaceful attrition of the analyst's couch."[18] Blackness, by contrast, is understood *a priori* as an uncultivated and primitive force, which is deeply eruptive through the sheer presence of its Otherness. For blacks to avail themselves of psychiatrists would not only be completely alien and a territorial transgression, it would, in Mailer's view, constitute a serious betrayal of what he perceived as the ontologically grounded "savagery" of blackness and, thus, of the potential for anarchy especially of black hipsters.

So, despite the fact that Mailer seeks to fashion his white hipster on his notion of black Hip, his white hipster not only is white and will always remain so, but he was an intrinsically white figure to begin with, with his shades of darkness remaining rooted firmly within white culture. But Mailer's surprisingly elaborate charting of a distinctly white pedigree for the hipster does not really contradict his intent to appropriate blackness. Blackness, in his essay, is sought out as a corporeal authentication for white middle-class males to groom themselves as anarchists. The dynamics by which Mailer attempts to appropriate blackness merit a closer look, for they not only shed light on the transformation of corporeal darkness into metaphorical darkness, but they tell us something about the trappings of using darkness as metaphor, even if it is summoned for an attack on whiteness.

The utilization of a blackness marked as corporeal in the construction of whiteness as an unmarked, even disembodied, universal condition prominently reflects how, according to Dyer, all concepts of race are concepts of the body and of heterosexuality.[19] In "The White Negro," Mailer avails himself precisely of this strategy to appropriate racial discourses from the top down in order to inveigh against square white middle-class America. This becomes particularly apparent in an early version of "The White Negro" that Mailer penned quickly to dare liberal newspaper publishers to print what, according to him, was the real reason for white America's resistance to forced racial integration in its schools. This draft of "The White Negro" reads as follows:

> Can't we have some honesty about what's going on now in the South? Everybody who knows the South knows that the white man fears the sexual potency of the Negro. . . . For the white, symbolically and materially, has possessed Negro womanhood for two centuries. Which is what all the literary critics mean when they talk about the blood guilt of the South.
>
> The comedy is that the white loathes the idea of the Negro attaining equality in the classroom because the white feels that the Negro already enjoys sensual superiority. So the white unconsciously feels that the balance has been kept, that the old arrangement was fair. The Negro had his sexual supremacy and the white had his white supremacy.[20]

By linking the blood guilt of the South with notions of black male sexual supremacy, and by endorsing racial integration as a means to compensate for this blood guilt and to catalyze what he regards as "the reversals of history," Mailer does not simply cite southern guilt as a political and historical phenomenon. In a very particular manner, he also deeply identifies with it and with the underlying racist assumption of black sexual supremacy. The reason Mailer's early draft did not find its way into "The White Negro" is not because Mailer, somewhere along the way, stopped believing in what the words essentially expressed, but because the draft drew sharp criticism. His friend and editor of *The Independent*, Lyle Stuart, sent the short piece to a number of prominent individuals ranging from Eleanor Roosevelt to William Faulkner, and the various objections these readers had to the piece caused Mailer to begin work on "The White Negro."[21] Faulkner's reply, in particular, prompted Mailer to admit to himself that he had to develop his sentiment into a more substantial argument. Mailer felt that Faulkner's criticism (which will be discussed a bit later with regard to Mailer's notions of gender and sexuality) had made him vulnerable to charges of imitating blackness. He felt that Faulkner had an image of him as "a noisy pushy middling ape who had been tolerated too long by his literary betters."[22]

For the version of "The White Negro" that was published, Mailer had thus moderated an out-and-out essentialist view of black masculinity in favor of a sociologically inflected quasi-essentialism. For example, he writes in the published version, "Hated from the outside and therefore hating himself, the Negro was forced into the position of exploring all those moral wildernesses of civilized life which the Square automatically condemns as delinquent or evil or immature or morbid or self-destructive or corrupt."[23] While Mailer could not possibly believe that white middle-class males could literally turn themselves into African Americans, he was convinced that they could identify with sociopolitical and historical aspects of African American oppression. Thereby, or so Mailer believed, they could assimilate crucial aspects of African American culture, enriching their own human and cultural potential, which they could then brandish on white, square society to cause havoc. Mailer believed that whites are able to appropriate certain aspects of blackness primarily by allowing themselves to be educated by the teachings of black hipsterism's mock scholarship,[24] realized mainly through the communicative capacity of art—in this case, jazz. As Mailer writes:

> Knowing in the cells of his existence that life was war, nothing but war, the Negro (all exceptions admitted) could rarely afford the sophisticated inhibitions of civilization, and so he kept for his survival the art of the primitive . . . and in his music he gave voice to the character and quality of his existence, to his rage and the infinite variations of joy, lust, languor, growl, cramp, pinch, scream and despair of his orgasm. For jazz is orgasm, it is the music of orgasm, good orgasm and bad, and so it spoke across a nation, it had the communication of art even where it was watered, perverted, corrupted, and almost killed, it spoke in no matter what laundered popular way of instantaneous existential states to which some whites could respond, it was indeed a communication by art because it said, "I feel this, and now you do too."[25]

Mailer's description of orgasm has caused much bemusement over the years, but it is important to understand that his equation of jazz with orgasm and his choice of words—"the infinite variations of joy, lust, languor, growl, cramp, pinch, scream and despair of his orgasm"—express what is essentially a *masochistic* infatuation with black culture. This masochism is brought out without any ambivalence in the early version of Mailer's essay, where he fantasizes that a black uprising would lead to "the *temporary* but nonetheless certain spiritual *enslavement* of the Southern white" (my emphasis), which, he believes, "ought to be nourishing for both races—not to mention the moral justice of it."[26] What becomes clear here is that while Mailer's fantasy constitutes the guilt-ridden wish to "make up" for history through a masochistic invitation to counter-colonization and counter-enslavement, this invitation is qualified in two ways: First, this counter-colonization entails for blacks neither a gain in power nor an improvement of material conditions (blacks may not actually ever come to power, as they never come into play, or, more accurately, they remain confined to playing[27]), and, second, it is temporary and thus less threatening to the ontological makeup of white society. At issue here is the concept of carnival, which celebrates a temporary destabilization of the oppressive hierarchical order of the world through which values and power relations are inverted for a brief period of time, only to reconsolidate the powers that be with increased force when the party is over.[28] For what is left disempowered in this cultural-spiritual osmosis is black people themselves. As Ned Polsky writes in a reply to "The White Negro," "Even in the world of the hipster the Negro remains essentially what Ralph Ellison called him—an invisible man. The white Negro accepts the real Negro not as a human being in his totality, but as the bringer of a highly specified and restricted 'cultural dowry,' to use Mailer's phrase. In so doing he creates an inverted form of keeping the nigger in his place."[29] Mailer's essay was provocative because, among other things, its author had successfully pinpointed the instability (and, thus, the constructedness) of whiteness, something that a long tradition of white supremacist texts had been suppressing.[30] In the imaginary triumph of "the white negro" we find an attempt to assuage white guilt by diabolically inverting the terms of the southern myth without abolishing the terms themselves. While the white hipster is a literary figure constructed to attack dominant white society, this construction clearly indicates Mailer's identification with that society. Mailer's guilt over the historical importation and enslavement of blacks produces psychosexual fantasies of the white self's masochistic subordination to blacks. Mailer's liberation of blacks is a predominantly intra-psychic phenomenon that has little to do with black liberation as a political cause. And since the self around which Mailer's phantasm proceeds is, of course, a white self, blacks come to be subjected to yet another incorporation—a phantasmatic incorporation of Otherness. Incorporation is thus the only conceivable discourse available to whiteness. The myth of the white South "that both most consciously asserts whiteness and most devastatingly undermines it," as Dyer describes it with regard to D. W. Griffith's white supremacist film *The Birth of a Nation*, becomes, in Mailer's essay, the myth that most consciously undermines whiteness and most devastatingly asserts it in the process.

Since the agenda of Mailer's essay is not the victory of black over white but of dark over light—that is, of white hip over white square, facilitated, as it were, via proliferation and expansion—the myth of southern guilt is too static to accomplish this goal alone. Mailer's essay thus supplements the southern myth with the myth of the West. As Mailer writes, "One is Hip or one is Square . . . one is a rebel or one conforms, one is a frontiersman in the Wild West of American night life, or else a Square cell, trapped in the totalitarian tissues of American society."[31] Dyer rightly points out that in contrast to the myth of the South, the myth of the West "is a success myth [that] allows us to experience a sense of white historical mastery of time and space" and that, in contrast to the myth of the South, takes "the project of whiteness for granted and achieved."[32] In this scenario, the hipster is a subversively sexualized westerner who reconquers white civilization through "black" qualities, features, and values, all the while remaining a white person. How pervasive this myth is in Mailer's essay, how aggressively imperialist its force, can be gleaned in Mailer's assertion that the anarchy of hip has already gripped many parts of the strata of American society:

> If it be remembered that not every psychopath is an extreme case, and that the condition of psychopathy is present in a host of people including many politicians, professional soldiers, newspaper columnists, entertainers, artists, jazz musicians, call-girls, promiscuous homosexuals and half the executives of Hollywood, television, and advertising, it can be seen that there are aspects of psychopathy which already exert considerable cultural influence.[33]

What is important for Mailer's effective engagement of both myths is that blackness itself is not only incorporated but also transubstantiated into a more general darkness, which can be claimed as the legitimate, authentic result of white masculinity's osmosis with black culture. The ease with which Mailer thrashes these concepts about indicates that Mailer shrewdly, perhaps intuitively, realized what Dyer recently conceptualized for whiteness in general—that is, that there need not be implied or even explicit referential blackness and that it is enough that there is darkness—except, of course, that this insight serves Mailer to consolidate white hegemony rather than abolish it.

In Mailer's pseudo-subversive essay, shards of blackness become shades of darkness and the latter can then be harnessed into a spatio-metaphorical topography in which it passes for ominous and anarchic. And something very similar can be said to transpire in the way Mailer uses whiteness's own sexual Others for the construction of hetero-sexuality—however alternative, subversive, and disruptive this heterosexuality is conceived to be. When Dyer points out that "dark desires are part of the story of whiteness, but as what the whiteness of whiteness has to struggle against,"[34] he does so to designate an explicitly heterosexual context. In this context, white heterosexual men have dark desires and their lives revolve around few options: giving in to what is rising up from below, harnessing these forces to the reproduction of the white race, or resisting them altogether. According to Dyer, "This furnishes the heterosexual desire that will rescue whites from sterility while separating such desire from what whiteness aspires to."[35] Dyer goes on to describe how the contradictions of a Victorian attitude toward sex are translated into potent clusters of metaphors, such as darkness/sex/rising-from-below and whiteness/temperance/control-from-top-down. Even though Mailer's essay appears to be an attack on the prudishness of American white middle-class society, in concrete political terms the racial pyramid implicit in "The White Negro" precisely replicates this hierarchization. Its top is still occupied by the heroic, lone white hipster, the phallic generator of all kinds of racial and sexual "subversions" of white square middle-class America. And the white hipster's priapic sexuality is being served from underneath by a whole range of dark Others, racial as well as sexual, whose disparate genealogies become occluded as they are subsumed under the umbrella category of darkness as metaphor.

It is precisely the umbrella nature of this category that glosses over the fact that the range of Others Mailer recruits into metaphor is extremely heterogeneous; and it is the nature of metaphor that makes it a tool for hegemonic appropriations of Otherness. Mailer's decision to characterize his own essay as a superficial reflection indicates a certain shrewdness. On the one hand, the performance of casualness and its desired effect of sangfroid deflect from the imperialist character of Mailer's appropriations, not to speak of their unfounded and unreasonable nature. On the other hand, it also serves Mailer to put some distance between him and his objects. With regard to Mailer's appropriation of race, this distance may well have been intended as a saving grace, communicating to the reader that Mailer himself knows best that there will always be a deplorable and unbridgeable rift between "white" and "negro." However, with regard to sexuality, this distance may have acted more like a safety zone, lest Mailer be taken up on engaging with certain sexual forms of Otherness too intimately. Among other things, this would have revealed that Mailer, finally, was lacking the courage of his convictions. For Mailer, as will be argued later in this chapter, it was impossible to absorb homosexuality into the spectrum of Others he deemed worthy of romanticization—and this was not only because its widespread practice might have posed an obstacle to "subversive" miscegenation, but because homosexuality for Mailer also designated certain gender aspects that may, in fact, have been inimical to the very concept of "The White Negro."

Returning to the reasons that prompted Mailer to develop his early draft into "The White Negro," we need to go back even further—into the early 1950s—when

Mailer was called upon by one of the editors of *One*, the homosexual magazine, to write an endorsement of homosexuals. "I didn't know the first thing about homosexuality I hurried to tell him,"[36] Mailer writes in his late 1950s commentary, or, as he calls it, "Advertisement for 'The Homosexual Villain,'" the piece he would ultimately write for *One*. The title "advertisement" was aptly chosen, for it allowed Mailer to go into detail in recounting how the members of *One* had sought him out as an up-and-coming intellectual in order to get endorsements for "the homosexual cause." As is often the case with straight liberals who endorse gays by recounting in confessional discourse their first encounter with homosexuality, Mailer flaunts his own ignorance about homosexuality to testify how this encounter put him on the path of self-knowledge and made him work through his own fear of association—only to emerge from this work as the better, more fully formed heterosexual. He writes, "When I was back in New York, my mind running wild in the first fevers of self-analysis, I came to spend some months and some years with the endless twists of habit and defeat which are latent homosexuality for so many of us, and I came to understand myself, and become maybe a little more of a man."[37] While Mailer in "Advertisement for the Homosexual Villain," a preface written in hindsight, gleefully admits to the square, liberal content of "The Homosexual Villain," his claim that writing the piece had a therapeutic effect on him and his craft is far from self-conscious. In fact, reading the essay and its hindsight preface side by side, we can see many parallels. In "The Homosexual Villain," Mailer writes:

> I did not know any homosexual because obviously I did not want to. It was enough for me to recognize someone as homosexual, and I would cease to consider him seriously as a person. . . . I always saw him as at best ludicrous and at worst—the word again—sinister. (I think it is by the way significant that just as many homosexuals feel forced and are forced to throw up protective camouflage, even boasting if necessary of women they have had, not to mention the thousand smaller subtleties, so heterosexuals are often eager to be so deceived for it enables them to continue friendships which otherwise their prejudices and occasionally their fears might force them to terminate.)[38]

This reads like a nutshell characterization of straight liberal hypochondria (see Chapter 3). Mailer claims that a purely cerebral encounter with homosexuality—reading Donald Webster Cory's *The Homosexual in America*—opened his eyes and a whole new world for him. This makes clear how Mailer sought to negotiate his wishes to engage with and to distance himself from homosexuality, a process resulting in the fact that he could now speak on behalf of homosexuals supposedly without being threatened by homosexuality,[39] that he could distance himself from homosexuality, having "worked through it" cerebrally and vocationally. As "a last remark," Mailer closes his essay this way:

> A last remark. If the homosexual is ever to achieve real social equality and acceptance, he too will have to work the hard row of shedding his own prejudices. Driven into defiance, it is natural if regrettable, that many homosexuals go to the direction of assuming that there is something intrinsically superior in homosexuality, and carried far enough it is a viewpoint which is as stultifying, as ridiculous, and as anti-human as the heterosexual's prejudice. Finally, heterosexuals are people too, and the hope of acceptance, tolerance, and sympathy must rest on this mutual appreciation.[40]

Mailer here instantiates the liberal discourse of mutually acknowledging and appreciating one's differences as essential but equal. In other words, he is willing to grant gays the status of full subjects and citizens. This status is not extended to the black male in "The White Negro," for that essay is about the phantasmatic appropriation of blackness, but not about the concrete development of a political agenda to further civil rights and fight racism. A line fashioned after the argument in "The Homosexual Villain" that would begin, "If the negro is ever to achieve real social equality and acceptance" would be strangely out of place in "The White Negro."

If one compares "The White Negro" with Mailer's hindsight commentary on "The Homosexual Villain," two things become clear. On the one hand, the latter actually contains brief flashes of euphoria that indicate the author's eagerness to treat himself to homosexuality the way he treats himself to blackness. In his "Advertisement for 'The Homosexual Villain,'" Mailer writes that what probably propelled him to seek out the therapeutic effect of writing the piece was that his fear of homosexuality was stifling his creative work and negatively affected certain characterizations in his most recent novel, *Deer Park*. "Given the brutal rhythms of my nature," he writes in "Advertisement for 'The Homosexual Villain,'" I could kill this inhibition only by jumping into the middle of the problem without any clothes."[41] As a homosexual wish fantasy, this bears a certain resemblance to Mailer's masochistic, more-than-skin-deep wish to assimilate blackness in "The White Negro." On the other hand, the comparison has its limitations, for "success" in each case is defined very differently. As far as blackness was concerned, Mailer, at least in the late 1950s, still believed that masochistic subordination to what he conceived blackness to be made significant parts of that blackness rub off onto him; with regard to the homosexuality, however, he believed that "naked" and masochistic exposure to homosexuality was successful only when it resulted in ascertaining one's essential difference from homosexuals. In other words, one doubts very much that writing "The Homosexual Villain" had any significant therapeutic effect on Mailer. Rather, it merely perpetuated his own hypochondriacally motivated relation to homosexuality. And this relation, still based on fear but now also heavily inflected by sexism, determined the method by which "The White Negro" plays out one Other (homosexuality) against another (blackness).

In his commentary on "The White Negro," Mailer recounts that he had spent the years leading up to writing his essay on drug binges, which had dissipated his energies and made him unable to write. Now, living in the country, a father-to-be, he was taking boxing lessons from his father-in-law, and his masculinity was on the rebound. As Mailer writes in the commentary, "Everything was good, exctpt [sic] that I could not write; my mind would have fine moments, but its powers of connection were dim; my brain seemed stuffed in cotton."[42] This comment indicates how Mailer felt both the influx of a re-masculinization and an anxiety resulting from the fact that this did not translate into his rebirth as a writer. Indeed, his words come very close to an oedipal scenario in which a male rival (his father-in-law) infuses him with a certain strength that he, however, fails to convert into actions that would redeem his own expectations implicitly nourished by this filial treatment. Given this context, it was then all the more disastrous for Mailer that another quasi–father figure, William Faulkner, whom Mailer admired very much, dismissed his first draft of "The White Negro" with the following response: "I have heard this idea expressed several times during the last twenty years, though not before by a man. The others were ladies, northern or middle western ladies, usually around 40 or 45 years of age. I don't know what a psychiatrist would find in this."[43] If this exchange is, as Mailer claims, what triggered him to write the eventually published version of "The White Negro," his own assessment of what Faulkner must have seen in him—"a noisy pushy middling ape who had been tolerated too long by his literary betters"—is a disingenuous, panicky attempt to cover up the real image created by Faulkner that Mailer understood all too well: that of a white, self-identified heterosexual whose romantic courting of black male sexuality testified not only to his sexual desire implicit in this courting but to his effeminacy. It is difficult to say which implication was harder for Mailer to take, but he responded only to the latter, attempting to throw the ball back at Faulkner. He writes: "Like many novelists who have created an extraordinary body of work, Mr. Faulkner is a timid man who has led a sheltered life. So I would not be surprised if he has had his best and most intense conversations with sensitive middle-aged ladies."[44] From this exchange it is clear, then, that Mailer's white negro may be many things, but not homosexual. Mailer asserts that many hipsters are bisexual, but this bisexuality is cautiously contained by an excessive masculinity that would never allow itself to be penetrated. In a reply to Ned Polsky, who accused Mailer's hipster of having premature orgasms, Mailer wrote: "Since he can hardly have had the requisite personal experience—'Uncle,' said a bisexual Negro to me once, 'I couldn't have more charge for that chick if I'd gone down on a platoon of Marines'—I wonder if Polsky isn't really just passing on a tyrannical assumption which is one of the cement blocks of the Square throne of psychoanalysis."[45] This "requisite personal experience" is enough evidence for Mailer that masculinity remains secured for the white negro, too. Should he really ever screw things up seriously, which Mailer calls "goofing" (as opposed to "swinging," which signifies the hipster's creative mastery of his environment), his masculinity is at stake: "If you goof (the ugliest word in Hip), if you lapse back into being a frightened stupid child, or if you flip, if you lose your control, reveal the buried weaker more feminine part of your nature, then it is more difficult to swing the next time, your ear is less alive."[46] Goofing or flipping for Mailer means that "one has lost one's will, one is impotent in the world of action and so closer to the demeaning flip of becoming a queer, or indeed closer to dying."[47] Note that queer here does not mean what it means today. In the late 1950s, it meant simply homosexual, "faggot." Finally, the whole affair between black male and white hipster, even when it takes place in the regions of bohemia, is an essentially, that is, conceptually, heterosexual affair. As Mailer notes in "The White Negro,"

> In such places as Greenwich Village, a ménage-à-trois was completed—the bohemian and the juvenile delinquent came face-to-face with the Negro, and the hipster was a fact in American life. If marijuana was the wedding ring, the child was the language of Hip for its argot gave expression to abstract states of feeling which all could share, at least all who were Hip. And in this wedding of the white and the black, it was the Negro who brought the cultural dowry.[48]

Bisexuality in this scenario takes on a function similar to blackness. It furnishes the white hipster with another cultural dowry, with a kind of sexual perversity that is disruptive enough to be usefully harnessed into the figure's overall economy of anarchic associations but that can finally be discarded in the same manner as blackness. What remains, predictably, is white and priapically phallic heterosexuality. Homosexuality actually never comes into play in this phantasmatic transference. Because homosexuality is equated with effeminacy, it needs to be nipped in the bud as soon as the associative track that produces the white hipster might spin out of control and take the wrong turn. In other words, homosexuality as a concept with such specific features as the desire for being anally penetrated remains darker than corporeal blackness in Mailer's fantasy—so dark that it remains unassimilable and cannot partake in corporeal blackness's recruitment into metaphor. Mailer's essay must be characterized by a newly coined, uniquely deserved oxymoron—*the systematic carnivalesque:* The blackness it appropriates not only serves to construct a new whiteness sufficiently flexible and resilient to respond to the challenges of the atomic age and consensus culture but also serves to stave off whiteness's own traumatic and unassimilable Other—homosexuality. But this also means that the Freudian equation of homosexuality with savagery (which informed early 1960s attempts at ethnicizing homosexuals) fell on deaf ears at least with those urban intellectuals who sought to appropriate savagery for their own, rampantly heterosexual, attempt at anarchy. If it is true, as Andrew Ross claims, that "Mailer's essay was an attempt to provide a political form for the disaffections of the hipster code,"[49] this code was obviously not disaffected enough to include homosexuality in its politics in any form other than the liberal pluralist "some-of-my-best-friends-are-gay" rhetoric. Dressing like a gay man does not make you homosexual, and so the white hipster deserves our pity, for his superficial posturing can hardly conceal his calamitous fate—that he is, in the end, all dressed up with nowhere to go.

I should probably curb my pity for white hipsters, though, only because I have not yet discussed the situation of homosexuals in relation to them. It may be argued that white gay men, too, partook in this figure for their own masculine self-stylizations—which may then, to a certain extent, also have determined their relation to nonwhite races. Designated, trained, and socialized simply as white men, white gay men have partaken in classic forms of incorporating the Other, and these incorporations may have been very similar to Norman Mailer's. An instance in which this seems to have been the case is the way blackness functioned in late 1950s male physique magazines. Because corporeal blackness has traditionally been overdetermined as racial Otherness, the black physique, as Tracy D. Morgan surmises, may have functioned to neutralize and "cover up" any other forms of Otherness, such as homosexuality, so that during the 1950s, it may have been all but impossible to represent the black male body as gay or queer.[50] Morgan argues that this might have determined the inclusion of black models in white gay male physique magazines of the period, a means by which these publications heterosexualized themselves sufficiently to eschew censorship and official queer-baiting. As Morgan notes, "The inclusion of 'too many' photographs of Black men might run the risk of de-homosexualizing the publication completely, while too few might draw attention to the magazine's queerness. A fine line thus had to be maintained, and the representations of Black men were crucial to its maintenance."[51] In this sense, blackness indeed seems to have functioned in the same way for late 1950s gay physique magazines as it did for Mailer: It was heterosexualizing, while also constituting an object of male-male desire.

However, even though Morgan, too, rightfully draws the connection to Mailer in this context, her argument also enables us to see how, on another level, there is at least an implicit difference between Mailer's and gay erotica's relation to blackness. Gay male erotica of the period suggests a very specific acknowledgment of male-male sexual desire—an acknowledgment that, though operating within the confines of homophobia and heteronormativity, was gay-authored and targeted at gay consumers and that stands in sharp contrast to the way homosexuality functioned in Mailer's construction of the white hipster. On the one hand, I agree with Morgan that it is absolutely justified to pay attention to the larger binary, in which blacks must be seen to be on the disenfranchised side and Mailer and white gay men on the other. I also agree with Morgan that the objectification of nonwhite races through racial stereotypes in postwar gay erotica (by evoking slavery and "tropical langour"[52]) unfolded within the parameters of white supremacy, for although fantasy is the operative idiom that infinitely complicates evaluations of these sexual representations, gay erotica's racial stereotyping nonetheless precisely indexes the historical, political, and cultural baggage that still determines the power relations between black and white. In this sense, white gay men must, indeed, be identified as nothing but simply white men.

On the other hand, I believe it is problematic to single out male–male desire as the baseline factor that links Mailer's treatment of blacks to white gay male erotica's treatment of blacks. Morgan argues that white gay male physique magazines deployed the black male physique *unconsciously* to protect themselves from queer-baiting, which enables her to draw the comparison to Mailer's own unconscious desire for the black male. However, this narrow comparison seems questionable when the implications on each side differ dramatically and produce different results. It might be just as useful to regard the recruitment of blackness in these magazines as but one element of a larger field of disciplinary productions, a field that also utilized blackness as but one part of its broader range of desirable displays (of which white male bodies constituted the larger portion). This field is complex and contradictory. We can witness the recruitment of blackness for the production of whiteness and masculinity within a heteronormative framework, but we also see the production of homosexuality, which, by definition, goes against some of the values of this framework. This perspective by no means intends to ignore white gay male racism. Rather, it is meant to enable a diacritical juxtaposition of Mailer and gay erotica that can stress commonalities and differences. While Morgan's comparison correctly targets aspects of white male *dominance*, it remains foreclosed to aspects of white male *hegemony*. In other words, a slippage is incurred that ignores another reality—that white gay men could only ever assume the status of undesirable freaks in Mailer's world.

The diacritical comparison between Mailer's and white gay men's relation to blackness raises certain questions: Does the idea that the values of whiteness, which include heterosexuality and masculinity, were fulfilled on one level and for a certain period of time by postwar gay erotica corroborate the assumption that blackness is as integral to white gay male self-stylizations as it is to Mailer's construction of heterosexuality? Does white gay men's racist adoration of the black male as noble savage reflect the same investment in masculinity and whiteness that can be witnessed in Mailer's text? Again, my intention is not to defend or rescue white gay men from charges of racism. Indeed, there appears to be no reason to assume that white gay men cannot be as racist as white heterosexuals. Of interest here are those structures that enable this racism, particularly the elements of sexuality that play into racist productions. Interrogation of these structures may broaden our scope of responses to the ways white gay men intersect with the regimes that both privilege and oppress them.

To the extent that white gay men may be said to contain a certain Otherness within themselves, they may well have a particular relation to the norms they are asked to inhabit and embody. On the one hand, it seems that white gay men have a very particular sense that these norms are imposed on them; their alienation from these norms, as discussed earlier in this book, has, among other things, produced specific forms of gay self-expression. On the other hand, because white gay men get subsumed under the category of "white men," the vocabulary for the visualization of white male homosexuality often tends to overlap with that which visualizes white heterosexual men. Indeed, some theorists such as Bersani might argue that visual media with their phenomenological trappings are not always the most effective means for articulating and displaying homo-specificity. This pertains especially to the context of the American postwar period, in which white gay men also partook en masse in a masculine-identified style for the productions of their selves in the public sphere. But while this puts white gay men and the white hipster "on the same radar," as it were, it is worth taking a closer look at how this radar is constituted from the perspective of a white gay image maker whose images belong to the historical moment of the white hipster. The reference here, of course, is to Andy Warhol.

APPROPRIATIONS OF DARKNESS

In 1956 Warhol's boyfriend, Ed Wallowitch, took a photograph of a young man on the street who is leaning against what might be the post of a lamp or a traffic light (Figure 6.1). The model has the distinctly macho look of a street kid or even street hustler, conveyed through his facial expressions, through the butch iconography of his clothes, belt, and leather boots, and even through the photographic prominence of the street itself. The photograph also indicates Wallowitch's desire for the young man and the young

Figure 6.1
Edward Wallowitch, Photo of young man leaning against pole, 1956. B/w photograph (14 × 11 inches). Courtesy of the Estate of Edward Wallowitch. Archives of the Andy Warhol Museum, Pittsburgh Founding Collection. © 2002 Andy Warhol Foundation for the Visual Arts/ARS (photo: Richard Stoner, 3/19/01).

man's willingness to pose for Wallowitch, suggested by the casual and playful way in which he leans against the post and places his hands behind his head.

Several of Warhol's drawings from the 1950s are based on photographs such as this one. Of interest here are the ways in which the Wallowitch photograph went through a subtle but important recoding in Warhol's minimalist tracing of its contours. Warhol used Wallowitch's photograph for the design of a book cover he submitted to Simon and Schuster for its publication of Walter Ross's novel *The Immortal* (Figure 6.2). The novel is a typical piece of 1950s pulp fiction, catering to a young readership by exploiting their attention to movies and popular culture. *The Immortal*, so its summary tells us, is about an up-and-coming movie star, Johnny Preston, who lives and dies in the fast lane, perishing in an accident with one

Figure 6.2

Book cover for *The Immortal* by Walter Ross, 1950s (8½ × 9½ inches). © Archives of the Andy Warhol Museum, Pittsburgh Founding Collection. © 2002 Andy Warhol Foundation for the Visual Arts/ARS (copy photo: Robert P. Ruschak).

of his sports cars. The novel engages and exploits the James Dean myth in several ways. It exploits Dean's death by accident and, along with it, rumors around the recklessness of Dean's lifestyle. It also echoes other rumors about the star by alluding to its own protagonist's sexual adventures, which, so the summary suggests, were not confined to girls. Its first sentence, "Johnny Preston was born into the crazy, mixed-up, beat generation," also reflects the designation by late 1950s culture of Dean as a hipster and beatnik. From there, it is but a short step to suggesting that Preston was the kind of psychopath in real life that he was expected to play on the big screen except that, as a Hollywood celebrity, Preston was able to afford a shrink. As written in the summary, "The analyst whose male patient first initiated Johnny into the 'gay' set had only to go to his detailed, clinical file." *The Immortal*, then, is coded and advertised as a racy adventure about a hipster-beatnik-psychopath-Dean-look-alike, but by suggesting Preston's alienation from his world, by alluding to the homosexualizing influence of psychoanalysis, and by intimating the possibility of his bisexuality, the novel may also be regarded as being targeted to the sad-young-man crowd, which adored Dean as much as straights did.

Warhol's image for the cover articulates these multiple and contradictory allusions in minimalist but suggestive manner. Warhol traced the contours of the young man in Wallowitch's photograph, flipped them into reverse, and deleted any indications of a street, house, wall, or other such environmental markers. Most notably, Warhol also deleted the lamppost. The overall effect puts this image in interesting relation to the eroticized images of white and nonwhite male models in postwar gay physique magazines of the kind Morgan discusses. The male figure in Warhol's image appears by himself, as is typical of the representation of models across different races in much commercial sexual representation (in postwar gay erotica as well as much of contemporary hard- and soft-core print pornography). Beyond this, however, Warhol's image negotiates aspects of whiteness as well as nonwhite markers for the production of what is ultimately a white boy with a "dark" side. Particularly the fact that Warhol deprives Wallowitch's model of his most important prop—the post against which he leans—has a contradictory effect: On one level, it rehearses the differentiation in the racial codings of male models in the physique magazines discussed by Morgan, where white models were classically shown without any props in contrast to nonwhite models, whose accoutrements (chains, shipping crates, straw hats, rum bottles) mark them according to historically specific racial and ethnic stereotypes and mark them, too, as threatening Others to whites.[53] Deprived of any props, the figure from the novel's jacket remains racially white. However, another aspect comes into play that ultimately modifies a reading of the image with regard to race. It is class, and particularly the markers of working-class masculinity, which Warhol's adaptation of Wallowitch's photograph polemically recodes into criminality. With the street post missing as physical support for the model's pose, the model now very much looks like he has just been apprehended by the police, who have ordered him to freeze and stick his hands behind his head. And here we note that this pose acquires a connotation that, paradoxically, runs counter to the codes of representing whiteness: Even though Preston has putatively been psychopathologized by the influence of psychoanalysis, the stark physicality of his pose may be said to convey an element of "willful," nonwhite violence, which is inscribed on an otherwise white-coded figure. In this sense, Warhol constructs an image of darkness that, while ultimately referring back only to whiteness itself, may also rhyme with racist projections of the *influence* of corporeal darkness on this hipster. The point is that, at least from the perspective of someone like Norman Mailer, this drawing might well visualize the middle-class "white negro's" determination to finally trade the Freudian couch for the violent externalization of anarchy—no matter whether inspired by blacks or by white hobos.

The most obvious means of Warhol's complex coding of markers of race and class in this image is the functional and metaphoric designation of black and white as color tones for the novel's jacket. Reversing conventional graphic design's rendering of black on white, the jacket presents Preston "in negative," photographically speaking. It infuses him and his environment with darkness, which then comes to function as a metaphor for the protagonist's vaguely ominous, sinister existence—his nonwhite aspects. This darkness, and the white lines that trace the figure's contours, constitute the enhanced metaphoric construction of a butch masculinity that, though racially white, is socially and, as we shall see, psychosexually nonwhite. This duality manifests itself in the way Warhol somewhat undermines a specific aspect of whiteness—heterosexuality. Some may argue that the contours of the male figure for the most part also heterosexualize him through the accentuation of butch aspects of masculine iconography (the cuff of the pants, the outline of the belt, the seams on pants, shirt, and jacket, and the wave of hair hanging casually in the figure's forehead). Yet, anyone who has observed gay male fashion will attest that gay sartorial style indicates that there is a certain glory to be found in exaggerating any lines, seams, cuffs, pockets, and collars. In this sense, the minimalist rendering of these applications and sutures may in and of itself already be read as gay—but also as black (black fashion has evinced similar proclivities, and it could even be argued that white gay fashion has, to a certain extent, modeled itself on black fashion). Both Others can be contrasted against Fifth Avenue's straight white sartorial finish, which, possibly for fear of coming apart at the seams, tends to efface the threads that hold everything together. The image of heterosexual masculinity is finally and forcefully thrown off kilter by the prominence of the fly of the pants, which not only is depicted as bulging but is also exaggerated through an irregular thickening of the line, somewhat unusual for Warhol's drawing style. This, then, makes the figure a bit too butch for his own good, suggesting a trace of sexual objectification and theatricalization that undermines the otherwise heterosexual coding. In this sense, this late 1950s/early 1960s drawing can arguably be read as a subtle gay effort of taking the "hetero" out of "butch." As such, it attests to the duplicitous marketing of the novel by its mainstream publisher, Simon and Schuster, and to the summary's intimation of the protagonist's bisexuality. Warhol's presentation of Johnny Preston as a white guy with a dark side then works in several ways: First, it evinces an effect similar to the one contemporaneous physique magazines incurred by producing a metaphorically potent darkness to exoticize their displays, and second, it harnesses subtle gay male codes into signifying masculinity in ambiguous manner, while the overall design never abjures semiotic recourse to the dominant, heteronormative categories of heterosexuality and whiteness.

We note, then, that Warhol's recoding of Wallowitch's photograph serves the novel's pitch well. The production of darkness as metaphor summons but also swallows up certain markers of several of whiteness's Others, while the image itself remains within the realm of whiteness. We also note that whiteness and butch masculinity are constructed through the same white lines, indeed, through the same discursive regime—whiteness itself—which is inevitably foregrounded in this image. In reference to the discussion of Warhol's minimalist drawing style in Chapter 5, a reading that stresses Warhol's subtle gaying of this image may acknowledge that this is an alienated rendering of white masculinity, with the stark contrast between the contours and the emptiness inside suggesting white gay men's distance from the discursive regime that had produced them. However, this alienation from the discursive regime of white heterosexuality still operates within the dominant framework of white appropriations of elements of non-whiteness and their articulation through darkness as metaphor.

In this sense, the male figure in Warhol's book cover design may be said to accumulate and negotiate the respective but dissimilar repressions by which white heterosexual masculinity produces its opposite signifiers with regard to sex, class, and race: Stereotypical markers of class and race become articulated within darkness as metaphor, sharing the same space with male homosexuality. But to the extent that white male homosexuality may harbor elements of abjectness (because it is anti-phallocentric) and to the extent that there would be an impulse to even so much as indirectly hint at or symbolize this abjectness in a visual representation (technically, abjectness is semiolinguistically unrepresentable), it would be difficult to do so on and within the white contours of white masculinity. Thus, this abjectness is signified as a structuring absence, and the dark empty space of this absence is taken up by what *has* historically been signified and strategically produced by the dominant—the Otherness of class and race. In this sense, the Otherness of class and race cover over the traumatic lack constituted by homosexuality. Structurally, this scenario is analogous to the way representations of working-class and black male physique function in white gay physique magazines, such as the ones discussed by Morgan: Heterosexualizing yet Other, they "fill" the space of sexual Otherness that was so traumatic to the phallocentric and heteronormative framework within which postwar gay erotica operated. By heterosexualizing the whole picture on one level, working-class and nonwhite male physiques then also helped consolidate the link between masculinity and whiteness, under which white masculine-identified homosexuality can always be subsumed (and which it can subvert in signification only to a limited extent). Harnessed into covering up the traumatic and abject aspects of white male homosexuality, displays of working-class and nonwhite male bodies in physique magazines lift the white gay male body into the signifiable and imbue it with however modest signifying power, which leads to the peculiar asymmetry between these Others.

That white gay masculine styles were, in fact, being recruited for the disciplinary production of the alternative, racy masculinity of the straight white hipster (as indicated in this Warhol image and its production context) also suggests that white gay masculinity and, indeed, white gay male identity were always already imbricated with the regulation of straight white masculinity's other Others. Hence, the fact that white gay masculinity was alienated from white heteronormative and phallocentric culture (with some aspects even downright inimical to the phallocentric imaginary) does not necessarily mean that white gay male identity had an intrinsic inaptitude for classism and racism. Even if white gay men shared the category of Other broadly with blacks and working-class people, the respective disenfranchisements pan out very differently. But we should not forget that heteronormativity has much to gain from the way it plays out its Others against one another. For example, its threatening presence accounts for white gay erotica's recruitment of corporeal darkness for the delimiting production as well as the containment of white homosexuality, as discussed by Morgan. Heteronormativity thus renders both corporeal darkness and white homosexuality extremely disciplined agents.

Blow Job, too, evinces some of the dilemmas incurred in the utilization of darkness as metaphor, but it also appears to evince certain conceptual similarities to Warhol's somewhat subversive appropriation of the skull as discussed in Chapter 5. The film blurs the boundaries between light and dark, between full and empty, and, to a certain extent, inverts these terms. The undulating shades that stream across the image signify that darkness in *Blow Job* is fluid and can, perhaps, be inhabited somewhat subversively by certain forms of the Other, even if the establishment of the Other's presence is still mostly predicated on the volatile application of metaphor, and even though any subversive and/or indigenous articulation of Otherness would be predicated on partisan discourses and interpretations brought to the image.[54]

The valences attached to white-authored metaphors of darkness are by no means fully abolished in *Blow Job*, nor does the film abolish the larger spatio-metaphorical framework in which darkness plays out. If *Blow Job* proffers a spectrum of myths that range from the teenage rebel to the psychopath and, eventually, to Mailer's white hipster, the film's hierarchical array of different degrees of brightness (from bright at the top to dark at the bottom) forms the very field in which light and dark receive their mythical-metaphorical connotations and valences, and these also bear on discourses that construct whiteness and its various Others. Richard Dyer has persuasively argued that whiteness uses light in a way that is meant to suggest rhetorically that white peoples themselves are literally and symbolically superior. Euro-American culture uses light to metaphorize its notions of political, spiritual, and geographical supremacy. It has developed what is called "Northern light," light that comes from high above and is reserved for the valorization of white values and of whiteness as such (which is seen to be "above" the south and its "lowly" cultures, "chosen" by God, and spiritualized by and suffused with celestial beams of light that whites may or may not pass on to those shrouded in darkness below them).[55]

An underground film made with crude and sparsely used technology, *Blow Job* partakes in as well as subverts this use of light. In fact, it is the film's mode of production that enables us to read *Blow Job* as a commentary on many of the aesthetic-rhetorical features that Western civilization's culture of light has utilized for the simultaneous construction and naturalization of whiteness. Because the film's light source is much closer to its object than those that produce Hollywood or "Northern" light, and because it has no naturalizing fill lights, its light is much harsher and casts deep, intrusive shadows, which then also help denaturalize the construction of the values of whiteness through Northern light. As discussed earlier, *Blow Job*'s lighting significantly contributes to the film's strategy of spatializing opposite mythemes. For example, the film counterbalances —almost symmetrically, it seems—its Christological discourse with its opposite, shades and metaphors of satanism. In addition, the brightness in the image's upper area— particularly when the poser throws his head way back into his neck in what could be sexual ecstasy—can then be read as a direct result of the dark forces from which hegemonic constructions of whiteness seek to distance whiteness itself.

Because *Blow Job* ironically inverts these terms, the film, at least potentially, or by default, also serves as a vehicle of identification for the white hipster, who has fantasized his assimilation of corporeal darkness via "osmosis" or "education" in order to turn himself into a spectacle of potent dark metaphors. *Blow Job*'s mise-en-scène does infuse the poser's whiteness with dark metaphors of *some* kind, which he both greets and catalyzes with his masochistic writhing, and the film's slowed-down projection speed stunningly conforms to the kind of nihilistic presentness of time at the root of the white hipster's dark, existentialist-inflected disaffections of cool. Significantly, however, these last two observations strictly concern the darkness that springs from a white imagination. Indeed, if *Blow Job* is a map for myths and mythical types, it simply reflects the white hipster as a popular type with his obviously white countenance and white genealogy reminiscent of the white psychopath as he has evolved since World War II. *Blow Job* has recourse to corporeal darkness no more than Mailer's "white negro" does, but this may not have presented an obstacle to early 1960s urban hipster culture which, in its own conceit of sheer presence, summoned corporeal darkness as an absent referent—something that, as Mailer might argue, has "rubbed off" on *Blow Job*'s poser. Similar to the dynamics in Warhol's cover design for *The Immortal*, *Blow Job* ultimately remains part of white dominant culture's conceit of being capable of—and entitled to—embracing forms of the Other by casting them as "subversive" visual metaphors that help whiteness understand itself better.

The same is true with regard to *Blow Job*'s metaphorization of sexuality. If one believes that the film is, in fact, "about" sex, and if this belief is formed "from within" whiteness's spatio-metaphorical topography, one may feel at least vaguely supported by *Blow Job*'s fluid and poetic fields of darkness. This darkness is most intense at the lower frame, conveying a sense of secrecy and illicit sexual activity. Indeed, *Blow Job*'s darkness feeds into the idea that heterosexuality is built on all of its dark and taboo sexual Others. But the impression that this darkness is emanating from below and creeping up on the poser is as constructed as the film itself—it is an impression produced by the same set of lighting codes whiteness has seized on to consolidate its dominant position. Literally throwing into relief the codes and tools by which white culture produces its own dark sides, *Blow Job* foregrounds whiteness as a construct. The film's mise-en-scène inverts the value system of asexual spirituality and whiteness, of Christ's transcendence of the dark, sexualized body. The qualities of "northernness" and "celestialness" are appropriated and cited as myths that rest on their opposites, instantiations of dark, demonic, and anarchic sexuality. However, because *Blow Job*'s avant-garde signature is the spatialization of opposite pairs, the film also upholds the discursive regime that it seeks to undermine. *Blow Job*'s image still operates firmly within the discursive regime that deploys darkness to signify sexual Otherness, no matter how much the film also carnivalizes this regime. Any effort to read *Blow Job* as an idiom that gives otherness depth and autonomy will have to bring something to the film from the outside. These efforts are appropriations by necessity and definition, attempting, as they do, to wrest the film away from whiteness's conceited attempts to engulf Otherness superficially, attempts to which the film always threatens to fall prey.

If, for white culture, darkness equals sexuality and sex in all its connotations, the carnivalization of light and dark in *Blow Job* is subversive to the extent that darkness always includes homosexuality in its spectrum of metaphors. That said, these metaphors hardly "salvage" homosexuality as a clearly identifiable category. They do not express what recent arguments have termed "homo-specificity." The definition of a homo-specific masochism—which arguably can be *juxtaposed* to the concept of the death drive—appears to be in sharp opposition to white hipsterism's valorization of precisely this concept. Norman Mailer, for example, seems to understand masochism as a strictly phallic construct, and he heavily invokes and romanticizes the white hipster's death drive. However, as argued earlier with regard to *Blow Job*, it is difficult to distinguish visually between different masochisms. The poser's sexualized writhing may, to a certain extent, fly in the face of whiteness if whiteness is understood in this context as a form of controlling sexual drives in men and stipulating sexual abstinence for women (it is precisely the poser's sexual pleasure that also feminizes him and makes us infer his desire for a more radical and transgressive passivity). Yet, the film's visualization of these aspects has clear limitations. If they are not censored altogether, they are converted into non-taboo figures: For example, abject femininity—which the nineteenth century associated with female prostitutes, who, in the 1930s, came to be the "original" psychopaths—is converted into the classic figure of the martyr. The various forms of censoring the Other are part and parcel of the overall disciplinary regimes that produce and engender the Other and that constantly threaten to swallow up the Other in the very environment in which it is defined. If white gay men in the early 1960s were at least half willing to remain under the spotlight that was shining on them by then, they nonetheless experienced very clearly that this spotlight also dictated the terms of their appearance: The dark nature of homosexuality itself—those dark, unassimilable desires that make for really good dark gay sex—became metaphorically recoded and neutralized at the same time.

The limitations of *Blow Job*'s self-reflexive approach to what whiteness deems its sexual Others can be gleaned further with regard to the way in which the film's lighting produces a figure/ground instability. The poser's fluid spatio-metaphorical relation to his backdrop conceptually diverges from the all too familiar setup of white masters in front of, and not within, the territory they command.[56] The film's lighting differs from the kind of lighting that represents white people not only as conquerors of foreign lands but as sovereign masters of their own property, that is, as full-fledged, fully acknowledged subjects-citizens in the public sphere of Western nation-states. In this sense, to the extent that *Blow Job*'s lighting codes do, in fact, place white gay men in relation to the broader category of white men, these codes function to express that white gay men only partially, unstably, share the sense of entitlement associated with white masculinity. However, the brick wall, which iconographically and symbolically stands for the kind of *public* America in which white gay men were attempting to claim their space, proffers a double-edged allegory: Blending in with this brick wall can mean "going underground," that is, existing as a gay man in the interstices of heteronormative structures; but it also means making concessions to these structures, validating their existence by choosing them as one's habitat. The overall effect is that even if assimilation does not occur in direct, linear fashion, subordination to the larger environment is predetermined and aptly visualized in the spatio-metaphorical makeup of the mise-en-scène.

There are, however, interesting inversions along the way, if we further allegorize *Blow Job*'s poser's sexually motivated leaning into the brick wall: The moment gay men experience their most intense sexual pleasure is also the moment in which they are threatened to be swallowed up by, to become passive particles of, the broader properties held out as obtainable goals by the myth of white male conquest, enterprise, and economic success.[57] This reading reflects Bersani's view that gay men's high point of passivity is the moment they are closest to abject femininity, itself linked by patriarchy to a particularly degraded form of commodity exchange, prostitution. But *Blow Job*'s poser reemerges from these moments with a certain regularity, holding out the possibility for white gay men to join the ranks of those entitled to own and command property rather than being part of it. *Blow Job*'s mise-en-scène becomes an allegory for the ways in which white gay men, to gain membership to white mainstream America, internalized the discursive regime that imposes traumatically experienced norms of gender and sexuality on them—even though the film, in its own deadpan way, does, in fact, make clear how these norms are constructed by one and the same regime. As a self-reflexive attack on white heterosexuality, *Blow Job* still upholds the larger dominant framework: By displacing a display of sex onto darkness as metaphor, the film, on the one hand, implies that any white man's struggle against his dark side is also potentially a struggle with homosexuality; on the other hand, it relegates homosexuality to a mere *subcategory* of dark perversions. In other words, *Blow Job*'s framing perfectly allegorizes how homosexuality is prepared for assimilation even before it is lifted out of the space of the Other. It receives equanimity with certain dark, anarchic aspects of heterosexuality only on the broadest, most superficial terms—and the conditions that underscore these terms are then likely to prevent rather than advance the explicit acknowledgment of homosexuality on its own terms. This last point becomes very important when one considers the historical context of the late 1950s, in which white liberal heterosexuals such as Norman Mailer launched their own subversive appropriations of darkness in order to brand it as a polemical weapon against white, square, middle-class America.

Blow Job's clearly limited visualization of the anti-phallocentric aspects of male homosexuality, then, seems to be nearly identical with the limitations of subversive straight-authored depictions of sexuality—the limit was a carnivalization that was part of 1960s culture in general and, as some have argued, of Warhol's Factory in particular, and that is also clearly reflected in Mailer's concept of the white hipster.[58] The film carnivalizes whiteness by designating darkness as a subversive, yet limited, space for Otherness as an umbrella category. Given the way Mailer links white hipsterdom with his own notions of sexuality, no one would applaud *Blow Job*'s carnivalesque play of light and dark more than Norman Mailer. In addition, the film's framing enables heterocentric liberalism to always subsume homosexuality a priori by converting it into transgressive heterosexuality. But a white hipster might not even be particularly threatened by the possibility that the camera could tilt down and reveal a male fellator. Someone like Mailer would simply interpret this as the hipster's prerogative to sometimes "dabble" in bisexuality.

Blow Job is thus no less a visualization of Mailer's "white negro" than of homosexuality. But if the film is also, as has been argued in this book, an allegory of white gay men's relation to the American public sphere of the late 1950s and early 1960s, it makes poignantly clear what price white gay men were paying for their membership in this public sphere. Their masculinities were alternative, yet not alternative enough to avoid such strange and scandalizing bedfellows as Mailer's "white negro." The scandal lies in the fact that Mailer's white hipster, while providing an umbrella category for alternative masculinity under which white gay men, among others, could find shelter, is a deeply homophobic and, as we have seen, a deeply racist construct.

If Norman Mailer has seen *Blow Job*, he probably liked it very much. The same aesthetic features that deny *Blow Job* the status of being an unambiguously gay film—those features that consistently force gay readers of *Blow Job* to *appropriate* the film as gay—are the features that make it embody, if only by default, Mailer's notorious literary creation. While the film's framing and the poser's ambiguous facial expressions function as discursive obstacle and psychosexual shield for homosexuality's radical implications, they work to the advantage of the hegemonic heterosexual hipster, who can appropriate the film's blind spots to eradicate his own blind spots. Rather than being threatened by a certain degree of unknowability, he can harness that unknowability to appropriate top-down a range of Others and play them out against one another, so as to make the Other fit his own hegemonic scheme.

Because the white hipster is a figure with a fairly broad range of connotations and embodiments that, like those of the figure of the psychopath from which he derives, harbor a spectrum of subsurface meanings, he threatens to subsume such other more marginal figures as homosexuals and Beats. And surely, the sum total of facets that made up white gay urban identity and also Beat did, to a certain extent, overlap with the white hipster. Most Beats, such as Jack Kerouac and Allen Ginsberg, and possibly no few homosexuals (Ginsberg being a member of both groups), romanticized "the negro" as much as they glorified jazz and drugs. But key members of the Beat movement knew better than Mailer: Kerouac abjured Mailer's violent phallicism, and Ginsberg giggled at his priapic posturing;[59] they also knew bohemia better than Mailer did and took it for what it was—a small geographical pocket (with really only two concrete referents: New York City's Greenwich Village and San Francisco's North Beach area) where sexuality and gender were the subject of much experimenting and where, for a brief period of time, this fluidity helped bohemians of all strands explore all possible combinations of male-male relations. While these experiments were enabled also by white male privilege, and while their explorations of darkness were also, at least sometimes, prompted by naïve adulations and pursuits of forms of the Other, the darkness they explored did not consume Otherness as an object the way Mailer does.

For example, such films as Warhol's *Haircut* (No.1) focus on the erotic aspects of darkness's connotative currency, which they identify, appropriate, and teasingly exploit as a *white*-authored, phobic construct. Others, such as Jack Smith's *Flaming Creatures*, bring in racial discourses but lend them a high degree of autonomy. These films belong to the same spectrum of experimental films as *Blow Job*, a cinema broadly labeled underground cinema. But they differ from *Blow Job* in the sense that they conduct their explorations of gender and sexuality by showing *relations* between several people. *Blow Job's* solipsistic minimalism does not furnish an image of group relations. In its minimalism and solipsism *Blow Job* remains as vulnerable to anyone's fantasy as any dark isolated figure would. If the film is about homosexuality, it remains about an image of *the* homosexual—an extremely delimiting construct. *Blow Job's* limitations then also circumscribe the analytical parameters of this study with regard to discussing male homosexuality's relation to community, identity, resistance, and anarchy.

In addition, while *Blow Job* is typical in many ways of the underground cinema of this period, it also differs from the late 1950s and early 1960s underground films that are closely associated with Beat in terms of their sensibility and aesthetics. As argued at the beginning of this book, *Blow Job* is firmly situated within the aesthetic and discursive parameters of Warhol's particular version of pop art. This version, too, engaged with some of Beat's concerns, including a celebration of drug experimentation, of life at the margins, of sexual fluidity, and of new forms of artistic expression. But while Beat lent these interests a forceful—if often also playful—authenticity, pop art is all play. Pop became a gigantic toy store in which, fueled by the New Sensibility of the 1960s, radically diverse discourses and artifacts all merited equal attention and lost any potential aspiration to seriousness.[60] What was romantic-authentic for the Beats became for pop the subject of coolly ironic reflexivity. This has its advantages: While Beat remained caught in the limitations of its own myth, pop became a tool that, in accordance with the exploratory zeal of the New Sensibility, was able to appropriate and visualize a whole slew of myths for comparison.[61] In the surface signification of a film such as *Blow Job*, the residually invoked ethereality of Buddhism overlapped with a mock invocation of Christian/Catholic iconography; the myth of James Dean is spatialized in its part myths, such as the juvenile delinquent, Christ, Satan, the sad young man, the psychopath, and the white negro. Because *Blow Job*, like much of pop, stops short of analyzing these myths—of "taking a stance" in the traditional sense of the term—and simply displays them, it invites two things: First, the film's display of myths enables us to use the picture plane as an aesthetic/discursive tool for the kinds of cultural analyses that we bring to the film; and second, as a particular mode of surface signification, the image invites equal access by a white gay male reader and a white heterosexual male one—by an Allen Ginsberg as much as by a Norman Mailer. And as the film refuses each reading a "finite" kind of authentication, it can be pulled into the realms of radically diverse partisan discourses, hegemonic as well as subaltern.

It is reassuring to know that the partisan discourse at issue in this book—white gay male identity—has clearly outlived some of the nastier, hegemonic partisan discourses, such as "The White Negro." But while *Blow Job*'s gradual appropriation by white gay men over time is clear testimony to the endurance and dignity of gay male culture in America and around the world, *Blow Job* also shows how white gay men have themselves partaken in key aspects of hegemony. These are aspects that make white gay male identity problematic and, sometimes, oppressive and self-oppressive; they continue to deserve our attention and concern.

NOTES

INTRODUCTION

1. *Blow Job*'s length, like that of the other minimalist films, has varied over the years because it has been projected at various speeds. The film is forty-one minutes long when projected at sixteen frames per second, which is the speed at which the film was originally projected in 1964. To reduce a flicker effect, the film was later projected at eighteen frames per second, which makes *Blow Job* thirty-six minutes long. This is the current projection speed. See Callie Angell, "The Films of Andy Warhol—A Selection," in *Andy Warhol 1956–86: Mirror of His Time* (Tokyo: Asahi Shimbun with the Andy Warhol Museum, Pittsburgh, 1996), 192.

2. For anyone interested in systematically analyzing *Blow Job* with regard to boredom, I highly recommend Leo Charney's *Empty Moments: Cinema, Modernity, and Drift* (Durham: Duke University Press, 1998), an excellent effort at theorizing and historicizing boredom within the context of cultural modernism.

3. *Blow Job* becomes a prime example for the way in which Warhol's early minimalist cinema enables new possibilities of metaphor, as Stephen Koch noted in *Stargazer: The Life, Work, and Films of Andy Warhol* (New York: Marion Boyars, 1973, revised and updated 1991), 21–23. The questions, "What does this film mean? What is it about? What do I see in it?" can be answered in any number of ways, making the viewer aware that one may well be part of the answer.

4. Linda Nochlin, "'Sex Is So Abstract': The Nudes of Andy Warhol," in *Andy Warhol Nudes*, ed. John Cheim (New York and Woodstock: Robert Miller Gallery and the Overlook Press, 1995).

5. For a complete overview of Warhol's filmmaking during the 1960s, see Callie Angell, "Andy Warhol, Filmmaker," in *The Andy Warhol Museum* (Pittsburgh: The Andy Warhol Museum, 1994), 121–146, from which the information in this book about Warhol's cinematic output has been taken.

6. Ibid. Angell points out that *Sleep* was edited according to an elaborate scheme in which different shots were excised from different parts and combined (125).

7. It should be noted, however, as Angell points out (ibid., 14), that in *Eat* material structure is disturbed by symbolic content: The mushroom Robert Indiana is eating does not become smaller over the course of the film but changes size erratically from one roll to the next, which means that Warhol assembled the rolls not in the order in which they were shot.

8. Ibid., 126.

9. Ibid.

10. Ibid., 130–131.

11. Ibid., 137.

12. Ibid. Angell singles out the Hudson Theater near Times Square, which offered to run as many films as Warhol could provide.

13. As noted by Callie Angell in *The Films of Andy Warhol: Part II* (New York: Whitney Museum of American Art, 1994), strobe cutting was Warhol's "trademark style of in-camera editing in which the camera (and tape recorder) were rapidly turned off and then on again, leaving a clear frame, a double-exposed frame, and an electronic "bloop" on the soundtrack" (28). Angell points out that this allowed Warhol to manipulate the sequencing of a film and at the same time preserve the full-length uncut thirty-three-minute reel as the basic unit of his filmmaking. *My Hustler* contains strobe cutting but no postproduction editing.

14. Ibid., 36.

15. Parker Tyler, *Underground Film: A Critical History* (New York: Da Capo Press, 1969).

16. On the prewar American avant-garde, see Jan-Christopher Horak's useful anthology, *Lovers of Cinema: The First American Film Avant-Garde, 1919–1945* (Madison: The University of Wisconsin Press, 1995). See also Richard Dyer, *Now You See It: Studies on Lesbian and Gay Film* (New York: Routledge, 1990), 109–111.

17. See P. Adams Sitney, *Visionary Film: The American Avant-Garde, 1943–1978* (New York: Oxford University Press, 1978), Chapters 1, 2, and 4.

18. On the complex artistic and avant-garde scene of the early 1960s, see Sally Banes, *Greenwich Village 1963: Avant-Garde Performance and the Effervescent Body* (Durham: Duke University Press, 1993).

19. See Carel Rowe, *The Baudelairean Cinema: A Trend Within the American Avant-Garde* (Ann Arbor: UMI Research Press, 1982). Rowe emphasizes that Baudelairean cinema seized on myth by visualizing certain myths, not re-narrating them completely (7). These visualizations enabled the spatialization of binary opposites, such as the loss of energy versus the renewal of energy, self-destruction versus purification, and decadence versus spirituality. Baudelairean cinema goes back to Baudelaire and the decadent/symbolist movement in France, which articulated both a fear of and a fascination with decay and chaos (13–14). In *Allegories of Cinema: American Film in the Sixties* (Princeton: Princeton University Press, 1989), David E. James points out that it was Jonas Mekas who first brought the term to bear on the American underground cinema (121). In a 1963 *Village Voice* review Mekas discusses four films that deserve this label: Ron Rice's *The Queen of Sheba Meets the Atom Man*, Jack Smith's *Flaming Creatures*, Ken Jacobs's *Little Stabs at Happiness*, and *Blonde Cobra* (Jacobs, Smith, and Fleischner).

20. Angell, "The Films of Andy Warhol—A Selection," 192. Angell mentions that Jonas Mekas had been arrested twice in 1964, once for showing Jack Smith's *Flaming Creatures* (1963) and once for showing Jean Genet's *Un Chant d'Amour* (1950). On the latter occasion, the police seized and never returned Warhol's film.

21. Dyer, *Now You See It*, 157.

22. Michel Foucault, *The History of Sexuality, Vol. 1, An Introduction*, trans. Robert Hurley (New York: Random House, 1978; Vintage Book ed., 1990), 51–74.

23. Ibid., 54.

24. Ibid., 55.

25. Ibid.

26. Ibid., 55–57.

27. Walter Benjamin, "The Work of Art in the Age of Mechanical Reproduction," in *Illuminations: Essays and Reflections*, ed. Hannah Arendt, trans. Harry Zohn (New York: Schoken Books, 1969), 217–252.

28. Ibid., 220.

29. Ibid., 226, 237–238.

30. Ibid., 221–223.

31. See Andrew Ross, "Uses of Camp," in *No Respect: Intellectuals and Popular Culture* (New York: Routledge, 1989), 141.

32. Douglas Crimp, "Face Value," in *About Face: Andy Warhol Portraits*, ed. Nicholas Baume (Hartford, Conn.: The Wadsworth Atheneum, 1999), 122.

33. Ibid., 114.

34. Hal Foster, *The Return of the Real: The Avant-Garde at the End of the Century* (Cambridge, Mass.: MIT Press, 1996), 130.

35. I fully agree with Crimp's critique of Stephen Koch's possessive treatment of the film as a rehearsal of the visual truth-discourse of pornographic voyeurism. But given this critique, it is somewhat surprising that Crimp claims to be able to identify unambiguously when orgasm takes place in the film and, further, to narrow down this point to what he calls "the decisive spasm" (114). Given this surrender to the faith in positivist visual evidence, it is even more surprising that Crimp claims in the very next paragraph that "we cannot look into this man's eyes and detect the vulnerability that his submission to being pleasured surely entails" and that "we cannot take sexual possession of him" (115).

36. Jonathan Flatley, "Warhol Gives Good Face: Publicity and the Politics of Prosopopoeia," in *Pop Out: Queer Warhol*, ed. Jennifer Doyle, Jonathan Flatley, and José Esteban Muñoz (Durham: Duke University Press, 1996), 125.

37. Ibid.

38. David E. James, *Allegories of Cinema*, 69, cited in Flatley, 125.

39. For an important discussion of the relationship between Warhol's sexploitation films and a growing gay male audience in North America, see Tom Waugh, "Cockteaser," in *Pop Out: Queer Warhol*, 51–77.

CHAPTER 1
----

1. Siegfried Kracauer, *Theory of Film: The Redemption of Physical Reality* (New York: Oxford University Press, 1960), 48.

2. One such analysis, to which my particular approach to *Blow Job* is indebted in this regard, is Christine N. Brinckmann's comparison of the aestheticization of documentary discourses in John Ford's *The Grapes of Wrath* (1940) to that in photographs of Dorothea Lange and Walker Evans. For her analysis of the tension between documentation and aestheticization in 1930s documentary photographs, Brinckmann draws on the film theory of Rudolf Arnheim and Siegfried Kracauer, as well as on the Gestalt theory of Christian von Ehrenfels, as formulated in "Höhe und Reinheit der Gestalt" (1916) and "Weiterführende Bemerkungen" (1922), both printed in *Gestalthaftes Sehen: Ergebnisse und Aufgaben der Morphologie*, ed. Ferdinand Weinhandl (Darmstadt, 1967). Von Ehrenfels argues that the aesthetic impression depends on the regular structure of the object, its Gestalt. Variations of plain structure within structures of overall complexity heighten the overall impression of Gestalt if the basic principle of Gestalt as ordering principle remains intact. This insight and the observation on the aestheticizing qualities of black-and-white visuals serve Brinckmann in her analysis of the aestheticizing effect of the contrastive black-and-white rendering of furrows in Lange's *Childress County, Texas/June 1938* and of the surface details in Evans's *Kitchen Wall, Hale County, Alabama/1936*. See Christine N. Brinckmann, "Zitierte Dokumentarität: Überlegungen zur Verfilmung des Romans *The Grapes of Wrath*," in Die Anthropomorphe Kamera und andere Schriften zur filmischen Narration (Zürich: Chronos, 1997), 32–61.

3. David E. James, *Allegories of Cinema: American Film in the Sixties* (Princeton: Princeton University Press, 1989), 66.

4. Ibid., 67.

5. Rudolf Arnheim, *Film as Art* (Berkeley: University of California Press, 1957), 15–16.

6. Stephen Koch, *Stargazer: The Life, World, and Films of Andy Warhol* (New York: Marion Boyars, 1973, revised and updated 1991), 22.

7. Thomas Elsaesser, "Dada/Cinema?" in *Dada and Surrealist Film*, ed. Rudolf E. Kuenzli (New York: Willis, Locker, and Owens, 1987), 23.

8. This tension, too, was by no means ignored by Dada cinema. Thomas Elsaesser has identified it as one of the key features of the Dada image, which thereby references cinema's shifting status from scientific ocular device to aesthetic medium. The dramatic evolution of modes and means of representation at the end of the nineteenth century indicated that mechanically produced objects are capable of producing aesthetic effects (ibid., 14). As Elsaesser writes, "The combination Dada/cinema is thus interlaced with the more general history of inventions and apparati, and with the crises provoked in the arts when it became impossible to separate technology from technique or scientific from artistic experiment" (ibid.). Elsaesser further points out that especially Duchamp's appropriation of the medium has aestheticized film. In his view, the transformation of a perceptual apparatus to an aesthetic medium can be regarded as constituting a response to the question posed by Georg Lukács as to how the apparently unmediated reality conveyed by the photographic image constitutes itself as a sign (22).

9. See Linda Williams, *Hard Core: Power, Pleasure, and the "Frenzy of the Visible"* (Berkeley: University of California Press, 1989, expanded edition 1999). In Chapter 4, "Fetishism and Hard Core: Marx, Freud, and the 'Money Shot,'" Williams discusses the money shot (the representation of male ejaculation) in relation to dominant heterosexual pornography's elision of female sexual arousal and satisfaction. This elision reveals that the hyperbolics of female performance in this genre are meant to compensate for the absence of a verifiable female orgasm; they have come to mask the fact that the "objective" quest for truth has run aground. While the money shot is actually no less artificial in its setup, male ejaculation outside the woman's body is meant to serve the phallocentric illusion that "authentic" pleasure has been obtained by both partners—the strategic production of making sex "speak" masks itself as natural by having male bodily essence juxtaposed to and substitute for female surface performance (93–119).

10. Ibid., 108.

11. One could also read the film's "coda," as Douglas Crimp calls it—its last roll, which features the poser in a more relaxed state, smoking a cigarette ("the cigarette after")— as a kind of delayed, metaphoric money shot. The allusive potential of this symbol, which allows us to reinscribe it into the preceding rolls and thereby to further imbue the film's documentation of orgasm with the quality of veracity, relates to the symbolization of male orgasm in Kenneth Anger's *Fireworks*, which, similarly, is achieved via the featuring of fire (in this case, a bundle of burning sticks, followed by a stream of milk).

12. Reported in Tom Waugh, "Cockteaser," in *Pop Out: Queer Warhol*, ed. Jennifer Doyle, Jonathan Flatley, and José Esteban Muñoz (Durham: Duke University Press, 1996), 67. Waugh identifies the information as an anecdote recounted by Neal Weaver in "The Warhol Phenomenon: Trying to Understand It," an article in *After Dark* (January 1969): 26.

13. Richard Dyer discusses the implications of the money shot in gay porn at several points in *Now You See It: Studies on Lesbian and Gay Film* (New York: Routledge, 1990). His discussion of Kenneth Anger's *Fireworks* asserts that for gay men the money shot in porn is important with regard to two aspects: "the emphasis on the male orgasm as something seen, as spectacle, and the exaggeration of how much fluid it produces and how long it lasts" (121). But Dyer also emphasizes that the money shot points to the importance of the visible in the construction of male sexual desire in general (ibid.), which is but one indication that gay men—socialized as males—partake in some of the same phenomena and dynamics as heterosexual men. It is perhaps because of this overlap of gay men with straight men, and because of the general stress gay men have placed on

male-identified masculinity, that, to my knowledge, no one has yet theorized whether the money shot in gay male porn can be wrested away specifically also from Marxist concepts of alienation.

14. Robert Stam, *Reflexivity in Film and Literature: From Don Quixote to Jean-Luc Godard* (New York: Columbia University Press, 1985; Morningside Edition 1992), 15.

15. Ibid., 12.

16. Jonathan Crary, *Techniques of the Observer: On Vision and Modernity in the Nineteenth Century* (Cambridge: Massachusetts Institute of Technology, 1990; first MIT paperback edition 1992), 4, 13–19.

17. See Rosalind E. Krauss, "The Photographic Conditions of Surrealism," in *The Originality of the Avant-Garde and Other Modernist Myths* (Cambridge, Mass.: MIT Press, 1985), 112. Surrealist photography and film, for example, denaturalize objects associated with motion by showing them stilled, which has the result, according to Krauss, of turning them into a sign of the reality they no longer possess. A photograph of a stilled train, for example, would thus become a representation of a representation. Or, as in the case of René Clair's film *Entr'acte*, the projected image could be read as that of either a stilled landscape or a filmed postcard. See also Stephen Koch, *Stargazer*, which compares the tension between stillness and motion in Warhol's films to Duchamp's painting, *Nude Descending a Staircase* (38).

18. The semiabstract nature of the fragments produced by the chiaroscuro of *Blow Job*'s image puts the film in complicated relation to the legacy of dadaism, for dadaist art was itself imbued with the contradictory (abstract vs. mimetic) effects of fragmentation. There is, on the one hand, the legacy of purely abstract precursors of Dada, such as the abstract films of Viking Eggeling, which seized on abstraction as a means to explore visual rhythm in the purity of nonmimetic art largely (if not completely) unburdened by the mimetic impulse. (See *Dada and Surrealist Film*, ed. Rudolf E. Kuenzli, 2.) Certain instantiations of dadaist art retained part of this legacy: While dadaist art was not anti-mimetic, it used abstraction as a means to achieve a radical break from cinematic illusion and to point to the film as a product of the camera (ibid., 2–3). On the other hand, especially the Berlin dadaists also had a clearly evident relation to mass media. The photomontages of such artists as Raoul Hausmann, Hanna Höch, and George Grosz, for example, cut up and rearranged a specific reality—the reality of mass media—which they exposed as an illusion. Kuenzli asserts that even though the Berlin dadaists did not produce a single film, such a film, had it been made, "would have consisted of a montage of carefully chosen cuttings from existing popular films and newsreels" (ibid., 7). In sum, within the spectrum of heterogeneous dadaist art, one can discern an oscillation between abstraction and mimesis that perhaps reflects Dada's own antithetical forces of destruction and construction. For our particular purposes here, the exact relation between these forces is perhaps less important than their combined effect for the dadaist legacy—the attempt to destabilize Western epistemology, science, and myth and the radical, tactile attack on the underlying philosophy of ocularcentric mastery.

However, *Blow Job* subsumes this aspect of the Dada legacy as but one single aspect under its overall rhetorical operations. In *Blow Job*'s image, fragmentation is always enfolded with realism, so that the antithetical forces in *Blow Job* consist of a simultaneous questioning and mobilization of ocularcentrism. The fact that the film never ceases to produce a unified image and the fact, too, that it produces its chiaroscuro and its pop icon simulacra not through actual collage-style cuts but as internal refractions of light are perhaps among the reasons why *Blow Job* (but also other early minimalist Warhol films) is usually not discussed with regard to this aspect of dadaism, even though critics are not shy in attesting a transformative vision to the film. While an analogy between

Blow Job and the aesthetics of dadaism is thus limited, the image fragments that emerge and reemerge in *Blow Job* may stand in a more suggestive relation to surrealism and, more particularly, to movie goers who, like their famous surrealist predecessors, appreciated moving images for what these were primarily—momentary and short-lived spectacles of light and shadow that can be appreciated in tiny, fragmented dosages without the larger plots, symbolisms, and ideologies into which they were usually harnessed. The surrealists appreciated realist-based mass culture literally in bits and pieces, as they derived libidinal meaning from single images or short sequences, as described, for example, by James Naremore in *More Than Night: Film Noir and Its Contexts* (Berkeley and Los Angeles: University of California Press, 1998), 18. It is almost as though *Blow Job* deliberately caters to this way of viewing film when its chiaroscuro mise-en-scène, minimalist and largely devoid of what we commonly call content, offers its limited set of basic image fragments to the ultra-selective viewer. He or she may seek out the film only for those moments when the poser's head is cast in shadow or when one of his ears is visible. Yet when briefly lingering in front of the screen on which *Blow Job* is projected (these days probably belonging to a college class room or a museum auditorium, in the 1960s more likely to a Greenwich Village basement), this viewer may well bump into a second afficionado, who, compelled by the particularities of his or her own taste, has sought out *Blow Job* only for its moments of celestial brightness, when the poser throws his head way back and into his neck.

19. Crary, 129–131.

20. Koch, *Stargazer*. The fact that Koch includes the following false observation in his description of the film is but one indication of the power *Blow Job* wields over the eye of its beholder: "A masculine shoulder covered with black leather skims the bottom of the frame, someone kneels invisibly, the action begins" (47).

21. Alfred C. Kinsey, Wardell B. Pomeroy, and Clyde E. Martin, *Sexual Behavior in the Human Male* (Philadelphia: W. B. Saunders Company, 1948). Kinsey's table of contents, printed in tiny letters over five pages, is an illustrative index of a broad range of sociosexual contexts and sexual possibilities and pleasures. The following items recur with regularity, as they mark subchapters of Kinsey's fieldwork: masturbation, petting to climax, premarital intercourse, marital intercourse, extramarital intercourse, intercourse with prostitutes, homosexual activity, animal contacts, genital stimulation (oral), and anal eroticism (xi–xv).

22. Ibid., 623.

23. Koch, 50.

24. See Linda Williams's landmark study on heterosexual pornography, *Hard Core: Power, Pleasure, and the "Frenzy of the Visible."* Williams traces the evolution of porn from a prehistory in Eadweard James Muybridge's motion studies of the 1880s (34–48) to the stag films of the 1910s, 1920s, 1930s, and 1940s (58–92) to contemporary hard-core fare. Tom Waugh traces a similar trajectory with regard to gay male sexual representation in his magnificently researched book, *Hard to Imagine: Gay Male Eroticism in Photography and Film from Their Beginnings to Stonewall* (New York: Columbia University Press, 1996).

25. Dean MacCannell, "Faking It: Comment on Face-Work in Pornography," *The American Journal of Semiotics* 6, no. 4 (1989): 154.

26. Ibid., 153.

27. Ibid., 155.

28. According to MacCannell, facial expressions signify asexual, emotional extremes by an upper/lower face agreement or complementarity. For example, joy and rapture are often expressed through wide eyes and a wide-open mouth; extreme disappointment and

pain are often expressed through a facial "crunch," in which the mouth and eyes are closed tightly and pulled toward the center of the face. By contrast, facial expressions that signify sexual activity are characterized by an upper and lower face muscular antagonism: The eyes may be wide open, but the mouth is closed (sometimes the teeth clench the lips to keep the mouth closed); the whole face may also evince a "bilateral asymmetry" with the mouth wide open on one side and closed on the other side. A distinctly pornographic effect is also achieved by a "surface/depth antagonism" of the mouth: The lips are pulled back and wide open; the teeth are clenched (159–161).

29. In this context, see Cathy Caruth's introduction to her book *Unclaimed Experience: Trauma, Narrative, and History* (Baltimore: The Johns Hopkins University Press, 1996). Caruth points out that trauma is characteristically constituted as a tension between knowing and not knowing: "It is always the story of a wound that cries out, that addresses us in the attempt to tell us of a reality or truth that is not otherwise available" (4). See also Michel Foucault's argument in *The History of Sexuality, vol. 1, An Introduction,* trans. Robert Hurley (New York: Random House, 1978; Vintage Edition 1990), that Western culture's sex discourse, which "established an entire pornography of the morbid" (54), did so to hide the thing it was speaking about. Foucault writes, "We could take all these things that were said, the painstaking precautions and detailed analyses, as so many procedures meant to evade the unbearable, too hazardous truth of sex" (53).

30. MacCannell, 162–164.

31. See Jacqueline Rose's introduction to *Feminine Sexuality: Jacques Lacan and the École Freudienne,* trans. Jacqueline Rose (New York: W. W. Norton; first Pantheon edition 1985), 42–43. Rose points out that Lacan reformulated the moment pinpointed by Freud when sexual difference is experienced as lack (the girl is seen to be lacking) as a linguistic trauma. As Rose states, "Something can only be *seen* to be missing according to a pre-existing hierarchy of values ('there is nothing missing in the real', PP, p. 113). What counts is not the perception but its already assigned meaning—the moment therefore belongs in the symbolic." To the extent that the symbolic is itself only an unstable and fluid ordering process, the anchoring of sexuality in this system is a process that constantly attempts to erect and consolidate meaning. This never-ceasing effort thus also implies the constant failure to anchor sexuality this way. Sexuality is thus never natural; it is always metaphorical and therefore also that which constantly fails.

32. Hal Foster, *The Return of the Real: The Avant-Garde at the End of the Century* (Cambridge, Mass.: MIT Press, 1996). Foster discusses such Warhol images as the 1963 *White Burning Car III,* a panel of five silk-screened reproductions of a black-and-white photograph that features a crashed burning car lying upside down in a suburb with a person (perhaps the driver) impaled on a tree next to it. Another example is *Ambulance Disaster* from the same year, a panel of two silk screens of a black-and-white photograph of a crashed ambulance with the corpse of a woman hanging out of one of the side windows, presumably killed on impact and ejected halfway out of the vehicle.

33. Ibid., 132.

34. Roland Barthes, *Camera Lucida: Reflections on Photography,* trans. Richard Howard (New York: The Noonday Press; Farrar, Strauss and Giroux, 1981), 43–47.

35. Foster's approach to Warhol is related to a reading of surrealism as traumatic realism. For his argument Foster cites Jacques Lacan's seminar "The Unconscious and Repetition," in which Lacan, an early associate of the surrealists, defines the traumatic as a missed encounter with the real. Because it is missed, it cannot be represented; it can only be reproduced. Foster writes, "Repetition in Warhol is not reproduction in the sense of representation (of a referent) or simulation (of a pure image, a detached signifier). Rather, repetition serves to *screen* the real understood as traumatic. But this very

need also *points* to the real, and at this point the real *ruptures* the screen of repetition. It is a rupture less in the world than in the subject—between the perception and the consciousness of a subject *touched* by an image. In an allusion to Aristotle on accidental causality, Lacan calls this traumatic point the *tuché*; in *Camera Lucida* (1980) Barthes calls it the *punctum*" (132).

36. Foster, *The Return of the Real*, 132.
37. *Blow Job* suggests that Warhol's silkscreens are not the only screens that get punctured according to the dynamics of what Foster terms "traumatic realism." In addition, it is worth briefly noting here that film theorists, too, have identified a sort of puncturing mechanism specific to film. In *The Imaginary Signifier: Psychoanalysis and the Cinema*. Celia Britton, Annwyl Williams, Ben Brewster, Alfred Guzzetti trans. (Bloomington: Indiana University Press, 1982), Christian Metz has theorized that the retina is a second screen (in addition to the screen of the movie theater), suggesting that there is not only a projective but an introjective gaze. It seems strange that Metz's theorization of the projective gaze is remembered more clearly by film theorists than the introjective gaze, since he argues that both coexist. Metz says that "a sort of stream called the look, and explaining all the myths of magnetism, must be sent out over the world, so that objects can come back up this stream in the opposite direction (but using it to find their way), arriving at last at our perception, which is now soft wax and no longer an emitting source" (50). Even though Metz's use of the concept of wax is suggestive, his introjective gaze is different from Barthes's punctum, because it is less concerned with the minute interplay between form and content and reads introjection as always already within semantic-symbolic patterns. However, the applicability of Metz'z theory to *Blow Job* is not foreclosed. Anyone interested in theorizing *Blow Job* in terms of boredom may do well consulting his work, for his introjective gaze enables a theorization of boredom as spectatorial masochism. Any minimal event in *Blow Job* (and, for that matter, most early Warhol films) can be re-conceived as a spectacle of the introjective gaze, a momentous whipping of the retina.
38. Foster, *The Return of the Real*, 136.
39. MacCannell, 168.
40. Art Simon, *Dangerous Knowledge: The JFK Assassination in Art and Film* (Philadelphia: Temple University Press, 1996), 109.
41. MacCannell, 167.
42. Ibid., 168.
43. Waugh, *Hard to Imagine*, 253–272.
44. MacCannell, 155.
45. Ibid.
46. Ibid.
47. Richard Dyer, *Now You See It*, 157.
48. Because of the sheer size of Warhol's cinematic output and the ongoing effort to find, identify, and preserve his films, it is risky to make claims about Warhol's overall cinematic body. However, my assessment of Warhol's and other underground filmmakers' self-censorship obliges me to make the following qualification: While the overwhelming majority of Warhol's films remained indeed safely within the boundaries of the permissible, Warhol made about a handful of films that even by today's standards would have to be categorized as pornographic. Among them are the 1965 *Couch*, which features group sex including fellatio, and the 1968 *Blue Movie*, which features heterosexual penetration. In addition, *Blow Job* is not the only blow job movie in the Warhol canon. (Warhol had certain favorite topics, such as kisses, haircuts, and blow jobs, and he continued to explore these themes in his filmmaking, producing groups, series, or clusters

of films with similar or identical titles.) As of this writing, one more blow job film, the 1966 *Eating Too Fast*, has been preserved and is now in distribution. *Eating Too Fast* is a black-and-white sound film that the catalog of the Museum of Modern Art Circulating Film Library describes as "an ironic remake, with sound, of Warhol's 1964 minimalist classic." The film features art critic Gregory Battcock, who is facing the camera in close-up. For most of the first of the film's two reels, the camera stays in classic static position, exploring Battcock's handsome features. Toward the end of the reel, the camera tilts downward, past Battcock's belly, revealing the back side of his dark-haired fellator of slight built. For a split second, we see Battcock's penis before the view is blocked by the fellator's back. It remains blocked for the second reel, which displays much hectic and in-consequential zooming and tilting. Battcock is sitting on a chair. He talks on the phone, he pushes his fellator's head gently into his crotch, he adjusts his tank top, he drinks water and wine, and he makes a considerable effort to perform boredom and disaffection to the camera. Even though, in featuring the head-on-crotch combination, *Eating Too Fast* is technically pornographic (if hardly sexually aggressive), and even though the first part succeeds as a portrait of Battcock, Warhol's decision to add sound (sometimes we hear sounds of sucking, gagging, and coughing) and below-the-waist camera movement make this one-hour film more prosaic but less interesting than *Blow Job*.

49. Bill Nichols, *Ideology and the Image* (Bloomington: Indiana University Press, 1981), 1.
50. Roland Barthes, "Myth Today," in *Mythologies*, trans. Annette Lavers (New York: Hill and Wang, 1972), 123.
51. Ibid.
52. Waugh, "Cockteaser," 61.
53. Barthes, "Myth Today," 122.
54. Ibid., 115.
55. Here, I am following Barthes's example from "Myth Today" of coining neologisms for mythical qualities. For Barthes, the saluting negro on the *Paris Match* cover signifies "Empire-ness"; the Basque-style French country house, "basquity" (124–125).
56. Ibid., 132.
57. Ibid., 135.
58. Ibid.
59. My terminology and conceptual approach here are inspired by Rosalind Krauss's essay, "Grids," in *The Originality of the Avant-Garde and Other Modernist Myths*, 8–22.
60. Foucault, 51–73.
61. In "Grids" Krauss notes this, for example, with art's relation to the Christian myth: "There is no painter in the West who can be unaware of the symbolic power of the cruciform shape and the Pandora's box of spiritual reference that is opened once one uses it" (10). But Krauss also notes that grids are special here—they do not so much relate the physical and the aesthetic to each other but rather make them visually and conceptually coextensive (11).
62. Jean Baudrillard, *Simulations*, trans. Paul Foss, Paul Patton, and Philip Beitchman (New York: Semiotext(e), 1983), 97–100.
63. Ibid., 115.
64. Ibid., 116–117.
65. Walter Benjamin, "The Work of Art in the Age of Mechanical Reproduction," in *Illuminations*, trans. Harry Zohn (New York: Schocken Books, 1969), 246, cited in Baudrillard, 118.
66. Baudrillard, 119.
67. Roland Barthes, "Change the Object Itself: Mythology Today," in *Image-Music-Text*, trans. Stephen Heath (New York: The Noonday Press, 1977), 166.

CHAPTER 2

1. Roland Barthes, "Myth Today," in *Mythologies*, trans. Annette Lavers (New York: Hill and Wang, 1972), 122.

2. Thomas Crow, "Saturday Disasters: Trace and Reference in Early Warhol," in *Modern Art in the Common Culture* (New Haven: Yale University Press, 1996), 53. Crow's essay is important because it was the first to attest emotionality to Warhol's silk screens, which had formerly been regarded as indifferent, distanced, or even coldly voyeuristic. See also Art Simon, *Dangerous Knowledge*, for an elaboration of the discourse of emotionality in Warhol's silk screens.

3. Barthes, 118. Compare to Claude Lévi-Strauss, *Structural Anthropology*, trans. Claire Jacobson and Brooke Grundfest Scheopf (New York: Basic Books, 1963), in which the author writes, "On the one hand, a myth always refers to events alleged to have taken place long ago. But what gives the myth an operational value is that the specific pattern described is timeless; it explains the present and the past as well as the future." (209).

4. In addition, *Blow Job* has neither the formal completeness nor the complexity of the large tapestries rolled out by Lévi-Strauss to analyze myths. There are, of course, several other methodological dissimilarities that also cause me to part ways with structural anthropology. Lévi-Strauss mainly analyzed myths that were unknown and "exotic" to him as a Western scholar. Even though the myths visualized in *Blow Job*'s image are hardly unknown, it is precisely their debased, visually poor character, their centrality in the larger canon of Warhol's images, and the significance they assume for certain spectators that compel me to accord much more significance to their symbolic implications than Lévi-Strauss ever would have accorded an individual myth or any small group of myths.

5. See Jonathan Culler, *Structuralist Poetics: Structuralism, Linguistics, and the Study of Literature* (Ithaca, N.Y: Cornell University Press, 1975), and Edmund Leach, *Claude Lévi-Strauss* (New York: Viking Press, 1970). The first of these insights is not unlike the one proffered by early film theory that our ordering process of reality through sense perception works by cutting up the continuous space of nature into segments. Our transformation of nature into culture, our inevitable perception of nature *as* culture, thus functions, among other ways, by redefining the space before us through opposite pairs and binarisms. Whatever we end up associating with the mise-en-scène's play of light and shadow, we engage in associative acts almost inadvertently. The second insight states that these binarisms can be correlated to more abstract oppositions. An example would be, according to Edmund Leach, the segmentation and symbolic harnessing of the color code by the semiotics of the traffic light (red equals danger/prohibition; green equals safety, permission, right of way) (15–21). Another example, which Jonathan Culler has pointed out, is the symbolic equation of light and good versus dark and bad/evil (43).

6. Juan Suarez, *Bike Boys, Drag Queens, and Superstars: Avant-Garde, Mass Culture, and Gay Identities in the 1960s Underground Cinema* (Bloomington: Indiana University Press, 1996). For the techniques by which American underground cinema appropriated mainstream texts, see especially Chapter 3, "The 1960s, Underground as Political Postmodernism: From the New Sensibility to Gay Cultural Activism," 87–140.

7. Wayne Koestenbaum, *The Queen's Throat: Opera, Homosexuality, and the Mystery of Desire* (New York: Simon and Schuster, 1993), 150.

8. Judith Butler, *Gender Trouble: Feminism and the Subversion of Identity* (New York: Routledge, 1990), 3.

9. See Steven Cohan's detailed study on 1950s masculinity, *Masked Men: Masculinity and the Movies in the Fifties* (Bloomington: Indiana University Press, 1997). Cohan

argues that notions of impetuousness and excess were linked during the 1950s to a renewed interest in the maturation of the teenager from boy to man. The term "boy" was often targeted at grown men who failed to fulfill normative standards of masculinity (238).

10. See Ray Carney, *The Films of John Cassavetes: Pragmatism, Modernism, and the Movies* (Cambridge, U.K: Cambridge University Press, 1994), 147–150. Carney comments on what he calls "the expressive gap" in American art: "Turning feelings into expressions involves a problematic act of translation, in which at times it seems as if not less than everything is lost" (147).

11. Consider, for example, the visually stylized and shrewdly choreographed knife fight on the planetarium terrace in *Rebel Without a Cause*. Director Nicholas Ray skillfully uses slanted angles and the full width of the frame to showcase the beauty of gang fight kinetics, even leaving enough space to show the valley far below the terrace. The purpose of this framing is to ethnographically exploit for mainstream audiences, in visually safe but highly stimulating manner, "a day in the lives of teenage gangs." But Ray harnesses the film's wide-screen format for ideological critique as well. Recall the metaphorically potent spatial constellation of Jim, Judy, and Plato on the bluff after the chicken race scene. The gang members have left, and Jim and Judy slowly move closer to each other with outstretched arms and longing gazes. Their union visually eclipses Plato ("the Other") who, from the camera's perspective, seems to stand between them. Ray is able to trace this near-mythical victory of heterosexual reproduction over deviant cultural forms with such bristling clarity by dividing the frame into a triptych in which all three protagonists occupy the center while the two wings are left empty. When Jim and Judy move into visual union, they dramatically extend these empty wings inward, draining the frame of anything "unimportant." This scene shows how well Ray (once a student of Frank Lloyd Wright) understood that wide empty spaces can be visually polemicized not only by filling them but also by choreographing their emptiness. I would like to thank Robert Sklar for attuning me to the subtle but pervasive reflexivity of the films of Nicholas Ray.

12. Richard Dyer, "Coming Out as Going In: The Image of the Homosexual as a Sad Young Man," in *The Matter of Images: Essays on Representations* (New York: Routledge, 1993), 86.

13. Steven Cohan notes that the derogative label of "boy" for a teenager or a young man must also be seen as a response to the teenager's ability to cross such anxiously guarded binaries as masculine/feminine, straight/gay, authentic/theatrical, young/old (252).

14. Dyer, "Coming Out as Going In," 87.

15. On Cagney's star persona, performance style, and screen characters, see Robert Sklar, *City Boys: Cagney, Bogart, Garfield* (Princeton: Princeton University Press, 1992).

16. Richard Meyer, "Warhol's Clones," *The Yale Journal of Criticism* 7, no. 1 (1994): 85.

17. Ibid., 82. Meyer cites Rainer Crone, *Andy Warhol*, and Patrick Smith, *Andy Warhol's Art and Films*, as sources.

18. Ibid., 92.

19. Benjamin H. D. Buchloh, "Andy Warhol's One-Dimensional Art: 1955–1966," in *Andy Warhol: A Retrospective*, ed. Kynaston McShine (New York: Museum of Modern Art; Boston: distributed by Bullfinch Press/Little, Brown and Co., 1989), 54.

20. Richard Dyer, *Now You See It: Studies on Lesbian and Gay Film* (New York: Routledge, 1990), 123.

21. This information is based on my own viewing of *Images in the Snow*. Raymond Durgnat, similarly, already identified the protagonist's mother with the Virgin and the suffering of the protagonist with that of Christ. See Durgnat's description in Dyer, *Now You See It*, 107.

22. Richard Dyer's study of the film contains a scene-by-scene breakdown that includes the titles of the songs and the recording artists.

23. Randy P. Conner, David Hatfield Sparks, and Mariya Sparks, *Cassell's Encyclopedia of Queer Myth, Symbol, and Spirit: Gay, Lesbian, Bisexual, and Transgender Lore* (London: Cassell, 1997), 190–191.

24. Ibid.

25. See Björn Krondorfer's introduction to his highly interesting anthology on the relations between Christianity, masculinity, and male sexualities, *Men's Bodies, Men's Gods: Male Identities in a (Post-)Christian Culture* (New York: New York University Press, 1996), 3–26.

26. Dyer, "Coming Out as Going In," 80.

27. Ibid., 78.

28. Ibid., 90.

29. If I say "iconographically," I refer to the content and array of the images, not their negotiation of visual clarity or depth of field. Note that these images display only one of *Blow Job*'s three visual constellations, the third one, which suggests the sad young man typology, but in a much more expressionist manner than in the film. The late Ed Wallowitch's brother, John, could not confirm any evidence that these photographs directly served Warhol as visual blueprints for *Blow Job*. According to him, they reflect his brother's obsession with Josef von Sternberg's use of light in his films with Marlene Dietrich. Ed Wallowitch tried to make Warhol look more glamorous by pronouncing his cheekbones. Author's correspondence with John Wallowitch, April 5, 2001.

30. Rosalind Krauss, "Grids," in *The Originality of the Avant-Garde and Other Modernist Myths* (Cambridge, Mass.: MIT Press, 1985), 13.

31. While *Blow Job*'s sexual trajectory is linear (and thereby apparently replicating the linearity of male sexuality), the poser's convulsions, frequently interrupted by white flares, do not project narrative progression. Although the poser's sexual pleasure seems more intense toward the end of the film than early on, an overall impression of narrative-like linearity can be wrought only in hindsight. A viewer uninitiated to the film and unaware of its length is likely to read every splice as the potential ending of the act, only to realize a few seconds later that the film is not yet over. Indeed, even the last roll's featuring of the poser smoking "the cigarette after" can serve as proof for the orgasm only by projecting it back into the already unspooled sequence. This interpretative move classically reenacts the retroactive structuring and interpretation of what one likes to perceive as "nature" via a cultural discourse. The overall slowed-down representation in *Blow Job* teases and frustrates spectators and, thus, additionally attenuates the impression of linearity.

32. Krauss, 13.

33. Walter Benjamin, "The Work of Art in the Age of Mechanical Reproduction," in *Illuminations: Essays and Reflections*, ed. Hannah Arendt, trans. Harry Zohn (New York: Schoken Books, 1969), 224.

34. See Carla Schulz-Hoffmann, "'Are You Serious or Delirious?'—On the Last Supper and Other Things," in *Andy Warhol: The Last Supper. Exhibition Catalogue*, ed. Carla Schulz-Hoffmann (Munich: Bayerische Staatsgemäldesammlungen/Staatsgalerie moderner Kunst, 1998), 10.

35. Corinna Thierolf, "All the Catholic Things," in Schulz-Hoffmann, 31.

36. Schulz-Hoffmann, "Are You Serious or Delirious?" 10.

37. Matteo Bandello, *Novella LVIII*, preface containing dedication to Ginevra Rangona e Gonzaga, Lucca, 1554, cited in Cornelia Syre, "Leonardo da Vinci's Last Supper: History and Reception," in Schulz-Hoffmann, 103.

38. Cited by Corinna Thierolf, "All the Catholic Things," in Schulz-Hoffmann, 48 (footnote 24). Original citation and translation by Alessandra Farkas, published in "Incontro con Andy Warhol alle Vigilia del Suo Arrivo a Milano Dove Presenta una 'Copia' di Leonardo," in *Corriere della Sera*, n.d., press folder issued by the Credito Valtellinese, Szanto (1997, 32).

39. As Thierolf notes: "The original is now so widely disseminated and used for so many different purposes as a glossy, high-class product and a cheap imitation that ultimately, if any thought is put on the matter at all, there can be no agreement as to where the picture actually belongs and what it shows" (34).

40. Ibid., 31.

41. D. A. Miller, *Bringing Out Roland Barthes* (Los Angeles and Berkeley: University of California Press, 1992), 31.

CHAPTER 3

1. Mikhail Iampolski, *The Memory of Tiresias: Intertextuality and Film*, trans. Harsha Ram (Berkeley: University of California Press, 1998), 15–16.

2. In her article "Pages of Whiteness: Race, Physique Magazines, and the Emergence of Public Gay Culture," *in Queer Cultures: A Lesbian, Gay, Bisexual, and Transgender Anthology*, ed. Brett Beemyn and Mickey Eliason (New York: New York University Press, 1996), 280–297, Tracy D. Morgan argues that "white gay people's race privilege enabled them to detach from their families of origin and form what today is known as the gay community. Restrictive covenants made it hard for Black homosexuals to do the same. Returning to their neighborhoods after the war, Black lesbians, gay men, and bisexuals did not disrupt the homophobically constructed geography of the U.S. urban sphere. Their queer identities were subsumed within the more dominant concept of 'the Black community.' They were also more fully integrated into the social fabric of the Black neighborhoods in which they resided" (283). However, this does not mean that the histories and lives of white gay men and black gays, lesbians, and bisexuals did not intersect. Indeed, white homosexuals were just as guilty of racism as white heterosexuals were. In his highly interesting article, "A Queer Capital: Race, Class, Gender, and the Changing Social Landscape of Washington's Gay Communities, 1940–1955," in *Creating a Place for Ourselves: Lesbian, Gay, and Bisexual Communities*, ed. Brett Beemyn (New York: Routledge, 1997), Brett Beemyn emphasizes that bars with a large gay and bisexual male clientele excluded not only women but also African Americans. Even after the U.S. Supreme Court ruling of 1953 forced restaurants and bars in Washington, D.C., to adopt desegregation, many establishments simply put "reserved" signs on the tables to continue to be able to reserve the right to turn away African American customers (187). See Beemyn's article also for valuable information on how black gays, lesbians, and bisexuals responded to the continuing racism within the white gay community and how they established their own networks and subcultures away from white homosexuality. See Chapter 6 of the present book for a discussion of the problematic position of white gay men with regard to race and racism.

3. George Chauncey, *Gay New York: Gender, Urban Culture, and the Making of the Gay Male World, 1890–1940* (New York: Basic Books, 1994). See especially 331–354, "The Exclusion of Homosexuality from the Public Sphere in the 1930s." Chauncey gives a host of reasons why and how homosexuality was made increasingly invisible, among them the State Liquor Authority's regulation and large-scale elimination of gay bars and the increasing coding of a wide range of behavior as homosexual, which gave authorities a host of opportunities to charge homosexuals with disorderly conduct.

4. Alfred C. Kinsey, Wardell B. Pomeroy, and Clyde E. Martin, *Sexual Behavior in the Human Male* (Philadelphia: W. B. Saunders Company, 1948), 659.
5. Ibid., 650.
6. Ibid., 665.
7. Ibid., 621–622.
8. Ibid., 622.
9. For a detailed historical analysis of the situation of gays and lesbians in the U.S. military during World War II, see Allan Bérubé, *Coming Out Under Fire: The History of Gay Men and Women in World War Two* (New York: The Free Press, 1990). Bérubé points out that the period between Hitler's invasion of Poland and Pearl Harbor became the crucial phase during which the military began to formulate attitudes, guidelines, and screening procedures with regard to the rejection of homosexuals from service. The psychiatric profession came to assume a crucial advisory function for the military, and it was during this time that homosexual classification in the United States crucially shifted status. As Bérubé notes, "Replacing the jargon of degeneracy with the jargon of psychoanalysis, [psychiatrists] used the term homosexual, which had originated within the psychiatric profession, and spoke of latency, tendencies, proclivities, and personality types" (15). A deeply ironic and poignant detail in this regard is that one of fewer than a handful of psychiatrists who had drafted and initiated these procedures for screening and classifying homosexuals, Harry Stack Sullivan, was gay himself. Sullivan believed that sexuality had little part in causing mental disorders. He and his colleague Winfred Overholser took a relatively "enlightened" view on homosexuality, somewhat foreshadowing the liberal, sociology-based view of such 1950s voices as that of Evelyn Hooker. Nonetheless, Sullivan, too, believed that self-confessed homosexuals should be excluded from the army because of their potential for causing disruptions and incurring punishment (10–11). Sullivan's initial recommendations to the military did not even include any references to homosexuality. But, according to Bérubé, Sullivan's plan was revised multiple times by a growing number of psychiatrists who sought to legitimize their profession by acting as military advisers and who added homosexuality to the list of pathological and classifiable categories. As Bérubé writes, "This bureaucratic process itself, by expanding the volume of directives, memoranda, and revisions, helped build the momentum of the military's wartime preoccupation with homosexuality" (ibid.). Even though the Selective Service, by the end of 1941, had shifted screening procedures away from local psychiatric examination boards to Army induction stations, "clarifications of previously vague psychiatric screening procedures suggested a tightening of anti-homosexual screening standards" (19), which led to the writing of a list of explicitly formulated "telltale signs" of homosexuality used for the clarification of rejection guidelines and procedures. The military also made it known through the press what constituted grounds for draft rejection (21), an act that, one assumes, enabled gays and lesbians to devise strategies with regard to their conduct during screening procedures.
10. Bérubé notes that the military also very consciously admitted homosexuals or found ways of circumventing or attenuating its own screening procedures. After all, in the wake of Pearl Harbor the United States was suddenly faced with the challenge of raising an army of millions instead of the one million anticipated by the Selective Service (19). According to Bérubé, "So many gay men were able to hide their homosexuality from examiners, while so many examiners were trying to find ways to let them in, that by the end of the war, after examining nearly 18 million men, the military had officially rejected only 4,000 to 5,000 as homosexual" (33).
11. Robert J. Corber, *Homosexuality in Cold War America: Resistance and the Crisis of Masculinity* (Durham: Duke University Press, 1997), 85–88.

12. Ibid.

13. Ibid., 91–95.

14. I do not mean to imply that Corber views *The Brick Foxhole* as a prominent or in any way detailed depiction of gay life. I agree with Corber that *Crossfire*, because of its very nature as a Hollywood film, would have given unprecedented visibility to gay men had Adrian Scott been allowed to retain homosexuality in the script. For a detailed account of how *The Brick Foxhole* was translated to the screen and of the battles with the censors, see James Naremore, *More Than Night: Film Noir in Its Contexts* (Berkeley and Los Angeles: University of California Press, 1998), 114–123.

15. Richard Brooks, *The Brick Foxhole* (Garden City, N.Y.: The Sun Dial Press, 1946). Brooks writes, for example, "The brow was good. The cheekbones high. The face was hungry. Jeff didn't know what the hunger was. He knew, however, that it wasn't for food. The man's clothes told him that, and the high-priced car" (85).

16. The novel describes Jeff's impression in this way: "The nude man was shooting an arrow from a large bow, and he seemed to be straining a little. However, the strain brought out the muscles and Jeff knew that was why the artist had the man straining. He wondered why a man would shoot a bow and arrow while nude. And then he decided he was too petty. He oughtn't to ask questions like that. Nothing had a reason and there he had to go and ask why a man painted a nude" (ibid., 90–91).

17. Ibid., 93. The identification between the straight protagonist and the homosexual comes out clearly in the passage that describes the group's ride in Edwards's car to his apartment: "Jeff wanted to warn Mr. Edwards. He didn't know against what. But the whole thing seemed evil to him. He wanted to tell the man to withdraw his invitation. There was something about the way Monty was talking that frightened Jeff. Jeff had heard about the pastime of some soldiers. Their treatment of sexual perverts. The way they regarded them. Jeff was afraid for himself, too. There was something clammy and unclean about the conversation. He wished he weren't in the automobile" (ibid., 88).

18. Richard Dyer, *Now You See It: Studies on Lesbian and Gay Film* (New York: Routledge, 1990), 121. For another useful and detailed discussion of Kenneth Anger's work in the context of American underground cinema, see David James, *Allegories of Cinema: American Film in the Sixties* (Princeton: Princeton University Press, 1989), 119–165.

19. Dyer, *Now You See It*, 121.

20. Ibid., 122–123.

21. Ibid., 124

22. On the close links between homosexuality and the cold war discourse on national security, see Robert J. Corber, *In the Name of National Security: Hitchcock, Homophobia, and the Political Construction of Gender in Postwar America* (Durham: Duke University Press, 1993). Corber argues that in the wake of Kinsey, gays and lesbians came to be regarded as a threat to national security because they were deemed emotionally unstable and susceptible to blackmail. They also fell victim to the classic homophobic double bind that, on the one hand, regarded them as sexual Others while, on the other hand, charged them with "converting" heterosexuals to homosexuality (9, 61–64). Corber argues that the contamination/conversion rhetoric was, in fact, crucial for the consolidation of state power, because it spread homophobic paranoia, which was then used as a rationale to keep all Americans "in check" (10). In addition, this state-authored paranoia also likened homosexuals to Communists especially with regard to secrecy, modes of communication and assembly, and a general antagonism to society that was deemed "unnatural." In these ways, gender deviance could be constructed as political subversion (19–21).

23. Barbara Ehrenreich, *The Hearts of Men: American Dreams and the Flight from Commitment* (New York: Doubleday, 1983), 50.

24. Tom Waugh, *Hard to Imagine: Gay Male Erotica in Photography and Film from Their Beginnings to Stonewall* (New York: Columbia University Press, 1996). See especially "The Kinsey Generation: The Golden Age of Magazines and Mail Order (1945–1963)," 215–252, and "The Movies," 253–272. Waugh's groundbreaking study throws light on the crucial links during the postwar years between what is called "physique culture"—the homoeroticization of bodybuilding—and the increasing visibility of homosexuality as an "open secret." His research establishes that many of physique culture's members, who were photographed nude or near-nude in increasingly homoerotic poses, had emerged from World War II military service and belonged to the demographic group of socially and geographically uprooted singles whom Kinsey had seized on for his research. Waugh points out that, in fact, many of the producers, consumers, and models of physique magazines had actually been interviewed by Kinsey even before the war began (215–216). On the success of physique magazines, Waugh writes that while *One*, the largest gay magazine with a somewhat political orientation, never printed more than 5,000 monthly copies, the circulation of such physique magazines as *Tomorrow's Man* and *Grecian Guild Pictorial*, although their actual circulation is difficult to determine, approximated mass-market proportions. The modus operandi of physique magazines and above-ground films that eroticized homosocial scenarios was the alibi that enabled the imaging of gay erotic fantasies without acknowledging their basic nature. This alibi structured itself into genre-type categories of which sports, art, and "nature" were the most prominent (219).

25. On the specific dynamics between hustler and john see Michael Moon, "Outlaw Sex and the 'Search for America': Representing Male Prostitution and Perverse Desire in Sixties Film (*My Hustler* and *Midnight Cowboy*)," *Quarterly Review of Film and Video* 15, no. 1 (1993): 27–40.

26. See especially George Custen, "Strange Brew: Hollywood and the Fabrication of Homosexuality in *Tea and Sympathy*," in *Queer Representations: Reading Lives, Reading Cultures*, ed. Martin Duberman (New York: New York University Press, 1997) and David Gerstner, "The Production and Display of the Closet: Making Minnelli's *Tea and Sympathy*," *Film Quarterly* 50, no. 3 (Spring 1997).

27. Judith Butler, *Bodies That Matter: On the Discursive Limits of "Sex"* (New York: Routledge, 1993), 58.

28. Juan Suarez, *Bike Boys, Drag Queens, and Superstars: Avant-Garde, Mass Culture, and Gay Identities in the 1960s Underground Cinema* (Bloomington: Indiana University Press, 1996), 138.

29. Corber, *In the Name of National Security*. See especially Corber's discussion of Hitchcock's *Strangers on a Train*, which displaces "the homosexual menace" onto a crime plot and reenacts the phobias and the juridical dilemmas that produced the term "the homosexual menace" in the first place (69–82). For a discussion of psychopathology, homosexuality, and murder in Hitchcock's *Rope*, see D. A. Miller, "Anal Rope," in *Inside/Out: Lesbian Theories, Gay Theories*, ed. Diana Fuss (New York: Routledge, 1991), 119–141.

30. Gerstner, "The Production and Display of the Closet," 14. Gerstner points out that the adaptation of *Tea and Sympathy* recodes Tom's queerness: It deletes the reference to Tom's socializing in the nude and replaces it with the moment in which two of the school's volleyball players "catch" Tom socializing with the faculty wives' sewing circle.

31. Custen, "Strange Brew," 122.

32. Ibid., 131.

33. See Richard Lippe, "Montgomery Clift: A Critical Disturbance," *CineAction!* 17 (1989): 36–42. Lippe explains that Clift's star persona was very complex in that it subsumed contradictory features: On the one hand, Clift personified the virility of youthful 1950s masculinity; on the other hand, this virility also often effeminized him. In their combi-

nation, these character traits set Clift apart from normative concepts of masculinity, but they did so in a palatable and attractive way. For an analysis of Clift's "intensity" and the construction/reception of his persona in fan discourses, see Steven Cohan's excellent chapter, "Why Boys Are Not Men," in *Masked Men: Masculinity and the Movies in the Fifties* (Bloomington: Indiana University Press, 1997). Cohan points out that Clift's own efforts to control his acting and his career by promoting himself as a performer with professional sincerity and integrity produced a unique effect: "For Clift, the qualities of integrity and intensity make 'acting' and 'being himself' equivalent terms" (225).

34. Cohan, 259.
35. Suarez, 138.
36. Butler, 111.
37. Richard Dyer, "Coming Out as Going In: The Image of the Homosexual as a Sad Young Man," in *The Matter of Images: Essays on Representations* (New York: Routledge, 1993), 73–92.
38. Ibid., 86.
39. Ibid., 78.
40. Ibid., 86.
41. Ibid., 88. In "A Queer Capital" Brett Beemyn points out that gay cruising in Washington in the postwar era implied many of the same rituals and dynamics that it has today: the lingering in parks and in front of store windows, the exchanges of looks and the casual signaling of a vague interest in the person cruised, and the asking of subtle questions along with the display of certain gestures and mannerisms. While these practices characterize gay cruising as a strategy of simultaneous camouflage and communication, Beemyn also emphasizes that gay cruising became widely visible as an overall phenomenon in postwar Washington D.C.'s urban areas—so visible, in fact, that it and homosexuality along with it became the subject of constant police surveillance and the subject, too, of the 1951 best-selling book *Washington Confidential*. Penned by Jack Lait and Lee Mortimer, the book singled out the presence of homosexuals as a negative consequence of the government's expansion of its bureaucratic apparatus. These findings are directly compatible with Robert J. Corber's analysis of the State Department's discovery and dismissal of homosexual employees. Part of the homosexual panic that broke out was the State Department's acknowledgment—even assertion—that homosexuals could pass as heterosexuals. See Corber, *In the Name of National Security*, 61–62.
42. The concept of the reverse discourse has become one of the staple elements of theories of the evolution of gay and lesbian sexuality and identity. The term "reverse discourse" was coined by Michel Foucault with regard to the classification, disciplining, and subversion of sexual identities. See Michel Foucault, *The History of Sexuality, vol. 1, An Introduction*, trans. Robert Hurley (New York: Random House, 1978; Vintage, 1990), 101. In an important recent critique of the political effectivity of reverse discourses, Eric O. Clarke argues that the concept "presents a theoretical repetition of the simultaneously historical and structural problem of formal equivalence itself," whereby the obtaining of equivalence becomes a teleological goal that glosses deeper problems of inequality that cannot be simply undone or "repaired" by often fairly narrow and schematic interventions of minority groups. See Eric O. Clarke, *Virtuous Vice: Homoeroticism and the Public Sphere* (Durham: Duke University Press, 2000), 88–95.
43. For a concise comparison of the different ideological positions within the Mattachine Society, the first postwar homosexual emancipation movement, see Jeffrey Escoffier, *American Homo: Community and Perversity* (Berkeley: University of California Press, 1998), 41–44. One such position was the argument that homosexuals are a cultural minority: They had been excluded from dominant heterosexual culture and had thus developed in different ways from that culture; their formation of subcultural networks

helped them negotiate their status as misfits and their own internalization of society's negative image of them. Therefore, homosexuals should embrace their status as a minority and should develop a distinct ethics and culture. Pitted against this was the so-called assimilationist position, which emphasized the similarities between homosexuals and heterosexuals. This argument recommended that homosexuals should make clear to the mainstream that they were not really different from heterosexuals and were thus worthy of social acceptance. Homosexuals, according to this argument, were also supposed to change or "reform," so that they would not continue to provoke the hostility of heterosexuals.

For a more detailed account of the early postwar homosexual emancipation movement, see John D'Emilio, *Sexual Politics, Sexual Communities: The Making of a Homosexual Minority in the United States, 1940–1970* (Chicago: The University of Chicago Press, 1983), 57–125. For a detailed biography and account of the ideas and concepts of Harry Hay, one of the cofounders of Mattachine, see *Radically Gay: Gay Liberation in the Words of Its Founder, Harry Hay,* ed. Will Roscoe (Boston: Beacon Press, 1996). Hay had a Communist background and modeled his construction of a minority discourse on Stalin's definition of a nation. Of Stalin's four criteria for what makes a minority— language, territory, economic life, and psychological makeup—Hay attributed the first and the fourth to homosexuals. Hay and other early cofounders of Mattachine were superceded as leaders in an ideological about-face in 1953, after which Mattachine increasingly adopted the assimilationist model.

For a discussion of another gay emancipation leader and proponent of the minority stance, Donald Webster Cory, in the context of postwar culture and, particularly, *The Brick Foxhole,* see Robert J. Corber, *Homosexuality in Cold War America,* 91–93. Corber argues that *The Brick Foxhole* is one of the few postwar texts that deals with homosexuality and implicitly extends the discourse of minority rights to gay men. It thereby anticipated Donald Webster Cory's 1951 study, *The Homosexual in America.* Different from Harry Hay's model with regard to what constitutes a minority, Donald Webster Cory's minority discourse is modeled on comparisons to other minorities, particularly African Americans. Corber notes that Corey was inspired by Gunnar Myrdal's analysis of race relations, entitled *An American Dilemma* (1944).

44. In his account of the situation of homosexuals in postwar Washington, D.C., Brett Beemyn mentions an interesting variant of a reverse discourse: In their sensationalist exploitation of gay life in the nation's capital, the authors of *Washington Confidential* provided a detailed geography of postwar gay life in Washington, D.C. that ended up serving as a guide for many gay men unaware of cruising sites (195).

45. Leo Bersani, "Is the Rectum a Grave?" in *AIDS: Cultural Analysis, Cultural Activism,* ed. Douglas Crimp (Cambridge, Mass.: MIT Press, 1989), 206, 215–219.

CHAPTER 4
- -

1. In *Bodies That Matter: On the Discursive Limits of "Sex"* (New York: Routledge, 1993), Judith Butler refutes the gender/sex binary, which conceives of gender as a cultural construct imposed upon a prediscursive, "hard" matter, sex. She argues instead that sex itself, similar to gender, is a cultural norm that governs the materiality of bodies. The subject is formed by going through the process of assuming sex (3–4). "Assuming," here, means that the subject assumes its sex in the same way that a law is cited, indicating that the subject seeks to consolidate its sexed position by reiteration. As Butler notes, "'The law of sex' is repeatedly fortified and idealized as the law only to the extent that it is reiterated as the law, produced as the law, the anterior and inapproximable ideal, by the very citations it is said to command" (14). Butler further argues that "the

symbolic ought to be rethought as a series of normativizing injunctions that secure the borders of sex through the threat of psychosis, abjection, psychic unlivability. . . . The presumption that the symbolic law of sex enjoys a separable ontology prior and autonomous to its assumption is contravened by the notion that the citation of the law is the very mechanism of its production and articulation" (15). In her groundbreaking study on the constructedness of gender, *Gender Trouble: Feminism and the Subversion of Identity* (New York: Routledge, 1990), Butler describes how gender, too, falls prey to the *fiction* of a separable ontology, since the gendered subject desires coherence and produces it as a *phantasmatic* essence.

2. This is then the second connotation of the term "assumption," which Butler deliberately collapses onto the first. In a passage that has become the mantra of postmodern gender studies, Butler writes in *Gender Trouble:* "Acts, gestures, and desire produce the effect of an internal core or substance, but produce this *on the surface* of the body, through the play of signifying absences that suggest, but never reveal, the organizing principle of identity as a cause. Such acts, gestures, enactments, generally construed, are *performative* in the sense that the essence or identity that they otherwise purport to express are *fabrications* manufactured and sustained through corporeal signs and other discursive means. That the gendered body is performative suggests that it has no ontological status apart from the various acts which constitute its reality. This also suggests that if that reality is fabricated as an interior essence, that very interiority is an effect and function of a decidedly public and social discourse, the public regulation of fantasy through the surface politics of the body, the gender border control that differentiates inner from outer, and so institutes the 'integrity' of the subject. . . . If the inner truth of gender is a fabrication and if a true gender is a fantasy instituted and inscribed on the surface of bodies, then it seems that genders can be neither true nor false, but are only produced as the truth effects of a discourse of primary and stable identity"(136).

3. Jeffrey Escoffier, *American Homo: Community and Perversity* (Los Angeles: University of California Press, 1988), 16.

4. Richard Dyer, *Now You See It: Studies on Lesbian and Gay Film* (New York: Routledge, 1990), 112.

5. Tom Waugh, *Hard to Imagine: Gay Male Eroticism in Photography and Film from Their Beginnings to Stonewall* (New York: Columbia University Press, 1996), 258–269.

6. Leo Bersani, *Homos* (Cambridge, Mass.: Harvard University Press, 1995), 18.

7. See Martin Meisel, "Scattered Chiaroscuro: Melodrama as a Matter of Seeing," in *Melodrama: Stage Picture Screen*, ed. Jacky Bratton, Jim Cook, and Christine Gledhill (London: BFI Publishing, 1994), 65–81. Meisel claims that melodrama has long been linked with "elemental contrasts of darkness and light." Melodrama lends itself to visualization because its designation of theme and morals via characters' emotional and psychological states parallels the way the human eye apprehends such basic elements as light and dark, form, contour, and movement. Meisel notes that melodrama exploits "sensitivity" textually and materially by capitalizing on such ocular phenomena as "'contour enhancement,' whereby receptors responding to different intensities of light exaggerate the differences, making for quicker recognition as well as firmer edges and emphatic boundaries between relative dark and light" (65–66).

8. See Gilles Deleuze, "Plato and the Simulacrum," trans. Rosalind E. Krauss, *October* 27 (1983): 45–53.

9. Judith Butler, *Bodies That Matter*, 81.

10. Ibid., 59.

11. This then also qualifies Deleuze's concept of subversive mimesis. See Marcos Becquer, "Snap!thology and Other Discursive Practices in Tongues Untied," *Wide Angle* 13, no. 2 (April 1991): 4–15. Becquer argues that drag queens constitute simulacra of gender,

but unlike Deleuze's concept of the simulacrum in which neither simulacrum nor copy can ever be as authentic as the model (and thus fall short of sameness to the model), drag queens displace the model by reinstalling sameness on the level of subjectivity (12). The claim to sameness becomes the democratic arena for the cultivation and celebration of multiple (gender/ethnic/class) differences and constitutes gender "realness" (9).

12. This discussion of the gay phallus is inspired by Judith Butler's very suggestive chapter, "The Lesbian Phallus and the Morphological Imaginary," in *Bodies That Matter,* 57–91.

13. Judith Butler, *Bodies That Matter,* 103.

14. Tom Waugh, "Hard to Imagine: Gay Erotic Cinema in the Postwar Era," *CineAction!* 10 (Fall 1987): 67.

15. Ibid.

16. Barbara Ehrenreich, *The Hearts of Men: American Dreams and the Flight from Commitment* (New York: Doubleday, 1983), and David Sterritt, *Mad to Be Saved: The Beats, the '50s, and Film* (Carbondale and Edwardsville: Southern Illinois University Press, 1998), 36–37.

17. Ehrenreich, *The Hearts of Men,* 50: "The playboy didn't avoid marriage because he was a little bit 'queer,' but on the contrary, because he was so ebulliently, even compulsively, heterosexual."

18. In this regard, see especially Steven Cohan's analysis in *Masked Men: Masculinity and the Movies in the Fifties* (Bloomington: Indiana University Press, 1997), 264–303, of the depiction of the playboy in such Hollywood mainstream films as *Pillow Talk* (1959), a sex farce starring Rock Hudson and Doris Day that constructed playboy heterosexuality in close relation to its doubles, effeminacy and homosexuality—the former produced through the playboy's effeminate (though putatively heterosexual) sidekick, Tony Randall, the latter produced as part of the playboy's own strategic combination of multiple personae (and, in fact, persons) for the broader goal of manipulating and winning the female. *Pillow Talk* is interesting for the fact that it inscribes the playboy and his double on the same performer. *That Touch of Mink* (1961), another sex farce starring Doris Day, fully displaces homosexuality onto the playboy's sidekick, Gig Young. Young sees a professional shrink, who, in a series of sitcom twists and turns, "misreads" him as developing homosexual tendencies, whereby, so the film implies, it is ultimately the shrink who is homosexual—because of his homosexual fantasies and his constant proximity to what the lingo of the day termed "fruitcakes." While this disengaging move must be regarded as a conservative reaction to *Pillow Talk*, it evidently freed up the scriptwriter of the film to greatly elaborate on homosexuality as a construction of the psychoanalytic profession. Homosexuality is once again deprived of any actual existence and becomes the film's most famous running gag. Hypochondria is here shifted from the patient to the doctor and recast as a combination of professional greed and paranoia.

19. Callie Angell, "The Films of Andy Warhol—A Selection," in *Andy Warhol 1956–86: Mirror of His Time* (Tokyo: Asahi Shimbun with the Andy Warhol Museum, Pittsburgh, 1996), 192.

20. D. A. Miller, *Bringing Out Roland Barthes* (Berkeley: University of California Press, 1992), 29. Notwithstanding Miller's overtly polemical presentation of the binary he observes, and notwithstanding my taking it perhaps a bit too literally, I should like to point out that Miller's reading works less well in Europe and South America, where the overwhelming majority of straight men have traditionally worn briefs. Miller's observation is qualified also by the daring sacerdotal forays of straight rock musicians, but such exceptions prove the rule, given that North American culture is one big erotic basket case.

21. Ibid., 31.

22. Bersani, *Homos,* 32.

23. Ibid., 6–7.

24. David Halperin, "More or Less Gay-Specific," *London Review of Books*, 23 May 1996, p. 24.

25. Leo Bersani, "Is the Rectum a Grave?" in *AIDS: Cultural Analysis/Cultural Activism*, ed. Douglas Crimp (Cambridge, Mass.: MIT Press, 1987), 217–218. Like many perversions, this one can be traced back to the infant stage of polymorphous perversity. Bersani argues that for the infant this perverse masochism functions as a defense mechanism, which helps the infant survive and, indeed, find pleasure in the impact of stimuli for which it has not yet developed defensive/integrative ego structures. He interprets infant masochism as a psychic strategy that partially makes up for the deficiencies of an as yet incomplete process of maturation. In its polymorphism, this masochism is very "basic" and synonymous with sexuality and sexual pleasure.

26. Bersani, *Homos*, 92, 99. Seizing on Freud's insight that human sexuality in general indicates "a certain rhythm of mastery and surrender" (99), Bersani speculates that the sexual appears to move broadly between a hyperbolic sense of self and a loss of consciousness of the self.

27. Ibid., 93–94.

28. Ibid. It should be noted that even though Bersani repeatedly uses the term "pleasure," he is far from conceiving of pleasure in, say, a Foucauldian way. As Tim Dean notes in "Sex and Syncope," *Raritan* 15, no. 3 (Winter 1996): 86, unlike many constructionist theorists (such as Halperin), for whom pleasure and *jouissance* are closely linked, for Bersani, they are conceptually antithetical. When Bersani talks about pleasure, he means the deeply eruptive and uncontrolled forces of sexual desire amplified into sexual frenzy. Halperin would never attach a utopian function to the notion of sexual pleasure or *jouissance*, whereas the utopian slant of Bersani's writing is based precisely on his notion of ecstatic sex, which he calls "pleasure."

29. Bersani, "Rectum," 217. As Bersani notes, Georges Bataille has proposed that the transgressing of the polarity between the assertion of the self in its exercise of power and the self's seeking of powerlessness may be at the heart of certain mystical experiences and of human sexuality. Bersani also stresses that Freud speculated that sexual pleasure may become independent of an external object of pleasure when a certain threshold of intensity is reached, as it may with the ecstatic oscillation between self-assertion and self-abdication. Sexuality becomes synonymous with masochism—an intrinsic link that might be traced back as far as the infant stage. Bersani explains, "From this Freudian perspective, we might say that Bataille reformulates this self-shattering into the sexual as a kind of nonanecdotal self-debasement, as a masochism to which the melancholy of the post-Oedipal superego's moral masochism is wholly alien, and in which, so to speak, the self is exuberantly discarded" (217–218).

30. Homo-ness for Bersani constitutes an intrinsically anti-identitarian identity, brought about by the shattering of the self, which is no longer interested in partaking in the discursive regimes of *scientia sexualis*. As a concept, Bersani juxtaposes it to the Lacanian definition of desire as lack. To cultivate homo-ness means to help qualify the processes of identification and desire that have suffered from a perception of profound sexual and gender difference. See, for example, his discussion of Marcel Proust in *Homos*, 146.

31. Bersani, "Rectum," 217.

32. Andrew Holleran, "Arrested for Sex," *Out* (May 2001): 70–75. Holleran's article provides a long list of such cases from the recent past and puts them in historical context.

33. Bersani, *Homos*, 101.

34. Theodor Adorno and Max Horkheimer, *Dialectic of Enlightenment* (New York: Social Studies Association, Inc., 1944; this edition New York: The Continuum Publishing Company, 1989). See, for example, their introduction, where it is argued that Enlight-

enment is totalitarian in its rationalism and empiricism: "For the Enlightenment, whatever does not conform to the rule of computation and utility is suspect" (6). Thereby, the simulacrum, initially conceived of in opposition to Platonic and Aristotelian metaphysics, has taken their place particularly with regard to its universalizing force.

35. See Chris Straayer's discussion of the recuperative aspects of the transvestite signification in these films, which she discusses as the genre of the "temporary transvestite film" in her book *Deviant Eyes, Deviant Bodies: Sexual Re-orientation in Film and Video* (New York: Columbia University Press, 1996). She notes, "The undermining of costume disguise by seemingly incongruous pitch relies on and reinforces the conception that one's voice represents the true self. Likewise, other physical qualities such as body language and hair length receive privileged authority" (46).

36. The poser's effeminacy is thus neither that of RuPaul nor that of the biblical ur-whore, but rather of Christ on the cross. Consider Kaja Silverman's characterization of Christian masochism in *Male Subjectivity at the Margins* (New York: Routledge, 1992) in relation to this characterization of the poser as suffering martyr: Silverman writes that Christian masochism always needs an external audience (heavenly or earthly), it needs to showcase the body as spectacle—a demand that is not incompatible with the dynamics of a film such as *Blow Job*. Even though the film only showcases the face, its aesthetic form is in line with Christian masochism's embrace of spectacularization as a viable rhetorical strategy. And even though *Blow Job* may prompt attempts at psychologizing the poser, these would remain futile, as the film also depersonalizes the poser, making him anonymous. This enables a foregrounding of suffering as a *mode* detached from any particular individual. According to Silverman, this, too, is very Christian and enables the shift from Christ to rebel/revolutionary (197–198).

37. Bersani, "Rectum," 209. Bersani's "rectification" of the subversive function of gay male sexuality comes partly in response to the claim of other theorists that straight men are threatened by gay male resignifications of their model. He singles out the argument Jeffrey Weeks makes in his study, *Sexuality and Its Discontents: Meanings, Myths & Modern Sexualities* (London: Routledge, 1985), 191. Bersani argues: "If, as Weeks puts it, gay men 'gnaw at the roots of a male heterosexual identity,' it is not because of the parodistic distance that they take from that identity, but rather because, from within their nearly mad identification with it, *they never cease to feel the appeal of its being violated*" (209).

38. Ibid., 211, 219.

39. *Homos*, 18.

40. Ibid., 59.

41. Hal Foster, *The Return of the Real: The Avant-Garde at the End of the Century* (Cambridge, Mass.: MIT Press, 1996), 156.

42. Ibid. Foster points out that abject art has responded to this aporia in two ways: One group of artists (often women artists who seek to explore the female/maternal body repressed by the paternal law) have sought to bring about identification with the abject, thereby probing the wound of trauma; the second group (often male artists—and Foster includes Warhol among them—who assume an infantilist position to mock the paternal law) have focused on "representing the condition of abjection in order to provoke its operation—to catch abjection in the act, to make it reflexive, even repellent in its own right" (157–159). With regard to Warhol's films, *Blow Job* may exemplify this aspect to the extent that the poser alludes to James Dean, the boy who, as Steven Cohan has noted, resisted becoming a man, which then becomes translated into the poser's repetitive attempts—and failures—to complete a patriarchally/paternally imposed linearity and to fulfill the assignment of gender. However, there are in Warhol's cinematic

canon some even more glaring examples of Foster's particular characterization. One might think of any performance by Taylor Mead or Mario Montez in a Warhol film. But since, as Foster notes, the signification of trauma in Warhol is complex, so is the signification of abjection. Yet another variant can be found in the famous scene in *The Chelsea Girls*, in which Ondine (the self-professed pope) violently slaps Rona Page, who called his bluff. Here we witness the operation of abjection and we are made to identify with the abject—even though the film also foregrounds our complicity in witnessing the spectacle we just saw.

43. I would like to thank Marcos Becquer for sharing with me his idea of gay men passing as men. Only he has the brilliance and originality of thought to develop this idea into a full-fledged theory. Even as a concise idea it has influenced much of what is behind my thinking on gay men in this chapter.

44. For a useful overview of various critiques of Bersani's discourse, see James S. Williams, "The Outlaw Returns: Homos vs. Tradition in the New Work of Leo Bersani," in *Gay Signatures: Gay and Lesbian Theory, Fiction and Film in France, 1945–1995*, ed. Owen Heathcote, Alex Hughes, and James S. Williams (London and New York: Berg Publishers, 1998), 91–109. The charge of conflation of ego and subject was made by Tim Dean in "The Psychoanalysis of AIDS," *October* 63 (1993): 83–116.

45. See John Champagne, *The Ethics of Marginality: A New Approach to Gay Studies* (Minneapolis and London: University of Minnesota Press, 1995), 52, 56.

46. Halperin, 26.

47. Halperin, 27.

48. Space constraints do not allow me to draw a detailed analogy between Bersani's argument and abject art. However, I will note that I am inspired by James S. Williams, who, even though he does not invoke the concept of abject, suggestively characterizes Bersani's theoretical move as a "spectacular, erotic exercise in 'turning back' on oneself at the very moment a display of the law of critical authority . . . is most called for" (100).

49. In his Deleuzian reading of performance and aesthetics in Warhol's work, Steven Shaviro argues that it is precisely repetition in Warhol that forecloses etiology, pathology, and ontology. See Steven Shaviro, *The Cinematic Body* (Minneapolis: University of Minnesota Press, 1993), 206.

CHAPTER 5
- -

1. John D'Emilio, *Sexual Politics, Sexual Communities: The Making of a Homosexual Minority in the United States, 1940–1970* (Chicago: The University of Chicago Press, 1983), 136–144.

2. Michel Foucault, *The History of Sexuality, vol. 1, An Introduction*, trans. Robert Hurley (New York: Random House, 1978; Vintage, 1990), 15–49.

3. D'Emilio (139, footnote 29) cites a *Newsweek* quotation (December 30, 1963) of A. M. Rosenthal, metropolitan editor of the *New York Times*, who wrote and published a front-page article on homosexuality after encountering a gay cruising area, where he perceived homosexuality as "unexotic" and "open." While I am aware that the terms "less-than-exotic" and "unexotic" have different connotations, I think there is a discrepancy between Rosenthal's personal choice of words and the broader style of representation of homosexuality on the part of the *New York Times* and other mainstream media. As late as 1966, *Time* magazine published an article denouncing and demonizing homosexuality. The article read, in part: "It is a pathetic little second-rate substitute for reality, a pitiable flight from life. As such it deserves fairness, compassion, understanding and,

when possible, treatment. But it deserves no encouragement, no glamorization, no rationalization, no fake status as minority martyrdom, no sophistry about simple differences in taste—and, above all, no pretense that it is anything but a pernicious sickness" (*Time*, January 21, 1966, p. 41, quoted in D'Emilio, 138).

4. D'Emilio (142) notes that deviance theory mounted the sharpest attack on traditional conceptualizations of homosexuality. Its most distinctly relativist perspective was provided by Howard Becker's *Outsiders*, which grouped deviants under the category of subculture and explained deviance as "the failure to obey group rules." D'Emilio notes further that in adaptational theory "'cure' remained the goal, but a society that produced homosexuals faster than professionals could treat them became the patient" (140). Interestingly, adaptational theory implied that the difference ascribed to the homosexual is constituted by factors external to homosexuality and that homosexuality, conceived of as a flight from masculinity, could potentially befall any man. This is a definite indicator that homosexuality had advanced from its position from Other to proximate.

5. See D'Emilio, 153. Kameny went on to say, "I do not see the NAACP and CORE worrying about which chromosome and gene produced a black skin, or about the possibility of bleaching the Negro. I do not see any great interest on the part of the B'nai B'rith Anti-Defamation League in the possibility of solving problems of anti-semitism by converting Jews to Christians. . . . We are interested in obtaining rights for our respective minorities AS Negroes, AS Jews, and AS HOMOSEXUALS. Why we are Negroes, Jews, or Homosexuals is totally irrelevant, and whether we can be changed to Whites, Christians, or heterosexuals is equally irrelevant" (D'Emilio, 153). This passage indicates that Kameny's rhetoric assumes a fully fledged homosexual identity as a basis for identity politics and direct action.

6. In this context, it is interesting to consider, as D'Emilio does, the role of Evelyn Hooker and her work on the depathologization of homosexuality. As early as during the 1950s, Hooker advocated a view that there was no difference between the psychological profile of heterosexuals and that of homosexuals. D'Emilio, who describes Hooker as an "observer, more in the tradition of anthropology and sociology, and not as a clinician," notes that she was "virtually the only mental health professional studying nonpatient, noninstitutionalized homosexuals" (141).

7. D'Emilio, 159.

8. It will take further research to see how, exactly, such gay-initiated discourses were contained and framed by nongay publications. D'Emilio describes especially the sensationalist aspects of ethnographic exploitation, noting: "The volume of material written about homosexuality grew large enough that the quantitative increase in itself represented a qualitative change. No longer the taboo topic of twenty years earlier, 'sexual deviance' was losing its ability to shock and frighten. In addition, the familiarity that came from more open discussion bred not contempt but a variety of viewpoints. The formula that mixed sin, sickness, and crime into a jumbled consensus justifying opprobrium and punishment retained its dominance, but not without challenges" (147).

9. I am purposely not saying that white gay men have simply remained white and male. With regard to the category of maleness (or masculinity, which I hold to be the same), my choice is determined by the complex relationship white gay men have had to the socially constructed category of "men," especially given queer discourses' theorization of this relationship as one of distance, alienation, and even dysfunction. White gay men's similarly complex relationship to the category of whiteness is discussed in Chapter 6.

10. Charles Brenner, *An Elementary Textbook of Psychoanalysis* (New York: Doubleday/Anchor Books, 1955; expanded ed. 1973), 41.

11. Diana Fuss, *Identification Papers* (New York: Routledge, 1995), 3.

12. Ibid.

13. Sigmund Freud, *An Outline of Psycho-Analysis*, in *The Standard Edition of the Complete Psychological Works of Sigmund Freud, vol. 23*, ed. and trans. James Strachey (London: Hogarth Press, 1964), 193.

14. Jacques Lacan, *The Four Fundamental Concepts of Psycho-Analysis*, ed. Jacques-Alain Miller, trans. Alan Sheridan (New York and London: W. W. Norton and Co., 1981), 243.

15. Jonathan Flatley, "Warhol Gives Good Face: Publicity and the Politics of Prosopopoeia," in *Pop Out: Queer Warhol*, ed. Jennifer Doyle, Jonathan Flatley, and José Esteban Muñoz (Durham: Duke University Press, 1996), 101–104.

16. Michael Warner, "The Mass Public and the Mass Subject," in *The Phantom Public Sphere*, ed. Bruce Robbins (Minneapolis: University of Minnesota Press, 1993), 234, cited in Flatley, 105.

17. Flatley, 104.

18. Ibid., 105.

19. Ibid., 112. In stressing the fictive character of Warhol's portraits and by comparing their aesthetic properties to those of the mask, Flatley seizes on Lacan's understanding that mourning functions for the subject like a masquerade. (See Juliet Mitchell and Jacqueline Rose, eds., *Feminine Sexuality: Jacques Lacan and the École Freudienne*, trans. Jacqueline Rose (New York: W. W. Norton and Company, 1982), 85. He cites Judith Butler, *Gender Trouble: Feminism and the Subversion of Identity* (New York: Routledge, 1990), 50, who characterizes the mask as the signifier for the subject having incorporated the lost love and thus mastered the refusal of love that was triggered by the loss. To the extent that the mask is the signifier for the phantasmatic, that is, hallucinatory preservation of the lost love, it is more closely associated with Freud's concept of melancholia than with mourning. However, as Flatley himself notes, Freudian discourse only initially juxtaposed the two as antitheses. He emphasizes that Freud came to suggest that a hallucinatory identification may be the only way in which the reality of loss can be negotiated and mastered (112). While melancholia in its extreme form is still considered mourning's dysfunctional double, in which the mourner fails to mourn (that is, he incorporates his own ego rather than the lost love), Freudian as well as Lacanian discourses have treated both as being proximate and not at all mutually exclusive. In this sense, it is not necessarily a contradiction that someone like Butler understands concepts of mourning, identification, and incorporation from a Lacanian perspective as being broadly melancholic, while a Freudian scholar such as Diana Fuss emphasizes in *Identification Papers* that melancholia merely represents mourning's "most violent continuation" (38) and that both exist on a sliding scale (ibid.).

20. See Tim Retzloff, "Cars and Bars: Assembling Gay Men in Postwar Flint, Michigan," in *Creating a Place for Ourselves: Lesbian, Gay, and Bisexual Community Histories*, ed. Brett Beemyn (New York: Routledge, 1997), 227–252.

21. See Patrick S. Smith, *Andy Warhol's Art and Films* (Ann Arbor: UMI Research Press, 1986). Patrick Smith has pointed out that many of Warhol's images from *A Gold Book* originated in photographs taken by Warhol's boyfriend from the 1950s, photographer Ed Wallowitch. The drawing of the juvenile delinquent in *A Gold Book* appears to be based on a photo of a young man leaning against a lamppost. However, Warhol made significant changes: The youth in the photograph does not smoke a cigarette; he has both feet on the ground and his hands are lifted up and folded behind his head. If the image from *A Gold Book* is based on this photograph, the "adaptation" is set apart from Warhol's more literal renditions of other Wallowitch photographs for the particular purpose of alluding to Dean. Patrick Smith's reading of the drawing's iconographic similarities to Dean (the blue jeans, the jacket, the cigarette) (67) may have been inspired and/or confirmed by his interview with Charles Lisanby, a close friend of Warhol in

the 1950s and 1960s, who identified the image as James Dean and mentions that it is taken from a photograph (377)—although it is not clear whether the photograph at issue here was the one taken by Wallowitch or a publicity shot of Dean.

22. Lacan introduced the concept of the mirror stage originally in *Ecrits* (1936). See also Jacqueline Rose's explanation of the concept as one that takes the child's apprehension of himself or herself as a coherent if fictional construct (fictional because, according to Rose, "it conceals, or freezes, the infant's lack of motor co-ordination and the fragmentation of its drives"). See Juliet Mitchell and Jacqueline Rose, eds., *Feminine Sexuality: Jacques Lacan and the École Freudienne*, trans. Jacqueline Rose (New York: W. W. Norton and Company, 1982), 30.

23. Unfortunately, I was unable to obtain a copy of *Two Girls Hand in Hand*.

24. Trevor Fairbrother, "Tomorrow's Man," in *"Success Is a Job in New York": The Early Art and Business of Andy Warhol*, ed. Donna M. deSalvo (New York: Carnegie Museum of Art, 1989). Fairbrother points out that these drawings already document Warhol's sensibility of being/wanting to be an "insider" and his desire to address insiders among the multiple audiences of his artworks. For example, the fact that Warhol refuses to detail the faces of the two young men from *a is an alphabet* stimulates the viewer's own narrative curiosity about their encounter or possible relationship (59). These drawings are analogous to the historically contemporaneous phenomenon of hypochondria, yet not so much in terms of the kind of heavy psychologization discussed earlier (which they refuse or, at least, displace from the image onto the viewer), but in their chimeric quality. Fairbrother rightly characterizes them as apparitions that "heighten both the sense of momentary revelation and the elusive narrative" (ibid.). In addition, the images' captions, written by "Corkie" (Ralph T. Ward), a friend of Warhol, produce a tension between image and text that manipulates the viewer (a concept that, of course, is still operative in *Blow Job*, even though the film has no credits that would announce its title to the viewer). The caption for the drawing of the two men from *a is an alphabet* reads: "S was a snake / who played with this young man / until his mother chased it with / a rake." Fairbrother rightly interprets the combination of image and poem as a spoof on "the classic psychiatric homosexual scenario: one of the men is a snake, an evil tempter, a stand-in for a penis; supposedly the strong-willed mother will put fear into the serpent, but will she have saved her son from the love that dare not speak its name?" (Ibid.)

25. Rainer Crone, *Andy Warhol—A Picture Show by the Artist* (New York: Rizzoli, 1987), 25–26.

26. Fuss, 34.

27. The real circumstances of Dean's car crash involved no brick wall whatsoever. Dean's Porsche Spyder, which he called "Little Bastard," collided on a wide-open road at full speed with another car that had come out of a side road.

28. Cited in Richard Meyer, "Warhol's Clones," *The Yale Journal of Criticism* 7, no. 1 (1994): 97.

29. Meyer, 97.

30. In the context of American visual/artistic representation, the tension between individuation and reification has been traced to mid-nineteenth century American painting. See David M. Lubin, *Act of Portrayal: Eakins, Sargent, James* (New Haven and London: Yale University Press, 1985), 13.

31. For a concise overview and useful historical contextualization of this debate, see David Sterritt, *Mad to Be Saved: The Beats, the '50s, and Film* (Carbondale and Edwardsville: Southern Illinois University Press, 1998). Drawing on David Riesman's *The Lonely Crowd*, David Sterritt observed that "the conforming or 'other-directed' person is 'too hard on himself in certain ways' and that 'his anxieties, as child consumer-trainee, as

parent, as worker and player, are very great. He is often torn between the illusion that life should be easy, if he could only find the ways of proper adjustment to the group, and the half-buried feeling that it is not." (24).

32. This scenario of identity formation and frustration has been analyzed in depth by Moe Meyer, "Under the Sign of Wilde: An Archaeology of Posing," in *The Politics and Poetics of Camp*, ed. Moe Meyer (New York: Routledge, 1994), 75–109.

33. For a discussion of these dynamics, see Art Simon's insightful analysis of the Jackie silk screens in *Dangerous Knowledge: The JFK Assassination in Art and Film* (Philadelphia: Temple University Press, 1996), 101–118.

34. Fuss, 38. Fuss cites Julia Kristeva, *Black Sun: Depression and Melancholia* (New York: Columbia University Press, 1989), 12.

35. Sigmund Freud, *Totem and Taboo: Some Points of Agreement Between the Mental Lives of Savages and Neurotics*, in *The Standard Edition of the Complete Psychological Works of Sigmund Freud, vol. 13*, ed. and trans. James Strachey (London: Hogarth Press, 1964), 144, cited in Fuss, 36.

36. Fuss informs us that the story of parricide enables Freud to apprehend more precisely the three major aspects intrinsic to the psychosexual dynamics of identification that were discussed earlier with regard to *Blow Job* and white gay male spectatorship. First, it designates the sons' love/hate relationship to their father as a kind of ambivalence central to all identifications: Identification with a love object can be based on a set of antithetical feelings that, in their combination, make identification so complex and contradictory. Second, the myth describes identification as an act of violence, a "monstrous assassination" of the other who is "murdered and orally incorporated before being entombed in the subject" (34). Third, the myth describes identification as a process of repetition and remembrance. The totem meal expiates the crime but it also repeats it, permitting the sons to celebrate victory and reappropriate the father's powers. "The whole unconscious process," Fuss writes, "functions as a form of psychical memorialization in which the subject must repeatedly kill and ingest what it wishes to preserve a remainder of inside" (ibid.).

37. Fuss, 34.

38. Fuss, 32–36; See also Brenner, 94.

39. Diana Fuss analyzes this rhetoric in detail. She notes, "Freud's theoretical reductionism in *Totem and Taboo* actually converges from two directions. From the one side, he employs an evolutionary schema to describe psychosexual development, analogizing the changes in sexual maturity to the "progress" of civilizations, while from the other side he relies upon a psychosexual paradigm to describe evolutionary change, ranking cultures according to a developmental scale" (35).

40. Fuss, 36.

41. Ibid.

42. Gretchen Berg, "Nothing to Lose: An Interview with Andy Warhol," *Cahiers du Cinéma in English*, no. 10, 1967. My citation is from the reprint in *Andy Warhol: Film Factory*, ed. Michael O'Pray (London: The British Film Institute, 1989), 56–57.

43. Fuss, 39.

44. Interview with Gretchen Berg, in O'Pray, 61.

45. Thomas Crow, "Saturday Disasters: Trace and Reference in Early Warhol," in *Modern Art in the Common Culture* (New Haven: Yale University Press, 1996), 56.

46. Fuss, 39.

47. Hal Foster, *The Return of the Real: The Avant-Garde at the End of the Century* (Cambridge, Mass.: MIT Press, 1996), 32.

48. I thank Matt Wrbican, curator and archivist of the Andy Warhol Museum, Pittsburgh, for this information.

49. Correspondence of author with John Wallowitch, Edward's brother, on March 14, 2001: John Wallowitch told me it is his strong recollection that his brother painted the skull and crossbones for the photographs he took of Warhol.

50. This remark was made by Warhol's assistant, Ronnie Cutrone, who retold it to Trevor Fairbrother. See Fairbrother's informative essay "Skulls," in *The Work of Andy Warhol*, ed. Gary Garrels (Seattle: Bay Press, 1989, for the Dia Art Foundation Series Discussions in Contemporary Culture), 96–97, 112 fn. 7. Fairbrother's essay renders a highly informative description of the painting technique Warhol applied for his skull paintings and puts the motif in relation to Warhol's overall canon of death-related motifs. Fairbrother also cites the following comment by Warhol from his own *The Philosophy of Andy Warhol: From A to B & Back Again* (New York: Harcourt Brace Jovanovich, 1975), 149: "Even when the subject is different, people always paint the same painting." See also Robert Rosenblum's introduction to *Andy Warhol: Philip's Skull* (New York: Gagosian Gallery, 1999), entitled "Warhol's Ultimate Vanity Portrait."

51. At issue here is the impact of Warhol's homosexuality on his artistic career. It is well known that there was a poor (in the sense of largely absent) reception of Warhol's only exhibition during the 1950s of his explicitly gay pre-pop work, the 1956 show, "Drawings from a Boy Book," at the Bodley Gallery. On this, see Trevor Fairbrother, "Tomorrow's Man," and Victor Bockris, *The Life and Death of Andy Warhol* (New York: Bantam Books, 1989). Bockris writes that Warhol's show at the Bodley Gallery was preceded by his efforts to have his drawings exhibited at the Tanager Gallery. But Warhol's friend Philip Pearlstein refused to act as a mediator between Warhol and the gallery because the drawings were too daring and explicit (84). Warhol's efforts to have a gay male art exhibit were thus marked by the experience of homophobia. In addition, there was the famous incident of Warhol learning that his revered artist colleagues Jasper Johns and Robert Rauschenberg considered him "too swish"—a discovery that, despite Warhol's own facetious account of it, must have been traumatic for the artist.

52. Fairbrother, "Skulls," 93. Fairbrother points out that Warhol made his skull paintings in 1976–1977, a time when one conceivable pair of binaries thus envisioned might have been between disco and punk, both of which the skull related to (the former being expressed through the paintings' coloring, the latter through the punk culture's appropriation of the skull as standard iconography).

53. Foster, 132.

54. Warhol returned to the spatial association of himself with the skull in the *1978 Self-Portrait with Skull* (acrylic and silk screen on canvas). (This image can be seen in *The Work of Andy Warhol*, ed. Gary Garrels, 182). In this late-1970s image, Warhol's association with the skull is somewhat different from that in earlier images—he places the skull on his shoulder, and the stark dual tone of the image privileges the likeness of artist and skull over a balance of sameness and difference.

55. Eve Kosofsky Sedgwick, "Queer Performativity: Warhol's Shyness/Warhol's Whiteness," in *Pop Out: Queer Warhol*, ed. Jennifer Doyle, Jonathan Flatley, and José Esteban Muñoz (Durham: Duke University Press, 1996), 135.

56. See Michael Bronski, *Culture Clash: The Making of Gay Sensibility* (Boston: South End Press, 1984). Bronski characterizes this British author as a contemporary of Wilde who "in an extreme form of Wildean self-invention, claimed to have been given the title "Baron Corvo," which he retained as a pen name" (64). Bronski goes on to say that this author's writing is "filled with overwrought prose and sprinkled with epigrams. His histories, such as *Chronicles of the House of Borgia* (1901), tell us more about his paranoid imagination than they do about Italian history. His best-known novel, *Hadrian the Seventh* (1904), in which a rather obscure English writer becomes pope, is a mixture of wish fulfillment and revenge upon those whom he felt prevented him from taking Holy Or-

ders" (ibid.). Most important, Bronski situates Rolfe in the Wilde tradition, which, after the Wilde trials, became more circumspect and reverted to established traditions of gay sensibility (ibid.).

57. W. H. Auden, Foreword to *The Desire and Pursuit of the Whole* (New York: New Directions, n.d.).

58. Leo Bersani, *Homos* (Cambridge, Mass.: Harvard University Press, 1995), 113–129.

59. Chris Straayer, being a feminist theorist who has explored some implications of women passing for male, defines passing via Jaqueline Rose's explication of Lacanian psychoanalysis, which has redescribed the psychosexual in linguistic terms. The subject's speaking position is linguistic as well as psychoanalytic. In Lacanian psychoanalysis, the phallus, which marks the Law of the Father, produces sexual difference as a "legislative category produced in language with no validity in the anatomic or visible" (Chris Straayer, *Deviant Eyes, Deviant Bodies: Sexual Re-orientation in Film and Video* [New York: Columbia University Press, 1996], 155). Gender crossings are here understood, first and foremost, as crossings of the linguistic divide between gendered speaking positions (ibid.). In linguistically informed psychoanalytic theory, this act of passing is then characterized as the deliberate and successful assumption of the speaking position of the opposite sex, which results in the passer's differential position.

CHAPTER 6

1. Steven Cohan, *Masked Men: Masculinity and the Movies in the Fifties* (Bloomington: Indiana University Press, 1997), 14–15.

2. Ibid., 119.

3. Ibid.

4. Ibid., 120.

5. Ibid., 118.

6. Ibid.

7. James Gilbert, *A Cycle of Outrage* (New York: Oxford University Press, 1986), 70–71, cited in Cohan, 115.

8. One might argue against this by referring to the scene in which Plato waits for his father to visit him but only receives the latter's check in the mail, handed to him by his black nanny. This might be construed as pointing to the economic conditions that make black fatherhood, in particular, so difficult, but the film alludes to this aspect only vaguely. Reading the film as I do, I do not mean to deny the existence of a black middle class in America during this period, nor am I trying to burden the film with the demand to mark any nonwhite characters as economically inferior to its white dramatis personae. Rather, I believe that the film, on the one hand, for much of its plot utilizes Plato's skin color and the fact that he has a nanny as vague, seemingly "self-evident" markers of his *overall* Otherness while, on the other hand, it *whitewashes* him by portraying his domestic background through the symbolic vocabulary of melodrama as a predominantly white genre. In this sense, Plato's nanny, too, signifies two things—her skin color is supposed to make Plato "black by association," while her very status as nanny is supposed to suggest that Plato's household and home are compatible with certain codes and demographics of whiteness. Ultimately, the film attempts to claim that Plato is "just a kid" like all the other—white—kids who live in the upper-middle-class white suburb.

9. Richard Dyer, *White* (London: Routledge, 1997). Dyer draws on the writings of Toni Morrison, who in *Playing in the Dark: Whiteness and the Literary Imagination* (Cambridge, MA: Harvard University Press, 1992) cites the inescapability of black represen-

tation to the construction of white identity, and on Edward Saïd's argument in *Orientalism* (London: Routledge and Kegan Paul, 1978) that Western culture has used the construction of the Orient as a way of making sense of itself (13). Sander Gilman, in *Difference and Pathology: Stereotypes of Sexuality, Race and Madness* (Ithaca: Cornell University Press, 1985), has argued that dark peoples have served as a screen onto which white culture could project its own taboo desires, which, according to Dyer, do not require even representations of actual black people (28).

10. Dyer, *White*, 23–24 and 72–75.
11. Ibid., 13.
12. Ibid., 28.
13. Ibid.
14. In her interesting article, "Beat Culture: America Revisioned," in *Beat Culture and the New America, 1950–1965*, ed. Lisa Phillips (New York: Flammarion and The Whitney Museum of American Art, 1996), Lisa Phillips divides Beat culture into three different phases: The first phase, the early to mid-1950s, saw the production and consolidation of much of what is usually referred to as "authentic Beat culture"; the middle phase, the mid- to late 1950s, saw the height of the production of Beat material, which also led to the mythologization of Beat and to its ethnicization in mainstream media; and the third phase, the early 1960s, saw an increasing commodification of Beat as style, constituting the high point of the white hipster (24).
15. Norman Mailer, "The White Negro: Superficial Reflections on the Hipster," in *Advertisements for Myself* (Cambridge, Mass.: Harvard University Press, 1959; first paperback edition 1992), 340.
16. Caroline Bird, "Born 1930: The Unlost Generation," *Harper's Bazaar*, February 1957.
17. Mailer, "The White Negro," 344.
18. Ibid., 346–347.
19. Dyer, 13–14.
20. Norman Mailer, "Sixth Advertisement for Myself," in *Advertisements for Myself*, 332.
21. Ibid., 334.
22. Ibid., 335.
23. Ibid., 348.
24. On the hipster's status as a mock scholar and on his appeal to the white intellectual (both are outsiders), see Andrew Ross, "Hip, and the Long Front of Color," in *No Respect: Intellectuals and Popular Culture* (New York: Routledge, 1989), 82.
25. Mailer, "The White Negro," 341.
26. Mailer, "Sixth Advertisement," 333.
27. In "Hip, and the Long Front of Color" (85), Ross cites Simon Frith, *Sound Effects: Youth, Leisure and the Politics of Rock 'n' Roll* (New York: Pantheon, 1981), 88, who argues that it was a "romantic version of racism," which imagines blacks as "pre-social, at ease with play," that reinforced white hipsters' idolization of black jazz musicians.
28. Notwithstanding the Beat's distanced relation to Mailer's essay, both have in common the carnivalesque as an underlying concept. This concept was most incisively formulated by Russian literary scholar and critic Mikhail Bakhtin. Drawing on Bakhtin's *Problems of Dostoevsky's Poetics*, trans. Caryl Emerson (Minneapolis: University of Minnesota Press, 1984), and *Rabelais and His World*, trans. Hélène Iswolsky (Bloomington: Indiana University Press, 1984), David Sterritt in his study *Mad to Be Saved: The Beats, the '50s, and Film* (Carbondale and Edwardsville: Southern Illinois University Press, 1998) likens the Beat's subversive influence on American culture to a carnivalesque destabilization of established hierarchies. He writes, "A key project of the Beats was to cultivate what Bakhtin called the 'image of the contradictory, perpetually becoming and unfinished being' within their own consciousnesses. Among the forms this project took were

Kerouac's embrace of spontaneous creativity, Ginsberg's nurturing of a transcendent visionary sensibility, and Burrough's decimation of linear thought patterns as a means of liberating the self from outwardly (and inwardly) imposed matrices of power and control" (60). However, it should also be noted that the Beat's propensity toward dilution and impurity was somewhat counteracted by the fact that Beat must, to a large extent, be regarded as a rejection of bourgeois values that emerged from within bourgeois frameworks, what with the middle-class backgrounds of many key Beat figures. This rejection then also took the form of a more or less systematic ideological force, which harbored in itself (and produced) the romantic desire for an authenticity and a purity of its own.

29. Ned Polsky, "2) Ned Polsky," published as part of "Reflections on Hipsterism," an exchange between Mailer and two critics of "The White Negro"—Jean Malaquais and Ned Polsky—which was republished under the title "Reflections on Hip" in *Advertisements for Myself*, 365–69.

30. However, we note via Dyer's observation in *White*, 36, that even such overtly white supremacist texts as D. W. Griffith's *The Birth of a Nation* indicate in their compulsive recourse to signifiers of whiteness that the whiteness of the American South was highly unstable.

31. Mailer, "The White Negro," 339.

32. Dyer, *White*, 36.

33. Mailer, "The White Negro," 345.

34. Dyer, 28.

35. Ibid.

36. Norman Mailer, "Advertisement for 'The Homosexual Villain,'" in *Advertisements for Myself*, 220.

37. Ibid., 222.

38. Mailer, "The Homosexual Villain," 223.

39. Ibid., 226.

40. Ibid., 227.

41. Mailer, "Advertisement for 'The Homosexual Villain,'" 222.

42. Mailer, "Sixth Advertisement for Myself," 331.

43. Ibid., 333.

44. Ibid.

45. Mailer, "Mailer's Reply," published as part of "Reflections on Hip," *Advertisements for Myself*, 369.

46. Mailer, "The White Negro," 351.

47. Ibid., 352.

48. Ibid., 340.

49. Ross, *No Respect*, 87.

50. Tracy D. Morgan, "Pages of Whiteness: Race, Physique Magazines, and the Emergence of Public Gay Culture," in *Queer Studies: A Lesbian, Gay, Bisexual, and Transgender Anthology*, ed. Brett Beemyn and Mickey Eliason (New York: New York University Press, 1996), 291.

51. Ibid.

52. Morgan, 290.

53. Morgan, 293. The specific function of these props as fetishes deflecting racial Otherness can be compared to a similar observation Linda Williams makes in *Hard Core* about early sexual representations of women. The endowment of women with props specifically reflects male castration fear, but props as markers of racial Otherness index a similar symptom—the fact that the body of the Other, in Morgan's words, "is always already spoken for, determined, delimited" (293).

54. By saying that light and dark must be read "mostly" but not completely in terms of metaphor, I mean to point to recent research that aims to establish a direct link between melodrama's textual and material exploitation of darkness, the material stratum of film working directly on the human eye and on consciousness. See Martin Meisel, "Scattered Chiaroscuro: Melodrama as a Matter of Seeing," in *Melodrama: Stage Picture Screen*, ed. Jacky Bratton, Jim Cook, and Christine Gledhill (London: BFI Publishing, 1994), who claims that melodrama seizes on the eye's "reading and scanning process, selective and discontinuous, favouring angles, edges and sharp curves; and on the level of representation, the habits of 'perceptual defence' (seeing what is likely, what is familiar and probable) and 'perceptual vigilance' (seeing what is anticipated, even dreaded)" (65–66). This is extremely suggestive even for a non-Hollywood film such as *Blow Job*, since the film's chiaroscuro does, indeed, produce a dramatic aesthetic effect.

55. Ibid., 117–126.

56. Dyer points out that this particular visualization of an equally particular topography is underscored by a broader shift in eighteenth century philosophy of what David Lloyd, in "Race Under Representation," *Oxford Literary Review* 13, no. 1-2 (1991): 62–94, has called the narrative of aesthetic judgment. In this narrative of human development, perception moves beyond the particular toward the universal, a move white people are apt to perform, since their own material conditions (as far as their economic status as landowners and their social status as members of the literary, philosophical, and scientific elite were concerned) enabled them to move to "a position of disinterest," implying abstraction, distance, separation, and objectivity, "which creates a public sphere that is the mark of civilisation, itself the aim of human history" (38–39).

57. In her important study, *Machine in the Studio: Constructing the Postwar American Artist* (Chicago: The University of Chicago Press, 1996), Caroline A. Jones theorizes a link between compulsory heterosexuality's homophobia and the industrial aesthetic of the 1960s with which, as she argues persuasively, Warhol's art engaged. In her words, "Overt homosexuality would have disturbed the operation of the industrial aesthetic ('business as usual'), but covert references might have fueled it. The success of the industrial aesthetic of the 1960s was predicated on its linkages with a larger economic order whose heterosexist, patriarchal nature went largely unchallenged—at least not explicitly—by Warhol's work" (244). This can certainly be usefully related to *Blow Job*'s own repressions, positing, as it were, the secret as one of the factors crucial to Warhol's engagement with the machine metaphor (see the discussion of Jonathan Crary's analysis of this metaphor in Chapter 1). However, we might add that even what is *covert* about homosexuality in *Blow Job* can also be regarded as articulating a deeply ambivalent relation to entrepreneurship and, if not to industrialism itself, then at least to male industriousness.

58. For a reading of Warhol's Factory as a site of the carnivalesque, see Annette Michelson, "'Where Is Your Rupture?': Mass Culture and the Gesamtkunstwerk," *October* 56 (Spring 1991): 43–64.

59. See Andrew Ross, *No Respect*, 89, and Maurice Berger, "Libraries Full of Tears: The Beats and the Law," in Phillips, 132.

60. For a historical contextualization of the top-down approach of pop and the New Sensibility, see Ross, "Uses of Camp," *No Respect*, 135–170.

61. I borrow the term "exploratory zeal" from Juan A. Suarez, who in *Bike Boys, Drag Queens, and Superstars: Avant-Garde, Mass Culture, and Gay Identities in the 1960s Underground Cinema* (Bloomington: Indiana University Press, 1996) gives a useful discussion of the impact of the New Sensibility on avant-garde and urban cultures in the 1960s (101).

INDEX